The Nature of Law

This book is published with the support of the Notre Dame Center for Citizenship and Constitutional Government. The Center aims to explore the principles and practices of a free society so that citizens and civic leaders are equipped to secure our God-given natural rights and liberties, exercise the responsibilities of self-government, and thereby dutifully pursue the common good. Among its initiatives is a partnership with the University of Notre Dame Press to publish excellent scholarship on the ideas and institutions of constitutional government.

THE NATURE OF LAW

Authority, Obligation, and the Common Good

DANIEL MARK

University of Notre Dame Press
Notre Dame, Indiana

Copyright © 2024 by the University of Notre Dame
Notre Dame, Indiana 46556
undpress.nd.edu

All Rights Reserved

Published in the United States of America

Library of Congress Control Number: 2024937291

ISBN: 978-0-268-20821-9 (Hardback)
ISBN: 978-0-268-20823-3 (WebPDF)
ISBN: 978-0-268-20820-2 (Epub3)

For my sons

CONTENTS

	Acknowledgments	ix
	Introduction	1
CHAPTER 1	Obligation	43
CHAPTER 2	Commands versus Rules—and Nazis	93
CHAPTER 3	Justification	143
CHAPTER 4	Authority and the Good	185
CHAPTER 5	We the Sovereign	279
	Conclusion	321
	Notes	329
	Bibliography	367
	Index	375

ACKNOWLEDGMENTS

This book came to completion during a time of excruciating personal trial and tragedy. I owe a tremendous debt, which I can never repay, for the support and prayers of so many friends and family members. I cannot name them all here, but I am eternally grateful to all of them. I will never forget their kindness. Special recognition, as always, is reserved for ΔΩΔ.

Much of my formation has come at the feet of Professor Robert George, whose instruction and example have shaped me into a far better teacher, scholar, and human being than I otherwise might have been. Being his disciple has been and continues to be one of the great privileges of my life. This is another debt I can never repay, but I hope to be worthy of all the gifts he has given me. Thanks also to the many excellent professors and teachers who imparted such a love for teaching and learning.

Part of the work for this book was done during a visiting fellowship at Princeton University in the James Madison Program for American Ideals and Institutions. For the opportunity to be a part of that program and advance my work, I am thankful again to Professor George as well as to Brad Wilson and the staff of the Madison Program, past and present.

Some work for the book was done during a visiting fellowship at the University of Notre Dame. I am particularly grateful to my sponsor there, Phillip Muñoz and his Tocqueville Program for Inquiry into Religion and Public Life. Additional support at Notre Dame came from Brad Gregory and the Institute for Advanced Study; Rick Garnett and the Program on Church, State, and Society; and Carter Snead and the Center for Ethics and Culture. Special thanks also to Nicole Gordon for a grant from the Charles Koch Foundation, administered through Michael Zuckert.

An earlier version of part of chapter 3 appeared previously in the *American Journal of Jurisprudence*. I am grateful to the journal and its publisher, Oxford University Press, for permission to adapt it here.

Several people read and commented on various versions of the manuscript. I am exceedingly grateful for their contributions. Their gracious efforts have significantly improved the final product. I especially want to thank Grégoire Webber, Adam MacLeod, and Emily Carson, who gave far more of their time than I deserved. I also wish to thank Suzanne Staherski and Daniel Meadvin for research assistance along the way.

I am very grateful to Megan Levine, my editor at University of Notre Dame Press, who is exceptionally kind and professional. Many thanks also to the director of the press, Stephen Wrinn, who matches those qualities and has elevated the press masterfully.

I can hardly do justice to the thanks I owe to my family. My brothers have been steady companions, especially during these hard times. To say that I would not be here without my parents is an understatement. Their love, encouragement, and generosity have kept me afloat.

Last but very much not least, I want to save a separate word for my sons: In the face of it all, you are the sweetest, funniest, cutest, most wonderful boys. I am so lucky to be your dad, and I promise to be, like Horton, "faithful one hundred percent." Thank you for bringing incomparable joy into my life. This book, and everything I do, is dedicated to you. I love you more than anything in the world ("except Hashem").

Introduction

THE DILEMMA OF AUTHORITY IS AT THE HEART OF THE NATURE OF LEGAL OBLIGATION

I often joke that legal philosophers concern themselves primarily with two kinds of law: traffic laws ... and Nazi law. (This juxtaposition is not based on anyone's feelings at having received a parking ticket.) Let me introduce the two kinds in turn, beginning with traffic laws and what I like to call the case of the mythical traffic light. Imagine you are driving in the middle of the night, in the middle of nowhere (so to speak) and you come to a traffic light. The light is red. There is a clear, well-lit, unobstructed view in every direction, and there are no vehicles or pedestrians—or really anything moving—for as far as the eye can see. There are also no police officers around. Do you have an obligation to stop at that light? Note well that I am not asking whether you *would* stop at the light. Nor am I asking whether *most people* would stop at the light. This is neither a psychological nor a sociological question. It is philosophical question of whether one *should* stop in the sense of having a moral obligation to stop. The reason for this contrived (yet fun!) example is that it allows us to isolate the question of what to do in cases when the reasons behind the law do not apply. Normally, there are at least two major reasons for traffic lights: to promote safety and to promote the efficient flow of traffic at intersections. In the case of the mythical traffic light, neither of these reasons is present. Therefore, if there is an obligation to stop at the red light in this case, then it is because the law says so and not because the reasons behind the law (such as the moral obligation not to hit anyone with one's car) happen to apply. Because there is no one and nothing else around, there is no reason to stop other than the law's say-so, if even that.

A related feature of traffic laws, as a category, is that they are entirely conventional, which makes the specific obligation at hand completely contingent on the positive law. Here is what I mean. When deciding to manage the flow of vehicles and pedestrians at an intersection, officials can choose any one of a number of devices: a traffic light, stop signs, a traffic circle (roundabout), or even just signs reading "proceed with caution." And so on. For whatever reason—whether after careful study or just by default—they choose a traffic light, and it is this choice and only this choice that generates the obligation to exercise caution in the specific manner of stopping at the intersection when the light is red. I take it as uncontroversial that there is an obligation to stop at the light when there are cars or pedestrians around, even if one judges there to be enough time to get through the intersection without causing an accident. Again, in the absence of a traffic light or any other traffic regulations, there is still a moral obligation to proceed through the intersection with due regard for the well-being of everyone else around. But, in the absence of official guidance about how, specifically, to proceed with due regard for others, such as a traffic light, there is no obligation to exercise caution in that particular way (i.e., to stop at the intersection for a fixed amount of time awaiting the illumination of an otherwise arbitrary signal). This perspective helps us see the usefulness of traffic laws in philosophy law: they provide a neat set of everyday, commonplace cases where the specific behavior required by the law (stopping at the red light) is required *only* because the law says so and not because there is any underlying obligation to do so even in the absence of the law requiring it. (There are other examples, to be sure, but everyone can relate to traffic laws. And everyone has an opinion!)

A universe away, mentally and morally, Nazi law serves as a convenient and useful point of reference because of the way in which the descriptor "Nazi" is appropriately synonymous with "unquestionably, uncontroversially evil." In the philosophical study of law, Nazi law stands as a ready example of that which seems to be both undeniably law and undeniably evil. For this reason, the presumed existence of a thing properly called Nazi law stands as the obvious counterpoint to the ancient maxim "an unjust law is no law."[1] And so Nazi law presents legal philosophy with one of its central debates: What is the relationship between law and justice? Do we deny that the Nazis have "law," or do we define law without respect to questions of morality? This, perhaps surprisingly, brings us right back to the matter of traffic laws because, if law can be defined without respect to questions of justice, then in what sense can we speak of the authority of law and the obligation to obey? Traffic laws are instructive because they capture scenarios where there is an obligation, if any, only because the law says so and not because of any underlying inherent obligation to stop at a red light as long as one is generally cautious and fair. This is unlike the way there is, by contrast, an obligation not to murder or assault, which the law forbids on top of the moral prohibition not to do the same. But if law is law regardless of whether it is just—that is, if Nazi law is law even though it is unjust—then in what sense can we speak of law imposing an obligation? Either we have to say that even unjust law is obligatory—thereby repudiating the simplest sense in which an unjust law can be said to be "no law," namely that an unjust law is *not* obligatory—or we must say that law in general is not necessarily obligatory. At first glance, neither option looks appealing.

Another issue that arises out of a consideration of the sense(s) in which Nazi law is law is the conceptually narrower yet still colossally consequential question of the war tribunals held for Nazi war criminals (and similar wrongdoers). In one telling, at least, these cases are vexed because people are being tried for acts that were legal at the time they were committed. (Let us assume, though it need not be true in every instance, the acts in question were not just permitted under the law but required—"just following *orders*.") Can people justly be punished for what they do under cover of law? My purpose, strictly speaking, is not to answer that question but, instead, to *understand* the question—that is, to clarify why it is such a difficult question and to show why others who have taken it up correctly identify the issue as a problem but fail to appreciate its full weight. As it turns out, we cannot do so without a proper understanding of the authority of law and the obligation to obey.[2]

The nature of legal obligation as strictly sociological or also normative is extremely consequential in real life because the difference between having justified authority and not having justified authority is the difference between justice and raw coercive power. H. L. A. Hart steps into the debate to rebut the conception of law as "orders backed by threats" and to recognize that people do not relate to the law first and foremost as an instance of coercive force.[3] In this way, a more specialized argument within analytic jurisprudence finds its roots in perennial questions of massive significance. The law-as-command theorists whom Hart takes up have an ancestor in Hobbes and his idea of a sovereign with powers of biblical proportions and before that in the partisans of the divine right of kings and the voluntarist turn after Aquinas. This long lineage traces back still further, as one strand with the long classical conversation about Hammurabi's Code, Creon's edicts in Sophocles's *Antigone*, and Hebrew and Christian notions of divine law. So, in addressing the concept of law, we are not only touching upon the most pressing matters today with respect to the legitimacy of government power under law but also engaging with a deep and wide tradition of thought about one of our most enduring human questions.

This brief foray into legal philosophy's popular topics of traffic laws and Nazi law brings us squarely to the issues at the heart of the field of analytic jurisprudence and especially this project. Most directly, I am asking, *Is there an obligation to obey the law?* That is, I am asking whether there is a moral obligation to obey the law just because it is the law or, elaborating a bit further, what concept of law supports the claim that there is an obligation to obey the law just as such. This, in turn, is tied into broader questions about the justification of authority, the basis of political legitimacy, the good of obedience, and so forth.[4] To repeat, the obligation to obey the law of which we are speaking is a *moral* obligation. To argue about a legal obligation to obey the law is senseless. By definition, there is a legal obligation to obey the law in the sense that the law demands obedience, rightly or wrongly. But the philosophically relevant and interesting question is whether the demands of the law have any normative purchase on us—that is, whether we *ought* to obey the law and whether we do anything wrong if we choose not to. In other words, to say that law is authoritative in this normative sense is to say that those subject to it have a moral obligation to obey, all else being equal. To borrow from a later discussion, what it means for the law (X) to have justified authority—and not just power—over a person (Y) is for Y to be morally obligated to comply with the directives of X. The reference to moral obligation distinguishes this case of genuine authority and obligation from an impoverished sense of those terms whereby X has "authority" over Y and Y has an "obligation" to obey X only insofar as Y complies because X has the power to coerce Y or punish Y for noncompliance.[5] If law is not followed out of obligation, then it must be coercion, or, if not that, then perhaps custom or habit.

As I show, this is how Hart gets into trouble: he rejects coercion, custom, and habit but cannot account for obligation, so his concept of law is incoherent.[6] Lacking the resources to answer our central question, Hart can demonstrate that people feel they have an obligation to obey the law but never why they feel that way or whether they actually have an obligation. Rather than proposing a theory about how people relate to the law, my aim is to develop a theory about the nature of law, meaning a theory about what law *is*. At first, this seems to put even more distance between Hart and me because my concept of law addresses the source of obligation while he starts with people's response to perceived obligatoriness. On closer examination, though, Hart's theory is not merely the descriptive sociology he says it is because he, too, is arguing about what makes law *law*.

For the purposes of this investigation, authority and obligation are two sides of the same coin, so we can properly say that the main question is when or whether law has the authority to obligate. If law (or a law) is authoritative, then law is obligatory. If there is an obligation to obey, then law has authority. (In general, I think the concepts are clearest when we use words to mean more or less what they usually mean.) I emphasize this here to endorse Andrei Marmor's goal of "harmonizing a long standing divide in the literature about political obligation, that I think many have found unsatisfactory, between the question of the conditions for the legitimacy of practical authorities, and the question of the general obligation to obey the law."[7] As I say, I do not believe that Marmor succeeds in his aim, but I do believe he identifies the right issue, namely what he calls the dilemma of authority. The dilemma is that, on one hand, for authority to be genuine, it must make a practical difference, which is to say, it must give subjects new reasons for action, which, for our purposes, means imposing obligations on them through the law. On the other hand, what justifies authority and obligation if not the correspondence of the law to reasons that already apply to the subject? Just how can an authority create "new" reasons for the subject if its justification depends on its overlap with reasons that already apply?

The tension between the justification of authority and the content independence of the obligation to obey poses a difficult problem. If there is to be authority at all, the idea of authority suggests that the very say-so of the authority should have the power to obligate; if not, it is hard to say why the sayer-so is properly seen as the authority. But at the same time, that authority must be justified—that is, tied to reasons that underlie the normative power. In that case, the power to obligate depends on the content of the directive (and therefore on conformity to the reasons that justify the power). Or, as Marmor explains the "dilemma of authority": "In other words, either an authoritative directive identifies reasons for action its subjects have anyway, regardless of the authority's directive, or else the directive purports to constitute such reasons. The former option makes it difficult to explain what practical difference authorities make, and why their say so matters. The latter option makes it difficult to explain how an authoritative directive can constitute a reason for action without assuming, as it were, that one ought to comply with the authority's directives."[8] If, in the end, authority depends entirely on the reasons for action that subjects already have, then it is hard to identify any "real" authority. And if there are new reasons for action, then it seems they must be weighed by the subject along with all other relevant reasons.

To resolve the dilemma of authority, we require an investigation into the need for authority, per se, meaning why authority is necessary and, to make the fullest case, why so even among intelligent, virtuous citizens. If authority itself is necessary in society, then there is room for content independence because then there is a reason to obey that does not depend on the content of individual directives. The content independence of authority must be underwritten by justification, namely by an appeal to the ends that authority serves.

The dilemma of authority has a close parallel in a paradox we find with obedience. On one hand, if one obeys, one must have reasons to obey, whether because what is required is good or even because obedience itself is good. On the other hand, as soon as one has reasons to obey (namely the good at which one aims in choosing to obey), then acting so appears not to be an act of obedience, strictly speaking. In other words, if the focal case of obedience means doing something on someone else's say-so just because it is that, then once one has reasons for doing so other than the fact of being required, it is no longer obedience.[9] It is as though whenever obedience is (recognized as) good, obedience vanishes. Yet there is a difference between doing something for independent reasons (meaning reasons other than the fact of being required to do it) and doing something out of obedience (on the authority's say-so) while knowing or believing that there are independent reasons for doing so. That is, one can still obey an authority for its own sake even if one is aware of other reasons for doing that same action. The purpose in such an act of obedience rests either in the goodness of obedience itself or in the belief that one is obligated to obey. And these two versions of why one obeys effectively collapse into each other given that obedience is obedience only if there is obligation. Put another way, we can say that the goodness of obedience is defined as the goodness of fulfilling one's obligation to obey, which, by definition, one can do only if one is obligated, where being obligated means being required, independent of one's own (initial) judgment in the matter. If obedience is good in this way, then that good can exist and be realized only if one is under an obligation; otherwise it is just a voluntary act taken with the guidance of the "authority." At the very least, we can say clearly that without an obligation to obey there can be no obedience.

JUSTIFIED AUTHORITY IS CONTENT INDEPENDENT AND PROVIDES A SECOND-ORDER REASON FOR ACTION

The solution, or the closest we get to resolving Marmor's dilemma, is to think about content independence not for individual directives but for authority as a whole. For authority to fulfill its purpose, to serve the good as only authority can serve it, it need not be correct in all of the particulars. That is, authority can sometimes require that which subjects do not already have reasons to do or even that which subjects have reasons *not* to do yet still be justified, provided that, on the whole, it otherwise satisfies the criteria for justified authority — in other words, provided that it generally acts for the common good. Again, this means that an authority can provisionally obligate subjects through directives that do not correspond to reasons they already have or even that are unjust. It can seem that a better solution is to claim that authority is justified only where the particular directive is justified, as Joseph Raz does. To claim this is also to deny the content independence of authority. *But to deny content independence is to deny authority altogether.*

If authority is justified only when it requires citizens to do that which they already have reasons to do, then it is not really authority. As Marmor says, on that view, authority makes no practical difference, as its directives create no new reasons for the subjects. There, the determination of whether to obey rests with, and can rest only with, the subject in judging whether or not the directive conforms with the reasons the subject already has. If that is the case, then it is not authority but advice, even if it is expert advice. As I argue, this is the real problem with Raz's theory, namely that in the end it does not amount to a justification of authority but only a justification of heeding advice rather than deciding for oneself. This is important to point out because we can use the term *authority* both in this sense of having authority over another and in the alternative sense of having expertise. The expertise of another gives us reasons to comply but not an obligation to obey. By definition, if the authority in question cannot impose obligations (or, equivalently, if the directives of the authority are not obligatory), then we are not speaking of authority in the relevant sense. Indeed, this definitional point provides us with an occasion to make a broader conceptual point: that the authority of law is predicated, in part, on the idea that people obey even when they disagree with the law. We can only speak meaningfully of a scheme as *authority* when the authority's directives are binding on the subjects independent of their individual judgments about the content of the directives.

To situate and sharpen the inquiry, we can reframe the core questions about authority and obligation in several ways, using jargon familiar in philosophy of law. Most of the time, I refer to the content independence of law's authority and a prima facie obligation to obey the law. Thus, we can ask: Is there a prima facie obligation to obey the law?[10] The idea of a prima facie obligation to obey refers to an obligation that is not absolute because it can be trumped by competing considerations. The prima facie obligation to obey is not an all-things-considered obligation to obey but an all-things-equal obligation. We can equivalently say that the obligation is provisional or contingent—contingent on the absence of competing obligations of greater weight. As I emphasize, the obligation is only prima facie because there is no argument for an absolute obligation to obey the law—that is, for an obligation to obey the law *no matter what*. Any serious theory of law and obligation must accept that there can be situations in which it is justified to disobey.

But the main reason for speaking of a prima facie obligation to obey is to make the "opposite" point—namely that there *is* an obligation to obey the law just because it is the law—while recognizing that there can be stronger reasons not to obey the law. For our purposes, an equivalent way of expressing this is in terms of a content-independent (versus content-dependent) obligation to obey the law. This idea of content independence is that there is an obligation to obey the law *independent of the content* of the law. We can say, relatedly, that the law gives the subject *independent* reasons for action because the reasons for action are rooted in the say-so of the law (or, more broadly, the authority) rather than in any reasons that already apply to the subject apart from the directive. The prima facie obligation to obey applies to all laws in that legal system. This means that the obligation to obey the law is content independent, not dependent on the content of some particular law or the assessment of anyone subject to it.

This notion of content independence illuminates just what we mean when we invoke the term *authority*, implying that the authority must be giving the subject new reasons beyond those that already apply to the subject. Otherwise, it is much harder to think of it as authority because it minimizes or erases the practical difference that the authority's directives make for the subject. If the existence of any obligation, even prima facie, to obey depends on the subject's assessment of the content of the directive (and, therefore, roots the obligation to obey in content dependence), then in what sense can we really be speaking of authority? At the same time, on what basis can we say that there is a prima facie obligation to obey the law regardless of the content? What is the ground of such an obligation? This is what the dilemma of authority seeks to highlight and presses us to resolve.

Another set of terminology that helps illuminate these issues is the language of first- and second-order reasons for action. For clarity, I mostly avoid switching back and forth between different terminologies, but this language is worth flagging here for completeness and for the times when it does come up. A first-order reason is a reason for acting (or refraining from acting). A second-order reason is a reason for acting (or refraining from acting) for a reason.[11] Let us say, for example, that I have (legal) information causing me to believe that the price of a certain stock is going to rise. Therefore, I have a reason to purchase the stock in an attempt to profit from the anticipated increase in value. In other words, I have a first-order reason to buy the stock. The information about the stock (or, more properly, the opinion I form of it) gives me a reason to act, namely a reason to buy the stock. Now let us add that, when I review the information, I am suffering from a migraine headache. And let us say that I know that the brain fog and impatience I regularly experience while having a migraine often lead to muddled judgment. As a result, I have a rule about not acting upon any investment decisions I reach while suffering from a migraine. The cloudiness of my mind at the time does not change the information I have about the stock, and it does not necessarily invalidate the positive judgment I form about the stock's prospects. But my rule of not trusting judgments I form while suffering from a migraine gives me a reason to refrain from acting on the reason I have for otherwise buying the stock. In technical terms, my belief that the stock is going up is a first-order reason to act—that is, a first-order reason to buy the stock. But my belief that I must not act upon an evaluation of the stock's prospects that I make while I have a migraine gives me a second-order reason, in this case a second-order reason not to act—that is, not to buy the stock. Forming a judgment while having a migraine gives me a reason not to act on that judgment, regardless of what it is, because that judgment is, as a rule, not to be trusted. Thus, I have reasons not to act on the reasons for buying the stock. This does not mean that the second-order reason can never be overcome; in this example, obviously I can reconsider the information when I am feeling better and form a revised judgment if necessary.

Similarly, we can introduce my stockbroker into the story in place of the headache and imagine that, regardless of my own assessment of the stock, I generally trust my broker to have sounder judgment about these matters than I do. If my stockbroker and I come to competing conclusions about buying or selling a particular stock, my judgment about the stock gives me a first-order reason to do one thing, but my view that my stockbroker's judgment is superior to mine gives me a second-order reason not to act on the first-order reasons in favor my own conclusion (to buy or not buy the stock). This is different from a scenario in which I come across conflicting information about whether to buy the stock. In that case, I am weighing reasons in favor of buying the stock against reasons in favor of *not* buying the stock—all first-order reasons—that is, reasons to act or not to act.[12] But when my judgment contradicts my stockbroker's, I am not weighing my reasons for buying the stock against her reasons for not recommending it. Rather, my stockbroker's judgment preempts mine because, by definition, I follow her advice over my own conclusions regardless of the substantive merits of our first-order judgments. To wit, I do not interrogate her reasons for forming her judgment and then weigh them against mine. I just take her judgment over mine. Of course, I can interrogate her view if I wish, but if I weigh all the information (the reasons for and against buying the stock other than the broker's opinion just as such), then I am dealing with first-order reasons only. Once again, as with the case of law, the fact that my information about the stock provides a first-order reason and my stockbroker's advice constitutes a second-order reason does not mean that there are *no* circumstances under which I can reasonably follow my own opinion over hers—just as there are circumstances under which one ought to disobey the law even though there is a prima facie obligation to obey.

The stock example is instructive for several reasons, and it foreshadows an example that Raz uses, but we can construct much simpler examples, too. Imagine that I am a middle schooler and wish to go out with my friends. I have reasons to go and reasons not to go, and, ultimately, I decide I want to go. But my parents tell me not to go. If I obey, it is (probably) not because I take into account their reasons for denying me permission, now weighing all of my original reasons along with all of their reasons for and against and then arriving at a new conclusion. Indeed, we can say that, if I do that and then plan to stay home because I arrive at the same conclusion as they do, staying home as they instruct is not an act of obedience. If I am obedient, I stay home precisely because they say so, not because I decide that a fuller consideration of the reasons (other than the fact of my parents saying so) militates against going out. It is this fact, the fact that I treat their decision as a second-order reason that preempts my first-order reasons regardless of my own judgment on the merits of whether to go out, that enables us to call it obedience in the first place.

We can draw a straight line from this example to our examination of legal authority and obligation. In order to say that law has authority, we must say that the law supplies second-order reasons. Take our case of the mythical traffic light. As I arrive at the traffic light, I have reasons for slowing down or stopping that have nothing to do with the presence of the traffic light. Whether it is my concern for safety or my concern for fairness—for example, that the drivers proceed through the intersection in the order in which they arrive—until I know there is no one at or approaching the intersection, I have a reason to slow down or stop. I also have reasons, better or worse, for not slowing down or stopping, such as my hurry to get where I am going or my assessment of the likelihood of anyone being at the intersection. These are all first-order reasons, which I weigh together as I decide what to do as I reach the intersection in the absence of any legal directives. In contrast, the law's requirement to stop at the traffic light when it is red serves as a second-order reason because it means to preempt my entire calculation about what to do. Therefore, in examining the nature of legal obligation, we are asking whether the law provides us with second-order reasons for action, which is to say, whether I have an obligation to obey that in some way preempts my own weighing of the reasons for and against doing what the law requires. If not, then we do not have genuine authority and certainly no obligation to obey the law just because it is the law.

We can recast the dilemma of authority in these terms as well. Does law function as a second-order reason? And the dilemma is as follows: On one hand, in order for law to be law (which is to say, to be authoritative), law must function as a second-order reason, preempting one's judgment of the first-order reasons. Again, in simple terms, this means that the law can require me to stop at the red light, independent of whatever view I have about stopping in that particular moment—that is, apart from my own judgment about whether it is safe, efficient, and so on to stop in the present circumstances. If I am free to disregard the traffic light whenever my judgment differs, then we cannot say that the law is authoritative. On the other hand, in virtue of what feature of the law can we say that the law functions as a second-order reason? If I do not consider the content of the law, why ought I to treat it as something that overrides my own judgment about the situation? How can any law be authoritative without consideration of its content? What, if not the content of each law, justifies the authority and generates an obligation to obey just as such?

LAW IS A SET OF COMMANDS ORIENTED TO THE COMMON GOOD

My thesis is that law, in its central case, is a set of commands oriented to the common good. The concept of law I am proposing restores to law both its "form" and its "content." We need both the "command" element of law—the form—and the "common good" element of law—the content. The normative valence of law comes from its relation to the common good. But this normative aspect must be wed to a descriptive aspect because there must be some specification of *whose* directives are authoritative. As I explain, without this, all we have is a variety of competing proposals for promoting the common good. All of them can be reasonable, but none in particular is authoritative. At the other end, if an authority promulgates directives without relation to the common good, then we have power but not justification.

Although not all laws are commands, *command* is still the right term to describe the central case of law. The main reason for this is that *command* captures the notion of obligation; in the central case, the directives of the authority mean to obligate, and, without obligation, we are not truly speaking of authority. Moreover, as I show, notwithstanding the impression left on contemporary jurisprudence by the deep and wide influence of Hart, even so-called power-conferring laws have a duty-imposing element. I hold open the possibility that not every single law can be reduced to a type of command, but a great deal of law does take this shape. In any case, command represents the paradigmatic case of law because of its direct relation to authority and obligation. Hart offers some valid criticisms of the thinking about law as command, but he mistakes erroneous yet extraneous elements of the old command model for the core, which we can preserve. In missing this, he throws the baby out with the bathwater.

Understanding law in this way enables us to resolve questions about law's authority and obligatoriness. On my view, there is a prima facie obligation to obey the law—that is, an obligation to obey the law just because it is the law. Law can function as a second-order reason because the obligatoriness of the law is rooted in the relation of the set of commands as a whole to the common good, which relation can hold even when a particular directive does not comport with an individual's judgment about its application in a particular context. As long as the set of commands as a whole—as long as the laws as a whole—are oriented to the common good, then the justifying feature of law's authority is present.

What, then, is the benefit of pressing my version of the concept of law? For one thing, it is worthwhile just to get it right. For another thing, if ideas *do* have consequences, placing an emphasis on the intrinsic relationship between law and the common good and noting that a legal system that strays too far from the common good is not worthy of the name can help to refocus officials on their central purpose.[13] Individual laws that do not serve the common good remain law, but each such one weighs down the system and potentially erodes its legitimacy. My concept of law also helps us better understand how we relate to unjust laws and civil disobedience in theory and in practice. For comprehending both properly, it is important to see that even an unjust law (within a just legal system) carries a prima facie obligation to obey.

But, for analytic jurisprudence, this project is necessary and important because of the way the field is misshapen by two giants, Hart and Raz. My return to the concept of law itself and the argument over foundational definitions is necessary because the persisting errors in conceptualizing law and its authority largely stem from the fact that the discussion is bounded by the parameters introduced by Hart and Raz, including, for all of their towering contributions, the ways in which they go badly wrong. Their influence remains dominant, and the ways in which more recent theories fail because of errors imported from them suggest that developing a superior concept of law necessitates going back to the basics. That is, beyond correcting some of where Hart and Raz went wrong, making the affirmative case for law's authority provides an occasion to revisit the concept of law and, specifically, the good of law's authority as it relates to the common good. Placing law in its proper context, namely as an instrument for promoting the common good, allows us to see why law must have authority and why law's authority (in a just system) is itself worth upholding. Unfortunately, too much of the current discussion of law overlooks this critical common-good element of the concept of law, leaving many other theories predictably inadequate.

In a critical move, Hart observes that people do not relate to the authority of law in the way they relate to other forms of coercion, including criminal coercion, because, unlike with those other sorts, they understand themselves to have an obligation to obey the law. This observation sets the thinking about the nature of law and legal obligation on a new course. If Hart is right about the sense of obligatoriness carried by law, then the central case of law is inseparable from notions of justification because authority without justification *is* merely coercion. Law as coercion is the old model, which Hart criticizes, that cannot account for this key feature of law, obligation. The problem, however, is that Hart's theory, like the theories of those who follow him, leaves no room for justification despite insisting that law is characterized by its obligatoriness. The conventional understanding of Hart is that, due to his aims, he leaves room for justification but does not address justification head on. My argument goes further than this, showing that Hart's concept of law is ultimately incompatible with any sound account of justification. Because law, for Hart, is strictly a sociological phenomenon marked by nonnormative criteria, it is impossible to add a normative aspect to law without contradicting Hart's positivism.[14]

This error carries into current scholarship and calls out for a new way forward. Because the leading contemporary accounts of authority build on the flawed theories of Hart and Raz, they never quite succeed. For all of the tinkering in later works, the foundational flaws introduced by Hart and Raz carry through. This is true for those who build directly upon Hart, such as Marmor in his institutional conception of authority or Scott Shapiro in his planning theory of law, as it is for those who follow Raz, including M. B. E. Smith, John Simmons, and Leslie Green, as well as those who try new approaches but remain limited by the reigning ideas, such as George Klosko and David Estlund. For this reason, it is necessary to recover a different description of law and marry it to a superior normative account of authority and obligation. In doing so, a major task is to show why each of the descriptive (command) and normative (common good) components is necessary and why neither alone is sufficient to account for law's authority and legal obligation.

The most influential attempt to account for the normative (justified) authority of law within the post-Hart landscape comes from Joseph Raz. But, whereas Hart ultimately offers an account of law without justification, Raz offers an account of justification without authoritativeness and obligatoriness. Though his intention is to account for the obligation to obey the law, Raz only demonstrates the circumstances under which it is morally permissible to obey, not the circumstances under which it is obligatory. Given this, one unsurprising result of his theory is the conclusion that there is no prima facie obligation to obey the law—that is, no obligation to obey the law just because it is the law. In other words, there is no obligation to obey authority just as such; the say-so of authority alone is never enough to generate an obligation. Instead, authority serves only to point the subject to reasons the subject already has for action. When, on balance, the reasons for action that apply to the subject, anyway, are dispositive, the authority's directive is justified because it corresponds to what the subject already ought to do. But there is no meaningful sense in which it is authority rather than advice.

Therefore, it appears that a theory of genuine authority must show that authority generates a special kind of second-order reason—which Raz calls an exclusionary reason—to obey the law: a reason to act on the say-so of the authority without weighing the underlying first-order reasons for and against that particular action.[15] In that case, authority generates a content-independent obligation to obey, an obligation to obey irrespective of the content of the particular directive. If so, then we must show that there are reasons to obey the authority that do not depend on what the authority requires in each case. That is, it appears that obedience to authority must supply its own reason for action apart from reasons behind the particular directive one is obeying. There presumably needs to be something good about authority itself or a reason for authority that stands apart from the substance of particular directives. Yet such reasons must exist if we are to explain why there is an obligation to obey the law just as such. If authority gives us no reason to obey just as such, then the obligation to obey depends on the content of each directive, as Raz has it.

The basic outline of the solution to this problem of how authority can create a content-independent obligation to obey is that justification depends on the goodness of the authority as a whole rather than the goodness of any particular directive. If the authority serves the necessary functions that authority alone can fulfill—particularly, if authority advances the common good, which authority alone can do in a relatively comprehensive way—then obedience to authority constitutes its own reason for action. Furthermore, because authority can function *as authority* only if it is authoritative *regardless of the particulars*, authority *must* present a reason to obey just as such.

This also explains why justified authority generates an obligation to obey that is not absolute but, instead, is a prima facie obligation, subject to override. As a second-order reason, an authoritative directive creates an obligation to obey just as such. As a first-order reason, the general obligation to obey sits on the scales with the rest of the reasons for and against action and can be outweighed by a stronger, contrary obligation. This is captured neatly by John Finnis when he writes, "The *equal* obligation in *law* of each obligation-imposing law is to be clearly distinguished from the moral obligation to obey *each* law."[16] There is an obligation to obey the law that applies equally to each law, but the all-things-considered decision to obey any particular law depends on the balance of competing considerations, only one of which is the general obligation to obey the law.

My aim is to present a concept of law based on these premises for a theory of authority and obligation. Specifically, my thesis is that a legal system is best described as a set of commands that is oriented, on the whole, to the common good. Such a legal system generates a qualified moral obligation to obey the law. Accordingly, in my model, the authority of law has a normative valence that other theorists of law miss, either because their theories have no normative valence or because it is partial and incomplete. Consequently, in keeping with the natural law tradition, I maintain that the "validity" and "legitimacy" of a legal system are necessarily coextensive. Natural law theory is so important here for its rejection of positivism and its insight that law is inescapably normative, without which normativity genuine authority and obligation elude us. The purpose of authority expressed through law is the advancement of the common good, and, therefore, if law largely fails to meet that purpose, we can say that it is not justified, but we can equally say that it is not a legal system but, instead, more like a bottle of poison with the label "medicine" pasted on it.[17]

In addition, because a legal system is a human construct based on naturally occurring moral norms, as it were, there must also be a descriptive criterion in the model to identify which scheme is authoritative. For this reason, my theory refers to the central case of law as a set of commands, which suggests that the directives originate from a commander.[18] Although it is the case that the identification of the commander depends on a social practice that designates a particular office or institution to bear the authority, my theory does not have the problems that Hart's has, owing in part to my choice of a different descriptor (a set of commands) and in part to the inclusion of the normative aspect (an orientation to the common good). While Hart's choice of rules rather than commands can also serve this function of identifying who is the authority, law as commands, unlike rules, captures the sense that law necessarily entails justified authority and obligation.

Although I expound more upon the natural law view(s) of the common good, an introductory word is in order here on what the common good is. In this project, it is not necessary to fill out the complete content of the common good, even if possible, but only, as I say, to suggest its contours. In a recent contribution to the literature on the common good, Matthew Wright begins, appropriately, by linking the common good to human flourishing, which "draws on the Aristotelian-Thomistic ethical tradition that emphasizes the rational cultivation of human capacities in an effort to fully enjoy the goods to which they are naturally inclined."[19] Like Finnis and others before him, he notes that the specifically *common* good comprises goods that are common to all as well as good pursued or instantiated in common.[20] Sorting out the different senses of the term *common good* is its own task (and there need not be only one correct sense), but Wright's larger purpose is to delve into the debate about whether the specifically *political* common good is instrumental or intrinsic to human flourishing.[21] In other words, Wright is asking whether the political common good is itself partly constitutive of human flourishing or whether the political common good is valuable only in securing the condition for the realization of other (basic) goods.

The good news is that we do not need to resolve that dispute in order to present a concept of law that refers to the common good. Even if Wright is correct, we do not need to go as far as he does, to his "definition of the common good per se," that "a common good exists most basically when common action is undertaken for a truly common aim, and most fully when the unity of the group itself is one of the intrinsic goods sought."[22] That is, even if the common good is best seen as an aggregation of individual goods, our understanding of the law does not change depending on which view we adopt. The central, unchanging point is that "natural law/natural right theories . . . *ground* the authority of law in its ability to promote the common good of the polity."[23] In our case as in Wright's, "the goal at this point is not to specify what precisely the substance of various common goods is, but rather what the formal characteristics are of goods that should be recognized as common."[24] Here, with Stefano Bertea, we can take a rather parsimonious-cum-capacious approach to defining the common good, whereby "the common good is defined by an arrangement of concerns which all participants in the legal enterprise ought to acknowledge as rationally valuable."[25] From there, we can say, again with Bertea, that "legal reasons are considerations that offer justification by appealing to the common good."[26] This is exactly right, and it echoes the natural law view of authority that Wright cites relating the justification of authority to the promotion of the common good.

THE BOOK AIMS TO UPEND THE CURRENT FRAMEWORK FOR THINKING ABOUT THE CONCEPT OF LAW

A significant contribution of this book is a demonstration of the depth and breadth of the flaws within current jurisprudence—and an attempt to offer a replacement theory. There are many critiques of positivism in general and of Hart and Raz in particular, but I extend the criticism further to show how deeply implanted Hartian and Razian ideas are in contemporary work. In doing so, I wish to present a thoroughgoing rejection not only of their core ideas but also of much of the apparatus constructed by them and others around those core ideas. In older work of those writing in a similar vein, such as John Simmons and Leslie Green, we can identify some of the same problems arising. In newer work, like that of David Estlund, George Klosko, Andrei Marmor, and Scott Shapiro, we witness the pervasive influence of Hart and Raz and the ways in which their errors doom later scholarship built upon them. Critics from the natural law school certainly recognize many of these issues, but none of them go far enough. And, indeed, I fear that the adoption of parts of Hart's and Raz's theories into the natural law view of law unwittingly imports some of their flaws.

Though not among the "hardcore natural lawyers," one contemporary scholar who neatly recognizes the inadequacies of Hart and Raz and offers a solid theory of legal obligation is Bertea.[27] Understandably, Bertea dismisses Hart and Raz relatively quickly. Yet, given their continued hold on the field, including partly among their critics, we need a more sustained and detailed analysis of the problems to dislodge their influence. Despite dismissing it, Bertea himself acknowledges that "Hart's theory lies at the origin of the currently dominant social practice account of legal obligation."[28] Therefore, although I wish to associate myself with many, though not all, of Bertea's conclusions, my own book is necessary for its more direct focus on the main culprits in jurisprudence. In attempting this audacious takedown, I turn back to key modern figures in the natural law tradition, especially Finnis and Simon, not to summarize all that has been said in response to Hart and Raz but to draw upon some of the most prominent recent figures in natural law theory, which characterize and are representative of a broader school of thought.

My work differs from Bertea's because of my concentrated critique of Hart and Raz and because of my firm reliance on natural law theorists (hardcore, I hope) to reconstitute the concept of law. And even though, as I say, I approve of much of what Bertea writes, exploring further difference between his latest work and mine can help to illuminate some important, introductory points. The two chief distinctions I want to address here involve, first, the direction or style of our approaches, and, second, our treatments of, if not our ultimate conclusions about, normativity, a critical concept in the debates over law. Drawing out these differences allows me to highlight the distinctiveness of my contribution and the ways in which this monograph goes beyond others in its engagement with the leading competition.

Not to overstate things, but one way to put the difference in approach is that, in order to understand legal obligation, Bertea is starting with what obligation is, and I am starting with what law is. That is, Bertea's overarching framework is to investigate the notion of obligation ("obligation *simpliciter*," as he calls it) and then to develop legal obligation as a species of that.[29] I heartily accept his point about "obligation *simpliciter*" as the genus and "legal obligation" as the species. Seeing legal obligation as a form of obligation more generally supports my conclusions about normativity and the way in which I propose a slight deviation from Bertea's framing. Yet, in contrast to Bertea, the point of departure in this book is a reformulation of the concept of law, from which flows our understanding of legal obligation. Although I also take up directly the matter of legal obligation by comparing it to religious and moral obligation, I place the concept of law at the center of my exposition, emphasizing that obligation is a necessary feature of any coherent concept of law. That is, I start with law and move to obligation to show how obligation is part of what makes law law. Bertea starts with defining obligation generally in order to discover what legal obligation is and whether, in fact, legal obligation really is a type of obligation.

My concept of law, stated again, is a set of commands oriented to the common good. This, of course, has resonances with what Matthew Wright rightly calls Aquinas's "classic definition of law—an 'ordinance of reason for the common good, made by him who has care for the community, and promulgated.'"[30] Bertea writes of legal obligation in a similar way, arguing that "legal obligation is a layered notion combining a categorical demand and a rational justification for that demand."[31] Here, like Aquinas, Bertea clearly recognizes the two-part nature of law, which combines both command (demand) and reason (justification). Similarly, Bertea states that "by virtue of the conceptual link which ties legal obligation to intersubjective reasons, on the one hand, and to mandatory force, on the other, legal obligation at once acquires non-prudential justificatory force and sets itself up as a rationally binding practical standard," again invoking need for both command (in a way) and reason.[32]

The appeal to rational justification, in parallel to the common good aspect of the natural law view, evinces Bertea's rejection of "Kelsen's nomological conception of normativity."[33] In this rejected view, "legal obligation is claimed to be categorically separate and autonomous from both (a) commands and the probability of incurring sanctions for non-compliance (two factual notions), and (b) *moral* obligation, in defining which the ideas of imputation, competence, and empowerment play no role. In light of these features, the formal account of legal obligation cannot be likened to either the empirico-positivist conception of legal obligation or the moralist conception of legal obligation espoused by hardcore natural lawyers."[34] Notably, although for Bertea the crucial point is specifically how Kelsenian thought gets normativity wrong, Bertea appreciates that, for Kelsen, legal obligation stands at a remove from both the empirico-positivist and moralist conceptions of law.[35] We cannot overlook that Bertea does not place himself with the hardcore natural lawyers, and I think that leaves us with something of a doubt about Bertea's full theory, which is incompletely "moralist." Yet, despite some final differences, the structure of Bertea's concept of law converges on my own in requiring both the "demand" and the "justification." Due to this convergence, yet bearing in mind the distinct directions of approach (Bertea moving from obligation to legal obligation while I move from law to legal obligation), it is not too much of a stretch to say that, for *certain* fundamentals of law, the difference is more of style than substance.

Speaking of a difference more of style than substance, I want to open my final, larger point about Bertea by turning to his comment that "intersubjective reasons have the potential to point out what can be argued to be not merely advisable, qua prudentially recommendable, but rather *right*," with the opposite conduct being "not necessarily considered unwise or foolish" but "*wrong*."[36] This emerges as a crucial piece for Bertea in the construction of his own theory of legal obligation. For reasons I am about to explain, I believe Bertea is entirely correct in relating legal obligation to true right and wrong. Yet, whereas Bertea's analysis leads up to this point, I wish to begin with it in mine. And this stylistic difference plays out in some substantive differences as well. But, before we come to those differences in our treatment of normativity, some background is in order.

Leading up to his own theory of legal obligation, Bertea provides a very helpful taxonomy of leading rival theories.[37] The main takeaway from Bertea's taxonomy is correct: most theories fail because they fail to properly capture law's normativity. I worry, though, that Bertea introduces quite a bit of unnecessary complication by tolerating too much ambiguous use of the notion of normativity. Theories that Bertea categorizes as normative are in fact nonnormative, and they fail for essentially the same reason as the nonnormative ones, namely that they do not properly capture the normativity of all. For this reason, those theories are better categorized as nonnormative. Calling them normative trades on an ambiguous use of the word *normative* that does a disservice to Bertea's otherwise clear grasp of the central issue. To be sure, I do not want to argue that there can be only one right way to define *normative*. Nevertheless, my preferred definition seems to be the one that motivates Bertea's conclusions as well, yet he does not apply it as uniformly as needed.

Before getting to Bertea's taxonomy, though, to put it in the right context, let me frame the question that connects the concept of law to the specific issue of legal obligation. In a point-counterpoint volume debating whether there is an obligation to obey the law, Simmons, who argues the negative side, explains, "A moral duty to obey the law would be a duty to do as the law requires because it is required by valid law (or because of what its being valid law implies), a duty to obey the law as such, not to do as it requires just insofar as it happens to overlap with independent moral duties."[38] As Simmons details, this is a duty to obey the law just because it is the law and not a duty to act as the law requires for reasons other than the fact that the law requires it, even if those other reasons exist. If there are other reasons to act as the law requires, then there can very well be "a moral duty or obligation to do (or to remit) what the law requires," but "this duty should not be seen as equivalent to a duty to *obey* the law."[39] Although I disagree with Simmons's conclusions, I believe his framing of the question is generally correct. The central question about law is whether there is an obligation to obey it. As Bertea puts it, "Traditionally, an issue concerning legal obligation that is closely related to its conceptualisation consists in determining whether the existence of a system of laws is in itself sufficient to provide those subject to law with a presumptive duty of obedience."[40]

The question of whether there is an obligation to obey the law can be specified, or at least tweaked, in the following way. In a collection of essays on political and legal obligation, Roland Pennock writes that the question of the book is "whether the obligation to obey and support the state and its laws is in any way distinctive and special. Or is it ... merely a set of moral obligations as they happen to apply to law and the state in a particular instance?"[41] Bertea sees himself engaged in a similar project, as he aims to "construct a *theoretical account* of obligation as it applies to the law, and hence to offer a *conceptualization* of legal obligation" and accordingly answer the question, "How should legal obligation be distinctly characterized?"[42] He wishes to "define legal obligation and ... establish what specifically distinguishes the specific sort of *legal* obligation from other kinds of obligation."[43] Taking all of this together, I argue that the answer to Pennock's question is and must be the second option, that the obligation to obey the law is a kind of moral obligation although without the ad hominem "merely" and "happen to." This is the only way that the authority of law can be truly normative—the only way it can have a real "ought." This is not to say that legal obligation cannot *also* be "distinctive and special," but it depends what we mean by those terms. Legal obligation can be a distinctive and special form of obligation, but the genus-species relationship still holds.[44]

Regardless of any disagreement here, the main thing is the consensus about the question at hand: the nature of legal obligation and whether there is an obligation to obey the law. Bertea articulates the same question as Simmons and Pennock for his project: "whether the existence of a system of laws is in itself sufficient to provide those subject to law with a (presumptive) duty of obedience."[45] The reason I mention yet another version of the same question is the way Bertea elaborates on the "the basic questions framing those debates," listing "the conceptualization of legal obligation, the duty to obey the law, law's claim to obligate, and the practical authority of law."[46] In my view, if we construe the notion of normativity rightly, then, for all intents and purposes, these are all different angles of the same question (or nearly so). If law has authority, then law obligates, and there is a duty to obey it. Authority and obligation are, in this way, two sides of the same coin.

This, now, suggests the broader point I want to make, that the answer to the question of legal obligation depends on our concept of law. What duties we owe to the law depends on what kind of thing the law is—that is, its nature. Bertea straightforwardly states that "a legal system is commonly understood to be an authoritative institution."[47] Then he goes on to say that "having authority, or claiming authority, in practical matters consists in having, or claiming, the legitimate power to affect the normative standing of others" and that "one of the paradigmatic ways" of doing so is "creating obligations for them."[48] In contrast to "some courses of conduct [that] are advisable, or recommendable, qua the sensible thing for an agent to do" (Bertea also uses the terms "recommended" and "practical guidance"), "obligations prescribe, require, necessitate, or mandate, as opposed to advising or recommending."[49] His language is as clear and unambiguous as can be. And he is right on target. Law, properly conceived, has authority; that authority is normative; and that normativity accounts for the law's ability to obligate. Moreover, this view of normativity is binary: either law is normative and generates a (presumptive) moral obligation to obey, or law is nonnormative, and it does not and cannot generate such an obligation. We can sum up the position with Bertea's stark declaration that "no non-normative conceptualization of legal obligation is theoretically tenable."[50]

Ironically, it is my very assent on this point that leads to my difficulty with Bertea's taxonomy. On one hand, Bertea makes precisely the right point, ruling out the possibility of successful nonnormative theories of legal obligation. On the other hand, Bertea declines to label certain theories, such as the formal and social practice accounts, as nonnormative even though he appears to dismiss them for essentially that reason. To fix this, I propose that Bertea's theory can benefit from a stricter definition of normativity (the one he seems to use otherwise!), which I believe puts us on much firmer ground for a coherent concept of law.

Bertea divides the theories of legal obligation into two categories: empirical and normative.[51] In the former category, which has its predictive and imperatival varieties, "no mention is made of what ought to be done."[52] In empirical theories of legal obligation, "that something is a legal obligation does not in itself mean that we should act accordingly."[53] Plainly, empirical theories cannot succeed on Bertea's (correct) terms because there is no obligation to obey in any meaningful sense except the tautological sense that the law requires it. The only chance for success is in normative theories.

Among the varieties of normative theories of legal obligation, Bertea begins with the formal account, which he associates with the "Kelsenian tradition of legal thought."[54] In this account, "legal obligation is constructed as essentially dependent on the formal validity of law."[55] This attempt to establish "formal" normativity goes nowhere. Bertea explains, "The reason why Kelsen takes empowerment to be the fundamental legal concept, making obligation secondary or derivative, is deeply rooted in his legal project, which is based on, and justified by, the possibility of keeping law separate from morality."[56] Thus, the very thing at the essence of the formal account is the reason why we cannot locate normativity it. In "Kelsen's nomological conception of normativity," "normativity is understood by Kelsen as a purely formal idea"—to wit, "Normativity exists simply as that which is lawlike."[57] This hews close to the problem of tautology. More to the point, this is not normativity, or it is, at best, a distorted use of the term.

The same problematic path is followed with the social practice account, which Bertea also categorizes as normative.[58] In this account, "the law binds legal subjects in the same way that social rules bind individuals and groups in society" because "institutions of this kind impose obligations on those who are subject to their rules."[59] The social practice account is Bertea's rendering especially of "Hart's jurisprudence," in which "a legal obligation arises through the existence of a legal rule understood as a social practice coupled with a widespread attitude to that practice."[60] Explicating Hart, Bertea states, "A legal rule ... is a standard by which to guide and judge courses of conduct—a standard at once broadly practised and accepted within a social group, and which is framed in a distinctly normative language."[61] Further, "This critical endorsement ultimately confers normativity," and "plain social conformity—the mere fact of acting in accordance with a standard of behavior—turns into a structured and considered pattern of justified behavior."[62]

I quote at such length here to show how profoundly at odds this accurate description of Hart is with Bertea's own criteria for normativity. Indeed, this opposition is Bertea's own conclusion and at the root of his dismissal of the social practice account. Bertea insists "there is no way to squeeze something normative out of a practice on the basis of social facts alone."[63] Likewise, "on the ground that a practice is widespread, people willingly participate in it and those who participate in it expect others to do so too, no obligation can be established."[64] Quite so. This is exactly why Hart cannot be right (and perhaps not unconnected to why Raz is wrong as well). For exactly the same reason, I find it puzzling, and incidentally misleading, for Betrea to count these theories as normative.

I think a hint as to why Bertea presents it this way can be found in the following passage. For Bertea, "obligation is a binding claim on our practical lives: the claim is *normative*, since it specifies a course of action in a realm of possibilities where we could choose to act otherwise; but it is also (and more specifically) *binding*, in that the course of action so specified is not just offered as generic guidance but as something that one is *required* to do."[65] The problem lies in the creation of a division between normative and binding. Those two terms ought to be coextensive in the sense that anything normative ought to be binding. The alternative, which seems to be operative here for Bertea, is that to be normative is to create nonbinding norms unless, for additional reasons, the norms also have the feature of being binding. Thus, in Bertea's formulation here, being normative and being binding are potentially distinct features. But if this is the case, then practices can be normative without being binding, in which case they are effectively suggestions, recommendations, advice, or guidance—but not obligatory. This guts the meaning of normativity and seems to fly in the face of Bertea's otherwise sound usage of the term in defining authority and obligation. This is what I mean by ambiguous use of *normativity*, which seems to possess both a binding and nonbinding sense.[66]

I propose that Bertea explicitly eschew the ambiguous use of *normativity*. In his own theory of legal obligation, despite some disagreement on other points, Bertea follow Finnis, who "conceives of legal obligation as a particular species of a broader genus, obligation *simpliciter*."[67] Bertea asserts that "a correct understanding of obligation is a necessary preliminary step in any comprehensive study of legal obligation," and this assertion forms a substantial part of his theory.[68] Accordingly, his version "constitutes . . . a specific instantiation of the general concept of obligation *simpliciter*."[69] In light of all the foregoing, Bertea's next language is unmistakable. He begins with "a concept of obligation understood as a normative claim in virtue of which we are bound to take some course of action, such that to fail to do so would be to commit a wrong."[70] Bertea explicitly links normativity with bindingness, which seems perfectly right, yet this remains irreconcilable with any other, nonbinding sense of the word. In a separate essay, Bertea writes that "legal obligation is theorised to be conceptually linked with what we *ought* to do, where 'ought' at least implicitly carries a value judgment of right and wrong, meaning that implicit in a claim that something is obligatory and so ought to be done is the idea that it is the right thing to do."[71] This is almost entirely correct, except that the idea that it is the right thing to do is not implicit. It is explicit. The rightness and wrongness of the actions required are at the heart of the very meaning of obligation, exactly as Bertea demonstrates in his elucidation of intersubjective reasons.[72] Bertea also recognizes that this view has "broad common-sense support: it seems intuitive that an obligation means that the behaviour it prescribes ought to be carried out."[73] This is perfectly well stated and needs to be assimilated into the rest of his theory. Normativity carries just this meaning, and all other, ambiguous uses are academic complications to a straightforward, if weighty, concept.

I dwell on my concerns about Bertea's taxonomy at such length to drive home the underlying point, that we need a firmer and wider rejection of Hart and Raz. My position on this depends on a fuller appreciation of where their accounts fail in general but particularly with respect to the scope of normativity and its role in legal theory. While in the end Bertea does land more or less in the right place, my goal is to root out the remaining confusion over normativity. Insofar as I can do this, my hope is that it represents progress for the field of analytic jurisprudence.

As a final footnote, I must be clear that the normativity of law's authority does not in any way contradict the claim that there is an all-things-equal but not all-things-considered obligation to obey the law. As Bertea writes, "Whereas the nature of legal obligation is rational and moral, the content of legal obligation—what is demanded by law—may not only differ from, but also conflict with, the content of the obligations that rational morality imposes on us."[74] In some cases, the law can be wrong when it requires something contrary to morality—though if it is wrong enough, systematically, then it ceases to be law. Relatedly, just as not everything that is legally required is morally required or permitted, not everything that is morally required is legally required. The laws leave much out, so "it is far from necessarily the case that one has a *legal* obligation to do what on the balance of moral considerations one *rationally* ought to do."[75]

THE ARGUMENT AND ARC OF THE BOOK

The starting point for paving the way for my concept of law is an aggressive attack on Hart's well-received reconceptualization of law more than half a century ago. This is admittedly a risky provocation, as many of Hart's insights have been embraced even by those who otherwise criticize his positivist framework. In his landmark text, Hart introduces what he calls the internal point of view, observing that people do not relate to the law as they relate to a mugger: they see themselves as not merely obliged (which is how they feel with a gun to their head) but as obligated. With this move, Hart astutely places the idea of obligation at the center of his concept of law, showing that obedience to the law surely runs deeper than a response to threats of punishments. At the same time, unfortunately, he sets for himself an impossible task by dismissing the idea of law as command and substituting, instead, law as rules based in social practice.

In my critique of Hart, I argue that Hart goes wrong due to his misconstrual of "command" and then compounds the error by adopting an alternative ("rules based in social practice") that is ultimately irreconcilable with his core insight about obligation. My critique of Hart extends from his rejection of law as command to his novel yet exaggerated distinction between duty-imposing and power-conferring rules to his treatment of the ethics at stake in post–World War II German war-crime tribunals, which misses the mark due to his failure to construct a coherent framework for legal obligation. This criticism of Hart is unique and original. Because of the way in which Hart dominates the field, my criticism is also highly provocative, as elements of his theory not only are widely accepted but also serve as the foundation for so much subsequent scholarship. Hence, my criticism of Hart is a necessary contribution to the field because of the way in which so much of analytic jurisprudence today is derivative of Hart, building on his flawed foundation, and therefore flawed.

After showing that Hart's concept of law does not provide the right elements for a coherent view of legal obligation, I next train my fire on the other titan of modern legal theory. Raz, in his theory of authority, famously and influentially argues that the obligation to obey the law depends on the law's reasons overlapping with reasons for action one has already. This means that, for Raz, there is usually an obligation to obey the law, but this obligation, I am certain, is neither as general nor as complete as Raz believes it is. Indeed, I argue that, on the basis Raz offers, we cannot properly speak of the authority of law at all. The exceptions he highlights demonstrate that law's so-called authority boils down to a form of expertise, the "authority" of which analogizes most closely to sound advice. With no true theory of authority, despite his conclusions to the contrary, Raz cannot ground the obligation to obey the law. Similarly, it is no surprise that other leading thinkers who reason in the same vein conclude that there is, in fact, no prima facie obligation to obey the law. As with Hart's work, the inadequate model that Raz sets forth for authority combined with Raz's towering stature in the fields means that all of the downstream theorizing continues to replicate the same errors and come up short on the subject of law's authority and legal obligation.

Having demonstrated the inadequacy of the prevailing views of the authority of law and legal obligation, I then turn to the construction of a new concept of law, wherein I contend that law is a set of commands oriented to the common good. This concept of law contains two main elements: the positivistic aspect, as it were, which sees law as a form of command, and the normative aspect, which ties law to the common good. The first element, law as command, is important because, while not supplying justification itself, command is the right "form" of law because commands intend to obligate. That is, while the fact of something being commanded by just any person (or entity) does not confer an obligation on the subjects of the command, commands intend to obligate and point to the authority of the commander as the source of obligation—though, again, that authority still needs independent justification. Starting with command is very unlike Hart's version (rules based in social practice) because the basis in social practice is explicitly a suggestion that the rules are merely conventional, in which case independent justifications of the rules' authority do not necessarily (and perhaps cannot) attach. The second element of my concept of law, the orientation to the common good, fills in the source of law's authority or, equivalently, the source of legal obligation. Crucially, the orientation to the common good applies to the legal system as a whole, as opposed to individual laws, which is how we can insist on a true normative justification for law's authority yet still maintain the content independence of law's authority that allows for a prima facie obligation to obey the law.

In order to motivate this two-pronged concept of law for which I advocate, I present religious obligation and moral obligation each as a partial model for legal obligation. While neither of these other forms of obligation fully explains legal obligation on its own, together they can help paint a complete picture. I describe one primary and familiar version of religious obligation as "commands without reasons." On this view, the divine commander is authoritative just as such—the ultimate paradigm of content independence. The lessons from religious obligation are useful because they help us arrive at how and why content-independent authority ever makes sense as a category and, further, why there must be content independence in order for us to speak of real authority. Legal obligation does not fit the model of religious obligation completely because a temporal lawgiver does not possess the inherent superiority of a deity to make its commands binding just as such or to make obedience for its own sake proper to the relationship between commander and commanded. Commands alone are not enough. Yet religious obligation does provide a compelling basis for the idea of content-independent authority (and obligation).

To be clear, I am not claiming that "commands without reasons" is the only way, or even the best way, to conceive of religious obligation. The classical tradition, perhaps most famously expounded by Aquinas, considers the way divine law, like natural law, corresponds to the eternal law. Yet, for our purposes, the key is to see how one construction of religious obligation can help motivate the idea that law has a content-independent aspect because of the way in which divine commands can be obligatory just as such—that is, just in virtue of being what they are. Some element of content independence is an essential component of authority, as I argue. Similarly, not all moral obligations need to be "reasons without commands." We need only recognize that moral obligations can and do exist without being posited by any authority in order to see that justification conceivably stands apart from position.

On the flipside, I describe moral obligation as "reasons without commands." This is because moral obligations (or the "reasons" behind them) apply regardless of whether there is any corresponding command, divine or otherwise. As with religious obligation, moral obligation on its own is inadequate as a model for legal obligation because law needs specification (command) among the range of possible options. Reasons for action alone are not enough. Yet moral obligation supplies the basis for the role of justification, in the case of law due to moral obligations surrounding the common good. Combined, parts of moral obligation and parts of religious obligation allow us to see a complete picture of legal obligation.

If this apparatus gives us the shape of the authority of law and the obligation to obey, the other major piece of the puzzle is the relationship of law to the common good. Drawing on natural law theory and particularly the work of Simon and Finnis, I argue that law is necessary for advancing the common good, no matter how virtuous and intelligent the people in that society, and that the advancement of the common good is the very thing that gives law its meaning and purpose. In other words, the advancement of the common good is the very reason for law, and, therefore, legal systems that advance the common good are valid and justified, and those that do not are not. To be sure, I emphasize that the law's orientation to the common good generates only a prima facie obligation to obey while also reminding us that the existence of such an obligation is a necessary feature of authority.

In anticipation of one important objection, I proactively acknowledge that my understanding of law's authority does not trade on democratic legitimacy. Controversially, I bite the bullet on this because I believe that this position is inescapable given the justification of law through its relationship to the common good. Of course, democratic governance can very well be be the most prudential method for ensuring that the law tracks the common good. More importantly, although the theory does not require it, my concept of law is fully compatible with popular sovereignty. In another original twist of the book, I import the work of Carl Schmitt to develop this theme. Although Schmitt is not normally part of the conversation in Anglo-American jurisprudence, I maintain that, properly construed, his work contributes to a correct concept of law. Despite some reputation as a positivist, Schmitt grounds his emphasis on decision (like command) on a normative basis akin to the way in which I propose to marry positivistic and normative elements. Furthermore, while similarly not arguing for democracy, Schmitt helps us see how a nondemocratic theory of authority and obligation aimed at the good properly accommodates democratic structures and ends.

My intention in this chapter is to hook the reader on the topic at hand with questions interesting to experts and nonexperts alike; to set forth the central philosophical problem (the dilemma of authority as it relates to the question of whether there is an obligation to obey the law) and to present it in multiple frames introducing key terminology; and to preview my thesis as the answer to the problem as well as some theoretical and practical entailments.

At the outset, I briefly set the project in the context of contemporary questions about law's authority and the obligation to obey. I raise the subjects of traffic laws and Nazi law to show that there are certain elementary legal-philosophical concepts that we (rightly) take for granted but that these premises also leave us with important questions about the nature of legal obligation. I then directly raise the question of whether there is an obligation to obey the law just because it is the law and the way in which the so-called dilemma of authority complicates our attempts to offer an answer. I also translate this thinking about law into the language of first- and second-order reasons, which restates the problem but does not resolve it. I next describe my thesis and suggest why my approach is key to understanding law's authority and the obligation to obey. I motivate the project by highlighting that the dominant theories in jurisprudence (especially Hart and Raz) put the field on shaky ground due to critical errors that are frequently adopted and transmitted through later works, and I thereby emphasize the need for a new concept of law.

In chapters 1 and 2, I present my frontal assault on Hart's jurisprudence. After summarizing some of Hart's key contributions, I focus on the central problem with Hart, namely that his theory cannot account for the obligation to obey the law. This is especially problematic given that one of Hart's most important innovations is his insistence on obligation as a defining characteristic of law. This conundrum is exacerbated by the fact that Hart's inability to account for obligation is closely linked to another widely accepted move of his, the rejection of the idea of law as command in favor of law as rules based in social practice. I argue that, even though Hart, as a positivist, mostly tries to avoid questions about the source of obligation, his reconstruction of the concept of law actually leaves his theory incompatible with any possible theory of obligation because social practice cannot be the basis of the sort of obligation he specifies. I similarly show that newer theories that build on Hart's foundation fail as well.

Instead, I suggest a return to seeing law as command—in part. I address various ways in which Hart is mistaken about the (in)applicability of the notion of command to law. In some cases, such as with respect to the idea of self-command, Hart overlooks the way in which people can operate in different capacities, allowing a self-governing people to be both commander and commanded. In other cases, Hart mistakes certain features of law emphasized by older positivists, such as sanctions or habits of obedience, as necessary to the law-as-command approach when they are not. He, therefore, fails to see how the appropriate dismissal of those features from the concept of law does not doom law as command more generally.

Another major development of Hart in his concept of law is his distinction between two types of law: duty-imposing and power-conferring rules. Hart believes that the existence of power-conferring rules strikes a deathblow to the idea of law as command. I challenge this and argue that the distinction is not as great as Hart suggests, and I demonstrate that power-conferring rules in fact do contain a duty-imposing element and, at the very least, are specifications of a duty to act justly. Furthermore, I suggest that Hart recognizes this inchoately in his central point about law being centered on obligation. He cannot have it both ways, claiming both that law obligates and that one of the two main types of law does not impose obligations.

Finally, I take up Hart's discussion of German courts trying Nazis after the last world war. This very gripping and concrete example helps to illuminate the perils of Hart's flawed jurisprudence. Although Hart is right to raise this as an example of an important real-life problem—people being tried for things that were legal when they did them—ironically his own theory ensures that he misses the true nature of the problem. Without the ability to account for legal obligation, Hart cannot really appreciate the moral quandary, namely the situation faced by those who possess a moral obligation to obey the law as well as a contrary moral obligation not to do what the law instructs.

Raz offers the most prominent and influential theory of law's authority, but, in chapter 3, I contend that his theory does not ultimately add up to a successful one. Raz locates the authority of law in the reasons behind the law, proposing that the normal justification for law's authority is found in the conformance of the reasons for the law to the reasons that apply to one already. That is, if the law aids one in acting upon the reasons that one already has for acting, then the law is authoritative. I write, however, that this deprives the law of true authority by reducing law's authority to a form of expertise and, therefore, advice or guidance. As Raz himself concedes, those who know better than the law in a particular instance have no obligation to obey it. But, per the dilemma of authority, if there is no obligation to obey the law just because it is the law, then there is no true authority in law. Likewise, I show that Raz's argument for authority from respect for the law does provide a reason to comply but does not add up to an obligation to obey.

A rejection of Raz's theory of authority opens the door for and, indeed, leaves us in need of a satisfactory account of the obligation to obey the law. Moreover, it points specifically to the importance of ensuring that any concept of law address and resolve the dilemma of authority. Otherwise, the use of the term *authority* is misleading and ultimately meaningless, as obedience reduces to case-by-case judgments by individuals about whether the law applies in those circumstances. Before closing the chapter, I extend my critique of Raz to other scholars who follow in Raz's wake and reach the problematic result that there is no prima facie obligation to obey the law. In my view, these authors repeat many of Raz's errors even when they more clearly see and state the conclusion that follows from the same premises that Raz adopts.

In chapter 4, I begin with my own concept of law, which defines law as a set of commands oriented to the common good. I explicate the duality of the definition, which contains both a descriptive element that depicts law as command and a normative element that links law to the common good. I argue that both elements are necessary and even complementary. I also argue that command is a superior way to describe law because commands presume to obligate (whether or not they in fact do), and obligation is, as Hart says, a critical feature of law. Therefore, a concept of law that sees law as command has room for an attendant theory that accounts for the obligatoriness of law. The justification of law's authority is supplied by the law's orientation to the common good. Law's promotion of the common good, often in ways uniquely available to the law, is what justifies law's existence; law's authority is, in turn, necessary for law to serve its function. This understanding also helps us to see why the authority of the law must be analyzed at the level of the legal system as a whole rather than with respect to individual laws. It is the legal system overall that must be aimed at the common good. Consequently, this means that laws in general have authority even if an individual law is unjust.

To motivate my concept of law, I build a model of legal obligation based on separate analogies to elements of religious obligation and moral obligation. Religious obligation provides an entry into the content independence of law's authority. Like divine commands, the commands of the law are authoritative just as such whereas moral obligation provides a model for justification. Admittedly, the sources of authority are quite different in the cases of divine and human authority, so I examine the useful points of comparison as well as the limits. I also draw upon Schmitt's political theology and his jurisprudence to bolster my usage of religious obligation as a partial model for legal obligation.

Having defended the idea of content-independent authority in the law, I immediately take up the necessarily limited scope of law's authority. No credible theory takes legal obligation to be absolute.[76] The obligation to obey the law must be recognized as prima facie only. This means that the obligation to obey the law (in a just system) always exists, but it can be trumped by stronger contrary obligations. This is important because content independence raises the specter of unlimited authority, which is indefensible. At the same time, one surprising and perhaps uncomfortable result is that there is a prima facie obligation to obey the law even when the law is mistaken. This tension is what lies behind quandaries like the one Hart (mis)identifies with the German courts.

The last part of the chapter takes up the law's relationship to the common good. In this section, the aim is not to break new ground with respect to the common good, per se, but to show how a correct understanding of the law's role in advancing the common good accounts for the authority of law in a way that is consistent with the content-independent authority of law. I draw on natural law theorists Simon and Finnis to show that law's authority is indispensable to the common good and that law's authority makes sense only when it takes the form I propose, contra Raz.

After arguing that a legal system is a set of commands oriented to the common good, in chapter 5 I address the glaring issue of popular assent. Although my theory does not require democracy, I argue that my nondemocratic justification of the authority of law is fully compatible with it. Moreover, I show that the natural law theories underlying my concept of law explicitly teach that proper authority promotes the kind of autonomy with which democratic norms are concerned. Moreover, because of the focus on the common good, my concept of law actually points away from authoritarian interpretations, even though justification does not strictly require the consent of the governed.

Continuing with this theme, I return to Schmitt to embrace the compatibility of his broader legal theory with my own. I show that Schmitt is not a positivist, and, more importantly, I show that his work, in parallel to mine, while not based on democratic theory, is compatible with it and supportive of the same fundamental ends. In this way, I offer more reason both to think that Schmitt's work is useful in bolstering my own and to think that natural law theories of authority are friendlier to democracy than they are otherwise assumed to be.

Finally, in the conclusion, I review the main arguments of the book, emphasizing that they are critical to a renewed and proper understanding of the concept of law and the nature of legal obligation.

I also expound upon an essay by Hannah Arendt, "What Is Authority?," to broaden our view of the implications of this sort of study.

In closing, I wish to borrow three qualifying remarks from Bertea that suggest notable parallels in the structure of our respective projects. First, Bertea holds that "a conception of legal obligation can aspire to be conceptually sound and theoretically adequate only if (i) it specifies the basic tenets defining obligation as a concept and, at the same time, (ii) it does not reproduce the mistakes made by" the other accounts of legal obligation he analyzes.[77] In that latter criterion, Bertea reveals that the search for a concept of law or a theory of legal obligation proceeds dialectically. I agree, and this leaves us in fairly good company. Simmons, though on the opposite side of the issue, admits the same structural point, conceding that "no a priori arguments are available to demonstrate the *impossibility* of a duty to obey."[78] Instead, Simmons sees his task as defeating each proposal one by one. Here, too, I intend to develop a concept of law dialectically by showing what is missing from the prevailing theories and thereby arriving at what must be in their place.

Second, I concur with Bertea about the limits of our claims. He, correctly in my view, accepts the position of Ernest Weinrib that "the systematic nature of law calls for a general conception of legal obligation."[79] Toward this end, Bertea notes that his is a "broad, or philosophical, approach" that seeks "a conception of presumptive, as opposed to conclusive, legal obligation."[80] In these respects, our methods and aims are similar. Owing to this, my concept of law, like Bertea's theory of legal obligation, does not resolve every outstanding question. As Bertea writes,

> In doing so, I implicitly admitted the programmatic, or constitutive, limitations of my argument concerning legal obligation. Such argument is ambitious since it deals with an idea—legal obligation—that has attracted the interest of several theorists at different times and it aims at providing a general conceptualization of that idea from a broad and philosophically oriented perspective; and yet the argument is limited, for it is not meant to address all the disputes concerning legal obligation and is rather

concerned with conceptualizing that notion when the notion is understood as the merely pro tanto demands legal systems place on those living under their jurisdictions.[81]

Third, and finally, Bertea accepts that his theory "reflects philosophical preferences that, however much they may be rigorously argued and clearly set out, cannot be supported by any logical or otherwise watertight argument. So I neither assert nor expect that the following argument will be found uncontroversial, command general consensus, or reflect the ordinary understanding of legal obligation, as this understanding emerges from the views of legal practitioners and laypeople alike. After all, theoretical statements are by nature highly contentious, and my account of legal obligation is unlikely to be an exception."[82] I deviate only from one part of this, as applied to my own project. Part of the appeal of my concept of law, I believe, is that it fits nicely with ordinary understandings of law and certainly does so better than the prevailing theories I refute. While such conformance is not proof of the theory's correctness, I do count it as a virtue. That caveat aside, I think Bertea's comment is a perfect way to describe how I leave things at the conclusion of this work, most of all because I choose to interpret his words as an invitation for further discussion and, better yet, disagreement.

CHAPTER 1

Obligation

HART'S INTERNAL POINT OF VIEW IS AT ODDS WITH RULES BASED IN SOCIAL PRACTICE

H. L. A. Hart's jurisprudence looms large. For better and for worse, his framework for the concept of law is the one on which the field rests today. Hart's work is so important to contemporary thinking about jurisprudence in part because he identifies the internal point of view—that is, the idea that subjects do not merely obey as one who is coerced but, instead, view themselves as having an obligation to obey the law. With this, Hart trounces sanctions-based theories of law, including John Austin's command theory. Similarly, Hart is correct that sovereignty is not determined by the presence of habits of obedience and other such features of the older ways of thinking about law. Following Hart, it is clear that legal theory must account for obligation.

Simultaneously, however, Hart concludes that the nature and scope of law make it impossible to understand law as command, even without sanctions, and says that law must be understood, rather, as rules based in social practice. If we accept this move, though, we can no longer find room for obligation and, therefore, have no way to explain why people have an obligation to obey the law. In turn, without any coherent account for an obligation to obey the law (indeed, eliminating the possibility of one), it becomes implausibly difficult to explain why people believe themselves to have such an obligation. Thus, in placing obligation at the center of law yet also excluding the possibility of grounding that obligation, Hart sets his theory on a collision course with itself. According to Hart, we rightly distinguish law from other demands—such as the demands of a mugger—through law's obligatoriness, yet we are unable to explain that obligatoriness because nothing about law is necessarily authoritative. Moreover, because of Hart's incredible influence, his mistake continues to carry forward, leaving, as I show, a troubled landscape in analytical jurisprudence in which law's authority presents this intractable problem in which it is impossible to square law's obligation-imposing nature with its lack of justified authority. Put another way, once Hart separates the fact of something being a law from the fact of it being authoritative (justified and, therefore, obligatory), it becomes impossible to claim, as he does, that obligation is a defining feature of law.

This central problem with Hart's theory stems partly from the fact that, in his rejection of the notion of command in favor of a notion of law as rules, Hart loses the framework that best supports a notion of obligation to the law. This is especially problematic, not to mention ironic, in light of Hart's key insight that the law differs from "orders backed by threats." The internal point of view reveals that law imposes (or purports to impose) obligation and does not merely oblige in the same way that a threat of force obliges one to comply. Hart observes that people do not obey the law because they feel "obliged" to comply in the same way they feel obliged to turn over their wallet to the mugger. Rather, they obey the law because they feel "obligated." This difference can be seen in the commonsense fact that one who escapes the mugger without giving up her wallet has not violated any sort of obligation, even though, staring down the barrel of the gun, she may have felt compelled ("obliged") to turn over her wallet. In contrast, a person who does not obey the law and manages to evade punishment has violated an obligation.[1] Unlike the mugger's would-be victim, when the lawbreaker does not heed, she has done something *wrong*.

To exemplify the obliged-obligated distinction, Hart uses the example of a traffic light that turns red. For the drivers approaching the intersection, he writes, "the red light is not merely a sign that others will stop: they look upon it as a *signal for* them to stop."[2] That is, the red light does not merely predict regular patterns of behavior, much as the mugger's victim is likely to turn over her wallet when confronted with a gun. Instead, the drivers see the red light as an indication that they must stop in the sense that they perceive an obligation to obey a rule to stop on red. People feel "obliged" by the do-it-or-else dictates of the mugger but "obligated" by the directives of the law, which they take to be not (primarily) a threat of coercion but a standard of behavior to follow.

Based on his insight into the distinction between being obliged and being obligated, which difference yields the internal point of view, Hart is right to fault command theorists of law for collapsing the difference between the commands of the law and the orders of a mugger, treating both as law because both are orders backed by threats.[3] In setting out his definition of law, what he calls the province of jurisprudence, Austin writes, "Laws proper, or properly so called, are commands."[4] Hart accepts that, in its proper sense, "a command is primarily an appeal not to fear but to respect for authority."[5] Because he knows that "to command is characteristically to exercise authority over men, not power to inflict harm," Hart appropriately distinguishes between Austin's concept of law as command and the demands of a mugger.[6] Yet if law is defined as orders backed by threats, then the law and the mugger have too much in common, and we can miss the important commonsense distinction Hart draws between being obliged and being obligated. Just as a mugger compels his victim to turn over his wallet at gunpoint, so, too, the law secures the desired behavior with the threat of sanctions. Hart, therefore, wishes to excise the notion of command from the concept of law.

In place of command, Hart offers another highly influential innovation, in which he sees law as rules based in social practice. Yet this devastates the coherence of his account of law. Hart's contributions in jurisprudence are a major step forward in the understanding of the law in part because of his introduction of the internal point of view (and the distinction between "obliged" and "obligation"). Again, this signature innovation, the internal point of view, draws on the reasonable insight that people do not relate to the law like they do to a mugger, complying with the latter only due to coercion and fear of consequences. At the same time, in viewing law as rules based in social practice, Hart makes the concept of law less suitable for explaining the sense of obligation that the internal point of view reveals. In this way, Hart's theory constitutes a step backward as well. Hart's idea here is that we can identify law in any given society by reference to rules in that society that specify what counts as a valid law. This can be anything from "passed by a majority of both houses of the legislature and signed by the executive" to "posted by the king on the royal bulletin board." The rules that tell us what counts as law exist just because they do, or they are the rules just because they are. To be sure, those rules can be identified with reference to further rules, but eventually the rules must be identified with reference to "what we happen to do around here."

This understanding of law invites the glaring question of what makes the law authoritative in the normative sense of obligation-imposing—that is, justified. His theory is meant to be descriptive, and, therefore, it is not Hart's aim to provide a justification of law's authority. Yet his descriptive theory at least ought to accommodate some theory of obligation precisely because one of Hart's key innovations is to show that, from the internal point of view, a person obeying the law understands herself to be "obligated," which is something more than to be "obliged." The problem is that Hart replaces the concept of law as command with the concept of law as rules based in social practice. While command alone is insufficient to justify the authority of law, viewing law as rules based in social practice is worse than insufficient; it excludes the possibility of a necessary link between law and justification. While some social practices behind law can in theory be justificatory, Hart *by definition* denies any such necessary link because his theory can identify as law rules based in social practice whether or not those social practices form an adequate normative basis for obligation. Thus, in some cases, law can be rules based in social practices that justify an obligation to obey the law, and, in other cases, law can be rules based in social practices that do not justify an obligation to obey the law. But if that is right, then from where does law universally derive the sense of obligatoriness that characterizes the internal point of view? It cannot be from coercion, custom, or habit because Hart directly attacks concepts of law that rely on those elements, so any appeal to those undercuts his own theory severely.

In short, there are two tasks immediately before us. I return later to my defense of command and then my own concept of law. But, first, I wish to show that Hart's concept of law is flawed and ultimately doomed. At first glance, we see that his theory is missing an answer to the critical issue that Hart himself puts at the center of his jurisprudential revolution, namely the issue of law's obligatoriness. On further inspection, though, we see that an answer to the question of why people have an obligation to obey (and therefore act that way) is not just missing but ruled out. That is, Hart's theory falls short because it claims that people have an obligation to obey the law (or at least that they act as though they do) but not why people think they do, let alone why and whether they actually do. Although Hart can claim a more limited scope for his project, the problem is that his theory excludes any coherent account of the "why." In short, he insists (correctly) that law is fundamentally characterized by its obligatoriness yet also deprives law of its normative basis.

HART CANNOT SHOW WHY PEOPLE TREAT LAW AS OBLIGATORY

With his repudiation of the command model of law and his introduction of the internal point of view, Hart revolutionizes the contemporary study of jurisprudence. By far, the most influential reconceptualization of law in the last hundred years comes with Hart's rejection of the command model. The imperative, or command, model, developed by earlier positivists such as Bentham and Austin, conceives of law as "orders backed by threats."[7] For positive law (human law), this means a directive given by a superior to an inferior and enforced with coercive sanctions.[8] That directive is authoritative in virtue of having been given by a superior capable of imposing such sanctions. In Austin's words, "*Command, duty,* and *sanction* are inseparably connected."[9] Hart, in his seminal work, *The Concept of Law*, decisively rejects the command model for insufficiently capturing the nature and scope of law. Hart argues that the command model cannot account for the so-called internal point of view of law's subjects, who understand themselves to be acting out of an obligation to obey, as opposed to being "obliged" by coercion.[10] Nor, according to Hart, can the command model account for the variety within the law, which includes both duty-imposing and power-conferring (nonimperative) forms, but I take up that issue separately. For these reasons, Hart rejects the command model and, instead, adopts a model of law as rules based in social practice. While this concept of law addresses some of the problems Hart sees in law as command, it creates new, insurmountable problems for his theory, chief among them the conflict with the internal point of view.

We can restate the core problem with Hart's theory this way. Like other positivists, Hart wishes to describe law without reference to normative criteria—that is, without respect to the justice of the laws and, therefore, the justification of authority. Hart's characterization of law and especially of the internal point of view allows us to see three distinct questions surrounding law's authority. First, there is the question of whether people feel they have an obligation to obey the law. Second, there is the question of why people feel they have an obligation to obey the law. Third, there is the question of whether people *in fact have an obligation* to obey the law and, if so, why. We must combine "whether" and "why" in the third question because it is a normative question, and we cannot know whether people have an obligation unless we construct a justification—that is, unless we establish why. By contrast, the first two questions are descriptive questions about the state and source of people's perceptions, so we can properly separate them. (I use the language of "feeling" because the point is that people have a sense of being obligated without necessarily having any developed thoughts on why they have that sense.) We can establish empirically whether people feel as though they have an obligation to obey the law that is distinct from the way in which they feel obliged to comply with the demands of a mugger. We can do this by asking or perhaps observing them. Then, if they do have that sense, we can separately determine *why* people feel that way. Of course, the questions are closely related. If the answer to the first question is in the affirmative, then we normally expect an intelligible answer to be available for the second, but that is not strictly necessary in order for people to have the feeling (of being obligated) and exhibit the observable behavior that results. Even so, it ought to be at least surprising and probably disappointing if no coherent answer can be found for the second question (why people feel they have an obligation) upon an affirmative finding for the first question (whether people feel they have an obligation).

This is where we arrive at the problem for Hart. Hart's theory, as descriptive sociology, prescinds from the third question of whether and why people in fact have an obligation to obey the law. Instead, Hart focuses on how law functions (i.e., as distinct from a mugger), not why, extrapolating from his affirmative answer to the first question that people feel obligated rather than obliged in the gun-to-the-head sense. He is massively influential in the field in framing the answer to the first question because of his powerful insight that people feel they have an obligation, as distinct from merely feeling obliged. With the respect to the second question, Hart proves far less interesting, not providing any sound basis for the phenomenon he observes—mainly focusing on the claim *that* people feel they have an obligation, not any claim about *why* they feel they do. Do they feel an obligation to obey because they correctly identify the law as obligatory, or is their feeling of obligation mistaken? As for the third question, Hart proves useless or worse. Not only does Hart offer nothing to address that third question, but also his theory blocks us from approaching a suitable answer. Indeed, as I show, Hart's avoidance of the third question leaves him unable to answer the second. Having no account of whether and why there *is* an obligation to obey the law, of course Hart also leaves us unsatisfied on the question of why people believe they have an obligation and, therefore, act *as though* they do.[11]

The problem for Hart here is actually twofold. First, ignoring the third question (namely whether and why people actually have an obligation to obey) leaves him without a good answer for the second question (why people feel obligated whether or not they actually are). But the second aspect of the problem goes further. The concept of law as rules based in social practice means that the answer to the third question is not just missing from Hart's analysis but that finding a satisfactory answer is excluded as a possibility. Once Hart tells us that we can identify law without normative criteria, then we have no solid basis for explaining why people treat the law as normative, which, per Hart's internal point of view, they do.

Hart's replacement of commands with rules based in social practice plays a main role in his theory being incompatible with any adequate theory of justification. Or, the way in which Hart addresses the first question undermines his ability to address the latter. This is because his replacement of command with rules based in social practice moves the concept of law too far from authority and obligation. This is well demonstrated by Hart's agnosticism on the third question (whether and why there is an obligation to obey the law) because that agnosticism makes it all the more difficult for him to address why people feel they have an obligation to obey and why they do not experience the force of law as the coercion of a mugger. Hart's version of law as rules based in social practice makes it much harder, even impossible, to account for obligation. On the basis of Hart's agnosticism on the third question alone, it is tempting to argue that Hart's theory is compatible with some adequate normative account. Yet his insistence on a wholesale rejection of thinking about law as command in favor of rules based in social practice deprives his new way of any basis for grounding legal authority and obligation.

Hart brings this upon himself when he invents the notion of the internal point of view in order to critique competing theories. By focusing on obligation, Hart correctly lays emphasis on this indispensable feature of law. At the same time, his description of law as rules based in social practice is, at the very least, not conducive to accounting for the very phenomenon he highlights (namely obligation). Hart sets the field off in an important direction by observing that law, unlike other forms of coercion such as armed robbery, is characterized by the sense of obligation attached to the law. On this basis, a descriptive theory must at least have room for a normative theory that accounts for the obligatoriness of law at the heart of Hart's theory. That is, a theory that ascribes a key feature of law—part of what makes law law—to the notion of obligation must admit some explanation about where that obligation comes from. That is, Hart's theory ought to be compatible with *some* normative account even if it does not provide that account itself, yet it effectively excludes it. His notion of law as rules based in social practice recognizes law wherever the rules of that society say there is law, which makes Hart's criteria for law necessarily independent of any judgment of the character (content) of the rules.

Ironically, a command model of law, which Hart rejects, can support the idea of the internal point of view while also leaving room for an account of obligation. So Hart is wrong in thinking he needs to scrap the command model in order to make room for his more sophisticated understanding of law in which the law leaves people feeling obligated rather than obliged. Indeed, the older concept of command, which he rejects, is a better concept for describing the central case of law. Of course, theories of law as command do not in themselves justify authority. Still, the concept of command suggests obligatoriness insofar as commands at least *mean* to obligate. One issuing a command intends to obligate, and one receiving a command understands that command as intending to obligate. We must consider whether any particular command in fact obligates the intended subject, but describing law as command at least provides the placeholder for the normative component. As I argue, we cannot speak properly (which is to say, normatively) of authority and obligation, including the authority of law and the obligation to obey the law, without speaking of justification—that is, that which imbues law with normative authority and thereby accounts for the obligatoriness of law. Justification is a necessary condition for law, and justified commands constitute the central case of law.[12] The irony is that this insight about the link between law and obligation comes from Hart (the internal point of view), even as his theory forecloses the possibility of offering a coherent account of that very phenomenon, in part due to his positivism and in part due to his substitution of rules for commands.

Thus, Hart's theory is flawed first and foremost due to its failure to account or, as I claim, even allow for law's obligatoriness.[13] To be sure, Hart deals extensively, if generally, with the topic of how to know what counts as authoritative within a legal system, sociologically speaking. This is the role of the all-important rule of recognition, which confers power to identify valid primary rules (which, in the central case, impose obligations).[14] But, although the rule of recognition answers the question of what counts as authoritative, it is silent on the question of why the law, or any law, is authoritative. If it is in the very nature of law that it imposes an obligation, then any complete picture must address that. To be sure, Hart describes *The Concept of Law* as an "essay in descriptive sociology," suggesting that he is off the hook with respect to actually providing an account of law's normativity (or lack thereof).[15] Instead, Hart's stated purpose is to characterize how law functions in society and how society relates to the law. But this leaves an important problem. While Hart eschews a normative analysis of law, not attempting to account for law's normativity, he still needs to have a theory that, though nonnormative, is compatible with the idea that law does in fact impose an obligation. But if law is merely what people accept as authoritative (because it is rooted in social practice), then there are presumably many cases where law, despite being treated as such, does not impose any obligation. In contrast, as I show, the command model, though on its face a descriptive account of law as well, is a better base on which to build a concept of law that accounts for authority and obligation.

SOCIAL PRACTICE CANNOT ACCOUNT FOR OBLIGATION AS A NECESSARY FEATURE OF LAW

In rejecting Austin's command theory of law, Hart writes that Austin "treats statements of obligation not as psychological statements but as predictions or assessments of chances of incurring punishment or 'evil.'"[16] It is revealing that Hart envisions obligation as a psychological, rather than metaphysical or ethical, reality. Strikingly, under Hart's analysis, the sense of obligation to the law cannot be accounted for as anything more than a psychological phenomenon because there is no room for a philosophical account. At the same time, the psychological phenomenon is, importantly, one of being under a nonsubjective obligation to obey the law. The obvious question, then, is whether that belief is an illusion or whether it has a real normative basis. This is the third question of the three main questions above, namely the question of whether and why there is an obligation. Even as a purely descriptive matter, Hart cannot describe obedience to the law as nothing more than a social practice ("what we happen to do around here") because, whether or not people are in fact obligated, those who obey generally understand themselves to have an obligation. Thus, at the very least, a good descriptive theory can account for the *apparent* existence of an obligation to obey the law—that is, why people believe they have an obligation, even if they do not (the second question).

Unfortunately, Hart overlooks this. Instead, for Hart, the distinction that "is crucial for the understanding of law" is the "distinction between social rules and mere convergent habits of behavior."[17] This is fine as far as it goes; surely Hart is correct that obedience to the law cannot be the same as that which people do alike more by chance than by design. Yet the notion of "social rules," which displaces the concept of law as command in Hart's telling, cannot sufficiently account for why people take the law as a reason for action. It is not necessarily mistaken for Hart to contend that people act a certain way because they know there is a social rule requiring that behavior. Yet it leaves the question of why people believe they ought to follow that social rule—not the question of why that is the rule but why there is an assumed obligation to obey it. In this vein, we can say that social rules operate more like habits of obedience than Hart wishes to admit, insofar as social rules seem to be more a matter of prediction of how people will behave than a standard for measuring behavior, as Hart refers to law. Without any normative grounding, the fact that the law is rooted in social practice mainly tells us that people are likely to follow the rule, not that they ought to or that they have good reason for doing so. By definition, that is what the identification of a social practice really establishes: that this is the way things are done around here. Despite Hart's claims, social practice is much less well connected to the idea that people treat a legal rule as a standard for measuring behavior than to the customs and habits that reflect "what we just so happen to do."

Because this is built into the very meaning of a rule based in social practice, it leaves Hart's theory on very infirm footing. To the question, "Why is it a rule?," Hart says we answer, "Because it is"—that is, because it conforms to the rules for making rules. When asked further, "Why do you obey the rule?," Hart says we answer, "Because it's a rule." In this way, the logic that underlies Hart's account of the law is essentially circular. It is, to adapt a phrase, social practice all the way down. This is adequate if we need to know only that people do, as a matter of fact, obey the law. But Hart's point is that people do not merely comply with the law in the way one complies with the demands of a mugger. His point is that people treat the law as though it confers an obligation on them. It is precisely his aim to make that distinction. But in recasting law as rules based in social practice (that which we do because it is the way we do things around here), he has hardly upgraded the law from its equivalence with a mugger. In fact, he has downgraded it to something more like a habit, which he strenuously wants to avoid, given his criticism of the place of habits in the concept of law. Thus, Hart's concept of law is much closer to the law-as-prediction model he wishes to reject. Without a normative basis—and without room for any normative basis—law can tell us what people are likely to do but not why they are likely to do it. To be sure, we do know why people in fact do it if we know they believe they ought to do it (simply: they do it because they believe they ought to), but, in Hart's version of things, they do so without any possibility of offering a coherent account of why they believe that. Any coherent account of obligation must appeal to something beyond the law's status as a rule based in social practice because some rules and practices ought to be normatively binding and some not, yet Hart excludes whatever more can stand beyond them.[18]

In this light, it is difficult to credit Hart's preference for the label "social practice" over "habits of obedience," the former of which he believes explains more about legal systems. Hart writes, "Continuity of legislative authority which characterizes most legal systems depends on that form of social practice which constitutes the acceptance of a rule, and differs, in the ways we have indicated, from the simpler facts of mere habitual obedience."[19] But if this is because Hart believes "habits are not 'normative,'" he should notice that neither are social practices.[20] In the relevant sense, namely with respect to the question of normative force (obligation), which Hart introduces into the analysis of law over and against theories of law rooted in habit, a social practice is just an elaborate habit. Hart notes the important distinction between rules and habits, specifically that a "social rule has an 'internal' aspect, in addition to the external aspect which it shares with a social habit."[21] On this view, rules are more than just habits because, under rules, people "have a reflective critical attitude to this pattern of behaviour: they regard it as a standard for all."[22] But on the question of what justifies that behavior, or why people take the rule as a standard for behavior, Hart's theory has nothing to say. That is, Hart can suggest that rules based in social practice have an internal aspect, but he cannot answer why they do or why they should, meaning he can satisfactorily answer neither the aforementioned second *nor* third question (neither why they believe they have an obligation nor whether and why they actually have an obligation).

Without any basis for law's obligatoriness beyond the fact of social acceptance, Hart sees an important distinction between legal pressure and moral suasion in the following way: on one hand, society exerts legal pressure often (or even primarily) through threats whereas "with morals on the other hand the typical form of pressure consists in appeals to the respect for the rules, as things important in themselves."[23] If there is a moral obligation to obey the law, then laws, too, are worth respecting in themselves, similar to moral norms. Yet Hart does not think that law necessarily carries moral obligation because we can identify rules based on social practice apart from their morality, so legal pressure and moral suasion are necessarily different things. This is particularly jarring considering Hart's own innovation, namely that people do treat the law as obligatory. Lacking a normative dimension, legal pressure must consist mainly of fear of "unpleasant consequences" or other material incentives.[24] Without an obligation to obey, the law can cajole and coerce, but it cannot make a justified claim to obedience. In failing to account for why people take the law to be a standard of behavior, Hart's theory must fall back on coercion to explain obedience, thereby reducing law to a mugger.

As with his rejection of "sanctions," Hart is correct to eschew the language of habits when it comes to understanding the law. Hart prefers to "conceive of the situation in terms of rules rather than habits."[25] Yet his focus on social practice, namely the adherence to rules (in place of the emergence of habits), improperly limits the discussion. Without explaining why this is the case, Hart avers that the "ordinary citizen manifests his acceptance largely by acquiescence in the results of these official operations."[26] If Hart means that the ordinary citizen acquiesces despite not recognizing an obligation to do so, then Hart describes a state of affairs that is both puzzling (because it leaves the acquiescence wholly unexplained) and clearly in tension with his own account of the internal point of view. Why, exactly, do citizens take the law as a standard for judging behavior if there were no obligation? If, on the contrary, Hart means that people obey out of a sense of obligation, then a better theory must, at a minimum, leave room for a satisfactory account of obligation or even tell us where that sense of obligation comes from. As things stand, Hart leaves no such room with his insistence on separating validity from justification. Social practices, like habits, can give reasons to comply but not confer an obligation. There can be many good reasons for complying with the law that fall short of generating an obligation. One can, for example, wish to accrue the benefits of compliance without believing one is obligated to obey. Indeed, precisely inasmuch as people see the "force" of law stemming from habits or social practices, they ought not to connect law and obligation. But this contradicts the substance of the internal point of view, which reveals that the law motivates compliance through something more than an appeal to "material" incentives.

In approvingly discussing what he calls the "*minimum content* of Natural Law," Hart explains that the argument for "a specific content" of laws and morals derives from the claim that "without such a content laws and morals could not forward the minimum purpose of survival which men have in associating with each other."[27] But if Hart accepts even these very basic premises, he thereby commits himself to a theory of the good that enables him to speak of what people's purposes are or what makes survival a worthy goal. (It also makes it all the more surprising that Hart seems fairly sanguine about the possibility of a legal system that produces a populace that is "deplorably sheeplike" and that "might end in the slaughterhouse."[28]) Indeed, looking a bit further, Hart ought to see that the same premises that enable him to recognize survival as a good point toward other goods that are equally natural and basic. Nor can the talk about the law's purpose be shrugged off as part of a detached analysis of natural law theory, rather than his own concept of law, since he writes explicitly, "Our concern is with social arrangements for continued existence, not with those of a suicide club."[29] Hart recognizes that "to raise this or any other question concerning *how* men should live together, we must assume that their aim, generally speaking, is to live," and he concludes that "there are certain rules of conduct which any social organization must contain if it is to be viable."[30] Hart does not appear to be saying that this is merely one way to think about the law; he is saying that this is the right way to think about the law—that the viability of the society is what gives the law purpose. Being aimed at preservation and not at destruction is an inescapably normative part of what makes it law at all. Though Hart wishes to avoid the conclusion, it is his emphasis on obligation as the characteristic feature of law that requires the authority of law to be based in something more than coercion or prediction or custom—or social practice.

THE INTERNAL POINT OF VIEW REVEALS HART'S FAILURE TO ACCOUNT FOR OBLIGATION

Hart defines the internal point of view as "the view of those who do not merely record and predict behavior conforming to rules, but *use* the rules as standards for the appraisal of their own and others' behavior."[31] For that very reason, Hart ought to be able to offer an account of why people do so. It seems strange to lay so much emphasis on that point yet sidestep the question of what explains why people treat the rules as standards for appraising their own and others' behavior. Even if the people are wrong about the justification of law's authority, surely Hart must think that they have some justification in their own minds. Otherwise, they are judging themselves and others against a standard that has no grounding. Once again, neither habit nor custom is sufficient to justify this because neither carries the sense of obligation implicated here.

A centerpiece of Hart's compellingly innovative approach to the concept of law is his distinction between the internal and external points of view. The external point of view is

> the view of one who, having observed the working of a traffic signal in a busy street for some time, limits himself to saying that when the light turns red there is a high probability that the traffic will stop. He treats the light merely as a natural *sign that* people will behave in certain ways, as clouds are a *sign that* rain will come. In doing so he will miss out a whole dimension of the social life of those whom he is watching, since for them the red light is not merely a sign that others will stop: they look upon it as a *signal for* them to stop, and so a reason for stopping in conformity to rules which make stopping when the light is red a standard of behaviour and an obligation.[32]

This is terribly astute, but the theory is incomplete—strictly in descriptive terms—if it stops without wondering *why* people take the law as a standard of behavior and an obligation, not least because Hart himself uses the term *obligation*. There must be some reason that people receive the dictates of the law differently than the dictates of a mugger, the former obligating and the latter merely obliging. Presumably, the red light is not a signal for them to stop merely in the sense that it warns that danger is ahead or in the sense that a fine will be imposed for failure to stop; rather, it is a signal of an *obligation* to stop under ordinary circumstances, regardless of whether the driver considers the danger of going through the light an acceptable risk or the fine an acceptable price to pay for the convenience of not stopping. In this way, the law is most certainly a command, and the internal point of view reveals that the laws' subjects regard it as such. (It cannot be that people merely have a "practical attitude of acceptance" because we can already observe and account for that with the external point of view.[33] On Hart's terms, the practical attitude of acceptance does not get us much further than Bentham's habits of obedience. All it tells us is that there is a regularized pattern of behavior, not how people relate to the law "internally.")

This internal point of view is the starting point for Hart's critique of the command model because, for Hart, the command model paints the law as a mugger. From the internal point of view, people understand themselves to be in a relationship with the law unlike the one they are in with a mugger even though, in both cases, compliance is usually attained through the threat of coercion. Though people's fear of punishment drives obedience to the law (to varying extents in different people), Hart offers that many or most people understand themselves to have an obligation to the law in addition to their desire to avoid punishment. This introduction of the internal point of view is crucial because Hart is saying that people understand themselves to have an obligation to obey the law (or at least act as though they do) and are not merely avoiding punishment. To be sure, Hart does not claim to provide an explanation of why people hold that understanding. After all, he just wants to observe that they do, and his insight is that they do so in a way that is distinct from the way they understand what they are obliged to do at the behest of an armed mugger. But, if it is to be viable, Hart's theory also must not rule out any possible coherent explanation for the important fact that he establishes. Yet Hart's definition of law—rules based in social practice—means that law is just whatever is accepted as law "'round here." This leaves the obvious question of why the internal point of view ever emerges. On a moment's reflection, any person can see that the fact that we happen to do things a certain way around here in many cases provides weak reasons (at best) to obey the law and never an obligation to obey the law just because it is the law.

Hart's theory falls short because it shows *that* people feel an obligation to obey the law but not *why* people feel they have that obligation. Put more precisely, although Hart, in his descriptive sociology, wishes to prescind from the question of why people feel a sense of obligation, his theory gets in the way of any coherent account for the phenomenon. So, while we can forgive Hart for not showing why people actually have an obligation (if in fact they do), the trouble is that his definition of law makes it hard for *any* successful account to be reconciled with his. Hart can say that he is agnostic with respect to why people see themselves as having an obligation to obey the law, but he cannot avoid the fact that, in its reliance on the internal point of view, his theory insists that there is such a perception. The internal point of view presupposes some sort of motivation (a belief about being obligated) other than mere avoidance of sanctions because that is precisely what distinguishes the law from a mugger. As people are not machines or rainclouds, their motivation must come from somewhere. For this reason, Hart's descriptive theory must at least be compatible with an adequate normative theory—that is, with a theory that can underlie people's sense of obligation. To repeat, by "compatible," I mean that Hart's theory must leave room for, and not effectively rule out, *some* normative account of law that can underpin the sense of obligation that people possess. But Hart's theory does rule it out.

Again, Hart's focus is on the fact of people's acceptance of law's authority, and, therefore, he goes only as far as examining the law's popular acceptance (or lack thereof) and not the matter of whether people *ought to* accept law's authority. That is fine as far as it goes, but it flies in the face of Hart's emphasis on the internal point of view in legal analysis. It is precisely because most people feel themselves to be under an obligation to obey the law that Hart distinguishes the law from criminal coercion.

A sense of obligation that motivates obedience to the law seems to be just what Hart is getting at when he argues that "those who reject the rules except where fear of social pressure induces them to conform . . . cannot be more than a minority" whereas "the majority live by the rules from the internal point of view."[34] While Hart's focus is on obedience to the law as a social practice, the internal point of view suggests that people ought to be able to give an answer to the question of why they participate in that practice and that that answer ought to rely on more than habit or custom. As Hart himself explains, habit and custom cannot explain obedience given that he understands people to be taking the law as—to invoke Hart's critical phrase—a standard for their behavior.[35] Unless people feel free to disregard the law when they have competing nonmoral motivations (such as subrational desires and so forth), which Hart seems to think they do not, then it must be that the requirements of the law are rooted in something deeper that produces a notion of obligation that does not arise from habit or custom alone. Any person reflecting on the matter can recognize that, in normal circumstances, habit and custom do not create an obligation to act, even if they provide other salient reasons to act. No one is bound by habit or custom (again, in the normal case). Therefore, in Hart's world, any person confronted with the sense of obligation also ought to believe there is a source of obligation beyond habit or custom, even if she cannot name it, or else she ought to identify the sense of obligation as mistaken, in which case Hart's internal point of view is illusory at best.

HART'S TREATMENT OF JUDGES HIGHLIGHTS HIS FAILURE TO ACCOUNT FOR OBLIGATION

We can find a good example of Hart's failure to account for the normative authority of law in his discussion of judges, which highlights this key flaw in his work. In his treatment of judges, we see the same problems highlighted by the three-question framework I set forth. The role of judges is not the centerpiece of Hart's wider project on the concept of law. As Hart repeats many times, law is not primarily about rules for officials. In Hart's words, "The principal functions of the law as a means of social control are not to be seen in private litigation or prosecutions, which represent vital but still ancillary provisions for the failures of the system. It is to be seen in the diverse ways in which the law is used to control, to guide, and to plan life out of court."[36] Yet Hart's inability to account for obligation causes trouble for any theorizing he does about judges. That is, Hart has the same trouble with respect to explaining judges' relationship to the law as he does with citizens'. Thus, the difficulty for Hart's theory in explaining the nature of judges' work further illuminates this central problem for Hart, namely his inability to account for obligation.

The context for his treatment of judges is his rejection of the command model, wherein Hart seeks to advance what he sees as a middle path that resists the "oscillation between extremes, which make the history of legal theory."[37] On one hand, he rejects natural law theories (and even Austin's positivism), which "leave insufficient room for differences between legal and moral rules and for divergences in their requirements."[38] On the other hand, he equally rejects the overreaction of the legal realists, for whom law is merely a prediction of what officials, especially courts, will do.[39] Instead, Hart seems to be in search of a place between the complete union and complete disunion of normative and nonnormative accounts of law. In dismissing legal realism, Hart contends that law cannot rightly be seen as prediction because "the judge, in punishing, takes the rule as his *guide* and the breach of the rule as his *reason* and *justification* for punishing the offender."[40] Hart's theory, unfortunately, offers no ground for supposing why the judge takes the law as a reason for action—why she takes it as a guide. Hart can show only *that* the judge does so. In this way, Hart's theory is descriptively incomplete. Because he points to a normative phenomenon, namely the taking of the rule as a guide, his description of law is incomplete without an account of justification or, worse, is impossible without room for one. This is precisely parallel to the difficulty with Hart's explanation of how the law's subjects relate to it.

In arguing against both natural law and legal realism, Hart tries to position himself in the middle. There are no necessary normative criteria for the law, yet judges are constrained somewhat in their decision-making. For Hart, judges remain "parts of a system the rules of which are determinate enough at the centre to supply standards of correct judicial decision" and which, on the judges' own understanding, "they are not free to disregard."[41] In describing the standards that limit judges, he adds, "This circumscribes, while allowing, the creative activity of its occupants. Such standards could not indeed continue to exist unless most of the judges of the time adhered to them, for their existence at any given time consists simply in the acceptance and use of them as standards of adjudication."[42] This exemplifies a key flaw in Hart's argument, which applies more generally to his concept of law. Because the system he describes rests on social practice, Hart can give no account of why judges take such standards as guides to their behavior: he can only observe that they do. But this tells us nothing about whether (and why) they are expected to do so in the future. And this leads to an especially problematic way of thinking about judicial precedents because the very idea of precedent presupposes that prior decisions have some force—that is, prior decisions serve as a standard in virtue of what they are rather than earlier and later decisions reaching similar results as "accidents" of convergent behavior.[43] In any given case, it is always possible that judges will abandon a rule, rightly or wrongly, but Hart's view implies that judges have no obligation to abide by the rule; the rule is a rule if and only if the judges continue to abide by it. This flies in the face of Hart's claim that "the basis for such prediction is the knowledge that the courts regard legal rules not as predictions, but as standards to be followed."[44] As before, if law is understood as social practice, then Hart cannot show why laws are taken as standards to be followed or even why any judge will act with confidence that they will continue to be taken as such.

SEPARATING VALIDITY FROM JUSTIFICATION MAKES IT IMPOSSIBLE TO BIND LAW TO OBLIGATION

Hart's discussion of legal validity and rules of recognition is a prime example of the tension and even contradiction within Hart's work. On one hand, he wishes to separate the identification of law's existence from the justification of law's authority. On the other hand, he wishes to set forth the obligation to obey the law as a key characteristic of law, as demonstrated by the internal point of view. Yet these two aims coexist very uneasily, at best.

The absence of any framework for justifying obligation is particularly clear with respect to Hart's discussion of legal validity, which is established by reference to the secondary rule called the rule of recognition. Rules of recognition are rules that establish the criteria for the identification of law, so they are used to identify which rules are valid parts of any given legal system. Rules of recognition are secondary rules, the classification of which is another major innovation of Hart's theory. The role of secondary rules is so important to the theory and practice of law that Hart sees their introduction into society (historically or conceptually) as "a step from the pre-legal into the legal world," indicating that secondary rules are necessary characteristics of any legal system properly so called.[45] Without secondary rules, a (pre)legal system suffers from being uncertain, static, and inefficient.[46] As Hart explains, "The remedy for each of these three main defects in this simplest form of social structure consists in supplementing the *primary* rules of obligation with *secondary* rules which are rules of a different kind."[47] First, uncertainty arises when there is no clear standard "as to what the rules are or as to the precise scope of some given rule" (92).[48] This uncertainty is resolved by a rule of recognition, which "specif[ies] some feature or features possession of which by a suggested rule is taken as a conclusive affirmative indication that it is a rule of the group."[49] Second, the system is static when it lacks a "mode of change" other than the gradual evolution (or devolution) of rules, leaving it with "no means . . . of deliberately adapting the rules to changing circumstances."[50] This defect is remedied with rules of change, which, as per the name, specify procedures for altering the rules.[51] Third and finally, inefficiency results from the absence of rules for definitively determining when violations have occurred and, separately, from the absence of an authoritative body for meting out punishment.[52] Rules of adjudication provide these capacities.[53]

Legal validity is the idea that a rule can be identified as law under the rule of recognition and, consequently, as part of the legal system. Legal validity, for positivists like Hart, depends on descriptive features, mainly procedural, such as the provenance of the rule. It is often contrasted with legitimacy (or justification), which, at least simplistically, refers to the normative force of the rule—that is, whether it is just and whether one ought to comply. Thus, where they are divorced, validity and justification refer, respectively, to whether something is a rule of the system and whether one ought to obey it.[54]

Hart's concept of law depends upon establishing criteria not for justifying law's authority but for identifying the existence of a legal system and its parts—that is, for identifying which rules count as law. Establishing legal validity means determining that the rule in question conforms to the rules for making laws, according to the rule of recognition. Simply put, in the United States, a federal law is valid when it is passed by both houses of Congress according to the proper procedures and then signed by the president. As a result of having emerged from this process, the rule can be recognized as a member of the set of rules known as federal laws in the United States. In each case, the rule of recognition tells us what characteristics the rule must bear in order to be a member of the relevant legal set. For example, "It must be passed by a majority of the parliament." "It must be decreed by the king while he sits on his throne." And so forth. Assuming the rule of recognition contains only procedural requirements (and Hart certainly assumes that is possible though not necessary), any rule, no matter how morally outrageous, can be a valid law; that is, it can be recognized as a law under the prevailing legal system because, like the others, it is adopted according to the proper procedures. But, for Hart, because of its immorality, the law can still lack justification and therefore normative force. If so, the law does not necessarily impose any moral obligation to obey. Under that scenario, the law can be valid but illegitimate (unjustified).[55]

For Hart, the rule of recognition is foundational because it is the rule by which other rules can be identified as valid: "By providing an authoritative mark it introduces, although in embryonic form, the idea of a legal system: for the rules are now not just a discrete unconnected set but are, in a simple way, unified. Further, in the simple operation of identifying a given rule as possessing the required feature of being an item on an authoritative list of rules we have the germ of the idea of legal validity."[56] The rule of recognition is meant to be a useful tool of jurisprudential analysis in that everything it identifies is law and only that which it identifies is law.[57] Or, put in terms of validity, "the statement that a particular rule is valid means that it satisfies all the criteria provided by the rule of recognition."[58] Nevertheless, Hart does not offer any legitimating source for the rule of recognition itself other than social acceptance. For this reason, although the rule of recognition can include or identify rules of change, meaning rules that specify what counts as valid changes to the law, the rule of recognition cannot explain changes to itself (or, for that matter, changes to the rules concerning changes to the rule of recognition), if there are any, except by appeal to social acceptance or, perhaps, to another rule of recognition, which only starts the problem again.[59]

Extending this logic, we can say that the rule of recognition itself needs to be subject to a rule of recognition.[60] The recursive nature of this reasoning is problematic because it demonstrates that, at some level of recursion, there must just be an acceptance by fiat of an ultimate rule of recognition.[61] Again, Hart is not (mainly) trying to account for why people treat the rule of recognition as authoritative (our second question). He is mainly pointing out that people do behave as though it is authoritative (our first question) and that this is part of what makes a collection of rules a legal system. But it also makes his theory far too much like the ones he wants to criticize insofar as it does not, despite Hart's intentions, account for the internal point of view. The rule of recognition, by definition, relies on nothing more than social acceptance. But social acceptance is a flimsy basis for treating the law as conferring obligation. If laws are valid on the basis of their conformity to the rule of recognition, then we ought to have no trouble identifying which things count as law, but we do not necessarily on that basis have a reason to treat them as a standard against which to measure our behavior and others'.

Hart's conclusion, succinctly put, is that a legal system exists when there are valid laws that are widely followed: "So long as the laws which are valid by the system's tests of validity are obeyed by the bulk of the population this surely is all the evidence we need in order to establish that a given legal system exists."[62] If the bulk of the population obeys laws that are not valid, Hart presumably thinks that this means the rule of recognition has changed and that the laws are in fact valid according to criteria that the people recognize, which recognition explains their obedience. In that case, the rule of recognition is determined retrospectively, as it were (or perhaps retroactively), depending on what people do. That is, the rule of recognition is defined by whatever facts about the law the people look to in order to know whether it is valid and, therefore, whether to obey it. Changing criteria for validity evince an evolving legal system. What this shows, though, is that, for Hart, the basis of law is reducible to what people happen to do. But, if that is the basis, we wonder, again, why people treat the law as imposing an obligation. In other words, because the "system's tests of validity"—the rules for identifying valid rules—are themselves merely sociological phenomena, any account of those rules' legitimacy (their obligation-imposing authority) is self-referential. The tests of validity are themselves valid because they are widely accepted, and they are widely accepted because they are valid. Or, they are widely accepted just because they are—they just happen to be. That can be correct as a matter of sociology, but it means that Hart's theory cannot offer an account of obligation wherever there is validity. But, because Hart distinguishes law from coercion, it does not suffice to defend Hart to say that he seeks a "concept of law which allows the invalidity of law to be distinguished from its immorality."[63] Law, on his theory, must include obligation, yet Hart here insists that we can have valid yet immoral laws. In other words, Hart's separation of invalidity and immorality is at odds with his signature distinction between being obliged and being obligated.

In sum, if Hart is right to distinguish validity from justification, validity's only meaning for legal analysis is that we can recognize or identify the thing in question as a legal rule in that society. This is because, for Hart, validity corresponds to the identification of laws as laws according to norms (like the rule of recognition) that exist apart from any consideration of the justice of the particular law (or the laws in general) or of the norms used to identify laws. But this means that, in the normal case, the fact that something is a law has no significant normative implications for whether one ought to follow it other than, perhaps, an expectation that there are consequences for obeying or disobeying—but this is law as prediction, which Hart strenuously rejects. Whether or not one *ought to* follow the law depends on an entirely separate normative analysis. In Hart's descriptive sociology, the identification of something as law in itself does not tell us whether there is a moral obligation to obey it.

This result is disastrous for Hart's theory because it introduces a disconnect between legal validity and the internal point of view, which Hart takes as a critical feature of law. To say that the law's validity entails an obligation to obey is necessarily to make a moral claim. More precisely, it is to make a claim that the definition of law includes some normative criteria beyond a recognition of what we happen to do around here. Even if we let Hart off the hook on our third question (whether and why there is an obligation to obey), the second question remains unavoidable (why people feel they have an obligation). That is, even if we recast the connection between validity and obligation in purely descriptive terms, namely that people *think* they have an obligation to obey a valid law (not that they necessarily have one, in fact), Hart's theory leaves us short because he disregards people's internal point of view about the basis of their obligation. Of course, Hart's version of validity does mean there is a legal obligation in the sense that the law expects obedience, but it is question-begging to say that a legal obligation means one truly *ought* to obey when the very issue is whether a legal obligation includes a moral obligation, or whether validity entails justification. If it does not, the most that can be said is that officials can be anticipated to hold people accountable for disobedience; nothing can be said about whether they do so justifiably. Yet if law does not, in general, coerce justifiably, then Hart commits what is by his own lights a grave wrong, failing to distinguish sufficiently between the law and a mugger.

DANGERS OF HART'S THEORY INCLUDE REDUCING LAW TO COERCION AND VALIDATING SHEEPLIKE COMPLIANCE TO COERCION BY OFFICIALS

The unintended consequences of Hart's attempt to define law as rules based in social practice, with the attendant flaws elaborated above, include some dangerous ways of thinking about power and coercion. In other words, in addition to the theoretical problems, there may be some negative real-world consequences to adopting Hart's view. The danger emerges, first, from the way Hart inadvertently reduces law to coercion, which is very much against the grain of what he is trying to accomplish, and, second, from the inadvertent encouragement to follow the law without reference to moral considerations.

Even for a positivist such as Hart—and even within his project of descriptive sociology—questions about what justifies law's authority are unavoidable because he addresses the meaning of coercion under the law. Hart believes that the coercion of some people is justifiable for the sake of the survival of the rest: "'Sanctions' are therefore required not as the normal motive for obedience, but as a *guarantee* that those who would voluntarily obey shall not be sacrificed to those who would not. To obey, without this, would be to risk going to the wall. Given this standing danger, what reason demands is *voluntary* co-operation in a *coercive* system."[64] Though that much is fairly uncontroversial on its face, presumably this coercion extends even to people who do not assent to being part of this system or who believe that they are not obligated by all parts of the system.[65] (Otherwise, there is no reason for the coercion.) Nor does Hart seem to think that this applies only when the malefactors threaten to directly endanger the physical safety of others, for the voluntary cooperators also risk going to the wall when it comes to paying taxes or refraining from polluting. For Hart, the possibility (and necessity) of coercion emerges from agreement among those who wish to cooperate and then force the regime on the rest: "Without their voluntary co-operation, thus creating *authority*, the coercive power of the law and government cannot be established."[66] But this view sheds little light on the justification for such coercion or even on whether the voluntary cooperators have any reason to *believe* (correctly or not) that what they are doing is justified. Indeed, in a similar passage, Hart expresses this more directly, adding, "A necessary condition of the existence of coercive power is that some at least must voluntarily co-operate in the system and accept its rules. In this sense it is true that the coercive power of law presupposes its accepted authority."[67] Given what Hart says throughout *The Concept of Law*, we can assume that the acceptance to which he refers is social practice and not any robust normative justification. This is specifically corroborated by other statements from Hart, such as when he writes, "Not only may vast numbers be coerced by laws which they do not regard as morally binding, but it is not even true that those who do accept the system voluntarily, must conceive of themselves as morally bound to do so, though the system will be most stable when they do."[68] Thus, the acceptance of the authority of the law is prudential, not principled. Here, Hart explicitly says that neither the people involuntarily subjected to coercion nor even the people voluntarily coercing must regard the law as morally binding (which is to say, obligatory). It is particularly provocative that Hart holds that even the people who are responsible for the coercion do not necessarily believe that the coercion is justified. For it is one thing to say that the people who accept the system do not believe they have a moral obligation to do so but instead participate voluntarily without assuming any obligations, but it is another thing entirely to say that those who force others to accept the system also do not believe there is any moral obligation to obey behind the laws for which they are coercing.[69] Hart thereby reduces law's authority to mere power.

This perhaps inevitable result of Hart denying that the justification of authority is a necessary, intrinsic part of law is devastating to Hart's claim about the internal point of view. Hart's theory centers on the claim that people take the law to be a standard by which to guide and judge their own behavior and others'. This main idea, that people treat the law as a standard, has great intuitive appeal, drawing as it does on his reasonable sociological observation that people do not relate to the law like they do to a mugger. But the idea is exceedingly hard to square with the above account of law and coercion. It requires great analytical strain to separate the notion that people *do* take the law as a guide from the notion that they believe they *ought to* take the law as a guide because it is, of course, the latter that explains the former. We cannot defend Hart by arguing that people believe they ought to take the law as a guide only in the instrumental sense of judging in particular cases that they are better off for doing so. This is not the kind of standard that Hart has in mind because that approach collapses his distinction between "obliged" and "obligated."

If compliance is tied instrumentally to the incentives in a particular instance, then obedience to the law can be reduced to a response to sanctions, which Hart emphatically wishes to avoid.

Thus, if the reduction of law to coercion does not make Hart incorrect, at least we can say it makes his theory dangerous. And there are further such concerns, especially in light of this idea of law emerging as the result of voluntary participants coercing the rest. Reading Hart closely, we learn that the group of voluntary participants may be limited to government officials. Hart's version of what constitutes a legal system, which he contrasts with the command model, comprises "obedience by ordinary citizens" and "acceptance by officials of secondary rules."[70] On this basis, Hart holds that, despite all of the sophistication of his theory in describing the form of law, "in an extreme case the internal point of view with its characteristic normative use of legal language ('This is a valid rule') might be confined to the official world. In this more complex system, only officials might accept and use the system's criteria of legal validity."[71] Hart's verdict follows: "The society in which this is so might be deplorably sheeplike; the sheep might end in the slaughter-house. But there is little reason for thinking that it could not exist or for denying it the title of legal system."[72] Contemplating the effects of the internalization of Hart's theory in real life, we can conclude that Hart unintentionally underwrites the rise of a society that is deplorably sheeplike in shifting the focus from the justification of law to the validity of law and thereby excluding questions about the morality of law as a necessary feature of the concept of law. To be sure, Hart purposely prescinds from a normative evaluation of the law. Yet it is he who suggests that the law is the set of social rules people follow just because it is "what's done around here." What is done around here does not *have* to be what people actually take as a rule for their behavior. But Hart is arguing that *it is law* precisely because it is "what's done around here" without any need for normative criteria. And that can be a powerful claim to those uninitiated in the nuances of analytical jurisprudence—that is, people who hear it is the law and, therefore, treat it as obligatory, just as Hart observes they do.

There is an instructive parallel in the work of John Simmons, who also expresses concern about potential sheeplikeness without realizing that, like Hart, his own theory risks exacerbating the problem rather than ameliorating it. In denying the existence of general political obligation, Simmons announces his preference for the alleged absence of an obligation to obey the law.[73] He thinks that widespread belief in an obligation to obey the law is government propaganda, for "what belief can better serve the interests of one's political leaders than the belief that all are specially bound to support their government and obey the law?"[74] It is the result of "not very subtle policies of political indoctrination to which we are all subjected."[75] Yet this may be something of an overstatement when we are speaking only of a prima facie obligation to obey, which is, perhaps, not as mesmerizing as Simmons supposes. The prima facie obligation to obey leaves plenty of room for competing reasons that militate against obedience to particular unjust laws.

Nevertheless, for Simmons, the belief in a general obligation to obey is in fact pernicious. He writes, "Surely a nation composed of such 'dutiful citizens' would be the cruellest sort of trap for the poor, the oppressed, and the alienated."[76] This normative evaluation of his analytic conclusion rests on empirical assumptions that do not necessarily hold. In the society Simmons imagines, the problem is too much deference to government. But it can just as easily be the case that the problem in any given society is insufficient deference. In fact, Simmons's perspective—fearing an overly submissive populace—is likely plausible because of the prevalence of the very belief in an obligation to obey that he decries. That is, perhaps Simmons has the luxury of attacking the presumption in favor of obedience only because the presumption is sufficiently widespread that his society can comfortably endure additional disobedience. But in a world that embraces his Razian conclusion of an absence of an obligation to obey where each citizen exercises individual judgment about each law, there can be an entirely different set of problems, perhaps worse than ones he perceives, leading to circumstances even less salutary for the poor, the oppressed, and the alienated.

HART'S CONCEPT OF LAW CANNOT ACCOMMODATE THE KEY FEATURE OF OBLIGATION

To recap, we recall that Hart's important innovation, the internal point of view, begins with the observation that most people do not relate to the law as to a mugger whom they obey out of fear and self-interest but instead take the law as a standard against which to measure their own behavior. That is to say, they treat the law as justified, and they take themselves to have an obligation to obey. Or, because we do not know their motivations, we can hedge just a bit and say they treat the law *as though* they believe it is justified or, equivalently, as though they believe they have an obligation. Hart falls short by failing to give an account of why people understand themselves to have such an obligation or, for those who insist that such an account is not Hart's responsibility, by constructing an account of legal authority based on social practice that leaves no room for a justificatory theory of law's authority. But unless the internal point of view is a mass delusion, then there ought to be some adequate source for the obligation to obey.

Two possible responses on Hart's behalf do not suffice. First, it does not do to say that Hart is off the hook because he argues only that people understand themselves to have an obligation and not that they actually have an obligation and, accordingly, that Hart has no need to identify or even leave room for any such source of obligation. Technically, it is possible that people generally understand themselves to be under an obligation even though no one is. But, for one thing, it significantly diminishes Hart's theory to say that his key insight about people's relationship to the law, widely taken to be correct, captures nothing more than a mass delusion.[77] If it is the case that the law is merely customary (or even habitual, which suggests even less cognitive engagement) yet people understand the law as something that creates obligation, then it is important to explain the enormous disconnect between the true nature of the law and people's understanding. If Hart wants to have it both ways, then his theory holds only if everyone is laboring under the illusion that law creates obligation when in fact it does not. In any case, if Hart's concept of law does not match people's understanding, this disconnect lands a severe blow to Hart's attempt to describe law as it exists in fact—that is, to engage in "descriptive sociology." More pointedly, if it turns out that people accurately understand the law to be rules based in social practice—that is, rules whose ultimate basis is just that "it's the way we do things around here"—it is all the more difficult to imagine the sense of obligation that Hart reports because then people believe that the source of law is not obligation imposing.

Second, it does not do to say that Hart's theory simply swings free of any normative theory, given his (allegedly) purely descriptive account. Indeed, Hart makes claims not just about how law functions sociologically but about what law *is*.[78] In describing the nature of law, Hart has a hard time getting it right if he omits or misjudges a central feature of it. To put it bluntly, Hart's theory cannot be a normatively agnostic model with room for a normative theory to be attached because, for Hart, the very thing that characterizes law is its standing as a rule, and the thing that makes it a rule is its social acceptance—no more.

For Hart, a socially accepted rule is law regardless of its pedigree or its merits, and, contrariwise, a standard that has fallen out of use, which can no longer be identified by the rule of recognition, is not law regardless of its justification under some normative theory. A law can be obligatory (or perceived as such) either because of social acceptance or, for example, because of some normative criterion, such as democratic legitimacy. It can also be obligatory (or perceived as such) due to both reasons, but there is no guarantee that the two overlap. That is, the law can be socially accepted but lack democratic legitimacy, or vice versa.

Limiting the basis of law to social practice works only if one is prepared to abandon Hart's revolution in jurisprudence and prepared to *fail to explain* why people take the law as a standard against which to measure their behavior and relate to the law differently than to a mugger—that is, why they take themselves to have an obligation to obey the law. To be sure, the absence of moral obligation can be reconciled with a more limited claim for Hart, namely that people only think they have an obligation to obey the law while Hart himself remains agnostic as to whether they do. But such a limited claim is tenuous for three reasons. First, as I say, it hardly seems as though Hart believes that most people suffer under a mass delusion about the obligation to obey. Second, it is too convenient if there is no obligation to obey yet most people conform to the same behaviors all for their own separate reasons, some believing they are obligated under democratic theory, some under tradition, and so on. Third—the point that is at the heart of my argument—Hart wants to identify law as rules based in social practice. On a correct understanding, it is the obligation to obey that differentiates the law from nonlegal rules (such as customs, manners, and so on). After all, people take the law as a standard against which to measure their behavior, as Hart says, in a way that is different from how they relate to habits or customs. The key problem, though, is that there is no room for obligation in Hart's theory because law is essentially defined by social practice, and social practice cannot generate an obligation in the sense required here. Put plainly, there cannot be an obligation to obey the law just because it is the social practice (at least not any more than there is an obligation to conform to any nonlegal social practice).

Instead, this sort of understanding of law requires a normative theory overlaid on top of it because the fact of the directive being a law, rooted ultimately in social practice, cannot itself imply an obligation to obey. For law to entail an obligation to obey (and, thus, for law to give people a reason to treat it as doing so), there always needs to be some additional theory that justifies the law or, in other words, supplies the obligation to obey. In that case, it is the features of that other theory and not a feature intrinsic to the concept of law itself that explain justified authority and obligation. That is, whatever gives a law authority in a particular case is separate from the concept of law itself, meaning that obligation is not an intrinsic part of law. But a key point of Hart's theory is to link law and obligation. This is the internal point of view, something Hart argues previous views of law miss.

To take an example, one candidate, among many others, for what could supply legitimacy (justification) in the minds of citizens, external to the concept of law itself, is liberal or democratic theory. On this understanding of Hart (where law and obligation are separate), there can be a democratically reached decision that is authoritative because, under this theory, it is some feature of democracy that creates obligations to obey but does not count as law if it does not conform to social practice.[79] Alternatively, there can be directives that count as law on Hart's view for conforming to the relevant social practices but are not obligatory for lacking the relevant democratic features, if, say, the rule of recognition encompasses nondemocratic legislative processes.

Because Hart sees law as social practice, he accepts the possibility of laws like the ones in that example that are valid but not normatively justified. But the example of a valid but unjustified law shows how complicated it is for Hart to propose his concept of law if it does not necessarily include an obligation to obey given that one of his central points is precisely that people *do* see the law as conferring upon them an obligation to obey. It is strange, therefore, if the obligation to obey does not come from the law but from any one of a number of other theories that stand independent of the concept of law (or, put another way, if the concept of law swings free of obligation). On these terms, it is even a stretch to say that law, by definition, entails some add-on justification, whether democracy or tradition or anything else, because even then there is little reason to view law as a separate concept in which laws are the standards by which people judge their own behavior when the explanation for why they do so is entirely parasitic on some underlying normative criteria that are not part of the central concept of law (for example, if it is the fact of it being the *consensus populi* and not the fact of it being actually legislated that makes it authoritative). If such a normative theory is part of the definition of law, then the proper identification of law depends upon satisfying the terms of that theory and not solely upon nonnormative features of the law. On the other hand, if normativity is not part of the definition, there can be some laws that meet the criteria for law and some that do not, but then Hart must be at pains to explain why the law, just as such, is taken as a standard against which to measure one's own behavior, rather than only the laws that possess the normatively salient feature being taken that way.

To be sure, although a theory with the correct view of law and authority explains why people have an obligation, it does not necessarily explain why people behave as though they do. That is, the correctness of a theory is no guarantee that everyone knows about it (or that they follow it if they do know)—as can be true of any moral obligation. Likewise, even if people believe they have an obligation to obey the law (and act accordingly), it does not mean they truly know why they have an obligation. Rather than proposing a theory about how people treat the law, though, I am developing a theory about the nature of law, meaning a theory about what law is. At first, this would seem to separate my theory from Hart's theory since my theory addresses the sources of obligation while he is dealing with the fact (or practice) of obedience. On closer examination, though, Hart's theory is not merely descriptive sociology, as he says, in the more limited sense because it is really an argument about what makes law law—about what law is. It is why his topic—and ours—is the concept of law.

MARMOR'S AND SHAPIRO'S ATTEMPTS TO IMPROVE UPON HART END UP REPLICATING THE SAME CRITICAL ERROR

Andrei Marmor, largely adopting Hart's view and working from within Hart's parameters, identifies well a problem at the heart of theories of authority that also exposes why so many theories go wrong. He calls it the dilemma of authority.[80] If, as Raz has it, justification depends on a confluence of the authority's directives with the reason for actions that the subject has already, then it is difficult to see what practical difference the authority makes. If, on the other hand, the authority's authoritativeness is content independent, it is hard to see how that content independence can be squared with any theory of justification because any meaningful theory of justification must be content dependent in some respect. In the face of this dilemma, Marmor adopts the Hartian option, choosing to recognize all de facto authority rather than distinguish between justified and unjustified authority. Marmor's theory is especially worth our scrutiny because it is a paradigm of applying Hart's core points; he does the best one can do taking Hart's work as his premises, and despite this (or because of it), he, too, fails to provide a compelling account of authority.

Like Hart, Marmor argues for understanding authority in terms of social or institutional practices and thereby purportedly avoids the need for a separate normative basis of authority—that is, a separate account of justification. He writes, "What it takes to have practical authority is determined by some social or institutional practice."[81] Though he risks sounding circular, Marmor claims that the normative power of an authority is rooted in the norms of the institution of which the authority is a part. He spells this out in "three theses: (1) to have practical authority is to have normative power of a certain type; (2) power, in this sense, is granted or constituted by norms, that is, some rules or conventions; and (3) power-conferring norms are essentially institutional—they form part of some social practice or institution."[82] Essentially, Marmor's claim is that the power-conferring norms that authorize the officials to obligate subjects are just part of the social practice or institution. The social practice or institution exists, and one feature of it is that it confers normative power upon the authority. While it is true that those who participate in the social practice or institution can understand it to confer "normative power of a certain type," just as we see with Hart, the identification of such practices and institutions is not enough to justify the power-conferring norms. Alternatively, if Marmor is using the term *normative* in a limited way that does not entail justification and a moral obligation to obey—we see something like this in Estlund—then his theory is unhelpful and does not properly address the nature of authority.

As Marmor sets forth at the outset, the kind of authority worth discussing is authority with normative power. That is the phenomenon that needs explaining because "mere" authority, the power to coerce, is at best insufficient for explaining what makes authority justified. Because, for Marmor, the existence of authority with normative power—which is to say, justified authority—depends on the justification of social practices or institutions, the key question is what confers that justification. In other words, the question is how social practices or institutions create an obligation to obey the authority. Marmor falters when he nearly suggests that it comes down to consent. Taking an example from his familiar university setting, Marmor asserts, "I am bound to comply with the dean's instructions because I have agreed to do so."[83] He is quick to specify that this is not consent in the sense of having directly given the dean his consent. Rather, his obligation is born of "a commitment to the institution, its members, and beneficiaries."[84] But this still depends on possessing that commitment—that is, on having given consent, albeit not in the narrowest sense. What Marmor really needs to explain is whether the dean's authority is justified even without Marmor's commitment to the institution.

In contrast to this weak spot, Marmor is on much firmer ground when he approaches his conception of authority this way: "The arguments about the obligation to obey the law pertain to the kind of institution law is, its functions in society, the moral obligations we may have in supporting these functions, and the extent to which the support needs to be realized by an obligation to obey."[85] Focusing on obligations in this way, Marmor can account for authority even in the absence of consent because we can recognize that some moral obligations exist without consent. Moreover, this framework for addressing the problem reveals why the law's authority depends on its justification as a whole, because it is about the function of law as an institution. The institution as a whole is either justified or unjustified. And this, in turn, exposes the central underlying question, namely what "kind of institution law is" and what "its functions in society" are. While Marmor does not attend carefully to this question, the answer that provides the most coherent account of law's authority is one that centers on its role in securing and advancing the common good.

Thus, the central problem, typical of any Hartian approach, is that Marmor cannot really explain authority without recourse to a more fully normative source or, failing that, without abandoning the very normativity that he seeks to explain. In setting out his definitions, Marmor writes that "to have practical authority is to have the normative power to impose obligations on another."[86] This is a fully normative claim. Similarly, Marmor is clear that he intends the moral usage of the terms *authority* and *obligation*, describing his concept of "systemic power" (or "S-power") as the "moral right to rule," or the "moral right to have authority under certain circumstances."[87]

Like Hart with his internal point of view, Marmor must be using this terminology in its normative sense. If by "obligation" he means anything short of moral obligation, then he is not speaking of a normative power to impose moral obligations but a coercive power to impose legal obligations merely in the sense of compelling certain behavior. But if political and legal obligation boil down to what one can be forced to do, then there is no need to explain or even refer to the normativity of law. Hart's key insight about the distinction between coercive power and legal power (being "obliged" versus being "obligated," in Hart's terminology) cannot stand on those terms.

Because Marmor follows too closely in Hart's line of thinking, he cannot finally account for this moral usage. In doing so, he runs into the same problem as Estlund and even employs similar language in his own defense. Much as Estlund writes, after what appears to be a long effort to justify authority, that "there can be authority without legitimacy," Marmor claims that his points "pertain only to the question of what it is to *have* a certain practical authority; they establish nothing about the question of legitimacy."[88] This is extremely problematic given his definition of practical authority just a few pages prior as "the normative power to impose obligations on another."[89] There is no coherent way to distinguish between legitimacy and the normative power to impose obligations if those terms are to have anything beyond trivial meaning. Unfortunately, this is something of an inevitable outcome as Marmor adheres to a descriptive framework anchored in social realities while also acknowledging the normative component of practical authority. Ultimately, he cannot dance at both weddings.

It is, therefore, not unexpected that Marmor runs into trouble again, saying, "The more we recognize the dependence of practical authorities on social practices or institutions, the easier it becomes to realize that the legitimacy of authorities is bound to depend on the legitimacy of the practice or institution in which they operate, each authority's specific functions in it, and, importantly, the general terms of participation in the practice or institution."[90] This is a helpful observation because he sees that the obligation to obey depends on the justification of the authority (the social practice or institution) as a whole.

Because of the institutional character of law—law serves a purpose as a system—the authoritativeness of individual directives depends on the authoritativeness of the institution of law as a whole. At the same time, the passage highlights the impossibility of separating authority and justification: the authoritativeness of the practical authorities or of the social practices or institutions on which they depend rests on the justification of those social practices or institutions. As Marmor set out in his own definition of law as the "moral right to rule," practical authority itself is meaningless without justification.

Marmor has the same problem when he tries to separate authority and what he calls the moral right to rule (what he calls S-power). In Marmor's view, "A moral right to rule, however, is not tantamount to having authority; it means only that one should have it or that it is good that one has it. Perhaps, all things considered, X should be in charge, not Y. But if the relevant powers are granted to Y, then Y is the one who has the relevant authority, even if Y should not have it (morally speaking, that is)."[91] It is true that one can have the moral right to rule yet lack de facto authority. And it is true that, conversely, one can wield power without justification. As Marmor says, one might be entitled to rule without anyone actually obeying (for any of a number of reasons).[92] But this is a puzzling point on which to rest his distinction between authority and legitimacy when the purpose of his theory is to unpack practical authority as a normative power to impose obligations—a normative power that ought to exist whether or not anyone actually obeys because it depends on having the right to rule and not on having the ability to coerce. Using Marmor's terms, someone with the right to rule has, by definition, S-power, meaning the power to change the normative situation, which is distinct from the power to bring about compliance through coercion. In other words, the person with the right to rule possesses *justified authority*. Even if having de facto power to force compliance is a necessary condition for S-power, it is clearly not a sufficient condition, so, contra Marmor, the one possessing such power (Y) does not have "the relevant authority." Or, if de facto power to enforce is sufficient for S-power, then Marmor needs to explain why this constitutes the power to change the *normative* situation. We can much more simply say that that person has the power to compel compliance. But if that, in turn, is an acceptable distillation of the theory, then Marmor is hard-pressed to distinguish between a government and a gang. Collapsing that distinction is fine if Marmor is seeking merely to describe just any de facto authority (situations in which there are rules and people in fact obey), but it does not extricate him from the dilemma of authority, the solution to which must include an account of justification. And it entails an abandonment of Hart's central insight about the internal point of view and the difference between being obliged and being obligated.

Marmor's separation of the moral right to rule from authority finally puts him in an impossible position. If he equates authority and the moral right to rule, he contradicts his statement that authority requires de facto power. If he divides them, he is left without any explanation for authority's normative power in the absence of a right to rule. Therefore, he ought to concede that having the moral right to rule is the same as having justified authority and that social practices or institutions can play a role in the designation of authority but that de facto authority is not required for the normative power to exist.

Instead of trying unsuccessfully to split authority and justification, Marmor ought to focus on truly accounting for the normative power of authority in his institutional conception. At bottom, he does recognize this, but, unable to accept a fully normative approach, he pulls back, claiming that he is speaking of authority but not justification. When he does address justification, however, he writes, "To determine when an authority is legitimate or not, we need a normative account for sure, but not about authorities in general; we need a normative theory about the legitimacy of social practices and institutions, what makes them good and just and worthy of our support."[93] He is terribly close to getting it right here: he sees that the kind of authority he is talking about, generated by social practices or institutions, depends on the justification of those social practices or institutions. But, in the end, the social practices or institutions are good for the ends they achieve through the authority they underwrite. So he cannot avoid a normative account about "authorities in general" while maintaining his other claims. Instead of getting it right, he ultimately falls into the same trap as Hart. Trying to separate authority from justification, Marmor finds himself with an incoherent account of authority and obligation.

Like Marmor, Scott Shapiro is sensitive to the key shortcoming in Hart's concept of law and tries to improve upon it with a stronger account of law's normativity. At the heart of Shapiro's book *Legality* is a thesis about the functions or purposes of law. In particular, Shapiro offers a description of the nature of law that emphasizes law's role in enabling planning. Shapiro wishes to avoid what he sees as the fundamental conceptual errors of two predominant ways of thinking about the law. One target is Hart and his followers, who "derive normative judgments about legal rights and duties from descriptive judgments about social facts."[94] Summing up the problem, Shapiro writes, "Normative judgments come out, but none have gone in."[95] Those theorists (Marmor among them, presumably) think they account for justified authority solely with the existence of rules based in social practice. But this cannot be done without a normative assessment of whether those social practices generate obligations, meaning it cannot be done merely by showing that the practices *exist*. As Shapiro rightly insists, in the legal sphere "there are no amoral concepts of authority and obligation and hence no middle ground between the descriptive and the moral that positivists can call their own."[96] For this reason, Shapiro calls "Hart's attempt to preserve the distinction between legal and moral thought and discourse ... an unstable compromise."[97] Unfortunately, although Shapiro puts his finger on the problem with thinkers like Hart and, by extension, Marmor, his own theory ultimately suffers from the same basic weakness. Like Marmor, Shapiro tries to split the difference between authority and justification in a way that simply cannot succeed.

Part of Shapiro's motivation to do so stems from his attack on his second target, natural law theory, which, in his interpretation, "rules out the possibility of evil legal systems."[98] Like Hart, Shapiro cannot accept a definition of legal systems that entirely fuses the descriptive and the normative given that, in his view, there plainly are evil legal systems. To deny a set of directives the name "legal system" due to the system's injustice is, in Hart's and Shapiro's views, simply to deny what is plainly in front of one's face. Hart and Shapiro identify legal systems by descriptive criteria. For them, a set of rules containing the appropriate nonnormative features—for example, in Hart's terminology, a union of primary rules (rules about duties, powers, and the like) and secondary rules (rules about those rules)—constitutes a legal system whether the system is virtuous or vicious, and no matter how thoroughly so.

As Shapiro indicates, the foundation of his theory is the search for an answer to the question "What is law?" Shapiro rejects the natural law approach precisely because he holds that it goes wrong on that critical question, denying the "truism" that legal systems are legal systems even when they are evil. Shapiro wants a theory that "better accommodates the *entire* set of considered judgments about the law."[99] Because he thinks that the natural law approach "amounts to no more than the defiant declaration that evil legal regimes are not possible," he prefers positivism.[100] But, as with Hart, the price he pays for being able to identify the legal systems of evil regimes is the inability to account for obligation as a central feature of the law.

So, despite his criticism of Hart and other positivists, Shapiro remains a positivist in this respect and searches for a better way to account for the authority of law. In explicating just what descriptive criteria define a legal system, Shapiro focuses on the planning function of law, which exists in both (morally) good and bad legal systems. He explains that "we cannot understand what laws are unless we understand how and for what purposes legal systems produce them in the first place," and he finds the answer in the planning function of law.[101] The immediate problem this raises, though, is that the end sought through planning is itself a normative goal. That end is the goal of the legal system, and the plan is a means to it. That is, planning is for the purpose of achieving certain ends that are preferred over other ends, for if the intended ends are not preferred, then there is no point in planning to advance them. In certain cases, perhaps, it can be that having a plan is itself the end, but, generally speaking, planning is not good for its own sake but for the ends sought through the plan.

This moral dimension of planning is evident in Shapiro's theory. He defines his "Planning Theory of Law" as follows: "*Legal systems are institutions of social planning and their fundamental aim is to compensate for the deficiencies of alternative forms of planning in the circumstances of legality.*"[102] And, in line with my own view, he acknowledges that "the aim of the law is not planning for planning's sake."[103] "Rather," he adds, "the law aims to compensate for the deficiencies of nonlegal forms of planning by planning in the 'right' way, namely, by adopting and applying morally sensible plans in a morally legitimate manner."[104] What makes the plans morally sensible, of course, is what they aim at (in addition to how they aim to get there). Though this is not exactly what we expect from a positivist, the real surprise here is not Shapiro's introduction of normativity as part of the definition of planning but that he ever proposes to do without it in the first place.

Following Hart's lead and hoping to avoid the trap that he thinks the natural lawyers fall into by combining law and morality, Shapiro also maintains that "the existence of legal authority can only be determined *sociologically*."[105] Because, in his view, "the fundamental rules of legal systems *are* plans," "the question of whether a body has legal power is never one of its moral legitimacy; it is a question of whether the relevant officials of that system accept a plan that authorizes and requires deference to that body."[106] As he says similarly later on, "To build or operate a legal system one need not possess moral legitimacy to impose legal obligations and confer legal rights: one need only have the ability to plan."[107] But that is difficult (or, really, impossible) to square with what he says about "adopting and applying morally sensible plans in a morally legitimate manner." Sociology cannot reveal whether the plans are morally sensible or deployed in a morally legitimate way. Again, it does not do to say that planning is moral only in the limited sense of being directed toward *some* end. As I say, perhaps in rare cases it can be better to have some plan over none, but, in the normal case, what is moral about being directed to any end is the normative preferability of that end. Thus, crucially, what makes any end (and, therefore, any plan) preferable cannot be established without reference to the morality of that end.

This problem of trying to describe plans without reference to legitimacy is exactly parallel to the problem of trying to describe authority without reference to justification. (That Shapiro does this is unsurprising, given that his theory is that the planning function of law is what gives law its authority. But the key point is that he sees his project as an attempt to avoid this problem.) To be sure, there can be de facto authority without justification, but this is mere power. The moral obligation to obey depends upon the presence of justified authority. In the same way, the authoritativeness of the plans—that is, the obligation to go along with those plans (namely, to obey the law)—depends upon the morality of the plans' ends. Surely Shapiro does not intend to say that there is an obligation to go along with plans just because they exist, completely irrespective of their content. And if he means to say nothing at all about obedience owed as a matter of moral obligation, then the authoritativeness of the plans must be rooted in coercion or voluntary compliance. It is only in that way that Shapiro can attempt to eschew what he calls normative jurisprudence in favor of analytic jurisprudence, which, "by contrast, is not concerned with morality."[108] That is manifestly not possible if legitimacy matters, which it must in order to give planning its salience in Shapiro's theory.[109]

Even Hart concedes that law has a moral component insofar as it must at least secure some minimal ends, such as survival.[110] Indeed, a similar element is reflected in Shapiro's discussion of the nature of law, itself an elaboration of what it means to plan. "What makes the law *the law* is that it has a moral aim, not that it satisfies that aim," Shapiro writes.[111] And, more broadly, "A legal system cannot help but have a moral aim if it is to be a legal system."[112] Shapiro wants to have it both ways, so his planning thesis is hard to reconcile with his insistence that the law cannot be understood without this moral referent. We cannot rescue him by arguing on his behalf that this remains purely in the descriptive realm on the logic that it is a definitional feature of plans that, in the self-understanding of the planners, plans have moral aims although nothing in the nature of law-as-plans depends on the actual goodness or badness of those aims. Shapiro claims, "It is part of the identity of law to have a moral mission, whereas it is not in the nature of nonlegal criminal syndicates to have such a mandate."[113] Clearly, criminal syndicates do have plans, even if they do not have moral missions, so Shapiro must mean that law not only has aims but also has good aims. But, equally clearly, some legal systems are evil, according to Shapiro. So Shapiro paints himself into a corner whereby legal systems that plan toward bad ends still have moral missions, but gangs that plan toward bad ends do not.[114] If this is the case, then Shapiro appears to maintain his position by assuming what he wants to prove: that it is possible to identify legal systems, both good and bad, with respect to descriptive criteria that distinguish legal systems from nonlegal systems in which de facto authority is also exercised. Yet, at the same time, he rests the distinction on a normative criterion: the presence or absence of a moral mission. He cannot have it both ways. The echoes of Hart—and Hart's central flaw—are unmistakable.

Still, Shapiro thinks that he avoids the problem (that he sees in Hart) of deriving normative judgments from descriptive facts by claiming, "To discover the content of law, one must begin by approaching social facts in a practical vein and forming normative judgments."[115] Thus, because of these normative judgments, it is possible for law to have its normative character even though law itself is identified solely on the basis of descriptive, not normative, facts. Showing that this solution traces back to Hart's theory, Shapiro turns to Hart's insight that "those who respond to the rule of recognition practically will form a normative judgment expressed as follows: 'What the Queen-in-Parliament enacts is law.'"[116] For Shapiro, to respond practically to the law is to adopt a practical attitude of acceptance. As his example of the judge shows, this does not entail accepting the rules as law in the full normative sense. It is entirely possible that one who responds practically to the rule of recognition *treats* it as law only in the sense of complying in order to receive certain benefits or, at a minimum, to avoid punishment. But this is insufficient to constitute a judgment that what the Queen-in-Parliament enacts is law in the full normative sense—that is, in the sense that one *ought* (morally) to take the law as a standard for judging behavior, as Hart puts it. This normative judgment entails believing that there is an *obligation* to obey whether or not it is convenient to do so. Such a belief does not arise simply from adopting a practical attitude of acceptance as Shapiro describes it; that is, this practical attitude of acceptance is, on Shapiro's own terms, not a normative judgment in the relevant sense.

Shapiro's attempt to account for the authority of law as a positivist draws heavily on his understanding of "perhaps Hart's greatest contribution to jurisprudential theory," the internal point of view.[117] Shapiro defines it as follows: "The internal point of view is the practical attitude of acceptance—it does not imply that people who accept the rules accept their moral legitimacy, only that they are disposed to guide and evaluate conduct in accordance with the rules."[118] In adopting Hart's position, however, he also inherits and in some ways even exemplifies the problems with Hart, especially the inability to explain why people who do not accept the moral legitimacy of the law are disposed to guide and evaluate their conduct in accordance with its rules. *Why do they do that?* They are disposed to do so either because they think they are obligated or because they fear punishment (or out of some other form of self-interest). While Shapiro, like Hart, can protest that he is only describing the fact of acceptance, this escape from the challenge leaves Shapiro without any recourse for distinguishing this kind of authority from de facto authority, or coercive power. And it thereby leaves him without room to distance himself from the very thing in Hart that he criticizes. Without at least a belief of moral legitimacy (to say nothing of actual justification), there is no reason for a belief in an obligation to obey (to say nothing of an actual obligation) to be a feature of law in the first place. Expounding on Hart's view, Shapiro agrees that "one can accept a rule for any type of reason, even a nonmoral one."[119] But it significantly weakens the conceptual force of the term *rule* if the judge, to take the example in question, accepts a rule "because it is in his long-term interest," such as "to advance his political career, or simply make a living."[120] This weakened sense is betrayed in Shapiro's language; it is not necessarily the same thing for the judge to accept something as a rule and to "treat" it as a rule.[121] Though the practical outcome can look the same in most cases, when a judge merely *treats* something as a rule, it means that she does not necessarily see the rule (or the source of the rule) as requiring her to treat it as such, whereas if she accepts it as a rule then she at least believes she is bound by it (whether or not she is in fact bound, morally speaking). That distinction is a fundamental difference. The difference can also bear out empirically if the "rule-treating" judge deviates when she believes that disregarding the rule will better advance whatever interests she is serving. The rule-accepting judge does not have the leeway to do this.

Shapiro's recognition of something like a content-independent obligation to obey the law accentuates the problem. Insofar as law gets its authoritativeness from its role in planning, Shapiro is correct when he writes, "It would defeat the purpose of having plans if I were to review their wisdom without an otherwise compelling reason to do so."[122] To a limited extent, that is true regardless of the content of the plans. But even then, the norm cannot be explained without recourse to deeper normative judgments. The purpose of a plan is to achieve the plan's ends. It is worth sticking to the plan, though, only if the ends are worthy. Otherwise, by executing the plan, one is merely more efficiently achieving something not worth achieving. The normative judgment that one ought to follow a plan (or, equivalently, that one ought to obey the law because it embodies some plan) rests on a normative judgment about the choice-worthiness of that plan—that is, a judgment based on *normative* facts about the plan. Without the choice-worthiness of the plan itself, the content-independent reason for sticking to the plan withers.

Furthermore, even if Shapiro is right that, in the absence of a compelling reason to deviate, there is a general, content-independent reason to adhere to one's plans due to the efficiency of adhering, that does not mean there is an obligation to adhere. Indeed, we can say that that position leaves the bar for departing from the plan so low as to make it effectively meaningless. If the planner, for example, simply decides that she feels like reconsidering, that seems like enough reason to do so in Shapiro's construction. If the plan's ends are no longer desired and if we assume nothing about the goodness of the plan's ends, then even the barest reasons are sufficient to warrant a reconsideration of the plan.

In sum, Shapiro is not able to solve the problems that jurisprudence inherits from Hart's positivism. On one hand, as a committed positivist, he strives to keep the identification of law's authority strictly sociological, which means not passing judgment on the moral merits of particular systems and, more broadly, reading normativity out of the definition of such systems altogether. Consequently, Shapiro offers dubious statements such as, "Since laws are plans, or planlike norms, they do not claim moral force either."[123] How can the plan-like law be normative, as he wishes to say, yet not claim moral force? Despite this (and without note of his own contradiction), he is sensitive to the incoherence of the modern positivists' account of authority shorn of an account of justification. Shapiro explains his Planning Theory as "affirming that it is part of the nature of law to have a moral aim, while at the same time denying that the failure to attain this end undermines the law's identity as law."[124] This falls short as a full explanation of law because it does not account for why a legal system that totally fails to achieve its moral aim is justified but a system with no moral aim is not. Simply having a moral aim is not enough to supply justification. The obligation to obey can follow only from the law's directedness toward some moral ends, so it is unlikely that any formulation of Shapiro's theory can avoid incoherence.

Shapiro's muddle underscores why Hartian jurisprudence cannot succeed. As suggested famously by Hart, a proper concept of law allows for a distinction between the coercive power of a mugger, who *obliges* a victim to obey, and the authority of the law, which *obligates* its subjects. Put another way, a successful definition of a legal system allows us to differentiate between gangs and governments even though both exert coercive power over groups of people, sometimes in an ordered fashion. For Raz, a hallmark of a legal system is that it claims legitimacy. For Shapiro, in a legal system, those who are part of the system, or at least those who administer it, believe it has legitimacy. This is why Shapiro can distinguish between the system having a moral mission and achieving it. But these frameworks are all insufficient because neither a claim of legitimacy nor a belief in it actually establishes legitimacy. If a belief in legitimacy is both necessary and sufficient, Shapiro is hard-pressed to explain the presence of de facto authority in a government that lacks the necessary moral mission or the absence of justified authority in a gang that, sufficiently, has a moral mission. In contrast, a better concept of law defines a legal system as actually having legitimacy—that is, as generating an obligation to obey the law—the full normative claim—and then seeks to identify the basis of justification.

Shapiro writes: "Augustine famously asked: 'Justice removed, then what are kingdoms but great bands of robbers?' Morally speaking, the answer may be nothing. But from a conceptual point of view, there is all the difference in the world."[125] The right rejoinder to Shapiro is that there is all the difference in the world from a conceptual point of view *because* there is a difference from the moral point of view. Shapiro thinks the difference is that the robbers do not have a moral mission, yet he does not offer a convincing argument for this. He suggests that it is the lack of a moral mission that makes them criminals and not legal officials, but it is not hard to imagine a criminal syndicate, like Robin Hood and friends, with a more lofty self-conception.

More broadly, the right response to Shapiro is that political and legal philosophy, unlike, say, sociology, ought to be able to demonstrate the moral difference between a kingdom and a band of robbers. That difference is one's justification and the other's lack thereof, the former deriving from the substance of its moral mission, namely the advancement of the common good. Perhaps, then, evil legal systems are in fact not legal systems but instrumentalities of great bands of robbers. In this respect, an evil legal system is like a hospital that intentionally kills people instead of healing them. The "hospital" looks the same in its physical plant, employs staff trained with all the same medical knowledge and skills, and so forth, but it is a hospital in name only. Indeed, it is not actually a hospital, much like Finnis says about a bottle of poison labeled "medicine."[126] What distinguishes the hospital and the "hospital" is their respective ends—that is, what purposes they serve. If a legal system is understood in terms of its purposes (which it must be if justified authority and obligation are to be meaningful parts of the concept of law), then the evil legal system is no more a legal system than the evil hospital is a hospital. Building on Hart's foundation, Shapiro simply cannot overcome the difficulties he sees in that theory and its progeny while also sustaining his commitment to positivism. His concept of law fails like Hart's does.

CHAPTER 2

Commands versus Rules—and Nazis

COMMANDS

The command model provides a superior description of law

With enormous impact on the field, Hart decisively rejects the command model of law. Yet, contrary to Hart's position, we ought to retain the notion of command in the concept of law. To rebut Hart, I offer both an affirmative defense with respect to why command is a useful component of the concept of law (because of the connection to obligation) and a negative defense with respect to why Hart's assessment of command is mistaken (because of his overemphasis on features of law, such as sanctions, that are separable from the concept of law).

In his thoroughgoing rejection of the command model of law, Hart argues "that the theory is not merely mistaken in detail, but that the simple idea of orders, habits, and obedience, cannot be adequate for the analysis of law. What is required instead is the notion of a rule conferring powers, which may be limited or unlimited, on persons qualified in certain ways to legislate by complying with a certain procedure."[1] Although Hart's theory has many virtues, it goes too far in rejecting the essential core of the command model. That is, while Hart is correct to critique some of the prominent features of the command model, including some of the key vocabulary associated with its understanding of law, he is wrong to reject the theory entirely. In doing so, Hart loses the framework necessary for a complete and proper analysis of law. Hart's new model, though an improvement in many ways, fails to account for law's central feature: its authoritativeness. Instead of rejecting the command model as Hart does, a better approach is to produce a revised version of the theory that accommodates his substantial critique without sacrificing the elements necessary for a complete picture of the law.

The command model is a more instructive framework than Hart admits because of the link between command and obligation. To be sure, a moral obligation to obey is not a logically necessary feature of the command model; identifying commands can simply be a way of identifying legally valid rules. This is how it appears in the work of Austin and others. But the command model—in a better, modified form—is superior to theories that throw out the notion of command because "command" implies the very thing that flows from the normative force of law, namely the obligation to obey. Though the fact alone of being a command does not justify authority, the notion of command inescapably implies the intended (though, again, not always effected) presence of an obligation. In other words, the notion of command suggests, without establishing, the morally obligatory nature of the directives. This is not the case for rules based in social practice ("what we do around here"), which do not possess the feature of being commanded and therefore do not necessarily imply any obligation.

While putting his finger on real problems with theories like Austin's and Bentham's, Hart errs in declaring that "command is, however, too close to law for our purpose," which is to say, he errs in rejecting that law is properly understood as command.[2] He writes, "The element of authority involved in law has always been one of the obstacles in the path of any explanation of what law is. We cannot therefore profitably use, in the elucidation of law, the notion of a command which also involves it."[3] Apparently, Hart's underlying objection is not to a concept of law that incorporates commands but to the idea that the commands of the law are rooted in authority rather than social practice. For this reason and further reasons I discuss, this leads Hart to reject law as command altogether. Unfortunately, in opposing an understanding of law as authoritative commands, Hart undercuts the explanatory power of his own theory with respect to the most important sociological feature of the law: the sense of obligation to obey the law that underpins its widespread acceptance and fundamentally characterizes the internal point of view—that is, the very thing that distinguishes the law from a mugger. Shorn of obligation, law must derive its force from coercion, or else the law is merely a version of custom or habit. Yet these are the very reductions Hart is trying to upend. To be sure, the problem here is not that Hart's theory itself does not account for the obligatoriness of law; as a descriptive theory, that is not its aim.[4] The problem is that, as a descriptive theory centered on the fact that people treat law as *obligating* (and not just *obliging*), it still ought to be reconcilable to a normative account in which law, by definition, includes the imposition of obligation. But this is no longer possible given Hart's jettisoning of commands in favor of rules based in social practice.

In the end, Hart's rejection of command has it backward: his own theory cannot account for obligation, but a better command model can. Unlike the concept of rules, which Hart favors, the concept of command accounts for obligation because authoritative commanding is built into the very nature of the relationship between the commander and the commanded, and it is in this obligation-imposing sense that "a command is primarily an appeal not to fear but to respect for authority."[5] The substance of the command may or may not be respectable (or justifiable), but law, in its general form, makes a claim on its subjects in that it proposes to impose obligations upon them that are obligatory just because they are the dictates of law. This obligation that the commander means to impose is not rooted in fear of the consequences of disobedience but, as Hart acknowledges, in the idea of authority.[6]

Therefore, in order to preserve the place of authority in the concept of law (and not rule it out by grounding law in social practice), the command model ought to be retained. The concept of a command, structurally, purports to impose an obligation; authoritativeness is built into the idea of command. Whether the command is in fact authoritative—whether or not it in fact imposes an obligation—depends on normative features yet undiscussed, but the key here is that nothing about the *form* of law as command (as opposed to law as rules based in social practice) excludes the possibility of obligation-imposing authoritativeness. On the contrary, the description of law as command assumes that there is such authority, and the job of the normative side of the concept of law is to explain when there is.

In contrast to rules based in social practice, which are (by definition) what we just happen to do around here, rules issued by a commander—in other words, commands—mean to obligate. In this way, command is a far superior description of law because command better captures what the law means to do: obligate. Again, this does not mean that a command always obligates; in some cases, it is not justified. But commands are made for obligating, as it were. In contrast, social rules declare themselves to be just what we do around here, thereby casting doubt on their own normative weight. Furthermore, even where the law does something other than directly impose duties, the essence of law's function is its ability to bind—that is, to put force behind whatever arrangement it requires (or permits) and to be justified in doing so. Even those who insist that some laws cannot be described as commands can admit that it is both correct and useful to see commands as the central case of law and to see other forms as peripheral. As I say, the very point of law is to bind. Some laws may bind in a modified or less obvious way, but they get their character as law from the central case of law, which binds. To fail to see this (like Hart) is to abandon obligation as the central feature of law and potentially to sacrifice the ability to account for it. And, as we know, without the element of obligation, Hart's internal point of view collapses.

Rejecting the command model, Hart takes an important step forward, but he also takes two steps back. On one hand, Hart revolutionizes the field of jurisprudence by recognizing some key respects in which the command model is lacking. On the other hand, Hart throws out the baby with the bathwater, abandoning aspects of the command model worth retaining, with the ironic result that he moves even further than Austin from being able to link law and obligation. Austin offers the simple (if not uncontroversial) proposition that "a law is a command which obliges a person or persons."[7] The extended version of this, which Hart of course denies, is, "Every *law* or *rule* (taken with the largest signification which can be given to the term *properly*) is a command. Or, rather, laws or rules, properly so called, are a *species* of commands."[8] In reply, Hart argues that some types of law do not function as commands at all. Following on his definition of law, Austin explains that "whoever can *oblige* another to comply with his wishes, is the *superior* of that other" and therefore that "*superiority* (like the terms *duty* and *sanction*) is implied by the term *command*."[9] Naturally, Hart rejects this as well because law, as command or not, derives fundamentally not from a superior commander but from social practice. Indeed, for Hart there is no need for anything that goes by the name of sovereignty. The law comprises rules that are identified by other rules that are, in turn, determined by social practice.[10] By implication, then, Hart also clearly rejects Austin's claim that "being a *command*, every law properly so called flows from a determinate source, or emanates from a *determinate* author. In other words, the author from whom it proceeds is a *determinate* rational being, or a *determinate* body or aggregate of rational beings."[11] Hart's rule of recognition or any other social practice certainly need not emanate from any determinate individual or group. On the contrary, Hart's writings imply the opposite, and it is far more likely that such practices develop organically.

Hart is right to reject Austin's conclusion that commands entail sanctions in the same way they entail obligation. Austin's observation that "whoever can *oblige* another to comply with his wishes, is the *superior* of that other" in its most proper sense must be taken to mean whoever can "create a moral obligation to obey" and not "coerce." This construal of Austin works even if we ought to accept Hart's language of "obligate" over "oblige" and even if Austin himself does not see it this way. Nevertheless, by going further and eschewing command altogether as a central feature of law, Hart makes it impossible to account for how law qua law confers obligation upon its subjects. Therefore, a better concept of law preserves the essential element of command while incorporating Hart's successful critiques and moving away from the separation of law and obligation behind this mess in the first place.

The command model can be retained without the element of sanctions

Among other reasons, as I demonstrate, Hart's overreading of the centrality of concepts such as sanctions and habits to the command model causes him to reject the model entirely. Because influential command theorists emphasize the ability of the commander to punish the noncompliant commanded or the role of habitual obedience in establishing authority, Hart rightly deems those theories as flawed. Yet we can import the command model without many of the problems that Hart believes go along with it. Moreover, Hart's replacement for commands, namely rules based in social practices, causes more problems than it solves. Setting aside the typical but unnecessary features of the command model as traditionally presented, such as habits of obedience or sanctions, we can distill the positivist command model into a directive from an authority that is authoritative precisely in virtue of being just that. Hart is right that thinkers from the natural law school, who see a close connection between law and morality, "might not be concerned to dispute our criticisms of the simple imperative theory" and "might even concede that it was a useful advance."[12] In some respects, Hart's critique of the prevailing command theories of that time is a helpful advance. He is right to ditch the earlier reliance in the concept of law on sanctions and habits of obedience and so forth. But because he goes further and rejects the command model entirely, thereby depriving the law of a sufficient connection to authority, Hart goes further than any sound theory can permit.

Stripped to its essentials, the command model fills an important gap left by Hart's theory, namely the ground for obligation that a valid legal system needs if it is to claim any normative force. Even though the command model is normally a descriptive theory, embedded implicitly in the command model is a claim about authority and the resulting obligation (the duty to obey) in the relationship between the commander and the commanded. This fundamental aspect of the theory can be obscured by the emphasis on sanctions by some of its proponents and critics, but the element of assumed obligatoriness is essential to command in a way that sanctions and other features are not. Accordingly, a revised version of the command model that incorporates important parts of Hart's critique can more clearly place the emphasis where it belongs: on the "command" part of law—that is, on the *orders* part not the *sanctions* part of orders backed by threat of sanctions. By abandoning the notion of command, Hart loses the critical element that can allow his descriptive theory to keep a placeholder for the normative aspect of law.

Hart believes that many of the features built into the notion of command make it ill-suited to describe law. Despite raising some sound concerns, he is ultimately mistaken because he does not realize that we can retain the notion of command without retaining some of its traditional accoutrements, such as sanctions and habits of obedience. Moreover, he misses the ways in which his own theory is vulnerable to some of the same criticisms he levels against the command model. In another respect, Hart is mistaken because he does not see the command model's ability to accommodate features that are essential to our understanding of law, such as the ability of a group of people to give law to itself and the persistence of law across a succession of lawmakers. I take up the matters of sanction and habits first and then return to the questions of self-governance and the persistence of law through succession.

In several respects, Hart's critique of the command model is correct and valuable. Perhaps his most important corrective is to Austin's insistence on the centrality of sanctions. Austin is mistaken, for sanctions are not an essential feature of law (at least not in the way Austin says), even if they are a ubiquitous one. Hart argues that reducing law to punishment also reduces law to prediction. When the focus is on punishment, law becomes fundamentally about what officials do in reaction to law abiding or law breaking. More broadly, the reduction of law to punishment focuses on a prediction of what people will do (owing to the incentives arising from how officials will react) and obscures the idea that people take the law as a standard for judging behavior. For Hart, behavior in violation of the law is not simply "grounds for a prediction" of how officials will react but also "a reason or justification for such reaction and for applying the sanctions."[13] That is, the law conveys a standard and, more specifically, a standard that is not reducible to a desire to avoid punishment—because it is a justification for the punishment. This is what it means to be obligated rather than merely obliged for Hart. Hart's reasonable distinction is evident in the fact that, theoretically, a standard for behavior can apply whether or not any sanctions attach for noncompliance. The subject can believe herself to be under an obligation to obey (and can, in fact, be under an obligation to obey) whether or not she believes there is a punishment for disobedience. This idea of obligation without sanctions is not novel. Moral obligations are normally understood in this way, so a moral obligation to obey the law can be just the same. By the same logic, there is no reason to say that legal obligations (even apart from the moral obligations that attach) cannot exist without sanctions.

Surprisingly, Hart writes that officials need not act with any belief that the execution of their offices is the right thing to do.[14] For this reason, Hart's legal positivism nearly collapses into the legal realism it is meant, at least partly, to supplant. If officials do not obey the law because it is the right thing to do—which is to say, because they have an obligation—then law is mostly prediction: a prediction of what officials will do and which incentives they will respond to in the execution of their "duties." In Hart's terminology, the law is a "standard" only because officials happen to follow it. Some can be more high-minded and some less, but, in all cases, they happen to follow it for reasons that swing free of notions of obligation.

Hart has a related worry that an overemphasis on sanctions reduces law to a system that primarily guides how officials react to subjects' behavior rather than one that primarily guides how subjects behave. Hart compares the law to a game for these purposes, illustrating that it would be equally wrong to see the rules of the game being more about how referees should keep score and assign penalties than about how the players ought to play.[15] This is a useful analogy, and Hart is right that such a predictive angle is devoid of (or at least deficient with respect to) the internal point of view, an analytic device that reveals that people relate to the law first and foremost as a standard for judging their own and others' behavior rather than as a guide to how officials will react to their behavior (though it can be that, too, secondarily). Furthermore, the focus on sanctions not only makes the theory more predictive than explanatory (predicting how people will behave rather than why) but also potentially trains our field of vision too narrowly on the behavior of officials rather than of everyday subjects. But, if all of the foregoing is correct, then the problem with the command model is not the element of command but the model's emphasis on sanctions.

In ways Hart does not explore, the analogy to sports further suggests that sanctions are not an essential feature of the law. The players are no less bound by the rules of the game when there are no penalties for infractions, even if the absence of penalties means they are less likely to follow the rules. And if they do follow the rules, sans penalties, no one thinks they are not playing that particular game. One could imagine a game of pickup basketball (informal, without referees) where infractions are overlooked but players adhere to the rules of the game for the sake of play. It is uncontroversial to say that the pickup players are playing basketball. In contrast, if there are no rules or if the players are free to make up rules as they wish (running with the ball, kicking it with their feet, etc.), they are not playing the same game. Thus, as long as we are willing to go along with Hart in dropping sanctions as an essential feature of the concept of law, we can retain the command model. In the same way that an obligation can be an obligation without sanctions, a command can be a command without sanctions because the authority of the commander does not reside in the ability to punish, just as the obligatoriness of an obligation does not reside in the existence of sanctions for violation.

The command model can be retained without the element of habits of obedience

Another major thrust of Hart's attack on older ways of thinking about the law is that, practically speaking, it is nearly impossible to predicate sovereignty and the authority of law on habits of obedience.

Habits of obedience are important to older versions of the command model because the authority of the commander is in the sovereignty that comes from being habitually obeyed and habitually obeying no one else. A sovereign whose sovereignty rests upon being habitually obeyed does not possess justified authority until habits of obedience are established: "There is nothing to make him sovereign from the start. Only after we know that his orders have been obeyed for some time shall we be able to say that a habit of obedience has been established. Then, but not till then, we shall be able to say of any further order that it is already law as soon as it is issued and before it is obeyed."[16] For Hart, this makes habits of obedience an unreliable or unstable (and ultimately unworkable) method of establishing sovereignty.

We can carry Hart's critique further than he does. If sovereignty in the command model depends on habits of obedience the way Hart construes it, the problems run even deeper than the fact that orders need to be obeyed "for some time" before a habit of obedience can be established. For one thing, there is the question of what impels people to start obeying in the first place if the would-be sovereign cannot yet properly claim authority. Short of coercion, how does a sovereign-to-be cultivate habits of obedience to herself before any such obedience is owed? For another thing, what if, after a period of obedience, habits of obedience are in decline? Sovereignty disappears, it seems. Presumably, it is impossible to know at any given moment whether the habits of obedience are still in place, especially if there is a gradual decline. (The same is true in the positive direction: it is difficult to know when casual compliance becomes a habit of obedience.) What this really reveals, though, is that habits can never serve as an appropriate marker for sovereignty given that habits can be judged only retrospectively. At any particular moment, if the behavior characterizing the habit is not repeated consistently into the future, the habit can retroactively be said to have disappeared. But this can be judged only in hindsight. We are especially dependent upon hindsight because the behavior itself can persist intermittently even when the behavior qua *habit* has disappeared; in a normal case, the habitual nature of the behavior likely dissipates before the behavior itself vanishes completely. Therefore, if sovereignty depends on a present habit of obedience, sovereignty is always in doubt.[17]

Hart's alternative to law as command is law as rules based in social practice, or "that form of social practice which constitutes the acceptance of a rule."[18] In his theory, the connection between social practice and authority is based on "the notion of an accepted rule conferring authority on the order of past and future, as well as present, legislators," which Hart takes to be "certainly more complex and sophisticated than the idea of habits of obedience to a present legislator."[19] Hart considers social practice to have a conceptual advantage over "habitual obedience" because the latter cannot account for various features of the law in his view. In some versions of the old command model that Hart criticizes, sovereignty is explained by habits of obedience: the sovereign is habitually obeyed and habitually obeys no one.[20] Hart is right that it is improper to think of obedience to the sovereign in terms of habits, but, like sanctions, habits of obedience also are not an essential feature of law's authority. Hart's position is that even a revised command model, as compared with other concepts of law, especially his own, does not better explain features of the law, and any explanatory value it does have comes at the cost of distorting concepts like command and obedience beyond recognition. The notion of obedience, as the corollary of obligation (subjects are obligated to obey the law's command), must be preserved, as obligation is a central aspect of the concept of law. But we can dispense with habits along with the old version of the command model.

Even for those who argue that law must have de facto authority in order to have de jure authority—that is, to be justified—popular acceptance need not be characterized as habits of obedience. Deliberate and thoughtful obedience (in contrast to unthinking obedience) can be consistent without being habitual. Joining Hart in his rejection of habits as a critical feature of sovereignty, we can say, instead, that a better version of the command model describes the sovereign as one to whom obedience is owed and who owes obedience to no one. Further justification is still needed to explain *why* obedience is owed, but on such an account, the justification of law's authority rests on normative features of the law, not on sociological trends.

In his denial of the explanatory power of habits, Hart proposes to ground the features of law, such as succession and the persistence of laws, in social rules. But people do not treat the pattern of behavior embodied in the social rules as the product of unthinking habitual behavior. Rather, people "have a reflective critical attitude to this pattern of behaviour: they regard it as a standard for all."[21] This reflective critical attitude is the difference, Hart explains, between observing that chess players tend to move pieces according to certain patterns and understanding that the players are guided by rules that require them to do so.[22] In Hart's terminology, a "social rule has an 'internal' aspect, in addition to the external aspect which it shares with a social habit."[23] While Hart criticizes an adaptation of the command model that leaves us with depsychologized commands, it is not obvious that Hart's account, which amounts to "depsychologized rules," fares any better against his own standard. Either Hart must recognize that rules based in social practice have no necessary normative force, being rooted in popular acceptance, or Hart must accept that these, too, are obligations without an obligator.[24]

The command model can account for succession and the persistence of laws across lawgivers

Another area in which Hart finds the command model deficient is with respect to the succession of rulers and the persistence of law's authority—the idea that laws retain their authority even as the people who issue them change—but this is because he focuses on elements of the command model that are not essential to it. Moreover, he fails to notice a comparable weakness in his own theory. Hart is right that a concept of law that centers on habits of obedience to a sovereign (one who is habitually obeyed and habitually obeys no one) cannot account for a right of succession because, as Hart correctly says, "habits are not 'normative.'"[25] Features of the law such as the "continuity of law-making power through a changing succession of individual legislators" are "a new set of elements of which no account can be given in terms of habits of obedience."[26] Habits of obedience are to a particular sovereign, and there is nothing about them that automatically translates into the authority of a successor. Rather, succession requires the establishment of new habits of obedience to a new sovereign. The problem for Hart's argument, once again, is that we can understand law as command without adopting a definition of sovereignty rooted in habits of obedience. Thus, while it is true that a definition of sovereignty based on habits of obedience is insufficient to account for some important features of law, a better, modified version of the command model can accommodate Hart's critique (while retaining the necessary elements of the notion of command).

At the same time, it is clear that social practice serves no better than habits for explaining succession. Hart writes, "Habits of obedience to each of a succession of such legislators are not enough to account for the *right* of a successor to succeed for the consequent continuity in legislative power."[27] In Hart's telling, we should abandon habits of obedience as the ground of authority, and, instead, we should consider social practices in the form of adherence to a set of rules that outlines the selection of legislators. Even though Hart is right about habits, the social practices that are meant to take their place explain only how it is that authority-holders can be identified; they do not explain why they are justified in their authority. Even if authority-holders have attained their positions by following a set of widely accepted rules, there is nothing to ground the legitimacy of those rules; they are merely accepted.[28]

A closely related point of attack for Hart is the role of habits in the enduring nature of laws, which parallels the succession of sovereigns. Laws, Hart observes, "pre-eminently have this 'standing' or persistent characteristic," which is to say they persist despite changes in the person of the sovereign or in the legislators.[29] According to Hart, the idea of a sovereign who is habitually obeyed cannot account for "*continuity* of the authority to make law" and "*persistence* of laws:" "The idea of habitual obedience fails . . . to account for the continuity to be observed in every normal legal system, when one legislator succeeds another."[30] The physical person of the sovereign, however, is irrelevant to the authority of the law. Instead, people are subject to the office of the sovereign, regardless of who occupies that office and regardless of whether it is a single individual or all the people acting collectively as sovereign. In this light, there is no difficulty in explaining the enduring nature of laws because the office persists regardless of changes in the officeholder. Thus, even insofar as Hart is right to reject habits of obedience as the core of sovereignty, he is wrong in implying that no version of the command model (which retains the idea of law as command while rejecting the claim that the commander's authority is justified by habits of obedience) can explain the continuity of law.

Obedience is owed not due to some intrinsic feature of the person or people serving in the capacity of sovereign but instead, as I show, because of the orientation of the law to the common good. The relationship between those serving in the capacity of commander and those serving in the capacity of commanded serves that end (even if they are the same people). The justification of authority and, therefore, the obligation to obey depends on the orientation of the law to the common good. With the normative aspect of law in place, a command can surely persist across changes in the personal identity of the commander. This is entirely in line with the ordinary understanding of commands. No one supposes that an order from a military officer is void just because she dies in battle. This commonsense view explains most cases of peaceful succession, where obedience persists because it is to the office of the sovereign rather than to the person of the sovereign. In other cases, sovereigns may be obeyed in virtue of who they are and not in view of the office they occupy ("We love Queen So-and-So because she's so virtuous"), but this kind of personal or charismatic "authority" does not inform the question of whether people have a moral obligation to obey the law because here the people obey out of loyalty, not obligation.[31]

Hart's reliance on rules is also inadequate, for it fails to explain why the rules can replace habits as the animating principle of law. For Hart, "continuity of legislative authority which characterizes most legal systems depends on that form of social practice which constitutes the acceptance of a rule, and differs, in the ways we have indicated, from the simpler facts of mere habitual obedience."[32] Yet he provides no explanation for what lies behind the acceptance of those rules. In light of Hart's critique of the concept of habits, he offers surprisingly little to guard his theory against the same attack that he launches. Hart suggests, "The notion of an accepted rule conferring authority on the orders of past and future, as well as present, legislators, is certainly more complex and sophisticated than the idea of habits of obedience to a present legislator."[33] For Hart, the authority of law persists because it is conferred by the acceptance of a rule. It is true that a legal rule can persist across time even though the officeholders responsible for issuing that rule do not remain in office indefinitely and also true that the acceptance of that rule may not be tied as closely to the person of the officeholder as in the case of habits of obedience to a particular sovereign. Yet Hart gives us no reason to think that acceptance of the rule will persist at any time under a single ruler (let alone across different rulers). The fact that there is more complexity and sophistication in this understanding of the law does not inoculate Hart's theory against the same problems he raises about others. Though the acceptance of the rule does not derive from any loyalty to the rule-giver, there is no guarantee that whatever factor does account for the acceptance of the rule will persist. Indeed, it is hard to say whether the absence of a rule-giver makes it more or less likely that acceptance of the rule will persist. This is especially true if we step beyond the overly narrow understanding of commands that Hart offers when he attributes their acceptance to a feature of the officeholder rather than a feature of the office. If we are not worried about the continued acceptance of the rule even when the rule-makers change, then we can also imagine continued habits of obedience, where those habits stem from something other than a connection to the person of the commander (though, of course, it is not my aim to defend the place of habits in the concept of law).

Hart wishes to remain agnostic as to the source of the rule's acceptance, but, in doing so, he passes over the question of the origins of its "internal aspect." As a result, an observer can say that the people appear to take the rule as a standard but cannot say why. Yet if the authoritativeness of the rule is based in social practice, then there is no basis for believing that the acceptance of the rule will persist any more than a habit will. We can say only at any given moment that the rule *is* currently accepted; we can have no firm expectation that

that acceptance will continue. It seems that if Hart wishes to vindicate rules over habits, then he has no choice but to presuppose some sort of normative underpinning for the rules, but he emphatically cannot (and does not) do this. There must be, at a minimum, a normative justification for the rule conferring authority on the sovereign (or the law); if so, one sovereign who succeeds another can be said to exercise authority by right. Authority persists regardless of who is in office when the normative justification for the authority-locating rule persists. But where the rule identifying who is in authority has force merely because of social acceptance, there is no reason to believe that the social acceptance will persist and, similarly, no way to reliably anticipate whether it will. Like with habits, the fact of a rule's social acceptance from one sovereign to the next or from one period to another can be ascertained only in retrospect.

The command model is compatible with self-government—that is, where the people command themselves

One line of objection for Hart regards whether the command model, which is predicated on the relation between a commander and the commanded, can accommodate a scheme where the person of the commander and of the commanded reside in the same being or beings. This is important because it helps us address the question of whether the command model can be squared with popular rule. That is, can the people command themselves?

In Hart's view, we must modify the command model in order to make it compatible with self-government. Yet he believes that the necessary modifications distort the command model beyond recognition (or, better, beyond any usefulness). Thus, in his view, we cannot salvage the command model at all. In any such revision, he writes, "we may find that the notion of general orders backed by threats has been transformed out of recognition."[34] For example, instead of the simple notion of a sovereign who commands and subjects who obey, a revised command model presents a "blurred image of a society in which the majority obey orders given by the majority or by all. Surely we have neither 'orders' in the original sense (expression of intention that *others* shall behave in certain ways) or 'obedience.'"[35] But Hart misses the mark here in two ways. First, the significance of the command model lies not in its other-regarding connotations (that law is an expression of how *others* should behave) but, rather, in its obligation-bearing connotations. This is the reason, or at least a main reason, why the idea of law as command can and must be preserved. By focusing on what is necessary about the idea of command for the concept of law, namely how law connects to obligation and not how law connects distinct persons through commands, we can recognize that the command model can be recovered and revised without blurring anything essential. In a way, it is surprising that Hart misses this given that he is the one who brings law's obligatoriness into focus with his idea of the internal point of view.

Second, insofar as "orders" and "obedience" sound like a funny way to describe people giving law to themselves, Hart neglects to see that the *demos* can act in different capacities as lawgiver and subject. While the notion of commanding or obeying oneself can seem strange at first, it is intelligible through the concept of capacities. Hart objects, "The relationship with law involved here can be called obedience only if that word is extended so far beyond its normal use as to cease to characterize informatively these operations."[36] In Hart's view, there is nothing to be gained by understanding lawful behavior as "obedience to a 'depsychologized command' i.e. a command without a commander."[37] Yet if people can function in different capacities, as both commander and commanded, then preserving the command element because of its connection to obligation is not problematic or misleading but is, rather, relevant and instructive because of the further connection of command to obedience. It is true that the revised command model does not envision commander and commanded in the same way as the old version, but the old version's vision of command simply is not necessary to preserve the importance of command for understanding law.

Hart objects to the use of command in the concept of law because he rejects the idea that the self can be seen in two parts, one part commanding and one part being commanded. While legislation by the people can be seen as an act of self-binding, it cannot be understood through the lens of command, which in Hart's view requires two distinct entities, one who binds and one who is bound. Hart believes the self cannot be split conceptually; it is necessarily just one entity. On this basis, Hart argues that "this complicated device" of an individual acting in two capacities "is really quite unnecessary" because "we can explain the self-binding quality of legislative enactment without it."[38] Legislation is like promises, he says: "We make use of specified procedures to change our moral situation by imposing obligations on ourselves and conferring rights on others."[39] Nevertheless, there is nothing strange about the same person acting in different capacities with respect to legislating. A promise and its fulfillment can be seen in two parts—in the exercise of two distinct capacities.[40]

Thus, this part of Hart's objection to law as command focuses on the self-regarding versus other-regarding nature of legislating, which he thinks is suitably captured by rules but not commands. For instance, he writes, "There is no reason, since we are now concerned with standards, not 'orders,' why he should not be bound by his own legislation."[41] But Hart offers no convincing reason why it makes any more sense to say one can set a binding standard for oneself than to say one can order oneself. Though that is not how we speak of it ordinarily, so it can seem a bit off linguistically (if at all), there need not be a deeper conceptual reason why it is unsuitable. If the essence of ordering is command—which is to say, imposing a duty—then a self-binding commitment can very well be understood as a command to oneself. Indeed, it is the element of duty (or obligation) that distinguishes a promise or other commitment from a mere intention, such as a personal goal or a New Year's resolution. If the key element is the imposition of duty, then there may be no significant difference between ordering oneself and binding oneself beyond what is or is not linguistically common.

Hart's doubts about the awkward usage of the language of "ordering" or "commanding" when it comes to oneself stem from his conceptualization of legislating as related to promising, where it makes far less sense to think of the self in two parts: the one that promises and the one that is bound. There is an important difference between promising and legislating that is highly relevant to this issue. In promising, the goal is to bind the self, and the reason promising works is that the self that does the promising is the same self that is bound. In legislating, the goal is not to bind the self qua self; the goal is for the commander (legislator) to bind the commanded (subjects), whether those parties are the same or not.[42] This is why the idea of the same body acting in different capacities fits perfectly here. Even if the people legislating are the same as the people bound by the legislation, the goal of the people doing the legislating is to bind the people who are subject to the legislation—just as it is when the sovereign and the subjects are entirely distinct entities. Put another way, even if the legislators and the subjects are the same, the subjects are bound by the legislation in virtue of being the subjects and not in virtue of being the ones who made the legislation. This is not the case for promising, where one cannot ordinarily promise for another. Therefore, while the analogy from law to promises is illuminating in some respects, it does not vitiate the utility of the command model, which better accounts for legal obligation while still permitting the people to be both sovereign and subjects.

In this way, the idea of a promise is probably less well suited to describe law than the idea of a command is, yet Hart believes that his own theory can easily accommodate self-government. As he writes, "Legislation, as distinct from just ordering *others* to do things under threats, may perfectly well have such a self-binding force. There is nothing *essentially* other-regarding about it."[43] Hart believes his theory is compatible with self-government precisely because he does not think of law as command, which, unlike self-binding, is inherently other-regarding in his view. Yet law needs to be more than just a form of self-binding if it is to rise above the level of a complex promise. Otherwise, all legislation becomes a version of promising to do something because it is just the people committing themselves to doing something. But if it is reasonable to view the law as an aggregated promise (wherein "I promise" becomes "we promise"), then it is no more distorting to think of the law as a self-command. We do not commonly think of a promise as giving ourselves a command and then obeying it, but, if we accept that the same person can serve in different capacities with respect to a single institution, then, in the realm of law, self-command is an adequate description of what it means to create a legal obligation. To form a commitment (to impose an obligation on oneself) is to choose a course of action (command oneself) and stick to it (obey oneself). At least, it is not more of a stretch than seeing the law as a complex promise, as Hart seems to do.

The notion of capacities makes sense of the way in which the same people can be both commander and commanded. The command model is, indeed, compatible with one body playing both roles. Some argue that, if "one identifies such a sovereign with the public, then the distinction between sovereign and subject, essential to Hobbesian theory, collapses," but there is no reason to rely on the Hobbesian view of sovereignty, even if the command model is linked to it historically.[44] The American model, per the opening "We, the people," of the Constitution, asserts a contrary possibility quite explicitly. Contra Hobbes, people can act in different capacities as both the creators and subjects of legislation.[45]

Hart's alternative possesses some of the same flaws for which he rejects the command model

Under Hart's theory of legal validity, obedience is found in the acquiescence to a rule that "constitutes a standard of behaviour for the group."[46] Yet if validity depends on popular acceptance, the concept has many of the same problems as the concept of habits. At what point is there sufficient acquiescence in the "results of ... official operations"?[47] And why does anyone begin to obey the law before there is sufficient acquiescence to prove legal validity? Put simply, if in the old model sovereignty obtains only once habits of obedience have been cultivated, in Hart's model validity also obtains only once there is acquiescence in the official operations.

Similarly, whereas Hart worries that an emphasis on sanctions makes the command model chiefly about instructions to officials, his depiction of his own theory suffers from the same flaw. Hart argues that a theory of sovereignty-by-habitual-obedience illuminates the "relatively passive aspect" of the legal system (namely the habitual obedience) but also finds that it "obscures or distorts the other[,] relatively active aspect" of the law, "which is seen primarily, though not exclusively, in the law-making, law-identifying, and law-applying operations of the officials or experts of the system."[48] He even writes that "in a modern state it would be absurd to think of the mass of the population, however law-abiding, as having any clear realization of the rules specifying the qualifications of a continually changing body of persons entitled to legislate."[49] In other words, Hart is saying that, while the command model can, indeed, capture how the aforementioned ordinary citizen relates to the law, the added value of Hart's theory is in the realm of how officials relate to the law. This is curious considering how concerned Hart is that a concept of law not be seen primarily as instructions to officials. This part of Hart's writing, though, suggests that the role of officials in the legal system is precisely the contribution of his theory that surpasses what the command model offers. And it steers the focus away from Hart's contribution of the internal point of view. That does not necessarily mean that Hart is wrong, but it does mean that his critique of focusing on the behavior of officials applies to his own theory as much as it does to others.

Ironically, Hart recognizes that it is "the strength" of the concept of "habitual obedience to orders backed by threats" that it highlights the "relatively passive aspect" of a legal system.[50] Implicit in this statement by Hart, correct but incomplete, is that, habits and sanctions aside, the command model captures a fundamental feature: the obedience owed to the law. This insight of the command model may be obscured by its earlier formulations, but it is the essential core and must be retained. Moreover, it is essential to Hart's key insight, the internal point of view, so Hart does himself a disservice—to say the least—by eschewing the command model.

RULES

Hart argues that the command model cannot accommodate the diversity within law

The first part of Hart's critique of law as command rests on his objections to that model's competing views of the *nature* of law and its purported features, such as habits, sanctions, and so forth. The second part focuses on the *scope* of law. Specifically, Hart argues that the command model cannot accommodate the full variety of rules that are appropriately characterized as law. For Hart, an advantage of his concept of law is that the notion of rules, rather than commands, better captures the variety of law, including both duty-imposing and power-conferring types. "Rules," he believes, better allows for this diversity, unlike "commands," which is an adequate descriptor for laws that impose duties but does not seem like a fitting title for laws that confer powers. Though Hart's critique of the command model in this respect is widely accepted, a fresh look at the concept of law enables us to see that law as command suffices to describe law in its different types because of the element of duty imposed in all (or almost all) laws. Moreover, it is the law's duty-imposing aspect that defines the central case of law over against other examples that count as law only derivatively. Ironically, my critique of Hart in defense of seeing law as commands dovetails well with Hart's key observation about the internal point of view, that law is marked by the sense of obligation that attaches to it and, indeed, fits it much better than Hart's notion of law as rules.

In this part of his argument, Hart writes, "what really is at stake is the comparative merit of a wider and a narrower concept or way of classifying rules, which belong to a system of rules generally effective in social life."[51] The wider concept comprises "all rules which are valid by the formal tests of a system of primary and secondary rules."[52] Hart proposes that, within this system of rules, the law comprises both duty-imposing rules and power-conferring rules.[53] Older theories of law, to which he refers as more narrow, incorrectly omit or exclude the latter type. Hart explains, "Nothing is to be gained in the theoretical or scientific study of law as a social phenomenon by adopting the narrower concept: it would lead us to exclude certain rules even though they exhibit all the other complex characteristics of law."[54] Hart thereby contends that the command model is too narrow because many laws, specifically the power-conferring sort, cannot be reasonably characterized as commands. Although many laws, especially the duty-imposing ones, can be fairly described as commands—though Hart still rejects that characterization for other reasons I address—many others do not seem like a good fit for the command model of law. For this reason, Hart wishes to resist past theories' strong "itch for uniformity in jurisprudence" that comes with reducing all laws to one type.[55]

Instead, Hart proposes a more capacious definition of law not as commands but as rules, a term he believes more comfortably encompasses both duty-imposing rules and power-conferring rules.[56] Duty-imposing laws are the kind of laws that ordinarily spring to mind when people think of law, the thou shalts and thou shalt nots: "Pay your taxes." "Don't jaywalk." And so on. As their name suggests, duty-imposing rules confer obligations (duties) on people to act or refrain from acting in certain ways. Unlike duty-imposing rules, power-conferring rules "provide individuals with *facilities* for realizing their wishes."[57] These are the sorts of laws that set the conditions for how one gets a driver's license or how one writes a will or how a legislature passes a law. Hart's understanding, along with many or most of those after him, is that, here, there is no obligation to do anything, just a way of doing things if one wishes. On that view, more precisely, the law does not confer any obligations in these cases; the law merely enables people to take actions that have legal effect if they wish to do so.

Anything short of a clean division between the two categories of rules, for Hart, is a distortion of how power-conferring rules function because "other devices, such as that of treating power-conferring rules as mere fragments of rules imposing duties, or treating all rules as directed only to officials, distort the ways in which these are spoken of, thought of, and actually used in social life."[58] Thus, Hart denies that power-conferring rules are essentially a form of duty-imposing rules and asserts, rather, that each is a distinct type of rule that cannot be assimilated or reduced to the other type.

The variety represented by these two different types of law makes it impossible, in Hart's view, to retain the command model. According to Hart, "The power thus conferred on individuals to mould their legal relations with others by contracts, wills, marriages, &c., is one of the great contributions of law to social life; and it is a feature of law obscured by representing all law as a matter of orders backed by threats."[59] Because power-conferring rules create possibilities for people and do not "require persons to act in certain ways whether they wish or not," Hart does not think they can be captured by the notion of command; after all, there is no immediate duty to do (or refrain from doing) anything.[60] Moreover, Hart writes, "The ideas of orders, obedience, habits, and threats, do not include, and cannot by their combination yield, the idea of a rule, without which we cannot hope to elucidate even the most elementary forms of law."[61] Thus, he prefers a rules-based model in which some rules impose duties and others offer opportunities by conferring powers.

Yet there is more going on with power-conferring rules than Hart acknowledges because they do impose duties but in a different way. First, power-conferring rules obligate people to create legal relations in certain ways if they wish to effect them at all. This makes the duty conditional, but the duty is still present. Second, power-conferring rules create obligations within those legal relations that require the parties to abide by the terms rather than to choose freely whether to uphold the arrangement they struck. That is to say, power-conferring rules provide the tools by which the parties bind themselves. Although it is true that, ordinarily, no one need enter into legal relations of the sort made possible by power-conferring rules, it is also the case that the law does not present a choice to those who enter into such relations, much as the law limits the ways in which one can create such legal relations to begin with. To repeat, the law imposes duties to act in certain ways if one wishes to act, *and* the law ensures that the terms of the legal relations into which one enters are nonoptional. (Thus, in some cases, laws add legal obligations on top of preexisting moral obligations, and in other cases, laws add legal obligations where equivalent nonlegal commitments create moral obligations where none exist previously.)

In sum, this part of Hart's challenge to the command model turns on whether he is correct that the command model lacks the resources to elucidate all forms of law. Contrary to Hart's claim, the modified version of the command model that I defend is up to the task because of the role that obligation plays even in power-conferring rules.[62] Furthermore, even if there are some examples of law that seem to skirt this point (and I deny that there are many, if any), obligation is an essential feature of law in its central case.

Power-conferring rules also impose duties

The duty-imposing aspect of power-conferring rules is most readily seen in the latter category, namely where power-conferring rules create obligations within legal relations. A contract, for example, is not normally a choice to abide by the terms of the contract or to accept the consequences. This is not the way the law understands itself, nor is it the way that parties to a contract understand the law. Rather, a contract creates an obligation to fulfill the terms of the agreement and imposes a legally enforceable consequence on those who fail to do so. This can be seen in everyday legal language that refers to nonfulfillment of a contract as a "breach." Similarly, it is surprising to find a party to a contract who has no expectations about whether the other party intends to meet the terms of the agreement but instead believes that, from the outset, the latter is equally disposed to fulfill the contract or pay the appropriate amount for breach. In general terms, a contract entails a duty to fulfill an agreement. While it is true that such duties are not imposed upon everyone—one first needs to voluntarily enter into such an arrangement—that does not make it any less of a duty.

Because there is no obligation to enter into a contract, we can object that such laws actually have two parts: a power-conferring rule that specifies the ways in which contracts can be created (conferring the power, but not imposing a duty, to create a contract) and a duty-imposing rule that obligates the parties to abide by the terms. For Hart, seeing the law in two parts this way is a distortion of its character because it sees power-conferring rules as "mere aspects or fragments of the rules of duty"[63] and because it thereby allows us to see both duty-imposing and power-conferring rules as essentially one type—the very sort of thing Hart wishes to avoid.[64] Yet the duty-imposing aspect of the law is inseparable from the power-conferring aspect because the obligatory nature of the legal relation is the very essence of what makes it a contract, and the obligatoriness is the thing that gives the act of forming a contract its very purpose. The obligation is what makes it a *contract* and not a suggestion. It is obligatory, not optional. In this light, the law's role is twofold, providing the way in which an agreement must be struck in order for the agreement to impose a legal duty and enforcing the duties embedded in the agreement. Hart is rightly concerned with pictures of the law that obscure more than they clarify. Exactly for that reason, though, we must recognize the unavoidable duty-imposing component of power-conferring rules.

Another way to grasp this latter duty-imposing aspect of power-conferring rules is to consider, as with contracts, that such a law primarily adds enforcement to an agreement that already has morally binding force.[65] Hart nearly makes this point when he states that "an elementary form of power-conferring rule also underlies the moral institution of a promise."[66] A better way to look at it is that, just as a promise is a form of agreement, so, too, a contract is a form of agreement given legal force by a power-conferring rule. This is not unlike the way in which duty-imposing rules, such as laws against murder, add a legal obligation to an existing moral obligation. The key here is to see that, just like a promise, any reasonable commitment made to another person is morally binding to some extent, even outside the context of the law. The power-conferring rule creates the possibility of adding the force of law to the agreement, but the possibility of entering into such an underlying, prelegal (or nonlegal) agreement and the morally obligatory nature of the agreement once it is struck both exist prior to and independent of the power-conferring rule. This is because one has a moral obligation to abide by agreements (promises, etc.) one makes whether or not they are enshrined in a legal contract. In this light, power-conferring rules "provide individuals with facilities for realizing their wishes" not by imagining arrangements they cannot otherwise create but by offering to enforce arrangements they can create. Indeed, the law does not create the possibility of entering into this (morally binding) arrangement or any other. It just creates the possibility of adding the backing of legal enforcement to the agreement. That is, with respect to power-conferring rules, the important thing that the law adds is the *legal* duty to abide by the agreement (because the moral duty is already present), which in practical terms mainly means the legal consequences that ensue if one does not. This reveals one way in which power-conferring rules really do impose duties. Where agreements between people take the form of contracts (or other private law devices), there is a legal obligation that is coextensive with the moral obligation that obtains. Indeed, Hart himself seems to be onto this when he accepts the idea of "thinking of the operations of making a contract or transferring property as the exercise of limited legislative powers by individuals," highlighting the affinity between agreement-making and law-making.[67]

At the same time, we can argue that the overlap between duty-imposing and power-conferring rules is compelling as long as we confine ourselves to the realm of private law, but once we consider the very important place of power-conferring rules in public law, the argument breaks down. Power-conferring rules also tell legislators how to legislate if they wish to do so: for example, "Legislate by majority decision." As before with contracts, although there is no specific obligation to legislate in the first place, there is an obligation to legislate in a certain way if legislators wish to do so. That much is clearly similar. But, unlike before, we can be less inclined to say that the legislation adds a legal obligation to a moral obligation that can be formed, anyway, in the absence of the legislation. There is no inherent obligation for a minority to abide by the decisions of a majority. Then again, we must remember that, in the case of self-government, at least, the whole system of governance is ultimately just an elaborate form of agreement. If everyone agrees to be bound by the decisions of the majority (or of the majority of the legislature), then they are bound, even if there is no law specifying how laws are to be made. We can, in fact, promise to be bound by the decision of the majority, and we can place on top of that already binding agreement a legal system that requires the very same thing, adding to our promises the force of law.

Power-conferring rules build upon a duty to act justly

The example of power-conferring rules within the realm of public law and specifically within the realm of law-making helps to reveal a deeper way in which power-conferring and duty-imposing rules converge. Even power-conferring rules impose duties as specifications of the obligation to act justly (or not to act unjustly). In the simplest case of a duty-imposing rule, the law adds a legal obligation to refrain from assaulting someone, for instance, on top of a preexisting moral obligation to refrain. In another case, the law can, for example, create a legal obligation to drive on the right side of the road. This latter case is slightly more complex for our purposes because the duty to drive on the right side of the road is conditional: the obligation applies only if one wishes to drive. And, even if one wishes to drive, there is no underlying duty (independent of any posited rules of the road) in the form of a moral obligation to drive on the right side of the road rather than the left. In that respect, it can be seen like a law that says "If you wish to create a contract, do it this way." Therefore, it can seem like a power-conferring rule. But it is only marginally different from the law that says "Do not assault" because there is in fact a moral obligation to drive safely. If everyone else is driving on the right side of the road, then it is reckless to drive on the left. Therefore, driving on the left is a violation of the moral obligation not to unreasonably endanger others. Insofar as the right-side-of-the-road law is a power-conferring rule at all, we can see how it conforms to the duty-imposing model that applies to contracts. The law adds a legal obligation on top of a preexisting moral obligation.

The rub, though, is that in the driving example, the law adds a legal obligation to the moral obligation to drive on the right side of the road that exists once that practice is settled upon. But what if the practice is not settled? In that case, the passage of the law serves as the occasion for settling on a particular practice. Yet perhaps there is no underlying moral obligation to settle on any practice, much less any particular practice (such as driving on the right side and not the left). In that sense, the rule that says "If you wish to specify one side of the road for drivers, this is how you should pass that law" may be exclusively power conferring and not also duty imposing in the way that most power-conferring rules are. But this conclusion relies on a partial picture.

There are two ways to see this rule imposing a duty. First, despite my suggestion just above, there can be a duty for all people to participate or at least acquiesce in some settlement of the "rules of the road" given the dangers that ensue from the absence of *any* settlement. Second, and more importantly, the rule that says how to pass the driving law is a specification of the more general rule, "If you wish to legislate, legislate this way (e.g., by majority vote)." Power-conferring rules of this sort tell authorities how to enact laws. We can call these power-conferring secondary rules because they are rules about how to create rules.[68] At first, these rules can seem to be the least duty imposing because, although they are the occasion for adding a legal obligation to an underlying moral obligation, they are also the occasion for generating the otherwise underdetermined settlement on a practice that creates the underlying moral obligation in the first place. In that sense, a law about legislating creates possibilities or opportunities (i.e., powers) rather than obligations. Looking deeper, though, we can see that each person has a duty not to endanger others with her motor vehicle, and the relevant traffic laws ("If you wish to drive, drive in the following safe manner") are one possible specification of the fulfillment of that duty.

Furthermore, we must take note that all of these power-conferring rules about how to legislate are specifications of the duty to do justice and, more narrowly, the duty to legislate (or govern) justly. Although there is no rule that says we must pick one side of the road, there is a rule that says how we pick one side of the road, just like there are rules governing all forms of law-making because we believe there is a duty in justice to legislate according to fair (agreed upon) procedures. Even in the case of a dictator, the power to make decisions necessarily rests on a claim of right, justified or not.[69] A law that says "Legislate by a majority" is a power-conferring rule. But, seen another way, this law imposes a duty to decide in accordance with a certain procedure (by majority) on top of the moral obligation to decide in a just manner, which is fulfilled not by the content of the decision but by the manner of deciding. To be sure, other voting schemes in the legislature can potentially satisfy the requirements of justice, but this is at least one way of discharging that obligation. The fact that the obligation to legislate in a just manner can be fulfilled in multiple ways does not mean the law imposes anything less than a duty when it specifies a particular way. Insofar as it is duty imposing in the way that I say, a law that says "Drive on the right side of the road" is clearly a duty-imposing rule even though a law that says "Drive on the left side of the road" acceptably fulfills the same purpose. In other words, where the law confers powers by specifying one mode of behavior among multiple morally permissible options for discharging a duty—in the case of legislating, a duty to act justly or not to act unjustly—the law gives shape to a moral obligation, and in this way it also adds a legal obligation where a moral obligation already exists.[70] Moreover, it imposes a duty to act a certain way even if we believe that there is no underlying moral obligation in that scenario. Either way, power-conferring rules impose a duty to act in certain way if one wishes to act, and the options are presumably constrained by obligations in justice.

Nullity does not undermine the duty-imposing character of law

Another way in which Hart denies the equation of duty-imposing and power-conferring rules is by showing how the violation of each kind purportedly differs. To do this, he distinguishes between legal duties and legal disabilities (or, equivalently, legal limitations), arguing that a power-conferring rule in the form of a constitutional limitation on legislative power cannot be seen as a duty-imposing rule because it does not work "by imposing . . . duties on the legislature not to attempt to legislate in certain ways; instead it provides that any such purported legislation shall be void," also known as nullity.[71] A legal limitation (or disability), according to Hart, "implies not the presence of *duty* but the absence of legal power."[72] For Hart, this demonstrates that power-conferring rules really do not reduce to duty-imposing rules. The violation of a power-conferring rule results in nullity. The violation of a duty-imposing rule results (in the normal case) in a penalty.

But Hart's distinction does not hold up. At bottom, the rules that specify both the form and substance of valid enactments create a duty not to do things otherwise. Although this can seem at first like a convoluted way to portray such limitations, it is important to consider what a legal limitation really is. Hart gives the example of a constitutional restriction on imprisonment without trial.[73] Now, it is true that this represents the absence of legal power to imprison without trial. Therefore, any sentence pronounced without a trial (i.e., in violation of the rule) is null and void. But this nullity, the lack of legal effect, is rooted in the duty not to imprison without trial, which is a subset of the duty not to imprison (or otherwise punish or harm) unjustly. The duty not to subject people to arbitrary punishment already exists. Laws that implement due process, such as laws that require the state to hold a trial, (merely) specify how this particular government chooses to fulfill the more general duty. There is an underlying duty to have due process even if there are many ways to fulfill that duty. In this example, perhaps all possible ways of fulfilling that duty necessitate a trial of some sort, even if it is underdetermined by the requirements of justice whether the trial should be by judge or by jury (and so on). In other instances, the laws that fulfill the government's duties can be even more underdetermined, but, at bottom, they still function in the same way.

Thus, we can see the role of duty on two levels: the nullity represents a duty to act in a certain way if the government wishes to act at all, and the required actions, though conditional on choosing to act, represent the fulfillment of an underlying moral obligation not to act otherwise (even if that obligation leaves open several possible paths for action). The government has a moral obligation to abide by fair procedures in any case (though, again, the specifics of those procedures can vary), yet it also has a legal duty to do so when so instructed by the constitution.

In this vein, if there is a requirement that the legislature pass all laws with a majority, this constitutes a legal limitation in the sense that the legislature lacks the power to pass laws with less than a majority. But it is equally a duty not to pass laws with less than a majority; doing so is a violation of that duty. This is true whether it is intrinsically wrong (morally speaking) for a minority to pass laws or whether it is simply determined in and by this society that valid laws require a majority vote in the legislature. Either way, there is a duty to abide by the settled procedures of that system (at least assuming they are not gravely unjust), a duty that is itself a specification of the broader duties of fairness, justice, and so on. Moreover, even if we stipulate that in a given scenario there is no underlying moral principle behind the legal rule, it is still true that a power-conferring rule creates a duty to do things a certain way. Once some procedure is specified by the law, an underlying morality enters into the picture, namely the morality of the rule of the law, which has its own inner morality created by reliance interests or other entailments of having announced a certain policy.[74] To be sure, in all these cases (of power-conferring rules), the duty is still subject to a conditional—"if you choose do X (e.g., legislate), then you must do it according to rule Y (e.g., majority vote)"—but there is a duty nonetheless. With legislating, the conditional is almost irrelevant to the picture because the legislature must inevitably act. With contracts and other aspects of private law, the conditional is more central, but the duty is still there, and, in those cases, the underlying moral obligation lies closer to the surface. Hart fails to see that even procedural requirements are not just limitations on powers but specifications of duties because his analysis stops at the level of the rule and fails to ask what is behind the rule or what justifies it.

In what he sees as a further difference between duty-imposing and power-conferring rules, Hart also rejects the idea that nullity can be construed as a sanction for the violation of power-conferring rules in the way that, for example, criminal penalties are a sanction for violations of duty-imposing rules.[75] In older ways of thinking about law, it is the attachment of sanctions (fines, imprisonment, etc.) to a command that defines law.[76] This way of thinking about law is incorrect, as it is plain that obligations can exist even without anything that can obviously be identified as sanctions. This is straightforward when it comes to duty-imposing rules (e.g., there is a duty to pay one's taxes whether or not there is a penalty for failing to pay one's taxes), but it is more complicated with power-conferring rules. According to Hart, power-conferring rules depend strictly on nullity because "if failure to comply with this essential condition did not entail nullity, the rule itself could not be intelligibly said to exist without sanctions even as a non-legal rule."[77] For example, if a legislature is required to pass laws by majority vote but laws that fail to garner a majority take effect nonetheless, then the power-conferring rule requiring a majority is effectively meaningless. Or, using Hart's analogy to sports games, "If failure to get the ball between the posts did not mean the 'nullity' of not scoring, the scoring rules could not be said to exist."[78] Thus, "The provision for nullity is *part* of this type of rule itself in a way which punishment attached to a rule imposing duties is not."[79] But if sanctions are not a necessary part of duty-imposing rules, as I argue, then it is much less of a problem that nullity with respect to power-conferring rules does not function as sanctions ordinarily do with respect to duty-imposing rules. This is because we do not need sanctions in order to have law. Thus, Hart can be right that nullity is not to power-conferring rules what sanctions are to duty-imposing ones. Nullity is merely a feature of power-conferring rules, which, in turn, are one type of duty-imposing rules.

Let us imagine a case where laws passed by a minority in a majority-rules legislature are treated as law by those responsible for enforcing the law. In that case, they are using their powers of enforcement unjustly. Hart's view is that such laws are invalid. Yet the fundamental problem of such measures taking effect is not that they are technically invalid, which is only a description of how they do or do not comport with some procedure, but that they take effect in violation of a moral (and legal) obligation for laws not to be passed in that way. Accordingly, it is unjust to enforce invalid laws. Further, the obligation not to pass laws with only minority approval is created by the rule that specifies the proper procedure for legislating. Therefore, Hart may not even be right that power-conferring rules cannot exist without a provision for nullity. Where such minority-passed rules are recognized by officials contrary to the rules for legislating (for whatever reason), the laws are not actually null, but their enforcement is unjust.

With this understanding of nullity in place, we can return to the subject of contracts to illuminate the conceptual similarity between duty-imposing and power-conferring rules because contracts exemplify the way in which power-conferring rules also entail obligations, in this case the obligation to fulfill the terms of the contract. To be sure, the focus on the duties imposed by contracts can seem, at first, to be a misleading way to make the point inasmuch as contracts are not themselves power-conferring rules but instead the creations of power-conferring rules. For those power-conferring rules, the law includes both rules about how to create a contract and rules (for officials, usually) about how to enforce that contract. It is the latter part that is more clearly duty imposing, but a keener view shows that the two are inseparable. What makes a contract more than a private agreement is that it has the force of law; shorn of that force, the idea of a legal contract is practically meaningless. Therefore, if nullity is an essential feature of power-conferring rules, as Hart suggests, it is because nullity plays an important role in the duty-imposing aspect of the rule. A power-conferring rule can offer the possibility for citizens to create contracts by specifying the requirements of creating valid contracts, meaning what counts as a binding agreement, even if it does not provide for the enforcement of those contracts in the event of a breach. (This is another instance of the possibility of law without enforcement, like duty-imposing laws that lack sanctions. Such laws can be inadvisable, but they are not invalid.) Although unlikely to occur, the government can specify what counts as a (valid) contract—that is, what counts as a binding agreement—without playing any role in the event that the agreement is not kept. The purpose of the law in this hypothetical situation is to specify when there is an obligation to keep agreements that are struck—that is, what counts as a binding agreement.

At first blush, this seems silly because, as long as all parties agree, they ought to be able to bind themselves through whatever mechanism they wish. But, looking more carefully, we can discern a role for government in specifying the required features of binding agreements to avoid the many possible scenarios in which parties dispute whether an agreement in fact exists or what the terms are. This can be a useful intervention of the law even if subsequent enforcement is not part of the picture.[80] Without a provision for enforcement, the law still adds clarity about what counts as and in an agreement. In this case, the prospect of nullity is the sole force of the law because the law establishes only whether there is or is not an agreement or whether a particular provision is or is not part of the agreement. In this respect, the prospect of nullity does impose a conditional duty on the parties to abide by certain standards in creating contracts. If they do not abide, then there is no legally binding agreement. On this understanding, it is not just the contract formed under the power-conferring rule that imposes a duty but the power-conferring rule itself, similar to the case of legislation where the legislator acts under a duty to legislate a certain way.

Hart risks falling victim to his own criticism of reducing law to instructions to officials

To the extent that Hart wishes to separate duty-imposing and power-conferring rules yet still consider them equally law, he is in danger of being guilty of the very thing for which he faults Hans Kelsen, namely reducing all law to instructions to officials.[81] Hart examines Kelsen's view that "law is the primary norm which stipulates the sanction"[82] and, therefore, that "there is no law prohibiting murder: there is only a law directing officials to apply certain sanctions in certain circumstances to those who do murder."[83] Hart's main objection to this is that "the theory involves a shift from the original conception of law as consisting of orders backed by threats of sanctions which are to be exacted when the orders are disobeyed. Instead, the central conception now is that of orders to officials to apply sanctions."[84] Hart argues that seeing law as rules for officials "conceal[s] the characteristic way in which such rules function if we concentrate on, or make primary, the rules requiring the courts to impose the sanction in the event of disobedience; for these latter rules make provision for the breakdown or failure of the primary purpose of the system. They may indeed be indispensable but they are ancillary."[85] Hart is right to criticize Kelsen, but his own theory is similarly vulnerable.

Granting Hart's introduction of the internal point of view, we can agree that the law does not function primarily as instructions to officials. People consider themselves to be under an obligation to obey the law. This can be seen in the fact that the law does not, in the eyes of its subjects, present a neutral choice with two options, compliance and noncompliance, along with instructions to officials about how to act in response to each choice. Instead, the law directly requires of subjects one mode of behavior (or a range of behaviors) and imposes a penalty for the opposite. Indeed, my theory vindicates Hart's internal point of view and rejection of Kelsen even more than his own because I maintain that law is law even without sanctions—that is, even without any enforcement by officials. But this same point does not work so neatly with Hart's theory. For Hart, power-conferring rules, unlike duty-imposing rules, are not to be seen primarily for the duties they impose. If that is the case, then the only alternative is that power-conferring rules must be seen for the way in which officials respond to them because the power these rules confer is little other than the power to invoke official sanction in the event of a breach, just to take the most prominent example. Again, especially if we set aside the way in which power-conferring rules impose duties on the parties who exercise the power being conferred (and even perhaps if not), then the main difference between a private agreement and a valid legal contract is the intervention of officials in the event of a breach of the latter. If the law is not imposing any duties on the contracting parties, then its main effect is to impose duties on officials to enforce the contract. Put another way, in Hart's world, a rule that offers the possibility of making a contract is ultimately an instruction to officials to enforce in a certain way what is otherwise a private agreement. This is a problem for Hart, however, because if power-conferring rules are primarily instructions to officials, then, per his criticism of Kelsen and his introduction of the internal point of view, they are not centrally law—though he holds them out as one of the two main types of law and something that a concept of law must encompass straightforwardly.

Hart's way out of this problem is an appeal back to the internal point of view, namely that citizens do not understand contracts mainly as instruments that specify how officials ought to react to their compliance or noncompliance with the terms; rather, they see contracts as standards governing their own behavior—that is, instructions to them, not to officials. But if that is Hart's view, then he ought to be willing to follow that logic to its conclusion and recognize that the citizen's view of a power-conferring rule is of a rule that says,

"If you wish to do X, you must do it in the following way." Numerous possibilities can be open for doing X under the law, but the conditional duties that are created are duties just the same. In other words, to avoid the problem of power-conferring rules mainly being instructions to officials, he must accept that power-conferring rules are versions of duty-imposing rules, at least with respect to the central, defining features of law.

Otherwise, Hart must reconsider why power-conferring rules constitute a central case of law alongside duty-imposing rules. Again, what separates a legal contract from any private arrangement is its nonoptional character under the law, both in that the law can specify ways in which the arrangement must be made and in that the law attaches enforcement (or at least a legal obligation) to it. Even without law, customs or social conventions are largely sufficient for creating opportunities otherwise created by power-conferring rules because they can specify how parties can strike agreements and so forth. That is, they can also confer powers by providing rules for behavior. In one culture, for example, it might be understood that a handshake forms an agreement between two individuals, sealing a shared understanding between them of mutual obligation. In another culture, an oath might be taken when one person places his hand on another person's thigh.[86] To take another clear example, cultural norms can allow for a marriage to be realized without the intervention of law; the moral obligations of marriage do not depend upon the presence of corresponding legal obligations. So the role of the law must be something more. This is not to say that duty-imposing rules and power-conferring rules function in exactly the same way as one another, but it is to say that the feature of legal *obligation* is what enables both types to be meaningfully seen as law.

Similarly, Hart explains early on that the "distinction between social rules and mere convergent habits of behaviour . . . is crucial for the understanding of law."[87] Presumably, what underlies the difference between social rules and convergent habits of behavior is the sense of obligatoriness that attaches to social rules.[88] But if obligation is what distinguishes rules from habits, how can Hart insist that power-conferring rules are in fact law while insisting that they are not a species of duty-imposing rules? They are law because they are rules, which is to say they are standards that spell out the requirements about how certain things must be done under certain circumstances. In other words, it is the duty-imposing element of power-conferring rules that enables Hart to distinguish power-conferring rules from convergent habits of behavior (whereas it is the *conditional* aspect of that obligation that allows Hart to distinguish them from duty-imposing rules). Hart can deny this and thereby concede that power-conferring rules are not a central case of law, or he can admit that power-conferring rules and duty-imposing rules are closer than he allows. The former is too devastating to his theory to be his choice, so his choice must be the latter.

Hart's view of the diversity of law undermines his focus on obligation

It is reasonable for Hart to be skeptical of the "itch for uniformity in jurisprudence" and to identify two distinct types of law.[89] His instinct to develop a taxonomy of law "free from the prejudice that all *must* be reducible to a single simple type" is understandable given that the old formulation of the command model does seem to constrict the true scope of law and distort the way in which some rules function, or, in Hart's words, "[distort] the different social functions which different types of legal rule perform."[90] On one hand, it does not seem, intuitively, that law is always about orders and sanctions (or the threat of sanctions). On the other hand, in elucidating the concept of rules, Hart scratches the itch too vigorously, failing to satisfactorily explain why both types of rules (duty imposing and power conferring) belong together under the same heading of "law." That is, in relieving the itch for uniformity, Hart obscures what the two types of law do have in common. Hart groups the two types together only insofar as both "constitute *standards* by which particular actions may be thus critically appraised."[91] "So much," he says, "is perhaps implied in speaking of them both as rules."[92] But, as Hart well knows, there are many social rules that serve as standards that qualify as law and many that do not; merely naming legal standards "rules" does not capture what is unique about them and therefore exclusive to law. After all, it is Hart, through his internal point of view, who teaches that law is centrally characterized by obligation. Yet it is not clear why this is true if power-conferring rules are a fully distinct type of law.

If power-conferring rules are not to be excluded from the category of "law," even Hart must concede that the itch for uniformity in jurisprudence has some merit; there must be some compelling reason that all of those rules count as *law*. Any analysis requires a unitary definition at some level, and, if so, the dispute is not really about whether it makes sense to have a unitary definition of law but over the degree of abstraction at which a definition of law ceases to be useful. Indeed, we must insist on criteria for identifying law that are neither trivial nor too narrow or too broad in scope. On a descriptive level, Hart offers us a picture of law as rules that people treat as standards though they can have no ultimate reason for treating law that way because law is, by definition, strictly conventional. In this light, Hart's account ought to equate law with any number of nonlegal social rules, which can influence behavior but do not confer any obligation. As a definition of law, Hart's theory stands as an impediment to normative analysis because it prescinds from concepts like justification and obligation and insists law can be defined without them. That is not to say that Hart's theory is flawed because it does not provide a full account of the normative basis of law; after all, that is not its task. Yet it does render a proper normative analysis of law impossible, coming full circle to the charge that his concept of law provides no basis for obligation and even rules it out.

NAZIS

Hart's errors about law undermine his analysis of postwar German war-crime trials

For Hart, one important upshot of getting the concept of law right is that, employing a correct (or at least adequate) concept of law, we can identify law wherever it exists.[93] Doing so, as Shapiro puts it, ensures that we do not deny any truisms.[94] In simpler terms, Hart and Shapiro want to be sure that our definition of law does not defy common sense, as they see it. Even evil regimes possess legal systems, so it is merely stubbornness in the face of reality to think otherwise just because "an unjust law is no law." Hart believes that his analytical framework correctly allows us to identify both just and unjust legal systems as law and steers us away from making the mistake of denying that an unjust system is law, in the tradition of those who say that an unjust law is no law.[95]

Elsewhere, however, Hart notes a more sophisticated and more accurate understanding of the relationship between law and justice, which is not that an unjust law is also invalid for being unjust but that all (valid) laws entail a moral obligation to obey.[96] Instead of focusing on the coincidence of legal rules and moral rules, the central claim of this approach is that "for a legal system to exist there must be a widely diffused, though not necessarily universal, recognition of a moral obligation to obey the law, even though this may be overridden in particular cases by a stronger moral obligation not to obey particular morally iniquitous laws."[97] This is a better interpretation of the natural law view because the unjust-law-is-no-law maxim, taken simplistically, can be misunderstood as a denial of truisms (namely the "obvious" existence of evil legal systems). Similarly, on my view, there is a prima facie obligation to obey, but it can be outweighed by a contrary moral obligation. This means that laws in a legal system properly so called confer an all-things-equal obligation to obey but not an all-things-considered obligation. Even an unjust but valid law (within a just legal system) confers a prima facie obligation to obey. When understood in this way, the partial separability of law and morality, which allows for the possibility of unjust yet valid laws, is at least as compatible with natural law thinking as it is with Hart's.

The problem with Hart's view, as with positivism in general, is that his concept of law requires a nearly complete severing of legality and legitimacy, or authority and justification. Yet a concept of law shorn of justification and, therefore, moral obligation is incoherent and unworkable. One place that this problem features prominently is in Hart's treatment of the "postwar German courts" that tried former Nazis.[98] Appropriately, Hart notices that these trials present a real quandary. But Hart misidentifies the nub of the problem. In Hart's opinion, what makes these cases so difficult is the fact that the immoral deeds in question were lawful at the time they were committed. How can we justly punish people for things they did that were legal at the time they did them? And so, for Hart, the question of whether the Germans on trial can be justly punished is a vexed one.

Hart's focus on the lawfulness of the acts at the time they were committed assumes that the question of desert and punishment depends on the question of lawfulness. Yet that makes sense only if lawfulness also tells us about the acts' moral permissibility or obligatoriness.[99] If lawfulness is severed from morality (justification, legitimacy, normativity), though, then the lawfulness of the Germans' actions poses little obstacle to just punishment. Hart's positivism does not void his question altogether, but it makes the problem much less difficult than he imagines. Again, Hart's problem is that the Germans on trial are being punished for acts that were lawful when they committed them. But, for Hart, lawfulness is disconnected from moral permissibility or obligatoriness. Therefore, the fact of the act being lawful has no bearing on the justifiability of the act or, to be fair, much less than Hart thinks. If the lawfulness of the act is tied to its morality, then we can see why its lawfulness presents a problem for punishing the actor. But the lawfulness of the act is not tied to morality for Hart. The lawfulness of the act depends solely on the not-necessarily-normative criteria specified by the rule of recognition. In short, due to his concept of law, Hart misses the force of his own example.

Thus, it is not just that Hart's theory has little to add to the analysis of such issues. More than that, it cannot account for what *is* in fact so interesting, which is to say difficult, about these cases. One of Hart's main tasks is to divorce questions of legal validity from questions of morality and justice. For instance, the question of "Are we to punish those who did evil things when they were permitted by evil rules then in force?," according to Hart, "cannot be solved by a refusal, once and for all, to recognize evil laws as valid for any purpose," for "this is too crude a way with delicate and complex moral issues."[100] Instead, Hart advocates a "concept of law which allows the invalidity of law to be distinguished from its immorality" and thereby "enables us to see the complexity and variety of these separate issues."[101] Otherwise, "A narrow concept of law which denies legal validity to iniquitous rules may blind us to them."[102] In this light, the validity of a law and the morality of a law seem separable; Hart argues against the unjust-law-is-no-law approach. As Hart sees it, there is "no contradiction in asserting that a rule of law is too iniquitous to be obeyed, and that it does not follow from the proposition that a rule is too iniquitous to obey that it is not a valid rule of law."[103]

Hart's theory simply does not have room to appreciate the quandary fully. Hart's concept of law is a theory of legal validity—distinct from legitimacy—that comes down to acceptance: laws are rules based in social practice. Fundamentally, whatever is accepted as law is law. His work is, as he says, an essay in descriptive sociology, which understandably limits his purview. But the most pressing parts of the questions that Hart believes are better illuminated by his theory, such as those faced by the postwar German courts trying Nazis, come down to matters of moral legitimacy, not of legal validity. For Hart, there can be a regime whose law is legally valid, internally speaking, but also morally monstrous. Hart spells out the criteria for identifying a legal system: "There are therefore two minimum conditions necessary and sufficient for the existence of a legal system. On the one hand, those rules of behaviour which are valid according to the system's ultimate criteria of validity must be generally obeyed, and, on the other hand, its rules of recognition specifying the criteria of legal validity and its rules of change and adjudication must be effectively accepted as common public standards of official behaviour by its officials."[104] Because this description can apply to Nazi law as much as to any other, Hart's theory provides inadequate tools for addressing the important questions he himself identifies, namely whether people can be held accountable for injustices they commit at the behest of or with the permission of unjust regimes. While Hart suggests that his theory provides a superior framework for analyzing the difficult questions raised by the legal systems of unjust regimes, his analysis actually offers no more and no better resources for parsing those questions than the theories and models upon which he means to improve.

Insofar as it abstains from moral analysis, Hart's form of positivism offers no advantage in being able to distinguish Nazi law from any other. To be fair, such distinctions are not Hart's purpose. Still, Hart thinks that a "concept of law which allows the invalidity of law to be distinguished from its immorality" is a better framework for addressing the questions that confronted the postwar courts in Germany.[105] This is because Hart believes that the nub of the problem in trying German soldiers after World War II is that their alleged crimes were at once legal and immoral and, accordingly, that it was ethically fraught to try those soldiers for acts they committed that were legal when they committed them. But if legal validity and moral legitimacy (justification) are separated, then the defendants can give no (in-principle) normative defense of their actions.

The real challenge of the German postwar trials is clarified when we understand, first, that the law entails a prima facie moral obligation to obey and, therefore, second, that, in the case of unjust laws, there is a prima facie obligation to obey the law competing with other moral norms that are violated by following the law. Hart does not see this, and therefore he has an incomplete grasp of the problem. In contrast to the positivists, we must recognize that where there is a legal system, there is also a prima facie moral obligation to obey the law. If we accept that there is a legal system in Nazi Germany, then the defendants in the German trials have a claim of doing what they were obligated to do. But we can see clearly the dilemma presented by the conflict of competing moral obligations and the curiousness (though not wrongfulness) of punishing people for doing something they had an all-things-equal obligation to do.

We judge them unfavorably because they failed to heed stronger contrary obligations. That is, they chose incorrectly because they had stronger moral obligations *not* to do what the law required or permitted. The problem Hart tries to identify exists precisely because those obligations (in effect to *disobey*) ran up against the prima facie obligation to obey the law. The defendants' predicament lies in the fact that they were acting within a legal system, as opposed to those not in a legal system and therefore without any prima facie obligation to behave as they did. This is why there is an intuitive difference between government officials and a crime boss's henchmen. Even if the government officials act wrongly, their claim to be following orders is intelligible, if not decisive in their favor. They have an obligation to obey those orders—not all things considered, but all things equal. In this light, we find the case to be legally and morally complicated, even if we ultimately judge their conduct to be blameworthy. By comparison, if a hitman for the mafia says he is just following orders, there is nothing to his claim. Those orders cannot plausibly be said to have force merely as components of the boss's criminal enterprise in the way that laws do have force as components of a legal system.[106]

Hart is right that treating as crimes actions that are required or permitted by the law at the time they are done is a vexing matter. But, crucially, for Hart, the legal status of the acts in question has no moral valence; there is no reason for anyone subject to those laws to consider the acts permissible or obligatory any more than they credit the orders of a gunman. Instead, the question is truly interesting when those who obey Nazi law claim to do so on the basis of having an *obligation* to obey the law. Only in that last case is there a clear case of conflicting moral obligations: the obligation to obey the law and the obligation not to harm others. If Hart's theory misses this point, it obscures more than it illuminates.

To be sure, in some respects, Hart's theory seems that it must incorporate some explanation of the normative force of law. Something of this sort must exist to support his distinction between justified and unjustified rules or directives—that is, the obliged-obligated distinction. For instance, Hart distinguishes the orders of a military officer, where there is an implied "right or authority," from the orders of a mugger, which are orders only insofar as they are directives with coercive force.[107] The victim is not morally "obligated" (though "obliged" via coercion) to relinquish her wallet. The demands of the mugger are unwarranted whereas the demands of the military officer are not. Hart points out the way in which language usage reflects these distinctions: "We might properly say that the gunman *ordered* the clerk to hand over the money and the clerk obeyed, but it would be somewhat misleading to say that the gunman *gave an order* to the clerk to hand it over."[108] The very fact of this distinction suggests a more strongly normative dimension to Hart's theory than he admits or than is consistent with his positivism.

While we can consider Nazi law to be like the gunman's coercive orders because we think it unjustified, unlike with the gunman, the problem with Nazi law is not the fact that the orders are given but the injustice of the orders. That is, unlike in the case of the mugging, the Nazi officer stands in a relation of justified authority to her subordinates. In other words, there is a legal system. Following Hart, we can say that the Nazi officer "gave an order" in a way we do not for the gunman. There is nothing misleading about saying that the Nazi officer gave an order to her subordinate, and that is because the officer's order, unlike the mugger's, is legitimate, which is to say justified with respect to the superior's authority to command her subordinates. This may be troublesome inasmuch as calling Nazi law "law," which carries obligation, seems to open the door to the just-following-orders defense of German soldiers. But our response is not that Nazi law has no presumptive (prima facie) authority. Instead, our response is that Nazi law carries an all-things-equal obligation but not an all-things-considered obligation. Therefore, Nazi laws that require certain immoral acts likely warrant disobedience in those cases. At the same time, Nazi laws that do not require immoral acts can be obligatory.

Despite what Hart seems to think based on his treatment of the question of the postwar courts, his theory does not shed much light on the matter beyond confirming the existence of a legal system on his own terms. A properly normative perspective on law, however, raises the question of whether there is a moral obligation to disobey (refrain from following) certain unjust laws or perhaps whether the injustice of the regime as a whole means that none of its laws are obligatory. If there is to be any connection between law and morality, the second option is harder to sustain because it means proposing a legal system in which some of the laws are valid but none of them binding. Such a position seems to vacate legal validity of any practical relevance because then validity plays at best a very minor role in one's practical reasoning. If the term *validity* is to have any significance, it ought to carry a sense of presumptive justification; otherwise, what is the purpose of calling the thing a law?

If we take the latter approach, namely that the injustice renders the whole legal system invalid, regarding Germany this means that all the laws presumptively lack justification (and, therefore, authority) in virtue of being part of the Nazi system. In that case, the orders of the Nazi officer *are* like the demands of the mugger and those receiving the orders are obliged but not obligated. But the former approach is better, under which we recognize a prima facie obligation to obey the law while insisting that the law's all-things-equal authoritativeness does not become all-things-considered authoritativeness when the obligation to obey the law comes into conflict with weightier moral obligations to do otherwise.

The reason Nazi law counts as a legal system and, therefore, possesses a prima facie obligation to obey exists because even Nazi law contemplates the common good of some set of people. If law, centrally, is a set of commands oriented to the common good, we can recognize that Germany under the Nazis has a legal system with respect to those under the law who are not targeted for elimination. This allows us to explain the commonsense observation that, for most Germans, ordinary laws, such as traffic laws, are obligatory, even though many other laws of the regime are unjust. On this line of reasoning, there is an all-things-considered obligation for ordinary German citizens to obey Nazi traffic laws in normal circumstances even when there is, all things considered, no obligation to obey (or perhaps even an obligation to disobey) certain other Nazi laws. The alternative is to say that the horrors of the Nazi regime mean that the law is not really aimed at anyone's common good, and, therefore, no one has any obligation to obey any of the laws, which are not, in fact, laws at all but rather the illicit orders of a mugger. This is plausible because the evil laws of the Nazi regime strike not only at the good of the victims but also the good of the perpetrators and enablers, but it is unsatisfying because, to mix Hart's disparate examples, it means that even ordinary laws like traffic laws in Germany do not have the status of law and do not carry any obligation to obey.

Similarly, in the context of rejecting the argument from gratitude, John Simmons quotes Jeffrie Murphy, who says that "those people who are systematically excluded from the benefits of a society do not have any moral obligation to obey that society's laws as such."[109] Simmons is right that gratitude is insufficient to support a claim for general political obligations, but he misses the way the construction of the argument from gratitude tracks the correct answer. Because the purpose of law is to promote the common good, those who are not included in the common good contemplated by the law are also not obligated to obey it. By the same token, those who are included in that common good are obligated generally.

Marmor essentially makes the same point, too, in describing his institutional conception of authority.[110] To the question of who is obligated under any given authority, his simple answer is, all those who are a party to the institution. But a more accurate and nuanced version of that answer is that it is all those who are a party to the institution insofar as the institution fulfills its function for those people. In better terms, the law obligates all those whose good it contemplates. Without filling out this substantive account, Marmor acknowledges the broader point. "Practical authorities," he says, "always have limited jurisdiction: their authority binds only those who are participants in the practice or institution in which they operate."[111] Those who are bound have a prima facie obligation to obey. But "such obligations are always conditional: They presuppose that there are valid reasons to participate in the relevant institutional practice and comply with its rules."[112] For Marmor, this is what it means to be a participant in the practice: to have valid reasons to participate. I think we can easily extend the point to say that those who do not have valid reasons to participate—that is, those whose good is not considered by the authority—are not bound. They do not "belong" to the social practice or institution in the way that Marmor means when he says that "authorities obligate only those who belong to the practice or institution that grants them the power they have."[113]

My position differs from Hart's because he wants to argue that even the evilest regimes can still be identified as having a legal system, irrespective of any normative judgments. Even Nazi law is law for Hart, not because he has judged any normative requirements to have been met but because no such judgments need be made. In contrast, I argue that a legal system failing to measure up to certain moral standards is not a legal system at all—an important departure from Hart.[114] To which actual regimes this applies is another matter. I must tread carefully here because my claim is not only very politically sensitive but also conceptually nuanced: Even Nazi Germany can have a legal system, and therefore even the German soldiers (or others) can have a prima facie obligation to obey the law. In that admittedly horrible case, Nazi law does contemplate the common good of the German citizens. This is distinct from the case of a rapacious ruler. Like the mafia, for example, the rapacious ruler rules for his own benefit at everyone else's expense. If the Nazi legal system is excluded as a legal system, it must be on the basis on its failure to be oriented to some common good. But the rapacious ruler does not contemplate a common good at all. Nor does it matter whether the rapacious ruler does nice things from time to time because that is incidental to the system (or perhaps merely instrumental to propping it up). In this way, my concept of law also helps us distinguish properly the legal system of a state from the internal rules of street gangs or organized crime. This is a significant point, as Hart thinks that the main distinction between a government and a gang is the complexity of the system and the attitude of the subjects. But the real difference is found in the normative justification of the authority (or lack thereof), as Augustine notes.[115]

Hart's vision is deficient when addressing the "delicate and complex moral issues," obscuring what is actually interesting about the question that faced the postwar German courts. That question is interesting precisely because of the conflict between the moral obligation to obey the law in general and the moral obligation not to do what those particular laws require. Anything short of that is, under Hart's view, merely the opposition of moral obligation and self-interest. Hart is not saying that the compliant Nazi soldier has any moral obligation to obey the wicked law, only that he does so for pragmatic reasons. Depending on the nature of the self-interest (for example, the understandable desire to protect one's family from Nazi retribution, as opposed to the desire for professional advancement), the court is faced with significant mitigating factors but not a moral quandary of the same sort. In other words, unless validity, which is to say legal obligation, somehow entails moral obligation, then the concept of validity adds much less of interest to the analysis of such moral issues than Hart thinks. Because law does not imply obligation (and Hart has no interest in arguing for the obligation to obey Nazi law), those who committed "wrongs" in obedience to Nazi law would have to claim that they had done so out of fear of punishment. If so, we can ponder whether they were justified in doing harm to others in order to avoid harm to themselves. Though that is not a small question, it is neither a unique problem nor one specific to the matter of law. It is even less interesting if they merely claimed that they obeyed in conformance with social practice, meaning that they complied with the laws because they were valid in virtue of being widely followed. That is a very weak justification for committing evil.

Hart gets the analysis of the German courts wrong in the end because he is limited by his own framework. Although Hart cannot reach this conclusion because of the limitations imposed by his own theory, the correct view is that the prima face obligation to obey the law gives some weight to the claims of those who were "just following orders"—and this is why the cases present such a dilemma. The accused are on trial for doing evil things that they *did* have a prima facie obligation to do. Such obligations can be in all cases defeated by contrary obligations, but it is the conflict between the two that makes the situation interesting and difficult (even if, as a matter of fact, knowing what is the correct thing to do in many particular situations is easy, especially when viewed in hindsight).

In contrast, the incompatibility of Hart's concept of law with a justification of law's authority and an obligation to obey means that he muddles some of the large questions that his theory means to illuminate. That is, his own concept of law fails to capture the most compelling issue in his example. For Hart, the question is whether it is just to try people for actions that were required (or maybe permitted) by the law when they committed them. But Hart, of course, does not believe that laws are obligatory just because they are valid, and he thereby minimizes the problem as fast as he identifies it.

CHAPTER 3

Justification

THE COMMAND MODEL NEEDS AN ACCOMPANYING NORMATIVE ELEMENT TO JUSTIFY AUTHORITY

One way to think about the contrast between theories of authority and obligation is to compare the command model, often associated with Bentham and Austin, where authority is located in the power of the commander, with Joseph Raz's approach, where authority is located in the force of the reasons behind the command. The command model is significant for two reasons. First, opposition to the command model is the starting point for Hart's theory and frames the development of his own hugely influential concept of law. Second, and relatedly, the overreach in Hart's critique of the command model provides the basis for my own concept of law and especially the recovery of the command aspect of law. Raz is so important because, like Hart, he looms large over all subsequent analytic jurisprudence, offering his own account of law's authority, which the command model and other theories fail to justify.

Older versions of the command model in which, for example, the sovereign is he who is habitually obeyed and who habitually obeys no one, are inadequate because they seemingly reduce all measure of political authority to power (and efficacy), thereby overlooking or at least obscuring questions of justification. This reductiveness creates a problem because, on one hand, it must mean either that even the worst dictator is as justified as the most worthy regime (i.e., that power justifies authority), or, on the other hand, it must mean that authoritativeness can exist without justification. Either way, this reduces authoritativeness to the simple fact of having power—of being able to cause others to comply—so there is no real distinction between justified and unjustified authority. This approach is unilluminating and does not provide or point us toward a satisfying normative account of authority because it merely attaches the name "authority" to coercion; it simply describes who wields power. On a more sophisticated level, it is unhelpful because it fails to explain why, short of fear of punishment (or desire for reward), anyone should or would obey authority. In that respect, such a view fails to take into account the fundamental difference between law and coercion, which Hart is at pains to point out in his distinction between being "obligated" to obey the law and being "obliged" to obey an armed robber.

After removing accoutrements of the command model such as sanctions or habits of obedience, which are flaws in the theory but are, it turns out, unnecessary for a correct concept of law, the main problem remains: the command model appears to ground obligation in nothing more than sheer will. In the "pure" version of the command model, the commander's directives are law because she stands in a relation of superiority to the commanded, as defined by the commander's ability to impose penalties (or another mark of sovereignty).[1] For some command theorists, all commands are justified simply by virtue of being the will of the commander. Thus, the command model is a theory of authority that offers insufficient justification for authority or no justification at all. A better theory demands an answer as to why the will of the commander binds. By what right does the commander bind the commanded? That is, what is the *justification* of authority?

At the same time, the leading theories that abandon the command model altogether are also inadequate because they, too, in a very different way, cannot account for or accommodate the normativity of authority. As I argue, for Raz, there can be reasons to comply with a law, but those reasons always fall short of imposing an obligation to do what the law says because the law says it.[2] Relatedly, for Hart, there can be many good reasons for acting *as though* the law imposes an obligation to follow the law, but, because the law finds its basis in social rules, there is no room for showing how there could be an obligation to do so.[3] On these currently dominant views, there is no model of authority in which the commands of a particular commander are justified as obligating reasons for action, either because no command can be justified or because authority cannot be located in a particular commander.

For Raz, authority is justified insofar as its directives conform to the reasons one has, independent of the authority, to act. The problem with his theory is that it is really not a theory of authority at all in the relevant sense of explaining the obligation to obey. To the extent that Raz's project is to reconcile authority with autonomy, he shows how it can be rational, and therefore morally permissible—but, crucially, not necessarily required—to defer to another's judgment. For Raz, while there can be a substitution of another's judgment for one's own, there is no substitution of another's will for one's own because the deference is justified only by reference to the fulfillment of one's own purposes.[4] At a minimum, for Raz, there is no taking of another's reasons for one's own. This is another way of revealing whether we have before us a notion of political authority that encompasses an ability to impose obligation in the sense that the commander's will (as an embodiment of the commander's reasons) substitutes for the will (or reasons) of the commanded as a reason for action. Raz's version of authority requires, essentially, that the subject who is commanded form an independent judgment about whether complying with the authority is consistent with her own reasons for acting. As such, Raz's theory can never produce an obligation to obey, only a reason to act as though one has an obligation by complying with the authority despite not having an obligation to do so (as when one takes the commands as a rule of thumb with which to comply only provisionally, not as a matter of obligation). Thus, Raz bequeaths a notion of authority devoid of obligation, or, in other words, no real authority at all.

RAZ'S THEORY OF LAW'S AUTHORITY FAILS TO JUSTIFY THE OBLIGATION TO OBEY THE LAW

Like Hart, Raz is a towering figure in the analytic jurisprudence of the later decades of the twentieth century. And, as with Hart, Raz's influence continues to be felt in the field, as much current work on authority and obligation is built upon his writings. Yet, also like Hart's, Raz's theory of authority falls short. It shows only that one can act in accordance with the law such that doing so is not in violation of the moral responsibility of autonomy, not that law has authority of the kind that generates an obligation to obey just because it is the law. Indeed, his theory does not show that there is ever an obligation to obey the law, only good reason to act in conformance with it. This is because law's expertise (broadly construed) is only enough to justify treating the law as a giver of sound advice, and it is not always wrong to reject sound advice, especially if one values deciding for oneself (among other possible motivations). Respect for the law (or the society that promulgates it) is enough to justify treating the law as authoritative as an expression of respect through complying, but there is no reason that such respect must entail an obligation to obey, especially if it involves no element of consent, as Raz maintains. Raz's failure to justify authority means that the prevailing theory of authority in philosophy of law is inadequate and that an understanding of legal obligation, if there is such a thing, requires firmer footing. In examining Raz's shortcomings closely, we can gain insight into what *is* needed to make a theory of authority work.

We can begin again here with the contrast to older ways of thinking against which Raz's theory is set. An exemplar of the pre-Hartian positivism, Austin sees law's authority in "whoever can *oblige* another to comply with his wishes, is the *superior* of that other."[5] There is no reason to deny that someone in a position to impose sanctions on another can, in practice, compel obedience. Obviously, though, such authority is not necessarily justified. It is authority only in the sense of power. To get beyond Hart's "descriptive sociology," concern about law's authority must take into account the question of justification. Among other things, justification of law's authority underwrites the justified (morally legitimate) use of coercion against lawbreakers. That is, justification is necessary to explain why the authority of law is distinct from criminal or other forms of coercion where, in Hart's terms, one may be obliged but not (morally) obligated to obey—why the law is different from a mugger.[6]

If Hart is right that law is distinguished in part by its ability to impose obligations (to *obligate* and not merely to *oblige*), then we ought to inquire into the source of law's normative (obligation-imposing) authority. As we have seen, Hart argues that the command model does not properly describe the nature and scope of law. As a descriptive theory, Hart's concept of law does not directly address the question of *why* there is (or is believed to be) a moral obligation to obey the law, only *that* there is. It is not Hart's aim to account for the rest. That question, instead, is taken up prominently by Raz, who offers one of the most influential accounts of law's authority. Unlike Hart, Raz goes beyond the descriptive matter of whether people treat the law as authoritative to the normative matter of whether people in fact have a moral obligation to obey the law. The normative side is important because it speaks to whether or not people act rightly when they treat the law as obligatory and wrongly when they disobey the law.

If the law is authoritative in the normative sense, then subjects under that law have a moral obligation to obey, all else being equal. (This leaves open the possibility that a competing obligation can override the all-things-equal obligation to obey the law.) In other words, what it means for X to have justified authority—and not just power—over Y is for Y to be morally obligated to comply with the directives of X. The inclusion of moral obligation distinguishes this sense of authority and obligation from a narrower sense—what we can call power—whereby X has "authority" over Y and Y has an "obligation" to obey X only insofar as X has the power to coerce (or induce) Y to comply or to punish Y for noncompliance. The prospect of coercion or punishment gives Y a reason to comply, but that is not the same as Y having a moral obligation to do so, and, therefore, it does not mean that there is (necessarily) anything morally deficient in Y refusing or otherwise failing to do so.

Before setting up his own theory for the justification of authority, Raz touches upon the distinction between having authority in this sense of being capable of forcing compliance and having authority in the sense of issuing directives that are morally binding (or at least claiming to): "A person needs more than power (as influence) to have *de facto* authority. He must either claim that he has legitimate authority or be held by others to have legitimate authority. There is an important difference, for example, between the brute use of force to get one's way and the same done with a claim of right."[7] On one hand, Raz may be incorrect: why does de facto authority depend upon an offered or accepted claim of right as long as there is compliance? Compliance can be coerced without any claim of right. On the other hand, his suggestion is important because it introduces the normative element to authority. At the same time, we can go further and recognize that there remains a critical distinction between claiming legitimacy and having it; obviously one can claim it without having it. So, too, being "held by others" to have legitimacy is not the same thing as having it, even if it does result in de facto authority over subjects who obey because they believe they ought to.

Pursuing this line of reasoning, Raz ultimately fails to muster an adequate account of justified authority. He succeeds in showing that there is often good reason to comply with the requirements of the law, yet he never shows that this amounts to an *obligation* to obey the law. There are, sometimes, moral obligations to act in ways that overlap with what the law requires. But having moral obligations that coincide with what the law requires does not amount to having an obligation to obey the law just as such—that is, to comply simply because the law requires it. And, indeed, we find that Raz denies there is a general moral obligation to obey the law—that is, a prima facie obligation to obey the law just because it is the law, which I contend must accompany justified authority. Without this general obligation, Raz cannot show that there is ever a moral obligation to obey the law qua *law*, and the authority of law vanishes.[8] Raz's central point is that law is justified—which means it is not a violation of one's autonomy to comply—when it requires that which one already has reason to do. This is an inadequate justification of law because, for law to have genuine authority, it must make a difference to one's practical reasoning by supplying a reason to act even when one lacks other reasons.

RAZ AIMS TO RECONCILE AUTHORITY AND AUTONOMY BUT DOES NOT JUSTIFY REAL AUTHORITY

As Raz makes clear, his chief concern about authority is not only (and not primarily) the obvious one, namely that power wielded through force alone is not the same as justified authority. Rather, Raz's main preoccupation is with the conflict between authority and autonomy. In one place, Raz opens his treatment of authority this way:

> The paradoxes of authority can assume different forms, but all of them concern the alleged incompatibility of authority with reason or autonomy. To be subjected to authority, it is argued, is incompatible with reason, for reason requires that one should always act on the balance of reasons of which one is aware. It is the nature of authority that it requires submission even when one thinks that what is required is against reason. Therefore, submission to authority is irrational. Similarly the principle of autonomy entails action on one's own judgment on all moral questions. Since authority sometimes requires action against one's own judgment, it requires abandoning one's moral autonomy. Since all practical questions may involve moral considerations, all practical authority denies moral autonomy and is consequently immoral.[9]

In other works, Raz's theory of authority is framed specifically as a response to the philosophical anarchists and in particular to Robert Wolff. In Wolff's view, "taking responsibility for one's actions means making the final decisions about what one should do"; furthermore, "the moral condition demands that we acknowledge responsibility and achieve autonomy wherever and whenever possible."[10] This necessarily sets up an opposition between the person and the state because the "defining mark of the state is authority, the right to rule," while the "primary obligation of man is autonomy, the refusal to be ruled."[11] Therefore, according to Wolff, "anarchism is the only political doctrine consistent with the virtue of autonomy."[12]

Introducing his edited volume on authority, which includes Wolff's essay, Raz wonders, "Can I not have absolute right to decide my own action while conceding an equal right to all? That is anarchy. But it may be that only anarchy avoids the problem of authority."[13] Continuing, Raz summarizes the problem:

> The duty to obey conveys an abdication of autonomy, that is, of the right and duty to be responsible for one's action and to conduct oneself in the best light of reason. If there is an authority which is legitimate, then its subjects are duty bound to obey it whether they agree or not. Such a duty is inconsistent with autonomy, with the right and the duty to act responsibly, in the light of reason. Hence, Wolff's denial of the moral possibility of legitimate authority. This is the challenge of philosophical anarchism.[14]

Raz's theory of authority is a response to this claim, an attempt to rebut the philosophical anarchists by arguing that authority can be consistent with autonomy under the right circumstances. His task, in other words, is to demonstrate that authority can be consistent with acting "in the best light of reason." Therefore, it is not altogether surprising that Raz's theory, when properly unpacked, amounts to a defense of the position that it can be permissible to yield to authority but does not add up to a claim that it is obligatory to do so.

Raz's theory of authority rests upon three main theses. First, there is the preemption thesis: "The fact that an authority requires performance of an action is a reason for its performance which is not added to all other relevant reasons when assessing what to do, but should exclude and take the place of some of them."[15] Authoritative directives mean to preempt the reasons to do or not do an action by excluding them from consideration. In this way, the authoritativeness of a directive is not weighed against the reasons for action but preempts them. In Raz's locution, a reason for action is a first-order reason while a reason to act or not act for a reason is a second-order reason. Law operates in this latter way, as a second-order reason. More narrowly, a reason to *not* act for a reason is a special kind of second-order reason called an exclusionary reason because it excludes at least some first-order reasons.[16] This is generally how law's authority is meant to work (as an exclusionary reason). Of course, the preemption thesis only describes the function of authority (to preempt); it is the other two theses that justify it.

Next is the dependence thesis. The dependence thesis states, "All authoritative directives should be based on reasons which already independently apply to the subjects of the directives and are relevant to their action in the circumstances covered by the directive."[17] Such reasons—that is, ones that already apply—are called dependent reasons, a category that includes the reasons for action that apply to the subject and any decisions that "sum them up."[18] Because the dependence thesis is "a moral thesis about the way authorities should use power," it "does not claim that authorities always act for dependent reasons, but merely that they should do so."[19] Adherence to the dependence thesis is one condition for justified authority.

The other condition for justified authority is Raz's third thesis, the normal justification thesis: "The normal way to establish that a person has authority over another person involves showing that the alleged subject is likely better to comply with reasons which apply to him (other than the alleged authoritative directives) if he accepts the directives of the alleged authority as authoritatively binding and tries to follow them, rather than by trying to follow the reasons which apply to him directly."[20] Therefore, authority that meets the terms of the dependence thesis and the normal justification thesis is justified because it does not require a sacrifice of autonomy. That is, because the directives are based on reasons that the subject already has for acting, and because the subject will better fulfill the purposes supported by those reasons, the subject is not doing anything other than that which she ought to do on the balance of reasons that apply to her, even if the subject is no longer acting *for* those reasons but because the law requires it. Although the normal justification thesis is "not the only" justification for authority, it is, eponymously, "the normal one."[21]

The main problem with Raz's justification of authority is that it can never produce an obligation to obey. The best that it can do is show when it is justified to defer to authority; it can never show that there is an obligation to do so. The source of this flaw is in the setup of the investigation: If the problem is that authority jeopardizes autonomy, then the solution requires that autonomy be preserved. By definition, autonomy is preserved any time it is merely morally *permissible* for the subject to defer to authority. (If it is morally permissible to defer to authority in some cases, then, by definition, it is not always morally impermissible to defer.) Therefore, to solve the problem at hand, Raz's aim is to show the permissibility of following authority, not to show the obligatoriness of following authority. In other words, Raz need not ever show that deference to authority is morally obligatory in order to avoid the alleged conflict between authority and autonomy. Autonomy and authority can be reconciled whenever it is permissible to comply with the law, even if it is never obligatory to comply. Raz never quite does show it is obligatory, and he recognizes this in his denial of a prima facie obligation to obey the law. Raz writes, "I shall argue that there is no obligation to obey the law. It is generally agreed that there is no absolute or conclusive obligation to obey the law. I shall suggest that there is not even a prima facie obligation to obey it. In other words, whatever one's view of the nature of the good society or the desirable shape of the law it does not follow from those or indeed from any other reasonable moral principle that there is an obligation to obey the law."[22] If so, Raz's theory shows when authority is morally acceptable because it is not in tension with autonomy, but it also never generates an obligation to obey the law just as such. If there is no prima facie obligation to obey the law, then there is no authority in the true sense, only further reasons to do what one already has reasons to do before the directive is issued.

In addition to this core problem with Raz's account, which I address in detail, there is a preliminary problem concerning Raz's understanding of autonomy that allows him supposedly to overcome the problem he sets up more easily than he should be able. Raz argues that deferring to authority is not an improper sacrifice of autonomy when the authoritative directives conform to reasons that the subject has for action, anyway. But this assumes, crucially, that what is relevant about autonomy is the outcome that results from deciding according to the best light of reason—emphasis on the *best light of reason*. Raz provides no explanation, though, for why, normatively speaking, the emphasis is not to be placed on the *deciding*. Perhaps true moral responsibility, and particularly the form of moral responsibility that concerns the philosophical anarchists, is found not in successfully acting according to the reasons one has for action but in independent decision-making.

In fact, this interpretation of the philosophical anarchists' problem with authority appears superior to Raz's. After all, if their main concern is for outcomes, then the philosophical anarchists' key point probably ought not to be the illegitimacy of all governments but instead an empirical doubt about whether governments are likelier to "get it right" than are the members of ungoverned societies, as required by Raz's normal justification thesis. If that is the question, then Raz and the anarchists can simply be on different sides of that empirical matter, Raz having more confidence than they about states' likelihood of getting it right. Yet it does not appear that the debate centers on this empirical disagreement. If the philosophical anarchists are defending autonomy in principle (for its own sake) and not only when authority leads to worse outcomes, then Raz is possibly wrong about the relationship between authority and autonomy.

Raz reveals his reliance on this critical assumption—that the compatibility of autonomy and authority depends on outcomes, not process—in passing once, writing, "So long as this is done where improving the outcome is more important than deciding for oneself this acceptance of authority, far from being either irrational or an abdication of moral responsibility, is in fact the most rational course and the right way to discharge one's responsibilities."[23] But it can very well be that, for the philosophical anarchists, the choice not to decide for oneself is the real abdication of moral responsibility. At the very least, the burden lies with Raz to explain why autonomy is primarily valued for enabling individuals to more successfully act on the reasons that apply to them (to get better outcomes) rather than for consisting in deciding for oneself even when it means getting things right less often than if one defers to authority.[24]

Raz's response can be that choosing to decide for oneself—despite the knowledge that deference to authority in some cases offers better outcomes—is not to take moral responsibility but to act irrationally. That is, if Raz maintains that it is not merely imprudent but irrational to knowingly choose a course that, on average, produces worse outcomes (defined as a less successful conformance to the reasons one has for action), then it makes sense for Raz to argue that there is no loss in deferring to authority in those cases. There is no loss because the exercise of autonomy in those cases is not valuable. At the same time, we also must not be too quick to assume that one can really know which path will produce superior outcomes.

But this dismissal of the centrality of deciding for oneself is a questionable, even question-begging, defense of Raz's position. To illustrate what it means for authority to produce better outcomes, Raz occasionally uses the example of "an authority on the stock exchange" or "financial expert" (I use "stockbroker") whose success rate is 20 percent better than her client's.[25] In that situation, if the client wishes to maximize her profits, she ought to defer to the broker's advice 100 percent of the time.[26] Occasionally substituting her own judgment for the stockbroker's results in lower returns on average. Nevertheless, the claim of irrationality in ignoring the broker's advice assumes that the client's only aim is to maximize profits. It is hardly a stretch to imagine an investor who sometimes wishes to win or lose on her own bets. She might value the "sport" of the actual decision-making—and not only because she believes she will learn the markets better from her own trial-and-error investing or because of the added thrill she gets from picking a winner herself but also because she finds intrinsic satisfaction in making decisions for herself, win or lose. To be sure, this example has its limits because the goal of investing, for most people most of the time, is to secure the best returns regardless of who makes the decisions. But there are many activities (including investing, sometimes) where part of the satisfaction and benefit comes from the activity itself apart from the success of the results, however defined.

I am not arguing that it is wholly unreasonable for Raz to maintain that consciously choosing a path that yields worse outcomes is reckless to the point of being irrational and, accordingly, forfeits any moral value that can otherwise be found in autonomy. Yet, as we have just seen, if this is Raz's argument, it builds in questionable assumptions about what counts as better and worse results or, in other words, what counts as reasons for action. Therefore, Raz can reconcile authority and autonomy only by assuming that each is valuable precisely in securing better outcomes in the particular sense that is captured by the example of earning higher investment returns.

Framing the problem of authority as Raz does in terms of autonomy reveals the absence of a distinct concept of law's authority—that is, of law being authoritative just because it is law. If the source of law's authority is the supposed irrationality (or unreasonableness) of acting contrary to the law in certain situations—that is, of acting autonomously—then the driving force behind one's compliance with the reasons one has for action is not the authority of law but the effort to act rationally (or reasonably). It is conformance with reason, not obedience to authority. To be sure, authority plays a role in identifying what is to be done in order to comply with one's own reasons, but, with that limited function, the law is really no more than a glorified stockbroker, an adviser who knows better, and cannot properly be seen to obligate. In sum, starting from the challenge presented by autonomy sets us on the wrong track for understanding authority. Furthermore, as I elaborate, comparing authority to a stockbroker roots authority's normativity in its expertise, but that approach actually deprives authority of its ability to obligate and therefore of its authoritativeness (and, therefore, it is not really authority).

GROUNDING AUTHORITY IN EXPERTISE DOES NOT YIELD AN OBLIGATION TO OBEY

My central claim against Raz's work on law's authority is that Raz proposes to justify law's authority but never fully does. This means Raz shows that it can be morally permissible to comply with an authority's directives (to forgo autonomy by substituting the judgment of the authority for one's own), but, contrary to what he says, he cannot and does not show that it is ever obligatory—that is, that there is ever an obligation to obey the law. His doubts about a general obligation to obey the law are, therefore, more consistent with his argument than his claim of justifying authority in the sense of grounding obligation. As I say, this incompleteness stems in large part from Raz's focus on answering the challenge of the philosophical anarchists regarding autonomy. Therefore, Raz's main theory does not reach the matter of obligation, strictly speaking. In other words, the normal justification thesis specifies the conditions under which it is morally permissible to yield to authority, but it does not necessarily follow that it is morally required to do so under those circumstances; that is, it does not follow that there is also an obligation to obey.[27] Raz often implies that the two (the permissibility of obeying and the obligation to obey) go together, and his occasionally ambiguous use of terms like *legitimate authority* to mean either "authority that it is permissible to obey" or "authority that it is obligatory to obey" reflects this confusion. In fairness to Raz, the question of the permissibility of deferring to authority can be, in some sense, conceptually prior to the obligation to obey, in which case it is understandable for Raz to address that first. But, if so, then the question of obligation remains unanswered.

Raz's failure to offer a proper account of legal obligation is a fundamental point. It is not just that there is in Raz's account no general obligation to obey the law, as he concedes, but that, even when he defends obligation more narrowly, it never adds up to an obligation to the law itself. There is a further difficulty because, despite his denial of a prima facie obligation to obey the law, Raz does speak as though there is an obligation to obey the law under certain circumstances. In other words, he needs an adequate account of the obligation to obey the law that covers at least those specific instances, but he does not have one. So Raz's theory suffers from the absence of a justification of authority to explain the prima facie obligation to obey the law (and therefore the authoritativeness of law qua law) and also the absence of a justification for obligation in the limited cases where he does recognize one.

Raz does argue for an obligation to obey the law in some cases, stating, "Those who do not voluntarily or semi-voluntarily place themselves under the authority of relatively just governments are under a partial and qualified obligation to recognize the authority of such a government in their country. In particular its authority should be recognized to the extent necessary to enable it to secure goals, which individuals have reason to secure, for which co-ordination is necessary or helpful, and where this is the most promising way of achieving them."[28] Unlike where he treats the permissibility of yielding to authority, here Raz clearly speaks of an obligation to obey, albeit partial and qualified. Similarly, Raz writes, "We are forced to conclude that while the main argument does confer qualified and partial authority on just governments it invariably fails to justify the claims to authority which these governments make for themselves."[29] The "claims to authority which these governments make" are claims about an obligation to obey the law. After all, no government claims merely that it is morally permissible to comply with its laws. If the failed claims to authority are claims of obligation, then, by the same token, the "qualified and partial authority," which is justified, also refers to obligation. What fails, according to Raz, is the claim to general authority. For Raz, the obligation to obey the law, while existing in a partial and qualified way, is narrower, notwithstanding the claims of government.

Yet even this limited obligation to obey the law is more than Raz's theory can sustain. In an echo of the normal justification thesis, Raz concedes only that "authority should be recognized to the extent necessary to enable it to secure goals, which individuals have reason to secure"—that is, reasons that already apply to the individuals in question.[30] The normal justification thesis, in combination with the dependence thesis, essentially means that law's authority is a matter of expertise, broadly construed. As Raz writes, "The main argument for the legitimacy of any authority is that in subjecting himself to it a person is more likely to act successfully for the reasons which apply to him than if he does not subject himself to authority."[31] Or, simply put, "The normal justification of authority is that following it will enable its subjects better to conform with reason."[32] This produces what

Raz refers to as "the service conception of the function of authorities, that is, the view that their role and primary normal function is to serve the governed."[33] By "serve the governed," Raz means that "the service conception establishes that the point of having authorities is that they are better at complying with the dependent reasons."[34] In yielding to authority in such cases, people can better comply with the reasons that apply to them than if they try to comply on their own without the assistance of the authority. This approach to justifying authority, which is finally inadequate, makes sense when we remember that Raz is mainly concerned to demonstrate when authority does not conflict with autonomy.

Authority can fulfill its function under the normal justification thesis by virtue of its expertise, which entails leading people to more successfully act on the reasons that apply to them.[35] Raz disfavors the term *expertise*, claiming that it is a misunderstanding to say "the legitimacy of an authority rests on its greater expertise" like a "big Daddy who knows best."[36] But taking the term *expertise* less cynically and less narrowly, it is entirely appropriate and useful for characterizing Raz's view. Raz identifies five main ways in which authority can produce better outcomes. First, authority can be "wiser."[37] That is, the authority can have greater knowledge or expertise in the relevant area. If so, the authority can know better than the subjects how they ought to act in order to comply with the reasons that apply to them. This is a classic example of expertise. But authority can have other advantages as well. The second advantage of authority, for example, is "a steadier will less likely to be tempted by bias, weakness or impetuosity," whether because the authority is not an interested party or because it is more insulated from countervailing pressures.[38] Third, subjects can often best "follow right reason" through "an indirect strategy," especially the indirect strategy of deferring to authority, whereby they "guid[e] their action by one standard in order to better conform to another."[39] Fourth, authority can aid an individual in avoiding the "anxiety, exhaustion, or . . . costs in time or resources" of deciding for oneself.[40] Fifth and finally, the authority is sometimes "in a better position to achieve . . . what the individual has reason to but is in no position to achieve."[41] That "some of these reasons are currently out of fashion in discussions of political authority" does not bother Raz; he maintains that "they all have their role to play."[42] In all of these cases, more or less, the role of authority is in exercising the distinct advantages it has in virtue of being an "expert": more knowledgeable, stronger willed or more disinterested, better positioned to formulate a plan, and so on—that is, all the advantages of a top-notch stockbroker. In this most general sense, authority *is* about expertise, simply insofar as the authority is better at guiding the subjects to act for their own reasons than they can manage on their own. The authority *is* an expert in the sense of being better able, where being better able possibly includes not only knowing more but also "knowing better," as in, knowing better than to act impulsively, and so on.

A key feature of such an account of authority for Raz is that it does not produce a prima facie obligation to obey the law. Put plainly, if authority is based on expertise, then there is no obligation to obey when the subject knows better than the authority.[43] But this is not a concession of Raz's theory—not a bug but a feature. As Raz explains, the scope of authority "depends on the person over whom authority is supposed to be exercised: his knowledge, strength of will, his reliability in various aspects of life, and on the government in question. These factors are relevant at two levels. First they determine whether an individual is better likely to conform to reason by following an authority or by following his own judgment independently of any authority. Second they determine under what circumstances he is likely to answer the first question correctly."[44]

On this matter of authority's limits, Raz offers some instructive examples. In one case, Raz writes, "An expert pharmacologist may not be subject to the authority of the government in matters of the safety of drugs, an inhabitant of a little village by a river may not be subject to its authority in matters of navigation and conservation of the river by the banks of which he has spent all his life."[45] Similarly, "One person has wide and reliable knowledge of cars, as well as an unimpeachable moral character. He may have no reason to acknowledge the authority of the government over him regarding the road worthiness of his car. Another person, though lacking any special expertise, knows local conditions well and has great insight into the needs of his children. He may have no reason to acknowledge the government's authority over him regarding the conditions under which parents may leave their children unattended by adults."[46] Thus, where law's authority rests on its ability to produce better outcomes, that authority is absent—that is, not authoritative—when the benefits conferred by the exercise of authority are absent. In Raz's examples, complying with authority does not lead one to better act on the reasons that already apply to oneself. Although the law is justified generally when "based in reasons which apply to its subjects," those particular laws have no authority over the particular subjects who "are able to do better if they refuse to acknowledge the authority of this law."[47] Their own views supersede the law precisely because of their expertise.

Moreover, in its full generality, the exemption from authority, as it were, does not necessarily have to do with any specialized knowledge, skill, or position of the subject, as in the case of the pharmacist or villager. Instead, the lack of authority has primarily to do with the law's failure to overlap with reasons that already apply to the subject. Even when the law requires something that the subject has a moral obligation to do (or refrain from doing) under other circumstances, the subject is free to disregard the law in specific cases where that moral obligation, apart from the demands of the law, does not obtain. In a hypothetical example about a law prohibiting river pollution, Raz argues, "If a sufficiently large number of people refrain from polluting the rivers, they will be clean, and each person has a moral reason to contribute to keeping them clean. But if most people pollute them and they are badly polluted there is normally no reason why I should refrain from polluting them myself."[48] In Raz's analysis, "It matters not at all to one's moral reasoning whether the practice of keeping the rivers clean is sanctioned by law. . . . It is the existence of the practice that matters, not (except in special circumstances) its origin or surrounding circumstances. On the other hand, suppose that the law requires keeping the rivers clean but that nobody obeys and the rivers have turned into public sewers. The moral reasons for not throwing refuse into them that we have been considering do not exist in such circumstances notwithstanding the legal requirement not to do so."[49] That is, because there is no separate moral obligation to refrain from polluting the river when everyone else is polluting it, the law itself cannot normally provide a reason for refraining.[50] According to Raz's theses of authority, if the law does not correspond to reasons that already apply to the subject—if the law does not overlap with a moral obligation that is apart from the one that would be generated by the law if the law could do so (what was referred to above as a "separate moral obligation," meaning separate from the law)—then it has no authority over that subject in that case. In sum, there is no obligation to obey the law just because it is the law; there are only reasons to conform when the requirements of the law overlap with what one already has an obligation to do. As before with his attempted reconciliation of authority and autonomy, Raz is left with no concept of the authority of law per se. Law can advise by pointing to a good course of action but never obligate.

Once again, the absence of any obligation to obey the law does not mean that authority makes no difference for one's practical reasoning, but it does mean that Raz is not speaking of *authority* in a meaningful way. Authority can make a difference in this way:

> The intrusion of the bureaucratic considerations is likely to lead to solutions which differ in many cases from those an individual should have adopted if left to himself. Reliance on such considerations is justified if and to the extent that they enable authorities to reach decisions which, when taken as a whole, better reflect the reasons which apply to the subjects. That is, an authority may rely on considerations which do not apply to its subjects when doing so reliably leads to decisions which approximate better than any which would have been reached by any other procedure, to those decisions best supported by reasons which apply to the subjects.[51]

Raz later explains, "This, to repeat a point made earlier, does not mean that their sole role must be to further the interest of each or of all their subjects. It is to help them act on reasons which bind them."[52] Hence, it is the preexisting reasons and not the law that binds the subjects. Yet, as Raz says, the law can make a difference, but, for him, the law does not make a difference by creating obligations. There is no authority of law, only the authority of the reasons, so to speak. We run the risk, then, of saying that, if the law makes any difference, it does so by compelling obedience to its solutions through force. While this de facto authority, grounded in the ability to compel through force, can be a necessary condition for de jure (justified) authority on Raz's view, it is certainly not a sufficient one. Therefore, Raz cannot speak meaningfully here of justified authority, either because law's authority is based on coercion, in which case it is not really justified, or because the law merely provides advice, in which case it is not really authority. In both cases, there is no moral obligation to obey.

My argument against Raz, that on his view there can be reasons to conform to the law but no obligation to obey it, is confirmed by what he says about the "paradox of the just law."[53] Raz explains the paradox as follows: "The more just and valuable the law is, it says, the more reason one has *to conform to it*, and the less *to obey it*. Since it is just, those considerations which establish its justice should be one's reasons for conforming with it, i.e., for acting as it requires. But in acting for these reasons one would not be obeying the law, one would not be conforming because that is what the law requires. Rather one would be acting on the doctrine of justice to which the law itself conforms."[54]

This analysis yields a puzzling situation, almost a paradox, in which there are two categories of people whose actions conform with the requirements of the law, yet for neither does the question of justified authority matter in their practical reasoning. First, there are people who recognize a preexisting moral obligation to act in a certain way (i.e., to act justly and, depending on the details, in conformity with the reasons that apply to them) and do so. Those people cannot meaningfully be said to be deferring to authority because they are doing that which they ought to do, anyway, without necessarily having any intention of acting that way because the law requires it.

Second, there are people who do not recognize the moral obligation but follow the law under coercion. They comply only because they feel forced to comply and not because they recognize the authority of the law as justified. If, alternatively, they recognize the justification of the law's authority, it is because they understand the law to require what they already have reason to do, in which case they are back in the first category—hence the paradox.

Raz makes this particularly clear in the river-pollution example, where "the moral reasons affecting such cases derive entirely from the factual existence of the social practice of co-operation and *not at all from the fact that the law is instrumental in its institution or maintenance*."[55] The law plays a role in creating those moral reasons insofar as it fosters the social practice from which the moral obligation stems. But the moral obligation exists with or without the corresponding law. If people keep the river clean, there is an obligation to refrain from polluting; if not, not.

At the same time, Raz has no problem with the law coercing those who fail to act on their moral obligations (though they are not moral obligations created by the law, much less, moral obligations to obey the law).[56] This stems from his thesis that authority is justified when it enables its subjects to better act upon the reasons that apply to them. Where those reasons are moral obligations, authority's justification need not depend on whether the subjects recognize those obligations. For Raz, if the obligations exist, the law can justifiably coerce. This, too, has nothing to do with law's authority per se. That is, the justification for coercion here does not rest on any obligation to obey the law. This can be seen in what Raz says about law's function in another respect: law as insurance (or, perhaps better, assurance). Although it is not the full story of authority, Raz writes that, simply speaking, "law's direct function is to motivate those who fail to be sufficiently moved by sound moral considerations" because "it forces them to act as they should by threatening sanctions if they fail to do so."[57] In this way, the law "reassures the morally conscientious. It assures him that he will not be taken advantage of, will not be exploited by the unscrupulous."[58] Importantly, though, Raz presents this "oversimplified picture" as a depiction of "the good a government *without authority* can do."[59] What Raz must mean by "government without authority" is that government need not possess justified authority over those subjects in order to justifiably coerce them. The justification for coercing those would-be lawbreakers is not found in the moral obligation the subjects have to obey the law (rooted in the justification of authority) but in their independent moral obligation to act in a way the law also happens to require.[60] For such purposes, the government need not have (justified) authority over the people it coerces.[61]

With the limited claims he makes about the obligation to obey the law, Raz's analysis fails to cohere. It is hard to account for what exactly he means by "authority." Common sense dictates that either the government has justified authority over certain subjects in certain situations and can justifiably enforce the law in those situations, or the government does not possess justified authority and cannot coerce. But Raz argues that government can justifiably coerce those not subject to its authority, or, put another way, coerce without justified authority.[62] This is a rather bracing claim, but it does seem that Raz argues that the government has authority because it has power. Apart from the concern about coercion, surely Raz does not want to suggest—or does he?—that the government is the same as any third party that enforces moral obligations inasmuch as anyone can justifiably enforce moral obligations against anyone else.[63] If Raz's argument is that the government is simply a third party enforcing moral obligations because it can, then law's authority has nothing to do with a justification of authority and everything to do with the government's superior strength.

This incoherence notwithstanding, Raz defends the law's enforcement of moral obligations without justified authority in the following way:

> The upshot of the discussion in this section is that the law is good if it provides prudential reasons for action where and when this is advisable and if it marks out certain standards as socially required where it is appropriate to do so. If the law does so properly then

it reinforces protection of morally valuable possibilities and interests and encourages and supports worthwhile forms of social co-operation. But neither of these legal techniques even when admirably used gives rise to an obligation to obey the law. It makes sense to judge the law as a useful and important social institution and to judge a legal system good or even perfect while denying that there is an obligation to obey its laws.[64]

It amounts to a puzzling combination of denying the authority of law to obligate its subjects and accepting the law's prerogative to coerce them. For Raz, the law is a centralized system for enforcing some of the moral obligations that people already have. In this respect, the law seems no different than any third-party enforcer, except that the law might be better at the job.

Yet, in light of this striking contention by Raz, the case of the polluted river raises an important practical difficulty about the possibility for the law to motivate social change, which Raz does seem to acknowledge as a significant role for law.[65] If the law can justifiably keep the river clean (by forbidding pollution), it also ought to be able to get the river clean (by forbidding pollution). Yet, in Raz's hypothetical, everyone pollutes the river, and therefore there is no moral obligation to refrain from doing so, regardless of what the law says. When one's actions can make a difference, though, such as when people do generally refrain from polluting the river, in which case an individual's pollution may affect the river appreciably, or when the government has successfully begun reforms, in which case one's cooperation may influence others and contribute to a general change in public behavior, then there is a moral obligation to refrain from polluting. Without the underlying moral obligation to contribute to the cleanliness of the river, the existence of which depends on the fact of one's actions making a difference and, therefore, on having a reason to act (to refrain from polluting), however, an antipollution law is not obligatory. Where the river is already "fully" polluted and continues to be polluted, from where can an obligation arise to refrain from polluting? It appears the law can keep the river clean but not get the river clean. If enough people happen to change their behavior, the new social practice of not polluting can confer an obligation to refrain from polluting. But that has nothing to do with law and authority. In that example, law's authoritativeness is not the source of the change and cannot be the source of an initial obligation that motivates the change because there is no obligation to refrain from polluting, law or no law, until there is a social practice to refrain from polluting.

If, on the contrary, people do not change their behavior—which is precisely the case in which the law's intervention is most needed—then government-led reform can begin only by forcing people to comply. This cannot be justified on Raz's terms, though, because even government with justified authority, let alone government without, is justified in enforcing only moral obligations that people already have. Where everyone pollutes the river, no one has an obligation to do otherwise, even when the law changes. The situation forms something of a catch-22 whereby, for lack of a certain social practice, there is no moral obligation, and, for lack of the moral obligation, the authority cannot justifiably coerce the behavior that can create the social practice. There are no dependent reasons to which the authority can appeal for justification because, as Raz clearly states, there is no reason to refrain from polluting the river when polluting the river is the norm. As a result, there seems to be no place for the law to effect change even in the most ordinary cases.

To sustain Raz's theory, we must assume that Raz believes the law can somehow catalyze this sort of change. But, even if we can render such a construction, the law is unlikely to be efficacious if there is no prima facie obligation to obey the law. Presumably, reforms such as a law banning pollution of a completely and continually polluted river work only if people believe—falsely, according to Raz—that there is an obligation to obey the law because, as stipulated in Raz's example, they have no other reason to refrain from polluting.[66] (Indeed, that they have no other reason is the *point* of Raz's example.) Yet Raz insists there is no prima facie obligation to obey the law. That leaves two options. The first option, as just mentioned, is the rather flimsy proposal that the law can effect change because people incorrectly believe they have an obligation to obey. The second option is to recast

Raz's position and insert an as-yet-undiscovered reason for action that obligates people to refrain from polluting and that, therefore, overlaps with a requirement in the law to do the same. In the absence of an obligation to obey the law, we can posit an independent (i.e., not stemming from the law) moral obligation to contribute to the creation of new social practices that are beneficial and, indeed, morally binding if they exist.[67] But if it is the case that everyone always has a moral obligation to start creating such social practices (again: ones that do not exist but are beneficial and, therefore, provide reasons for action if they exist), then there is always an obligation to refrain from polluting the river. Yet Raz explicitly says this is not so, so he evidently does not count an obligation to start beneficial social practices among the reasons people already have for action. If so, the law is impotent in the situation of the polluted river because it cannot make a practical difference.

In any event, it adds far too much difficulty to the theory to allow for a moral obligation to help create as-yet-nonexistent social practices that, if they exist, generate moral obligations to conform to those practices. For one thing, it makes moral obligations multiply impossibly. There are infinitely many nonexistent but potentially beneficial social practices, and the mere possibility of their existence cannot confer an obligation on everyone to start participating in all of them, perhaps even when it is reasonable to expect others will go along. And if, on the contrary, we allow for a moral obligation to create such social practices, then the space between Raz and his opponents vanishes because then there is always a separate moral obligation coinciding with the law because the law almost always overlaps with a social practice that is beneficial if it comes into existence. In other words, in that case, even with no prima facie obligation to obey the law in principle, there is one in practice. In effect, the law picks which social practices ought to be initiated, and each law is justified (and obligatory) because of its inevitable overlap with one of the infinitely many moral obligations to initiate various potentially salutary social practices. Yet we cannot accept a construction of Raz's theory that yields a prima facie obligation to obey the law, so the problem for Raz remains.

RAZ'S APPEAL TO RESPECT AS A JUSTIFICATION FOR AUTHORITY ALSO FAILS

In addition to his central justification of authority, Raz also offers an argument for authority and the (presumably partial and qualified) obligation to obey the law rooted in the notion of respect. He develops this through an extended analogy to friendship. Friendship itself, Raz claims, provides reasons for action, and the choiceworthiness of relevant actions derives from those actions' suitability to such a relationship.[68] The reasons for action created by friendship are called expressive reasons "because the actions they require express the relationship or attitude involved."[69] Like with actions that express friendship, respect for the law or consent to its requirements can be expressive of loyalty to or identification with one's society, what Raz calls "an attitude of belonging and of sharing in its collective life."[70] Respect for the law follows naturally from this attitude because "a person identifying himself with his society, feeling that it is his and that he belongs to it, is loyal to his society. His loyalty may express itself, among other ways, in respect for the law of the community."[71] To be sure, Raz is quick to point out that "even if loyalty to one's community is obligatory, respect for law is not."[72] Respect for the law may come easily to those who identify with the society, but no one *has to* respect the law. The question is what it means for the law in terms of obligation when one does respect it.

In the above passages, Raz's language evinces the same ambiguity as between having *reasons* to do what the law says and having an *obligation* to do it. In another treatment of the topic, Raz speaks of "acceptance" of an authority: "Identification is a common and often proper ground for accepting authority.... Acceptance of an authority can be an act of identification with a group because it can be naturally regarded as expressing trust in the person or institution in authority and a willingness to share the fortunes of the group which are to a large extent determined by the authority."[73] In that rendering, where "acceptance" replaces "respect," there is also no notion of obligation. Much as acceptance of another person's guidance can be an expression of trust without entailing any obligation to obey that person, acceptance of authority can express trust without entailing obligation.

In another place, however, Raz speaks very directly of respect for the law engendering an obligation to obey it: "Yet those who respect the law have a reason to obey, indeed are under an obligation to obey. Their attitude of respect is their reason—the source of their obligation. The claim is not merely that they recognize such an obligation, not merely that they think that they are bound by an obligation. It is that they really are under an obligation; they are really bound to obey."[74] Even though Raz does not mean here a prima facie obligation to obey the law, he obviously does understand there to be some sort of obligation, probably what he calls elsewhere a partial and qualified obligation. The problem, though, is that Raz does not account for how respect produces this obligation.

The closest thing to an explanation that Raz offers is his comparison of respect for the law to the notion of consent. Raz writes, "But in a reasonably just society this belief in an obligation to obey the law, this attitude of respect for law, is as valid as an obligation acquired through consent and for precisely the same reasons. . . . Therefore, people who share it have an obligation to obey the law that they acquire through their conduct of their own lives, as part authors of their own moral world."[75] Here, we can think he is assimilating "acceptance of authority" to consent, yet Raz is careful to say that an attitude of respect is not the same thing as consent. While consent to the laws is another way to express an attitude of loyalty or identification, respect, Raz insists, "is not consent. It is probably not something initiated by any specific act or at any specific time. It is likely to be the product of a gradual process as lengthy as the process of acquiring a sense of belonging to a community and identifying with it."[76]

Thus, two points about respect and consent: First, respect does not necessarily entail consent, and, second, where there is respect, consent is not a necessary condition for the existence of an obligation to obey. Respect alone is sufficient. Because the justification of authority depends upon its ability to enable subjects to better act according to the reasons that apply to them, "a just government can exist even if its subjects are not bound by a general obligation to obey it. Therefore, consent cannot be justified as a necessary means to establish a just government. Moreover, to the extent that in order to establish or preserve a just government a qualified recognition of authority is necessary, such recognition in itself, independently of consent, is sufficient to establish a suitably qualified obligation to obey."[77] Nevertheless, in distinguishing between consent and respect, Raz undercuts his claim that the obligation to obey the law that is generated by respect "is as valid as an obligation acquired through consent and for precisely the same reasons."[78] Inasmuch as it differs from consent, respect falls short of generating the same obligation.

The argument from respect has several problems. First, there is a question of whether respect is not effectively the same thing as consent, despite Raz's protestations to the contrary. Raz writes, "Identification with one's community is, though not morally obligatory, a desirable state, at least if that community is reasonably just. Of course consent to obey the law is not a necessary condition of such an attitude."[79] Yet, according to Raz, respect for the law, which may follow from identification with the society, constitutes a reason to obey and a source of obligation.[80] How does respect function in this role? Because he explains respect by reference to consent while still distinguishing it, Raz must show another mechanism (apart from consent) by which respect can generate an obligation. But this proves difficult, and Raz falls back on the language of consent in describing the connection between identification with (and the ensuing respect for) one's society and the obligation to obey the law: "Undertaking an obligation to obey the law is an appropriate means of expressing identification with society, because it is a form of supporting social institutions, because it conveys a willingness to share in the common ways established in that society as expressed by its institutions, and because it expresses confidence in the reasonableness and good judgment of the government through one's willingness to take it on trust, as it were, that the law is just and that it should be complied with."[81] But what else can "undertaking an obligation" be but consent? Language such as "undertaking an obligation" as well as "willingness" strongly suggests some form of consent, even if not a discrete declaration of such.

So, too, Raz says that "to the extent that in order to establish or preserve a just government a qualified recognition of authority is necessary, such recognition in itself, independently of consent, is sufficient to establish a suitably qualified obligation to obey."[82] Here, the term "recognition" strongly suggests some form of consent. If not, Raz needs to explain what it means to *recognize* authority in a way that justifies it but does not involve consent. If, on one hand, Raz intends to say that one recognizes the already-existent justification of the authority, then the argument is circular because the justification is meant to rest on the recognition. If, on the other hand, Raz intends to say that one recognizes the authority's satisfaction of the terms of the dependence and normal justification theses (the satisfaction of which is the ground of justification), then all the questions about law as expertise arise, and it turns out that the argument for authority from respect is not a separate argument at all. Otherwise, we have no argument for how recognition generates obligation apart from consent.

Second, apart from the questionable distinction from consent, the core problem with the argument from respect, like with the argument from expertise, lies in connecting the dots from respect for the law as a reason to obey the law to respect as the source of an obligation to obey. Raz attempts to do this by equating belief in an obligation to obey the law with respect for the law.[83] Even if we grant that those who respect the law believe they have an obligation to obey it, it is not the case that that believing in an obligation is the same as having an obligation. Moreover, his reasoning is unconvincing in part because Raz himself argues that no one has an obligation to respect the law. In explaining the "proper attitude to the law," Raz asserts: "There is no general moral obligation to obey it, not even in a good society. It is permissible to have no general moral attitude to the law, to reserve one's judgment and examine each situation as it arises. But in all but iniquitous societies it is equally permissible to have 'practical' respect for the law. For one who thus respects the law his respect itself is a reason for obeying the law."[84] If there is no obligation to respect the law, those who do respect it are unlikely to translate that into a belief that they have an obligation to obey it. Rather, they are likely to see themselves as having the option to express their respect by doing what the law says when and where they believe that conforming to the law will express that respect. (And, again, even if they did believe what Raz proposes, it would not mean they actually had an obligation.) To emphasize, Raz speaks only of the permissibility of respecting the law in a way that he believes generates an obligation. Even for Raz, there is no obligation to hold the attitude that, in turn, yields an obligation to obey the law.

In introducing his argument about respect, Raz explains "that there is an attitude to law, generally known as respect for it, such that those who have it have a general reason to obey the law, that their reason is their attitude, the fact that they so respect the law, and that it is morally permissible to respect the law in this way (unless it is a generally wicked legal system)."[85] In other words, "respect is itself a reason for action."[86] As before, respect for the law is a *reason* to obey, but it still falls short of creating an *obligation* to obey. When Raz refers above to a "general reason to obey the law," he seems to mean something closer to a reason to comply—in the way that one has reasons to comply with a stockbroker, but never an obligation. At first, Raz seems to acknowledge this difference when he writes, "A person who respects the law expresses in this way his attitude to society, his identification with and loyalty to it. Such a person may find it appropriate to express these attitudes to society, among other ways, through his attitude to the law. He may feel it is a fitting expression of his loyalty to acknowledge the authority of the law. He will then obey the law as it claims to be obeyed."[87] But Raz continues, "In any case, for the person who respects the law, there is an obligation to obey. His respect is the source of this obligation."[88] This claim demands explanation. An attitude of respect explains why it makes sense for subjects to act *as though* they have an obligation to obey the law; they act in the same way they do if they have an obligation to obey (and are fulfilling it) insofar as they comply as an expression of respect. But this respect does not self-evidently account for the existence of an actual obligation. As with friendship, other relationships (and one's attitude toward them) give reasons to act a certain way but typically do not confer an obligation to do so. This fundamental flaw appears as well in Raz's primary account of obligation:

law's expertise provides a reason to defer to it—a reason to comply—but not an obligation to obey.

It is instructive to see the way Raz elides this difference between having a reason to do something and having an obligation to do it. In one case, Raz first writes, "It is not difficult to see why practical respect might be thought of as a proper expression of loyalty to the society. It is a manifestation of trust. A man who is confident that the law is just and good believes that he has reason to do as the law requires."[89] This is plausible because one who trusts the judgment of the law does well to follow it, no less because he believes it requires the right things of him than because it is one way of expressing his trust. In nearly the same breath, though, Raz adds, "If a person places absolute trust in the law then he will acknowledge the authority of the law. It is natural therefore that loyalty to one's society can be expressed by behaving as one would if one trusted the law implicitly. Hence the attitude of respect is a manifestation of loyalty since it gives rise to such an obligation to obey, to such an acknowledgment of authority."[90] But behaving as though one has an obligation and actually having that obligation are different; Raz conflates them too easily.

RAZ CANNOT DEFEND AN OBLIGATION TO OBEY THE LAW JUST AS SUCH

One line of defense for Raz is that having an all-things-considered reason to act is just what it means to have an obligation and, accordingly, that this is what Raz intends when he talks about the reasons generated by the law's expertise or by respect for the law—that is, that expertise or respect provides the all-things-considered reason to obey (improbable though that may be). If that is Raz's meaning, then it closes the gap between reasons to act and the obligation to obey. Yet, on Raz's terms, there can never be an all-things-considered reason to obey the law just as such. An all-things-considered reason to obey the law just because it is the law is, in essence, an all-things-considered reason to be law abiding, but Raz definitively excludes the possibility of such a reason existing. To the contrary, Raz's argument assumes that being law abiding is never its own reason for action. If being law abiding is its own reason for action, not only is there an obligation to obey the law in some cases, but there is also a prima facie obligation to obey the law, which Raz denies. Nor can Raz suggest that respect for the law generates an all-things-considered reason to be law abiding because that, too, supports a prima facie obligation to obey (for those who respect the law). If one respects and, therefore, obeys the law of a good society just because it is the law of a good society, which, as Raz teaches, is one way of expressing loyalty to and identification with that society, then one has an all-things-considered reason to obey all of the laws of that society (at least until the injustice of obeying outweighs the obligation to obey, as in my theory). It does not do any good to defend Raz by arguing the prima facie obligation to obey is limited to those who respect the law and, therefore, consistent with his denial otherwise of a prima facie obligation (and different from what I am claiming) because his explanation and all of his examples (polluted rivers and so forth) do not have room for this distinction.

SMITH'S THEORY OF LAW'S AUTHORITY EXEMPLIFIES RAZ'S ERRORS

In large part due to Raz's work, or at least in concert with his ideas, many prominent theorists conclude that there is, in fact, no prima facie obligation to obey the law, which is to say, no justification for authority in general and therefore no power to obligate just by virtue of being the authority. One prominent, representative example of this way of thinking is found in M. B. E. Smith's article "Is There a Prima Facie Obligation to Obey the Law?" The errors we find in Smith's work help us see how critical it is to reject Raz's proposals for the justification of authority as well as related theories such as Smith's. In the article, Smith rejects various common arguments for authority based on fairness, consent, and so forth. He is correct that none of these other theories adequately account for the obligation to obey the law. Yet, failing to find any adequate theory, he concludes that there is no prima facie obligation to obey the law—that is, no obligation to obey the law just because it is the law.[91]

Nevertheless, he undermines his conclusion that there is no prima facie obligation to obey by trying to have it both ways, writing, "The government of the United States counts as having legitimate authority over its subjects because within certain limits there is nothing wrong in its issuing commands to them and enforcing their obedience."[92] The basis for this statement is his belief that "the questions 'What governments enjoy legitimate authority?' and 'Have the citizens of any government a prima facie obligation to obey the law?' both can be, and should be, kept separate."[93] But claiming that there is "nothing wrong" with the government issuing commands and enforcing them, that the government is morally justified in coercing its citizens to obey the law (within certain limits), suggests that people *do* have some obligation to obey. And if they do not have an obligation to obey the law just as such, in what sense is the authority of the government justified? In what sense is the coercion justified? Rather, justified authority and the prima facie obligation to obey are corollaries of one another and cannot be separated in the way Smith thinks.

If Smith is proposing that the legitimacy of the government in coercing citizens extends only to obligations they already have independent of the law, then he is not really dealing with the legitimacy of government per se. Rather, he is just arguing that it is sometimes legitimate to coerce people to fulfill their obligations. Moreover, in limiting the government's prerogative to issue commands of that sort (if this is what he means by "within certain limits"), his concept of justified authority is too narrow to shed any light on the nature of legal obligation. Without a prima facie obligation to obey, the justified authority of the government to coerce stands apart from the concept of legal obligation because the justification of the authority inheres in the fact that the person already has an obligation to act that way and not in the fact that the directive to do so is law. In other words, if Smith wants to separate justified authority from legal obligation, then legal obligation vanishes altogether.

It is, therefore, no surprise that, according to Smith, there is no obligation to obey when "obedience to the law often benefits no one."[94] "Perhaps," Smith continues, "the best illustration is obedience to the traffic code: Very often I benefit no one when I stop at a red light or observe the speed limit."[95] Although Smith is speaking there in the context of the argument from fairness, he accepts this conclusion with respect to his broader theory as well. Smith argues that there is no obligation to obey in these circumstances, and he maintains this even if there *is* an obligation to obey due to considerations of fairness because of the lack of any benefit from complying and therefore the lack of any independent reason for acting that way.

At the same time, Smith also argues that "if there is a prima facie obligation to obey the law, it is at most of trifling weight."[96] Obviously, this is not identical to the claim that there is no prima facie obligation, yet Smith ultimately adopts that position, concluding that "considerations of simplicity indicate that we should ignore the supposed prima facie obligation to obey that law and refuse to count an act wrong merely because it violates some law. There is certainly nothing to be lost by doing this, for we shall not thereby recommend or tolerate any conduct that is seriously wrong, nor shall we fail to recommend any course of action that is seriously obligatory."[97] Moreover, Smith adds, "there is much to be gained, for in refusing to let trivialities occupy our attention, we shall not be diverted from the important questions to be asked about illegal conduct."[98] Ironically, this line puts us in mind of the way Hart gets wrong the matter of the postwar German trials — the irony being that it is the very path that Smith endorses that leads to incomplete or mistaken views of the "important questions" he invokes.

There are several problems with Smith's statement about the triviality of any potential prima facie obligation to obey the law. First, as just noted, Smith does not show that there is no prima facie obligation, only that it is, in his view, trivial. This is a more significant concession than he acknowledges, for the importance of the prima facie obligation is not found in its weightiness but in its existence. As a starting point, we are concerned with whether the prima facie obligation to obey exists at all because of what it tells us fundamentally about the nature of authority and the concept of law. The first order of business is to understand whether law's authority creates a prima facie obligation to obey at all. Smith is wrong to dismiss the matter just because he believes the obligation is minimal. For analytical clarity and because of the principle at stake, it is more consequential whether there is or is not *any* obligation to obey the law than whether that obligation is light or weighty.

Second, Smith can be underestimating the weightiness of the prima facie obligation to obey the law. He sets up this prima facie obligation, conveniently, against wrongs like murder, and it is true that the obligation to obey the law just as such (in any one mundane instance) is trivial compared to the obligation not to murder. But the triviality of the obligation to obey the law is less apparent when that obligation is compared to less severe wrongs. Put another way, even a light prima facie obligation to obey the law can make a practical difference when weighed against lesser wrongs. In addition, Smith can be underestimating the poor judgment with which people discern which of their violations are sufficiently trivial. Part of Finnis's view is that people ought not to break the law even when they believe the harms to be nonexistent or trivial precisely because people are, as experience has always taught, bad judges in their own cases. This problem cannot be avoided by saying that people can exempt themselves when their violations are truly harmless or undetectable because the ability to discern that accurately is precisely what is in question.

Third, Smith's view leads him to miss the point about civil disobedience. According to Smith, "We can then treat civil disobedience just as we regard many other species of illegal conduct," meaning "judge it in the same way we judge most other kinds of acts, that is, on the basis of their character and consequences."[99] Although Smith wishes to "escape the air of mystery that hovers about most discussions of" civil disobedience, he fails to see that civil disobedience is in fact unique because part of its expressive value is exactly in the breaking of the law.[100] Civil disobedience is not merely a protest against, say, racial discrimination. It is a protest against the legal enforcement of racial discrimination. And that is why it generally entails an intentional, public violation of the law just to make that point. Without the obligation to obey the law just as such, it is harder to make sense of this. The objection to legal enforcement of injustice can be registered even if enforcement of the law does not have the backing of moral obligation. But the moral obligation to obey is necessary for understanding why civil disobedience is a morally fraught question (even when justified), and it helps makes sense of the norms we attach to it.

For Smith, the legitimacy of the government (and, therefore, the obligation to obey) extends only to cases where there are other reasons to comply, meaning reasons independent of the fact that the law says so—notwithstanding his conclusion above that "the government of the United States counts as having legitimate authority over its subjects because within certain limits there is nothing wrong in its issuing command to them and enforcing their obedience."[101] Excepting that puzzling conclusion, he seems to share Raz's view of authority. Therefore, like Raz's view of authority's justification, Smith's, such as it is, cannot be sustained.

SIMMONS DENIES LEGAL OBLIGATION YET INADVERTENTLY CONCEDES A MAIN POINT

In *Moral Principles and Political Obligations*, John Simmons considers and rejects the standard accounts of political obligation. Contract and consent theories fail, as do those based on duties of justice, fair play, and gratitude. He concludes that there is no prima facie obligation to obey the law, or no general political obligation.[102] Contra M. B. E. Smith, and correctly in my view, Simmons recognizes that these two formulations are substantially the same. Like most others, he does maintain that there are, "even in the absence of political obligations, still strong reasons for supporting at least certain types of governments and for obeying the law."[103] Nevertheless, those reasons can always be understood separate from political and legal obligation and without admitting such concepts. As with Raz, those "strong reasons" do not amount to political or legal obligation. Rather, they are reasons for action that one already has and that overlap with what the government requires. Thus, we see the underlying problem with Raz repeating again although, in this case, Simmons does not deny that this leaves us without authority and obligation. At the same time, while Simmons arrives at the wrong conclusion, his analysis reveals the germ of a correct theory of authority and obligation in resting people's compliance with the law on the distinction between governments that do and do not deserve support.

Plainly, the consequence of this is that, according to Simmons, there is no distinct normative conception of the authority of law and, correspondingly, legal obligation. On the contrary, Simmons writes, "The fact that I have a 'legal obligation' or a 'duty of citizenship' will be a morally *neutral* fact," and, furthermore, "We will want to distinguish between 'the obligation to obey the law,' which is a *moral* requirement, and our 'legal obligations,' which are not."[104] Clearly, Simmons is understanding the phrase *legal obligation* specifically as something along the lines of being subject to the power of the state, as distinct from having a moral obligation to obey. If Simmons is correct that having a legal obligation is morally neutral, then he only reinforces the question for Hart of why people believe themselves to have an obligation to obey the law, if in fact they do believe that. And, of course, they do believe that according to Hart, as this sense of obligation is one of Hart's central observations and a significant part of his revolution in contemporary jurisprudence.

From Simmons's perspective, people do not have an obligation to obey the law. At most, they have preexisting moral obligations that overlap with what the law requires. All that legal obligation can mean, then, is that the law requires certain behavior and may disincentivize (by punishing or otherwise censuring) noncompliance and incentivize compliance. What it does not mean, however, is that there is a moral obligation to obey the law. Therefore, it must be the case either that people do not believe that they have an obligation to obey the law just as such or that they do believe they have an obligation to obey but are mistaken. If it is the former, then their law-abiding behavior must be motivated by self-interest (whether to avoid coercion or what have you) or by a recognition of overlapping but independent moral obligations. Either way, this undermines the key move by Hart (and all of analytic jurisprudence after him) to distinguish law from both coercion and suggestion because of law's characteristic obligatoriness, real or perceived. Without the benefit of Hart's insight, which seems unavailable according to Simmons, latter-day positivists must be back to saying that law is merely orders backed by threats, as the older positivists' command model had it.

Even though he dismisses the idea of a prima facie obligation to obey the law, Simmons reveals the contours of what such an obligation can look like. Simmons cites Hanna Pitkin: "It is part of the concept, the meaning of 'authority,' that those subject to it are required to obey, that it has a right to command. It is part of the concept, the meaning of 'law,' that those to whom it is applicable are obligated to obey it."[105] In the same vein as my critique, Pitkin highlights that authority must be tied to justification if the concept is to be anything more than a descriptive term equivalent to *power*. The right to command that Pitkin mentions is the authority to impose a moral obligation on subjects through directives.[106] Philosophical anarchists hold that justified authority is an oxymoron. But if it does exist, then it must entail the power to obligate.

In the absence of justified authority, Simmons prefers that we "distinguish between governments that *deserve* our support, or that are worthy of it, and those that do not (or are not)" with "no presumption in favor of obedience."[107] Ironically, Simmons unwittingly hits upon an important point here that upends his own conclusion. He is right that we ought to discern which governments deserve our support and which do not. What he misses is that the ones that do deserve our support, presumably the ones that promote the common good, possess justified authority and, therefore, the normative power to obligate. Thus, despite rejecting the very thing we are trying to prove, Simmons lays the groundwork for arguing that some governments do deserve support and, therefore, that people *ought* to obey them—in the exact sense that we mean when we speak properly (normatively) of legal obligation. Moreover, in raising the question of which governments deserve our support, Simmons implies that he agrees that the assessment of the government takes place at the level of the system as a whole: either the government as a whole deserves support or not. In my concept of law as well, the justification of authority depends on a view of the government as a whole, which can deserve support despite promulgating some laws that overstep.

GREEN'S POSITION DEMONSTRATES THE UNSUSTAINABILITY OF DENYING LAW'S AUTHORITY WHILE TRYING TO GROUND OBEDIENCE

In *The Authority of the State*, Leslie Green takes a very similar line to Simmons, concluding that there cannot be a prima facie obligation to obey the law and, equivalently, that the authority of law cannot be content independent. A practice of obedience, which he associates with a prima facie obligation to obey, "will therefore have to be, in some sense, a discriminating one, for it must not encourage acquiescence in the face of serious injustice."[108] And he insists, with some merit, that it is "wildly implausible that the range of tolerability can in fact be identified in a content-neutral way."[109] In particular, Green is right that there cannot be a content-independent way to identify the justice of individual laws and their all-things-considered obligatoriness; otherwise, we have a contradiction in terms. But there can be a content-independent prima facie obligation to obey the directives of a justified authority, meaning an obligation that is independent of the content of individual directives. Again, this is because the normative assessment takes place on the system level, which is where the authority's justification rests. This system-level analysis accords with the way that authority is commonly understood. A parent or an official is not authoritative in virtue of the content of the directives issued. Rather, that person is authoritative in virtue of occupying a particular station (parenthood, officialdom) of justified authority. To be sure, the station-holder can exercise authority in such a way as to undermine the justification (by failing to fulfill the functions that justify the station's authoritativeness in the first place), but in the normal case, the parent or official does wield content-independent authority.[110]

Strictly speaking, the content-neutral criterion for when to disobey that Green invokes does not necessarily exist. But this is not the decisive point Green thinks it is. It is not some degree of intolerability that triggers the weighing of options; it is the injustice of any directive. If a law is unjust, then the subject has to decide whether the obligation to obey the law is defeated by the obligation not to do what the law requires. But this is true for any concept of law that recognizes authority and obligation. The difference is that, in my theory, there is an obligation to obey the law that is part of the decision of whether to do what the law requires whereas Green and others (like Raz) discount that factor.

Green gives up on finding any formula for justified, content-independent authority. "Obedience cannot be the virtue we seek," he writes.[111] Instead, Green counsels the "virtue of civility," which "at no point requires a surrender of judgment."[112] Because civility is marked by self-restraint, it provides stability and "in circumstances of imperfect motivation and moral uncertainty it helps to sustain valuable institutions."[113] But, in a way, Green falls into the same trap as Simmons. Of course, civility is valuable and, where it is closely associated with self-restraint, perhaps essential for a free society. Civility, however, suffices only against a background of obedience. Where people generally obey the law, it is easy to rest obedience on individual judgment; the danger is low when most of the people obey most of the time (even for reasons unknown).

Therefore, Green may be too sanguine about the prospects for law and order in a society where obedience rests first and foremost on people's individual judgments of the balance of reasons in each case, even among people who are fairly civil. Green believes that civility will provide for "mutual tolerance of minor and occasional injustice," which are "an essential part of a shared commitment to political institutions."[114] (Incidentally, or perhaps ironically, a prima facie obligation to obey the law also supplies these benefits.) But there is an opposing danger as well. In Green's view, people are not bound to the scheme as a whole but only bound to the individual directives they find worthy, and they will feel this all the more acutely if the aforementioned shared commitment to political institutions erodes. This, in turn, can manifest as a decline in the shared commitment to political institutions, meaning not only that people will fail to excuse minor injustices but also that they will fail to contribute to the promotion of justice.[115]

If we look at Green's point about civility from another angle, we can see that he is caught making either one of two errors. Either Green is repeating Raz's error, reducing all behavior under the law to morality without the authority of law (because the authority of the law depends on the applicability of the law's reasons in the instant case), or Green is caught effectively conceding the prima facie obligation to obey. In relying on civility, Green is essentially saying that subjects use their own moral judgment without reference to a background obligation to obey the law. In the first possibility, if they reason about their actions without reference to legal obligation, then the law cannot be said to have real authority because subjects are acting for reasons that apply to them, anyway. If, in the alternative, civility, arising from a shared commitment to political institutions, leads to a toleration of mild injustice by the law, then the fact that people obey the law even when it is (mildly) unjust means that there is, for all intents and purposes, a prima facie obligation to obey the law. Again, on Green's own terms, either he must be denying the authority of law even more than he admits, or he must be unwittingly conceding the very point he wishes to deny, namely that we can account for authority's content independence.

In the end, Raz's theory—and certainly Smith's, Simmons's, and Green's—do not provide a sufficient account of authority. To the extent that law does possess authority, it is only in the sense of giving people reasons to act but not an obligation to obey. This almost parallels Hart, who points to a phenomenon of the appearance of obligation but cannot account for any actual obligation. One possible conclusion is that there is less of an obligation to obey the law than even Raz imagines and perhaps none at all. Another possible conclusion, though, is that Raz's theory is incomplete because he fails to consider other sources of law's authority. The challenge, though, is to identify a justification for law's authority that neither empties it of all meaningful content by attributing that authority to other moral obligations that overlap with the law, as Raz does, nor strips law's authority of its justification by attributing its force entirely to will or coercion. The search is on for a middle way.

CHAPTER 4

Authority and the Good

LAW

The concept of law lies "in between" the different incomplete theories

In their different ways, Hart, Raz, and their intellectual progeny are unable to capture the concept of law. This is true despite the advances they make beyond the old command model, which, in its positivist formulation, is insufficient to justify authority. In the search for a definition of law, one approach is to ask whether there is any conceptual space between two competing poles. On one hand, there are theories, like the old command model, that attempt to account for the obligation to obey the law by attributing authority to sovereigns or commanders but, in doing so, implicitly justify all de facto authority, thereby failing to distinguish between just and unjust authority. On the other hand, there are theories that offer normative analyses of authority that can make that critical distinction, but their narrower grounds for justification leave us with philosophical anarchism (in effect) because they cannot underwrite the obligation to obey the law just as such.

Another way to put it is to ask whether there is room between the two models of "authority without reasons," which recognizes all de facto authority as law, and "reasons without authority," which denies law its general authoritativeness (and, therefore, the prima facie obligation to obey the law) through a requirement of case-by-case justification for each individual law. We are looking in between because our aim must be to find a definition of law under which law has content-independent authority—that is, where law has authority qua law yet under which we can also distinguish between justified and unjustified authority.

Similarly, in the search for a satisfactory concept of law, we can say we are looking in between theories like Austin's or Bentham's command models on the one hand, which go too far in rooting law's authority in the sheer power of the sovereign (the power of the commander over the commanded) or the fact of obedience, and theories like Raz's on the other, which go too far in rooting law's authority in the reasons behind each law (and whether they apply to the subject). Neither side provides an adequate basis for justification and, therefore, for a compelling view of true authority, which must have a normative basis and also provide the subject with new reasons for action. A simplified but useful way of thinking about the two poles for authority is, on one hand, commands without reasons and, on the other, reasons without commands. Austin and Bentham represent the former, commands without reasons, or what we might call a content-independent theory of law's authority. To a close enough approximation, Raz represents the latter, reasons without commands, or a content-dependent theory of law's authority. He locates the authority of law and the obligation to obey in his normal justification thesis. According to Raz, law has authority when it requires what the subject has reason to do, anyway. This is not exactly the same thing as reasons without commands because there are the law's directives, but it is reasons without authority because the directives do not possess authority just because they are law. Each of these models contributes something important, but neither, on its own, is sufficient to account for legal authority and obligation, which is why we need a middle way.

The difficulty with such a "middle" position is that any compromise seemingly threatens to collapse into one of the poles. Positivistic (descriptive-only) definitions of law, devoid of normative criteria, can give us a sense of content independence by assigning the name of law and law's authority without regard to the substance of the law while normative definitions of law risk reducing to the "unjust law is no law" maxim. Doing so seems to rule out content independence and, per some positivist critiques, denies the name of law to that which positivists see plainly as law. Separately, the most prevalent normative justifications of law's authority risk being unable to account for the authority of a particular official or directive among qualified options that all meet the normative criteria. Issues of the last sort return us to the problem with Raz: that, at best, authority, according to Raz, lies with whoever has the best reasons at that moment, and not with a recognized authority whose directives preempt alternative proposals, notwithstanding their relative merits. Thus, a middle position that balances elements of both must deal with vulnerabilities in either direction.

Law is a set of commands oriented to the common good

My concept of law, which occupies this middle position, defines law as a set of commands oriented to the common good. Any adequate concept of law (and law's authority) must combine descriptive and normative aspects, incorporating the necessary features of each. My theory has two interlocked parts: law as a set of commands, and law as oriented to the common good. First, on the descriptive side, we need the aspect of command. The idea of command is necessary to the concept of law because it captures the obligatoriness of law in a way that rival descriptions of law do not. As I argue with respect to Hart's rejection of the language of command, a concept of law that does not center on law's authoritativeness misses law's central element: obligation. Moreover, as I show in response to Hart, the idea of command does not suffer from the defects that he attributes to it. The notion of command supplies the right descriptive element for the concept of law because command implies obligation. This is because commands plainly intend to obligate. Nevertheless, not all commands (or sets of commands) are necessarily authoritative because the authority behind those commands is not necessarily justified. The idea of commands without reasons that we get from divine authority and religious obligation is only a partial model, to be joined with another partial model, moral obligation, which supplies the idea of reasons without commands.

The second necessary aspect, on the normative side, is an orientation to the common good. Crucially, and distinctively, this applies not to individual laws, which can be just or unjust, but to the laws as a whole—that is, to the legal system. This substantive criterion ensures that not just any act of commanding (much less coercing) is authoritative, and in this way, of course, my theory is unlike Austin's command model or any positivist theory.

The law, therefore, is best understood as a set of commands oriented to the common good. Although it is instructive to analyze the two aspects of law, descriptive and normative, separately, it is also true that they are conceptually linked. The (descriptive) validity of law, as Hart has it, and the (normative) legitimacy, or justification, of law's authority converge upon one another. We cannot speak of law's validity wholly apart from justification because, without justified authority, we do not have law. Even so, my theory is not coextensive with a simplistic version of the "unjust law is no law" maxim—that is, that all unjust laws are invalid—because I hold that there is a prima facie obligation to obey even an unjust law when it is part of a legal system oriented, on the whole, to the common good.

A successful concept of law requires both elements of the definition

It is important to note that the normative aspect of the concept of law, concerning the common good, which provides the justification of authority, is not doing all the conceptual work under the cover of the descriptive aspect (concerning command). The evidence for this is that not every instance of a proposal (or set of proposals) oriented toward the common good is authoritative. Instead, the normative side must be wedded to the aspect of command, such that, in the central case of law, only a directive from a superior to an inferior in a system oriented to the common good is authoritative. It cannot be the orientation to the common good alone that renders one of the parties the superior—and therefore authorized to command—and one the inferior—and therefore obligated to obey—or else the substantive criterion really is doing all the work, in which case authority follows whoever knows best. That incorrect path invites many of the same problems that Raz's theory faces, in particular with the identification of authority, meaning in whom authority is located.

The dual criteria for law and its authority, namely the descriptive aspect of command and the normative aspect of the orientation to the common good, enable us to avoid the problems that compromise any single-sided definition. Neither earlier positivist theories like Austin's or Bentham's nor contemporary ones like Hart's (or the many based on his work) offer sufficient basis for distinguishing, say, law in a liberal order from that of a dictatorship, whether benevolent or cruel and capricious. For Austin, all are equally authoritative when directives take the form of orders backed by threats and are obeyed. For Hart, all is equally law when the directives have the backing of rules based in social practice. In keeping with their positivist approach, the orders or rules carry the name of law equivalently when morally good and when morally bad. For Hart, the concept of a legal system and the moral obligation to obey the law are separable. The key thing is that law is identified by the rules of that system, whatever they are. In this way, positivists deny a necessary relationship between the law and justice. My theory, however, treats as authoritative only the law of those regimes oriented toward the common good.

So, too, my theory can explain why an orientation to the common good does not suffice as a stand-alone criterion for law. Individuals who rise to the occasion in moments of urgency do not possess authority even if they do, as Andrei Marmor puts it, display leadership.[1] When there is a fire in a crowded theater and a patron takes charge, directing people to the exits, or when a passenger organizes entry into lifeboats on a sinking ship, she most certainly is acting for the common good, but she possesses no authority per se. There is no meaningful sense in which she can be characterized as a superior issuing directives to an inferior.[2] The test for whether she possesses authority is to ask whether anyone has an obligation to do as she says because she says so—that is, whether anyone has a reason to treat her directives as authoritative, just as such. The answer is plainly no. This lines up with Hart's obliged-obligated distinction. Indeed, this example possibly does not even rise to the level of "obliged." But it is clear we cannot speak of obligation for reasons that parallel the reason that Hart introduces the distinction in the first place. It may very well be that everyone in the theater or on the ship has very good reasons to listen, for instance, in order to facilitate an efficient escape. But the leader in those situations cannot obligate anyone to obey. If, for example, some people have to be sacrificed for the common good, the leader cannot obligate anyone in particular to serve in that role. Prudence may strongly commend compliance with the leader's directives, but this is markedly distinct from an obligation to obey. Even if we go further and say there is a moral obligation to do whatever best conduces to the common good, which is unlikely given the impossibility of knowing the answer, we cannot say that the failure to do so in this case is a failure to respect authority. At most, we can say that the circumstances generate an obligation to act in a certain way that the leader cannot generate. (In any case, the one-must-do-what-is-best source of obligation, like Raz's theory, yields an unworkable concept of law where "authoritative" directives are always subject to immediate preemption by better suggestions.) In contrast to the case of spontaneous leadership that arises in an emergency, in the case of conscription, taxation, or the like, a government regularly and, one hopes, justifiably decides whose life, liberty, or property is to be sacrificed for the common good—that is, decides on the distribution of benefits and burdens attendant to life together in society.[3] That is, the law does have the ability to obligate in a way that the leader in the burning theater does not.

In this way, Marmor's theory is extremely useful in pointing to the need to identify particular practices or institutions that are authoritative among those that can possibly claim justification. One problem with some normative theories, including Raz's, is that they do not explain why particular individuals or groups meeting the normative criteria are authoritative (that is, have the power to obligate) while others do not. For example, there can be any number of individuals or groups that possess the expertise that, for Raz, confers authority by enabling the subject to better comply with the reasons that subject already has for acting. As Marmor correctly sees, "Not every solution to a collective action problem—even if it is a collective action problem that the relevant parties are morally obliged to solve—amounts to an authoritative relation."[4] In fact, as I argue, Raz's theory seems to suggest that any individual or group with the requisite expertise (or, in the case of collective action problems, coercive power) can be authoritative. Marmor is sensitive to this problem when he writes that "power conferring norms must assign the power *ex ante*, designating certain individuals or a body of individuals the right to alter the obligations or rights of others."[5] Similarly, Marmor states, "For A to have authority over B in matters C, is for A to have the normative power to alter the rights and obligations that B has in matters C. To have authority, in other words, is to have normative power. Power, in the relevant sense, is essentially an institutional construct: its existence and scope is constituted by rules or conventions."[6] Without this institutional aspect, a theory of authority cannot specify where the normative power lies. Therefore, Marmor adds, "My main point was to show that there must be some institutional setting that mediates between the general reasons for having the relevant kind of authority, and the practical difference that the authority makes on particular occasions."[7] In this respect, Marmor takes the opposite approach of Raz, who at least attempts a justification for this sort of authority that Marmor cannot reach. Despite this advantage, Raz fails because, among other problems, he cannot explain which qualified "authority" actually counts as authoritative.

Law must entail declarations among various just options or proposals

Another way to see this point, of the need for proposals oriented to the common good to be embodied in the directives of an established commander, is to consider a gap in some accounts of law as fairness.[8] One familiar argument suggests, essentially, that law is an arrangement for the fair distribution of benefits and burdens in society. When one breaks the law, one violates an obligation of fairness to one's fellow citizens by taking an unfair benefit for oneself that others have forgone for the sake of the common good. To invent an example: While everyone wants to park in the available space in front of the fire hydrant, everyone refrains from doing so and spends extra time looking for a different parking spot so that the space in front of the hydrant can remain clear in the event of an emergency. To park at the fire hydrant is to benefit unfairly from everyone else's forbearance, or to fail to share fairly in the burden. Yet, while fairness of this sort can account for some important features of the obligation to obey the law, it is also insufficient as an explanation of law's authority in general. First and foremost, fairness does not, on its own, explain why one particular fair scheme is authoritative over another. As with competing proposals for advancing the common good, there can be many ideas about how to fairly distribute the benefits and burdens in society, but only one is treated as authoritative — that is, as law. Therefore, there must be a further component in the understanding of law that reflects the designation of a particular scheme as authoritative.

Second, fairness cannot fully make sense of the nonoptional nature of law. On the view of law as fairness it makes no difference in principle whether one complies with the law or pays the penalty for noncompliance because the penalty ensures that the fair distribution of benefits and burdens is restored when one, for example, takes an unwarranted liberty by parking at a fire hydrant.[9] As long as the penalty is adequate, the payment of the debt to society rectifies the imbalance. Though the law can operate this way, giving subjects an open choice between compliance with the directive and payment of the "penalty" for noncompliance (though "price" is more apt than "penalty" under this arrangement), from its own perspective, as it were, the law does not offer a neutral choice between compliance and restitution. Rather, the law quite obviously requires one course of action and holds out the alternative course (the penalty of a fine, prison time, and so on) as a consequence of noncompliance that restores the distribution of benefits and burdens (or serves some other purpose under other theories of punishment).[10] So we need a concept of law that captures the idea that the law, like a command, requires a particular course of action. Fairness alone does not get us there. In line with my point above, that essentially amounts to having the normative aspect of law without the descriptive aspect.

In sum, the concept of law properly contains two parts, which, loosely speaking, address its "form" and "substance." Law needs the form of command, or a directive from a superior, because not every suggestion or even system that conduces to the common good yields obligation. A proposal is not authoritative simply because it is oriented to the common good, or else anyone can obligate anyone else merely with a good idea (which approaches, if with a bit of warranted caricature, Raz's notion). The concept of law also needs the substance, an orientation to the common good, because commands issued by a superior do not automatically bestow a moral obligation to obey simply because they are issued nor, critically (given the history of the concept), because coercion is possible. An orientation to the common good is part of the very nature of law, what gives law its purpose. To be clear, my point is not that there is a neat division between normative and descriptive components of the concept of law. Rather, both are integrally and inseparably part of the nature of law, and the concept of law becomes untenable without either.

The distinction between different uses of "authority" tracks the two components of the concept of law

In a way, these two aspects of law—command and the orientation to the common good—track a well-worn distinction between being "in authority" and being "an authority."[11] Ordinarily these terms are introduced by way of contrast to each other. Being in authority is normally used in the sense of being an official, and being an authority is used in the sense of being an expert. A monarch is in authority because the people obey her word whereas a scientist is an authority because she possesses advanced knowledge about a particular topic. The former is the sort of person who issues directives (for better or worse), and the latter provides special insight into some topic. Despite this commonplace distinction, I think we can further illuminate the concept of law by focusing on the terms' interconnectedness. Though the parallel is not perfect, being in authority is close to having de facto authority while being an authority is closer to de jure authority (though certainly not the same thing, per my critique of Raz). Being in authority suggests the ability to attain compliance with one's directives; it refers to one serving in a position of authority—having authority in the sense of having power. But, plainly, simply having power—that is, being able to obtain compliance through threat of punishment—is not the same as having justified authority; power does not serve as a justification. Rather, de facto authority complements the necessary de jure authority, insofar as we can think of "de jure" capturing the justification of authority. Loosely, this parallels what we can say using the other terms, that justified authority, being not only *in* authority but also *an* authority, marries power to justification. The normal case of authority is power plus justification, being in authority and being an authority (loosely).[12]

The distinction between de facto and de jure authority also has a lesson for us with regard to the separation of power and justification. Because obligations can exist without enforcement (i.e., without carrots or sticks), law is no less justified for the authority's inability or unwillingness to enforce it. If a new government is elected but the previous administration refuses to step down and the newly elected officials proceed to govern in exile, their directives are authoritative, which is to say, justified and requiring of obedience, even if the recalcitrant regime controls the military and makes enforcement impossible. More generally, because law has a normative aspect, like other moral obligations, its authoritativeness does not depend on compliance or enforcement. A justified command is authoritative whether or not it is obeyed, just as a moral obligation exists whether or not it is fulfilled (or enforced).

The government-in-exile example shows us a case of de jure authority without de facto authority. But this does not mean that de facto authority is superfluous to the concept of law. This is because there is still the matter of the descriptive angle: *whose* commands count, whose directives count as law. There needs to be an identification of who is the authority. The conceptual role of de facto authority is relevant in a couple of ways. First, there is the problem of who authorizes the authorizers (or the authorities). If consent-based theories are insufficient for explaining law's authority, which they are, then somewhere back up the line there must be an initial "seizure" of power that precedes all subsequent authority. Such power is effectively de facto authority without de jure authority. John Finnis argues that "those general needs of the common good which justify authority, certainly also justify and urgently demand that questions about the location of authority be answered, wherever possible, by authority," but he recognizes that this is not always possible because authority must originate somewhere.[13] Historically speaking, it is likely that in most cases there is no initial authorizing event; indeed, in most cases, it is effectively impossible for there to be so. Instead, de jure authority traces back somewhere to de facto authority. Finnis describes the difficulty of establishing the initial authorizing procedure: "*Whose* say-so, if anyone's, are we all to act upon in solving our coordination problems?"[14] In theory, unanimity can be required for such a decision because no authoritative framework is already in place. Given the unlikelihood of unanimity in most cases, an initial, unauthorized act of authority may in practice be necessary to ensure that the procedure for locating authority in the future is authorized.[15]

Second, taking the orientation to the common good as a central component of authority, we must accept that de jure authority without de facto authority (like the government-in-exile) severely undermines the authority's ability to support the common good.[16] For example, authority plays an indispensable role in solving coordination problems; an inability to impose solutions or otherwise gain compliance diminishes the value of authority in those situations. The ability to secure coordination contributes to our ability to distinguish authority from all other proposals about how to advance the common good. (Part of the problem with Raz, as I say, is precisely the inability to ground this distinction.) As Finnis writes, the "first and most fundamental" requirement of "practical reasonableness in locating authority" is that it "is to be exercised by those who can in fact effectively settle coordination problems for that community."[17] For this reason, "the sheer fact of effectiveness" is "presumptively" though "not indefeasibly" decisive for understanding authoritativeness.[18] In a way, though, this need for de facto authority (i.e., power) bolsters the case for keeping the de jure aspect of authority—which requires an orientation to the common good—in consideration. For, as Finnis notes, the directives of an authority who offers "schemes thoroughly opposed to practical reasonableness" are not authoritative; the authority cannot claim to be fulfilling the role that makes authority desirable and necessary in the first place and, therefore, cannot claim to be justified.[19] If the only thing that matters is de facto authority, then legitimacy (the justification of authority) depends solely on whether the authority can elicit obedience. Yet merely having power is plainly insufficient for justification. Rather, this ability to produce compliance and, therefore, the ability to advance some agenda must be paired with an orientation to the common good.

Nevertheless, the absence of power does not vitiate the justification of the authority, say, in the case of a government in exile. That is to say, there can still be justified authority without power because the directives can be oriented to the common good even if inefficacious and because the directives are still commands even if they cannot be enforced under the circumstances. If the normative aspect is to be salient—if it is to be central to the concept of law in equal standing to the descriptive aspect—then authority's justification turns not on *whether* people obey but on whether they *ought to*. This point is further valuable because it helps us see another important caveat, that the authority's orientation to the common good is not fatally undermined by the inevitability of mistakes in advancing the common good. Those mistakes are to be accepted. As Yves Simon writes, "A man of good will may well err as to the *thing which is* right. . . . Such occasional failures are compatible with moral perfection," and in such cases there is still a *"steady tendency"* toward the good.[20] This is as true for the authority as it is for the individual.

Finally, the role of power in contributing to justification finally helps to illuminate the role of being an authority. At its simplest—and this is why the term *an authority* is not just synonymous with de jure authority—being an authority entails neither any actual power nor any justification in the sense of being able to obligate others. Rather it implies a sort of expertise, as the term is commonly used. Even so, the idea of being an authority remains connected to the idea of being in authority—evoking the inseparability of the descriptive and normative aspects of the concept of law—if being in authority means, as it should, occupying a position of power to serve the common good. Certainly, being *an* authority on the common good equips one well to fulfill the conditions of justified authority.

To be sure, this does not mean that justified authority necessarily requires any kind of philosophical, sociological, or other expertise. One's directives can be oriented toward the common good without any specific expertise. Anyone can be an authority on the common good inasmuch as it does not require any narrowly technical knowledge, at least not in the broad scheme of things. Nevertheless, a superior sense of how to advance the common good, something akin to statesmanship, can certainly be an important component of authority, much as the power to implement can be as well, though neither is essential for justification. In Simon's words, the "truly able leader . . . is supposed to be a man of higher excellence" and, similarly, "Responsibility is in the hands of the most able."[21] Celebrating the virtues of authority, Simon states, "To work under a leader whose qualifications are equal to his task is a happy experience," noting later on that, under authority, "the man of good will who wants to do the thing that the common good demands, actually knows what that thing is and does it."[22] Thus, being an authority can be the complement of being in authority.

Law is better understood when we take the legal system's orientation to the common good as a whole

My concept of law has the advantage not only of including theoretically necessary elements (both the descriptive and the normative) but also of illuminating some of the elements of law's authority better than other theories do. For example, as we see, it can explain why a government in exile can possess justified authority without the ability to force compliance. So, too, it can explain how an unjust law can remain obligatory as part of a broader system that is oriented to the common good.[23] For the prevailing (Razian) theories of law's authority, when the moral status of an individual law is under assessment—that is, when we ask when a law ought to be obeyed—the relationship of that particular law to the common good is at best a secondary consideration. For example, if a law requires a person to kill unjustly, the primary problem with the law is not the damage to the common good but the injustice to the intended victim (which, in turn, harms the common good but which is impermissible even if, counterfactually, it does not).[24] That strong reason to disobey the law, namely the wrong of murder, defeats competing reasons to obey, including the prima facie obligation to obey the law just because it is the law. So the weighing of the obligation to obey any individual law mainly relies on an analysis of the harms to particular goods (and the good of particular persons) before reaching the question of the common good.

But when the starting point in an analysis of authority and obligation is the legal system as a whole, then the law's necessary connection to the common good rises to the fore. This does not vitiate the preceding analysis (in which we find the wrong of murder as grounds for disobedience of a law commanding it), but it sets it in a new light. Once we have the correct understanding of law, we see that the question of whether there is an obligation to obey any particular directive starts with the question of whether it is part of a legal system that is oriented to the common good (or whether it is part of a system that is not oriented to the common good and, therefore, that merely pretends to the title of "legal system"). If the system is just, then there is a prima facie obligation to obey even an unjust law—although, in case it needs to be said again, that obligation can be defeated by the wrong proposed in the law.

This leads to an important insight into our understanding of unjust laws. Critics of the classical view that an "unjust law is no law," like Hart, are correct that some unjust laws are part of what is apparently identifiable as a legal system. As part of a legal system (which, as a set of commands oriented to the common good, is by definition "justified"), even unjust laws impose a prima facie obligation to obey.[25] As with any all-things-equal obligation, that obligation can be overridden by other considerations. As Finnis explains, "The *equal* obligation in *law* of each obligation-imposing law is to be clearly distinguished from the moral obligation to obey *each* law."[26] Accordingly, "Like the obligation of promises, the moral obligation to obey *each* law is variable in force."[27] Significantly, this is different from saying that there is simply no obligation to obey because the unjust law is "not law." It is "not law" only if the directive is not part of a legal system in the first place due to the lack of an orientation to the common good at the system level and, therefore, due to the system's failure to meet the definition of law.[28] (The very purpose of a legal system is the advancement of the common good, and, therefore, there simply cannot be a legal system that does not meet this requirement.) As I show, this distinction between being an unjust law in a valid system and being an invalid law (because unjust) is important because it accounts for the prima facie obligation to obey in my concept of law.[29]

Furthermore, my concept of law highlights the way in which the common good is part of what makes a legal system what it is and not merely one consideration in deciding whether to obey the law. The effects on the common good are not just one factor among many to be weighed in deciding whether to obey a particular law but, instead, at the heart of what constitutes a legal system and therefore what determines whether the law is authoritative (justified) in the first place and whether there is any prima facie obligation to obey apart from the reasons to comply that one might have, anyway.

This also helps to make sense of the idea that a law that advances the common good at the expense of the private good of an individual who is subject to the law can be obligatory. It is hard to see how Raz, in contrast, can account for this. While he can suggest that the individual's reasons to support the common good outweigh the reasons to protect her own good, such an outcome, at least in difficult cases, seems to depend on rigging the calculation in advance in favor of the common good. Surely there are some cases of genuine opposition between private good and the common good that favor the former. As with other "escape routes" for Raz that I address, his contribution is underwhelming if it yields no practical differences from the theories he opposes due to all considerations related to the common good always automatically being folded into the reasons that apply to one, anyway. If there are such differences, meaning if Raz's treatment of the common good does not produce outcomes identical to his opponents', then it seems Raz's theory cannot explain why any given individual would have to comply with a draft order, for example. We can concoct some scenario in which losing one's life in the war is preferable to surviving and losing the war (and, therefore, one already has reasons to do what benefits the common good), but this needs to be fairly contrived compared to the central case where the sacrifices of war-fighting clearly require the individual to put the common good before her own. Perhaps Raz bites the bullet on this and, to preserve his theory's distinctiveness, minimizes the weight of people's obligations to the common good. If so, the resulting conclusion, that there rarely is an obligation to put the common good before one's own, counts as another point against his theory.

Thus, one result of my concept of law is a different way of conceptualizing unjust laws within a legal system. Another, related consequence is the way we think about so-called legal systems that, on the whole, are not oriented to the common good. Those are not legal systems. Thus, my concept of law points to the conclusion that there can be systems mistakenly understood as legal systems under the prevailing theories. Because the very purpose of a legal system is the promotion of the common good, a "legal system" opposed to the common good is unworthy of the name.[30]

Positivists protest that insisting on a normative aspect in the concept of law means improperly denying the existence of some legal systems. One way to adjudicate that claim is to ask which definition of law has a steeper price. Let us grant, just for the sake of argument, that the selection of either definition of law entails a tradeoff between certain conceptual advantages and disadvantages. Adopting my concept of law requires us to deny that certain things that go by the name of law in popular discourse are, in fact, law. Yet the normative aspect is unavoidable. If the defining feature of law is its obligation-imposing nature, then the definition of law must comprise a normative aspect. In contrast, Hart's concept of law makes it impossible for the concept of law to do the work Hart wishes it to do. The concept of law cannot be built on a massive house of cards, one in which everyone recognizes an obligation to obey the law in a system that can give no substantial account of that obligation. In this critical respect, my concept of law brings greater conceptual clarity, which is a decisive advantage even if it entails the sacrifice in the sense of being unable to capture certain systems that a different theory recognizes as law. And, in any case, I continue to deny those systems' status as law. At most, we need to see some systems as central cases of law and others as peripheral, but this is probably true of almost any theory—and certainly of Hart's.

RELIGION

Legal obligation combines elements of religious obligation and of moral obligation

Neither theories like Austin's nor theories like Raz's amount to adequate theories of *legal* obligation on their own, but they do correspond, respectively, to two other kinds of obligation. The benefit of drawing comparisons to other forms of obligation is that each of those kinds of obligation has something to contribute to the proper understanding of the concept of law even though neither suffices as a model for legal obligation on its own. That is, from these two other kinds of obligation, religious obligation and moral obligation, we can draw many of the ideas necessary to understand legal obligation.

In this vein, we can think of legal obligation being in the middle, in between religious obligation and moral obligation, combining elements of each.

For the purposes of understanding the concept of law, the command model best parallels a notion of divine authority and religious obligation.[31] Religious obligation provides us with a paradigm for the content-independent authority of what we can call "commands without reasons." There is a directive from a commander, but there is no reason to obey other than the fact of it being the commander's directive (or at least that fact is the primary reason to obey). At the other end, the reasons-based model of obligation, or "reasons without commands," most closely parallels the notion of moral obligation.[32] Because it appeals to justification without the content-independent authority of a command, the idea of rationally apprehended moral obligations provides us with a paradigm for obligation as reasons without commands. There are reasons to obey the moral norm at hand but not because of (and without) any directive from a commander specifying the obligation. The obligation is just there, so to speak.

Combining both models, we can resolve the apparent paradox of law's authority (and, correspondingly, legal obligation), which entails both content independence and justification. Put another way, the notion of command supplies the right descriptive element for the concept of law because command implies obligation: commands plainly intend to obligate. Nevertheless, not all commands (or sets of commands) are necessarily authoritative because the authority behind those commands is not necessarily justified. The idea of commands without reasons that we get from divine authority and religious obligation is only a partial model, to be joined with another partial model, moral obligation, which supplies the idea of reasons without commands.

In contrast to religious obligations derived from divine authority, which can be seen as commands without reasons (or at least not necessarily with reasons), there are the inherent moral obligations the authority for which is found exclusively in their reasons, lacking altogether any source in command or other divine or human positive law (notwithstanding any parallels in such). Such laws, whether called

Authority and the Good 203

natural law or the moral law or anything else, are no less authoritative for lacking an origin in command. Those to whom the laws apply are obligated to obey, and they do wrong when they do not obey. We do not speak of authority here because the obligations are freestanding. Legal obligations, however, do not exist until they are specified, so we cannot rely on reasons alone to describe them. Thus, neither moral obligation (reasons without commands) nor religious obligation (commands without reasons) alone provides an adequate model for legal obligation, which is to say, the moral obligation to obey the law just because it is the law. Commands without reasons lack justification, that normative aspect that distinguishes a government from a gang; reasons without commands make it impossible to identify authority, per se, and, accordingly, deprive putative authority of much of its utility.

So, a third way must be found for legal obligation. If the moral law represents reasons without commands and divine law represents commands without reasons, then human law (what we usually just call "law") sits in the middle, combining aspects of both. Legal obligation requires both commands and reasons because not every good reason is authoritative and not every command is justified. Law, in the sense of a legal system, is a set of commands oriented to the common good. As a concept, it combines commands and reasons. The "reasons," which is to say the normative justification of its authoritativeness, are the legal system's underlying orientation to the common good, which is the animating principle of law. The "commands" are the directives of the legal system that derive from the relevant commanders. Accounting for this aspect of legal obligation based on a comparison to religious obligations (stemming from the commands of a divine authority) is more complicated because, in human affairs, there is no inherently superior individual or group akin to God in divine authority. Rather, there must be some individual or group in the role of commander. With those two components, the concept of a legal system is complete, and the law that springs from it generates a prima facie obligation to obey the law.

To be clear, "legal obligation" refers to a moral obligation to obey the law. The central issue, to remind ourselves, is whether one *ought to* obey the law, in Hart's terms whether one ought to take the law as a standard against which to measure one's own or others' conduct, or whether, having chosen not to obey the law, one has done something wrong—not wrong in the sense of having disobeyed someone with the capacity to punish the disobedience but wrong in the sense of having not done what one ought to have done. It is not illuminating to investigate, in general terms, whether there is a legal obligation to obey the law because law typically requires compliance by definition. That is, the very act of creating a law is normally to create a legal obligation to adhere to the law; requiring certain behavior is the very purpose of the law, and, therefore, legal obligation is built into the definition of law (again, in the ordinary case).

Importantly, even though we are talking about a moral obligation to obey the law, legal obligation cannot be described merely as a species of moral obligation in the form of reasons without commands. Moral obligations have the interesting feature of existing without being posited by anyone (and whether or not there is any kind of incentivization or enforcement). For law, the command aspect remains necessary in order to generate the specific content—that is, the directive that carries an obligation; unlike moral obligations, legal obligations do not specify themselves.

Indeed, my claim is not merely that the command aspect is contingently necessary but, rather, that it is a necessary feature of law. Raz's failure to account for legal obligation helps illuminate this point. Raz cannot account for religious obligation (and perhaps has no interest in doing so), but he also cannot account for legal obligation because he sees no room for law's content-independent authority. Law's authoritativeness cannot be located in reasons without commands. Reasons alone—that is, reasons that apply to the subject without any source in a commander or other issuer of directives (i.e., they exist without being commanded)—are enough to generate moral obligation, but because legal obligations are not self-specifying and can extend further than reason alone can require, something more is necessary.

So, even though the force of the obligation is a moral obligation, the source of the law must be an authority, in whatever form.

Nonlegal moral obligations do not require such a provenance because they can, in some cases, be self-specifying, as, for example, with all the ordinary obligations at the core of basic morality (the obligation not to murder, assault, and so on). Thinking of Hart, one can object that *some* laws evolve organically, as customs, for example, that became legal rules and therefore also do not require specification by a lawgiver. But, first, this is surely a peripheral case of law as compared to directives by a lawgiver. It is the obligation-imposing aspect (or at least intention) of law that characterizes it most fundamentally. Second, such an objection is question begging because the issue in play is how to account for obligation: customs are not morally obligatory merely because they have become deeply entrenched. They have to be converted into law by some official act, even if that means only recognition by officials as law when a specific case comes to court, as with so many common law norms.

Further, we cannot defeat this objection by positing a dichotomy within laws, for example in the form of statutes on one hand and obligations on the other. On that view, we separate law and obligation by supposing that the statutes themselves require certain behavior, irrespective of any moral claims, and then that the moral obligation to obey attaches separately. But, even if we leave aside the conceptual difficulty of sustaining such a division, this approach fails to see that the creation of the law itself entails the imposing of obligation. The element of imposing obligation is built into the very project of making law. Obligation is intrinsic to law. Hart gets this right, even if he gets much else wrong. Because it is the command that specifies the legal obligation, to say that there cannot be law without a moral obligation is also to say that there cannot be law without command. From another angle, we can say that legal obligations generally are not self-specifying, so without command there is no moral obligation, and without moral obligation, law is just coercion or suggestion (depending on whether and how the law is enforced). But legal obligation cannot stand free of all of this, evading the normative dimension that explains the wrong in disobedience. Otherwise, legal obligation reduces to one of these two unacceptable forms. If law is mere coercion, there is no moral obligation to obey, and one has done something wrong only in the older, discredited sense of being punished for failure to obey, an interpretation which, as I show, fatally undermines Hart's argument for the internal point of view. Moreover, without moral obligation, in a hypothetical, if unlikely, legal system that does not punish but at most censures or condemns, the expectation of obedience can be no more than customary. There can be good reasons to adhere to customs, all things being equal, but that is different from saying one has violated a moral obligation by breaking them. Similarly, if law is mere suggestion, then the law advises and even goads, but, once again, one has done nothing wrong, morally, by disobeying any more than one has done something wrong by failing to heed a piece of sound advice.[33] Thus, without moral obligation, legal obligation is no more than a prediction of punishment or of censure. This is why, in Hart's theory, despite his efforts, the fact of something being law says nothing about whether there is a moral obligation to obey it.

This leads us to two contrasting models for obligation: divine authority and religious obligation on one hand, or law rooted in commands without reasons, and moral obligation on the other hand, or law rooted in reasons without commands. The task for us is to figure out where legal obligation fits in, or, put better, what these models of obligation can tell us about legal obligation. If fellow persons lack the superiority of a divine authority, which is an uncontroversial assumption (not least because God in this argument is posited as the being possessing such superiority by definition), then nondivine command alone is insufficient to generate an obligation. At the same time, reason alone is inadequate as a general basis for legal obligation because the reasons behind the laws (besides laws that are coextensive with preexisting moral obligations, in which case it is that latter obligation that supplies the morally binding force) provide reasons to act but not necessarily obligations to act. This, as we see, is a core flaw with Raz's theory for the simple reason that it means that anyone with a good idea can obligate others. Moreover, reason alone does not provide for a definitive choice between various proposals regarding how to achieve the law's aims or which aims to choose among competing reasonable proposals. Neither command nor reason is enough on its own: not every reason for action (even good ones) is authoritative, and not every commanding authority is justified.

The content independence of divine authority makes religious obligation a useful framework for the concept of law

Like Carl Schmitt, Austin recognizes an important comparison between divine command and human command, in respect of which both are law: "In the comprehensive sense above indicated, or in the largest meaning which it has, without extension by metaphor or analogy, the term *law* embraces the following objects:—Laws set by God to his human creatures, and laws set by men to men."[34] This echoes the ordinary availability of the term *law* to refer to divine law, human law, and so forth. Although the justification of human law does not depend on any reference to divine law, divine law serves as a helpful model for the "command" aspect of human law.[35] Chiefly, the model of divine authority and corresponding religious obligation helps make sense of the idea of a content-independent obligation to obey. This is because, on at least one plausible version of divine authority, God's authoritative commands obligate just as such. Indeed, on that model, obedience is not only required but also good. By definition, one ought to obey a being whose very superiority warrants obedience. Relatedly (or alternatively), obedience is good because it is proper to the relationship with a being of that sort.

Yet we must recognize immediately that the challenge in learning from divine authority lies in describing the obligation to obey God in a way that remains possibly relevant for the concept of human law. The possibility of seeing religious obligation as instructive for understanding legal obligation is especially difficult with belief systems that do not presuppose the goodness of God's commands or its knowability, which is to say, that do not presuppose the ability to understand the commands' goodness through human reason, or even that do not presuppose God's goodness altogether.[36] But this also gives us the clearest picture of content independence. The more we posit the goodness of God's commands, the easier it is to tie justification of divine authority to the reasons behind the commands, and, accordingly, the less useful it is as a model for commands without reasons. Of course, this is not to suggest we can truly reach the far end of one extreme because, at a minimum, the fact of God having commanded it must serve as the basis of obligation and a reason to obey. But that bare "reason" carries us quite a way conceptually because it does allow us to abstract from the content of the commands themselves.

On a strongly voluntarist view, obedience to God's will is obligatory strictly because it is God's will, and the reasons for God's commands, if any, need not be accessible to humans even in principle. Undoubtedly, we balk at connecting this kind of authority and obligation with the idea of justification, much less a Razian one. In this example, there are no reasons to which one can appeal outside of God's will for justification. Instead, obeying God must be good for its own sake, meaning that obeying God is something that people have reason to do just as such, and, therefore, divine authority is justified without reference to the reasons behind God's commands. If this is so, then it seems that the goodness of obeying God is somehow rooted in God's relationship to the subjects of divine authority because any appeal to the content of the commands is already ruled out. Instead, the authority must be rooted in a feature of the relationship (to wit, God's superiority), not in the content of the commands. There are no "reasons," in the ordinary sense, and the commands are authoritative only because they are God's will. In this version of divine authority, we arrive at the starkest expression of commands without reasons. That is fine (perhaps) as far as religious obligation goes. But we must ask whether we can still offer an account of authority and obligation under that construction that is relevant to legal authority and obligation. If so, we may have something useful to learn about the concept of law. If not, then obedience to divine authority is, at best, sui generis and, at worst, unreasonable.

To be sure, I introduce the concept of religious obligation not in order to make any claims about the existence of God nor, therefore, for the existence of any actual religious obligation. Instead, I wish to use the easily recognizable idea of religious obligation as a basis for understanding for a form of authority that is best captured by at least one plausible conception of divine authority. What is important here is the utility of the *idea* of divine law and religious obligation as a partial model for human law and legal obligation. The application to human law derives from my use of divine law as a paradigm of commands without reasons. On this conception, divine law is authoritative because of God's intrinsic authority, which emerges from God's intrinsic superiority. Under this not-uncommon conception of divine authority, the fact of the law being commanded by God is what makes it authoritative, namely what generates an obligation to obey. In this view, it is in the very nature of God's superiority for divine directives to be binding on those who are commanded. This view is reasonably associated with biblical religion, even if thinkers in that tradition actually disagree about the basis of divine authority. One simple reason for the biblical association is that the original commands of God to humans in the Bible presuppose humans' understanding of the nature of commandedness. The Bible offers no suggestion as to how or why humans understand themselves to be obligated by God's commands. This is highlighted by the fact that the first directives in Eden are obscure in their purpose, offered without clear reason. Rather, God's authority to command seems to be implicit in the nature of the relationship between God and those humans. The God of the garden presumably intends people to take divine law as authoritative just because it is divine—that is, just because of the superiority of the commander over the commanded.

In this regard, one helpful analogy is parental authority, insofar as parents possess an acknowledged authority over their children that confers upon them at least partially content-independent authority to make decisions for their children. This means children have a prima facie obligation to obey their parents. Like any analogy, though, this one has its limits. One limit to the analogy of parental authority is that parents are thought to have authority only insofar as they make decisions in the interests of their children. Perhaps the same can also be said for divine authority, in which case the problem is not with the analogy but with the idea of locating God's authority in the sheer fact of superiority.

In some religions, there is a belief that God is always and only good, which means in turn that divine commands are always good. If this is the case, then it is possible that divine authority is not rooted in the nature of the relationship between commander and commanded as superior and inferior but in a more Razian notion of justification. If God cannot but be good (in addition to omniscient and omnipotent), then God's subjects always have reason to follow divine directives, resting assured, as Raz requires, that the directives instruct them to do that which they have reason to do, anyway. But, for our purposes, the key is that the superiority of God can obligate even absent a belief in God's omnibenevolence. That is, despite this legitimate consideration about God's goodness being the source of justification, it is not difficult to conceive of a religious obligation to obey God's commands just because they are God's commands. In this way, we can conceive of commands without reasons as a foil opposite Raz's version of law's authority.

Yet we do not need to adopt a fully voluntarist approach to show the conceptual usefulness and distinctiveness of divine authority and religious obligation as a model for the content independence embodied in commands without reasons (and, therefore, as one piece of the concept of law). Even a rationalist understanding of divine authority and religious obligation can stand apart from Raz's theory of authority and provide some basis for content independence. This is important because we want to construe divine authority in a way that makes it as plausible as possible as a model of obligation without watering down the content independence so much as to make it merely derivative of Raz's view of authority. Obeying authority when knowing the reason and for that reason, as Raz has it for human law, is different than obeying authority when one merely believes there is a reason—or even, perhaps, when one knows the reason but obeys primarily because it is commanded.

Attempting to apply this model of divine authority to the political or legal realm highlights the difference. Much as Razians (not to mention many others) presumably demur if the government tells them to do something for which there is no reason, they likely also object if they are told that there is a reason but that the government cannot tell them it. There are exceptions, for example in the realm of defense and security, but these cases are different in part because the reasons are known generally even if the particulars are not known. It is hard to think of a realistic example in any area of human law where the subjects are completely in the dark about the reasons, as opposed to being unaware of certain specifics. Yet this is not difficult to imagine in the realm of divine law, where mystery abounds. More so, divine and human directives are different because, as in the security example, the withholding of certain information is necessary for the achievement of the end itself; that is, the reason for withholding the reasons for the law is intrinsically linked to the reasons for the law—that is, the same security that depends on obeying the directive is compromised by revealing the specifics behind it. But we cannot necessarily say the same for opaque divine commands, where it is not necessary to think that knowledge of the reasons behind the command undermines the purpose(s) of the command.

Moreover, even the commands of an unfailingly good God do not fit the Razian model because the whole logic of obligation, according to Raz, entails the judging of reasons, whether first-order reasons or a second-order rule of thumb rooted in yet further reasons. For Raz, it is the understanding of the law's consonance with one's own reasons that generates the obligation, which cannot be for the case of the unexplained command even of an omnibenevolent god, where there can be a belief in the command's goodness without an inkling of its reasons or effects (and therefore how it relates to the reasons one already has). Taking it on faith that there are reasons is substantially different from having reasons because, in the former, there is no access to the reasons and, therefore, no ability to judge whether the command in fact satisfies the normal requirements of justification. While it is true that people who obey human law do not obtain or examine the reasons in every case, they certainly have access to them in principle and, as in the security example, are aware of their general contours—whereas this is not necessarily the case with divine authority. It may be, then, that Raz's theory cannot accommodate the idea of an obligation to obey divine authority. Perhaps Raz sees obeying divine authority as irrational or even impermissible. But if it is rational to obey divine authority for some other reason for which Raz does not account—that is, if I can defend a reasonable version of commands without reasons that does not collapse into some version of reasons without commands—then we do have in commands without reasons a model that can stand as one part of building a concept of law.

Rooting divine authority and religious obligation in the commands themselves as opposed to the reasons behind the commands does not imply that there are no additional reasons that generate a moral obligation to obey divine authority. Indeed, there may be as good and as many reasons (that generate a moral obligation) to fulfill particular religious obligations as there are for any other moral obligation.[37] The difference between religious obligations and nonreligious moral obligations is that religious obligations potentially carry the command aspect and, therefore, do not depend on reasons other than the fact of being commanded to supply an obligation. To be sure, every true obligation, in the normative sense, is a moral obligation, precisely in the sense that one ought to perform or abstain from a certain act (or thought) and in that the failure to do so can be properly termed "wrong." If there is no moral obligation to obey, then in failing to obey, whatever one has done, one has not done something "wrong."[38] This is true whether it is a moral obligation to do what God says or what the law says or what any justified authority says. The idea that every true obligation (obligation properly so called) is normative is why Hart's government-mugger or obligated-obliged distinction (the internal versus the external point of view) makes sense in the first place. One is obligated to obey the law, and it is wrong to disobey; one is merely obliged to obey the mugger, and one who disobeys is taking a risk but cannot be said to be doing anything "wrong." The difference with religious obligation is that, on one possible model of divine authority at least, the commands and not the reasons for the command generate the obligation. In other words, there can be content independence. This is the significance of investigating divine authority: looking for a different account of authority from the more familiar reasons-based one that we can easily see in freestanding moral obligations. To be sure, none of this necessarily means that the obedience that is a proper response to divine authority is also a proper response to human authority—that is, to any relationship other than the one with God. Nevertheless, it is a good starting point for understanding divine authority and its concomitant obligations and how it can partly shed light on the nature of legal obligation.[39]

Obedience for its own sake is proper to the relationship with a superior being

The next step, then, is to ask whether obedience to God can be reasonable for its own sake—that is, how close we can get to a model of content-independent authority and the corresponding obligation to obey—and then to see whether it can inform our view of human law and, if so, how. Again, my argument is that we need some grounding for content independence in our concept of law; otherwise, we cannot say that law is authoritative qua law, only that individual laws are authoritative when they meet certain conditions, such as those set forth by Raz in his normal justification thesis and the like.[40]

The first place I turn to buttress this argument about religious obligation is to John Finnis. Separately, Finnis provides a solid foundation for my claims about the relationship between law and the common good, but, for our purposes here, the important part is that he also indirectly provides support for the reasonableness of obedience to God—that is, of treating God's commands as authoritative. We find this in his elaboration of religion as a basic human good.[41] The basic good of religion in its most general terms need not entail any particular kind of deity or higher power, but in his closing chapter of *Natural Law and Natural Rights*, Finnis examines this basic good in light of more conventional notions of God. Although he surely favors the version of divine authority where God is reasonable over the version where God's directives are entirely inscrutable yet authoritative nonetheless, Finnis's view here is at least loosely compatible with the voluntarist view because he views the good of religion to include harmony with (or the attempt to harmonize with) God, which can include even a God whose goodness is not known to us in any particulars.[42]

The key takeaway is that Finnis's account of the good of religion underwrites an understanding of the relationship with God that justifies obedience as something proper to that relationship. Finnis characterizes the good of religion broadly as bringing "one's life and actions . . . into some sort of harmony with whatever can be known or surmised about that transcendent other and its lasting order" if there is, indeed, "a transcendent origin of the universal order-of-things and of human freedom and reason."[43] Even those who begin with an atheistic premise often appeal to principles that amount to "a recognition (however residual) of, and concern about, an order of things 'beyond' each and every one of us," or "concern for a good consisting in an irreducibly distinct order."[44] Although this understanding of the good of religion does not need the concept of God as commander or any sort of divine command, it does suggest the goodness of bringing one's actions or even will into line (into harmony) with something transcendent outside of oneself. Depending on the nature of that transcendent other, obedience can be the proper mode of that harmony. Harmonizing or cooperating with God means being in line with, or obeying, the divine will. This is all the more compelling if we contextualize God's transcendence as a form of superiority. Obedience is proper to the relationship precisely because God is superior.

Touching on more commonplace notions of God as an entity, Finnis suggests that the good of religion can entail more than generic harmony with the cosmos; it can be a real relationship with God, in which case one can cooperate with God as an aspect of that relationship in addition to the other reasons one has to pursue the further goods instantiated through that cooperation (such as the well-being of oneself or others). On this understanding, cooperation with God, or participation in God's will, is equally well termed "obedience." Just as one can say that the point of living a religious life is to serve God, to be in harmony with the divine, rather than to earn reward or avoid punishment, all the while knowing that those consequences attach, one can also say that obeying God's commands is the proper mode of relating to him.[45] If every kind of relationship has a particular mode most appropriate to it, then the mode most appropriate to the God-human relationship is one of obedience, or at least it can be. Seeing obedience at the heart of the relationship is embedded in the simple theological observation that a transcendent God does not need people's prayers or animal sacrifices. Rather, these offerings are "meaningful" to God and serve the relationship insofar as they are acts of service.[46] God does not need obedience, either, just as a friend does not need favors or other tokens of friendship. Instead, these are expressions of, or, better, instantiations of, the relationship.

This line of thought is brought into sharper relief where Finnis expands on his notion of religion, in which the question of why to obey God "has no bite" because obedience is simply the behavior proper to the relationship: it is its own reason for action.[47] In Finnis's construction, the correct concept of God (or the placeholder, D) is "an entity and state of affairs that by its existing explains the existing of all entities and states of affairs in all four orders of contingent being."[48] Furthermore, Finnis adds, "How D (or God) thus is the explanation of all this is not known; what is considered to be known is simply that D (or God) is whatever is required to explain them. Already, therefore, it should be clear that to ask for an explanation of D (or God) is to miss the sense and reference of claims made about D (or God)."[49] Finnis goes on to say that there are further beliefs "beyond what can be affirmed about D on the basis of philosophical argumentation" that underpin claims for obedience to God.[50] He writes, "In the context of such beliefs—and it is only in such a context that claims about the authoritativeness of God's will for man to be are plausibly made—the question 'Why should God's will be obeyed?' has no bite."[51] But the possibility of God's authoritative superiority already seems to follow from the previous part even before the beliefs in question are added. In the same way that it misses the point to ask how God is the explanation for existence, because God is posited as that explanation, meaning God is whatever is needed to explain existence, so, too, God's superiority is entailed in the very nature of divinity.[52] That is, as a model for authority, God (or D) just is "whatever is required" to be superior enough to command authoritatively.[53]

Religious obligation is relevant despite obvious differences between divine and human authority

Simon raises an obvious problem about the comparison of religious and legal obligation, namely that "there is something paradoxical about having the power to bind the conscience of another man."

Continuing, he writes, "Of course, a man cannot do such a thing. God alone can. And God can bind a man to obey another man. This he did by the creation of the human species, which is naturally social and political; for the necessity of government and obedience follows from the nature of community life."[54] Notably, Simon does not say that God commands humans to obey their fellow humans. Rather, Simon claims that the obligation to obey is built into humanity in virtue of the human being's social and political nature. This means Simon's position can also be argued by those who deny that God exists or that any feature of human existence comes from God. That is, if humans' "boundedness" is part of their nature, it does not necessarily matter, for our purposes, where it comes from; the relevant point (and debate) is about human nature, not its source. Simon suggests this as well, recapping from an earlier section that "the need for government is so rooted in the nature of society that government would be needed even in the ideal case of a society made only by enlightened and virtuous people."[55] He adds, "If government, as distinct from unanimity, is made necessary by the very nature of things, the obligation to obey has its roots in the nature of things, in the very nature of man and of human society."[56] Again, it is worth noting that Simon's emphasis is on the "nature of things," which has its implications whether or not one sees God in the background of the picture. Simon's claim is that human nature makes authority necessary and that, because authority is necessary, it has the power to obligate. Therefore, we must understand this basic human need for authority under the law.

While divine authority and religious obligation serve as a partial model for legal obligation, they are, of course, not its source. We must ultimately root the authority of law in facts about human nature and not in a strong correspondence between divine and human authority because there are important, often obvious differences between God's commands and the government's. Instead, we will need to explore why, human nature being what it is, the authority of law is necessary and therefore good. But even before reaching that point, the comparison to divine authority and religious obligation can help us to see to what extent obedience itself is good. Insofar as the goodness of obedience to the law falls short, we must turn to the goodness of authority to justify legal obligation.

The primary difference is that, because government never possesses the intrinsic superiority that God does, "because I said so" is never enough. Plainly, the government's authority needs to rest on something more than command alone. In the divine authority model, God possesses the requisite superiority to obligate. Implicitly, no such superiority exists outside of God because no other entity has intrinsic superiority (contra the divine rights of kings) or perfect knowledge of the common good. Perhaps for this reason, Yves Simon writes that the authority of human law actually derives from God.[57] For him, the problem is that "on the one hand, it seems impossible to account for social life without assuming that man can bind the conscience of his neighbor; on the other hand, it is not easy to see how a man can ever enjoy such power."[58] The plain reason for the doubt is that, while directives from another person can provide reasons for action, seemingly they can never be binding *just as such* because one can justifiably choose to act otherwise for other reasons. If someone receives very sound guidance from a friend, it can be foolish to ignore it, but we cannot say that the person violates any obligation if she does otherwise, even if the reason for choosing another course is as weak as "I didn't feel like it."

Nevertheless, there is, perhaps, a case to be made for obedience that is independent of the origins (divine or human) of the authority. It can be that commands without reasons in fact do have a reason: training subjects in habits of obedience that serve the purpose of disposing subjects to obey commands that do have good reasons behind them. We can imagine that the government requires everyone to wear a yellow shirt on Tuesdays not because there is any underlying benefit to that practice but simply because it trains people in habits of obedience to the government. That is not, in itself, wholly irrational, but it is discomfiting. It makes sense when God does such a thing because we are more confident in the goodness of divine commands. Alternatively (or additionally), obedience to God for its own sake can be good in a way that is not the case for government because of the way obedience is proper to the relationship with an intrinsically superior being—that is, because obedience to God can be good in itself insofar as it is fulfilling of the relationship with God.[59] For human authority, though, obedience to the government is instrumental to promoting the common good. Government is not the sort of entity that ought to command just for the sake of obedience. Yet it is not unreasonable for the government to conclude that, in general, it is better if everyone is in the habit of obeying it (provisionally). One can argue that it is better for citizens to have habits of obedience to the government so that they err on the side of obeying when they otherwise underestimate the importance of obeying in a particular case.

Even so, this is only an instrumental justification, not a claim that obedience to the government is good for its own sake in the way that obedience to God can be. Therefore, to issue directives that serve no other purpose than training people in obedience seems too far given that there are plenty of opportunities to practice obedience (following laws that do have a purpose) and given that obedience to human law does not necessarily have any intrinsic value the way obeying God can. Moreover, because the requirements of human law, on the whole, ought to be more intelligible to us than the requirements of divine law, we are likely to need less training to ensure obedience. Even when the government's reasons cannot be offered under special circumstances, this is not meant to be the norm. And even in those cases, they are not reasons that cannot ever be known or cannot be known in principle. In contrast, commands rooted in unknown or unknowable reasons make more sense in the realm of divine authority. This does not make it necessarily wrong for the government to cultivate habits of obedience, but it does raise questions.

Though it is harder to make the case for a content-independent obligation to obey human law than divine, we can see the relevance of religious obligation as a partial model for legal obligation precisely because it exemplifies the content-independent authoritativeness of the law. With respect to divine authority, it makes sense to say that we obey God's commands just because they come from God. Whether we believe in God's infinite goodness (and therefore the necessary goodness of every command) or inherent superiority (and therefore the ability to bind us in all cases), divine authority is a prime model for an obligation to obey the law just because it is the law. But can this translate to human authority? Can human law generate obligations like that?

To be sure, relying on God's (definitional) superiority to explain the authoritativeness of divine commands reveals an obvious and important difference between divine and human authority. One difference between the commands of God and of, say, the government lies in the issue of whether one ought to bring one's will in line with the authority's will (or at least strive to). It might seem that in the realm of politics and law, one might yield to the judgment of the majority, for example—that is, act in accordance with the majority's will—without attempting to bring one's own will into conformity with the majority's, meaning without (actively) desiring the ends for which those actions are intended although willingly cooperating in their realization. With divine authority, however, perhaps it is implicit that one is meant not only to perform what is required but also to take God's reasons, insofar as they can be known, as one's own reasons for action, or to will (or wish to will) whatever God wills, even granting that God's reasons are not or cannot always be known.

This challenge helps to alleviate, if not fully resolve, the paradox of obedience, because it shows at least one way in which the obedient character of acts of obedience is not undermined by reasons. The paradox is that once one takes another's reasons as one's own, then compliance is no longer really obedience; rather, it is doing what one has reasons to do independent of the command. Nevertheless, if one takes an authority's will as a reason for action just because it is the authority's will apart from any separate judgment about what is willed (or takes the other's reasons as one's reasons just because they are the other's), then it is still obedience, notwithstanding the fact that one necessarily does so because one judges it good to take that will as a reason for action. That last part, the cognizable good of taking another's reasons or will as one's own just because they are the other's, must be built into obedience as a minimum because to choose to obey necessarily entails making a judgment that it is good to comply with the other's will for *some* reason, even if the only reason is that the other is acknowledged as superior.

Again, though, this suggests a major distinction between possible conceptual understandings of divine and legal authority because we do not ordinarily think it is good to obey a human authority for no other reason than the fact that that person (or group) is in authority. Perhaps it makes sense to take another's will as one's own just because it is the other's only when the other is God. At the same time, there is an important similarity between divine and legal authority in this aspect of the nature of the obligation. In deferring to human authority, one can do so contingently, or, perhaps better said, cynically, in which case one can try to cheat when violations of the law will go undetected. But if the authority is justified, then one can correctly grasp an obligation to obey the law even when one can get away with disobeying. In that case of true authority, we can construe the situation as one in which the authority of the law substitutes the judgment of the law for the judgment of the individual. This results in a prima facie obligation to obey the law, so the prevailing public judgment (of the law) does not admit of exceptions on the basis of greater expertise or the like, as Raz would have it. In Finnis's language, it is a substitution of public judgment for private judgment that in its very nature rules out individual discretion.[60] Indeed, on this view, the whole point of the law is that substitution of public judgment for private judgment rules out individual discretion. One does not have to will what the law wills in the sense of truly preferring what the law requires as an original matter, but one can still accept the law as genuinely authoritative—that is, as producing a (prima facie) obligation to obey.

Obeying God counts as obedience even when God's will is directed at the good

Finnis's framing of the good of religion as a form of relationship provides the structure for understanding the value of obedience to God for its own sake because of the way obedience is the proper expression of that relationship. Obedience for its own sake is the paradigm of content independence. At the same time, the most paradigmatic instance of content independence also seems the most removed from justifications for the authority of law because of the yawning gap between divine and human authority. Yet if we make room for God's goodness in the picture, then we can further unpack the good of obedience and close the gap somewhat to legal obligation without completely forfeiting the element of content independence. If the relationship with God can be compared to a friendship (or a similar relationship where one takes the other's will as a reason for action), and if God, out of goodness, favors the common good, then there is an additional reason for people to favor the common good, namely God's will. Finnis writes, "This would not entail that we no longer favoured the common good for its own sake, nor that we no longer loved our friends for their own sakes. Rather, it would mean that 'for their own sakes' would gain a further (and explanatory) dimension of meaning."[61] Similarly, in my argument about law's authority, the concern is not primarily about obedience to God specifically as participation in friendship; rather, the takeaway point here from Finnis is that cooperating in or fulfilling God's will can be its own reason for action, without appeal to further goods, apart from the reasons that already exist for favoring the common good (which is advanced by obeying God's commands).

It is true even in an ordinary friendship that cooperating in the intentions of the other person is one constitutive part of the friendship, but here such "going along with" is ostensibly obligatory. There are, of course, already reasons to help advance the common good, but if this is to be a reason that *obligates*, then there must be something about the relationship ("friendship") with God that renders it different from a friendship with another person who also favors the common good. God's perfect knowledge means that what God favors is definitively the common good, as opposed to our more approximate intentions, but this alone does not seem to be the source of obligation given that (relatively) definitive knowledge of the common good does not otherwise usually generate obligations. Finnis's question remains: "In what sense are we to take it to be *necessary* to favour that common good, which after all will end, sooner or later, in the death of all persons and the dissolution of all communities?"[62]

He continues, "In friendships one values what one's friends value ... for no other reason than that they value it."[63] Once again, as in my criticism of Raz's argument, this generates a reason to value it — that is, to value what God values (in this case, the common good). In the relationship with God, the valuing of what God values takes the form of obeying divine commands. Examining divine authority and its entailment specifically rather than just any form of friendship is important because, in the concept of law, we are searching not merely for reasons to act — which are not necessarily obligatory — but for actual obligation.

To reiterate, the worry is that if God's reasons (and commands) are always good and known to be so (even if the reasons or their goodness are not apparent), then, by some lights, there is neither real authority nor real obedience but instead a free choosing of the good by the subject who perceives the goodness. Yet, there is a crucial difference between acting because God commands it (while still believing in God's goodness) and acting because it is good. That is, the classification of the act as obedience or not depends on what motivates the act. Reducing all adherence to divine authority to acts of choosing the good shifts the character of such acts away from obedience insofar as choosing and obeying are never fully compatible. In contrast, complying with God's commands just because they are the divine will is obedience, even if one believes the commands to be good. Obeying involves complying because it is the will of the commander, even if one disagrees with the command, notwithstanding the fact that one happens not to disagree. There is no possibility of construing Raz's theory of human authority to fit this conception of obedience because authority is unnecessary and unjustified where one knows a certain course of action to be best independent of the authoritative directive.

By analogy to another basic human good, the good of play, Finnis explains obeying God this way: "The requirements of practical reasonableness (which generate our obligations) have a 'point' beyond themselves. That point is the *game* of co-operating with God. Being *play*, this co-operation has no point beyond itself, unless we wish to say that God is such a further 'point.'"[64] So we can understand obedience in terms of the requirements of practical reasoning or as part of a basic good (friendship, play, cooperation with God, and so forth) that itself provides a reason for action. But, again, unless this is a special kind of relationship, cooperation with God generates no more obligation than any other cooperative enterprise, including a relationship with someone very wise about the common good. In other words, if there is an obligation to obey God because of God's unique access to knowledge of the common good, then that same authority to command extends in Razian fashion to others who know the common good (so to speak) as well. Moreover, if the obligation to obey God entirely collapses into the obligation to act for the common good (whatever that is), then it is never really a matter of divine authority, except insofar as one believes that God has an epistemic advantage in knowing what best conduces to the common good. By that reasoning, it is never really a matter of law's authority but, as in Raz, a question of whether the law overlaps with reasons that already exist.[65] Therefore, with divine authority, there must be something about this particular relationship (with God) that generates obligation. This returns us, then, to the distinguishing feature of the relationship with God, namely that it is with a being possessing an intrinsic superiority.

This portion of Finnis's view is helpful in two respects. First, Finnis roots cooperation with God in a concern for the common good, both in itself (the value of the common good that each person can recognize) and as the object of God's concern (the value that a person attaches to the common good as an expression of cooperation with God who values the common good). This is important because it highlights the dual nature of human law, for which divine law serves as a partial model in my theory. Human law, too, must incorporate the will of the commander (expressed as directives) and a concern for the common good. Both features together combine to make sense of the obligation to obey. Second, Finnis's view helps illustrate that the emphasis on command in my theory is not a return to positivism but part of its critique. The utility of the command model, as shown through the example of divine authority, is not that it gives us a theory of rules for rules' sake but rather that it illuminates a necessary component of law. In human law, there still must be an underlying point to the rules as a whole, and that point must be the common good. In the final analysis the authority of law is not content independent because it swings free of any normative considerations. Rather, the content independence is with respect to the individual laws because of the orientation of the law as a whole to the common good.[66]

Schmitt's political theology supports both the command model and the claim for normativity

In his work dating from the first half of the twentieth century, Schmitt anticipates some of the key problems and themes at the center of the discussion over authority and obligation in the second half of that century. Although not ordinarily considered alongside postwar analytic jurisprudence — that is, the conversation revolving around Hart, Raz, and company — Schmitt's political theology is instructive in this area. In painting a picture of legal obligation that draws on the idea of divine authority and religious obligation, Schmitt lends support to a concept of law that is rooted in the commands of a sovereign. That is, he helps us see how religious obligation is useful as a partial model for legal obligation. Because of the very different context in which he is writing, Schmitt approaches these problems and themes from a different angle than Hart and Raz, so it is especially worthwhile to recognize his contributions to this topic, which otherwise go overlooked. To be sure, in my own theory, I insist on marrying the command model to the requirement of an orientation to the common good in a complete concept of law. Yet the partial overlap with Schmitt's theory is helpful because it points to the notion of a content-independent obligation to obey the law. As with any sound theory of (human) authority, Schmitt's writings are not a brief for an absolute obligation. Thus, although he envisions a system in which there is great leeway for the sovereign, he, too, views law through the lens of its normative character, so his understanding of authority also contributes to the idea of law as a set of commands oriented to the common good.

At the heart of Schmitt's argument about sovereignty is the claim that politics is both analogically and genealogically related to religion.

In what is perhaps the second-most-famous line of his work *Political Theology*, Schmitt writes, "All significant concepts of the modern theory of the state are secularized theological concepts not only because of their historical development—in which they were transferred from theology to the theory of the state, whereby, for example, the omnipotent God became the omnipotent lawgiver—but also because of their systematic structure, the recognition of which is necessary for a sociological reconsideration of these concepts."[67] In Schmitt's thinking, divine authority is *the* starting point for thinking about the authority of the state. As before, I raise this not to support any claims for divine authority, per se, but to show how religious obligation can serve as a partial model for legal obligation.

In the context of seeing religious obligation as a partial model for legal obligation, Schmitt's work also supports my concept of law in part because his political theology provides ground for an understanding of law that incorporates an updated version of the command model. Schmitt depicts the "systematic structure" of governmental authority against the backdrop of theological conceptions of divine authority.[68] Schmitt's famous starting point regarding sovereignty is, "Sovereign is he who decides on the exception."[69] This "decision" of the sovereign, which is the essence of sovereignty, mirrors God's creation *ex nihilo*. "Looked at normatively," he writes, "the decision emanates from nothingness."[70] For Schmitt, sovereignty resembles God's creation in that both depend on no prior existence or creation and in that both are in principle illimitable.[71] In his foreword to Schmitt's *Political Theology*, Tracy Strong explains: "Political power is to be understood on the model of God's creation—which is how Hobbes understood it. Power is to make something from that which is not something and thus is not subject to laid-down laws."[72] Sounding a similar note, John McCormick notes in his introduction to Schmitt's *Legality and Legitimacy* that, for Schmitt, "the President possesses a world-making, God-like fiat of exceptional legislative authority."[73]

In speaking of the decision emanating from nothingness, Schmitt is not directly addressing the singular issue of authority originally stemming from a first, unauthorized authority. That issue fits this as well, but Schmitt is addressing, rather, every real "decision" of the sovereign, the making of which is an ongoing occurrence or at least a possibility. For Schmitt, the *ex nihilo* character of the sovereign's power is not just found in some distantly past starting point but rather reproduced in each exercise of "decision," much as ancient traditions suggest that God renews creation in each moment of sustaining the world. But, for the very reason that the decision—the truest expression of sovereignty—extends far beyond the initial establishment of authority, the concept of command as sheer will is all the more salient in Schmitt. Schmitt writes, "The exception reveals most clearly the essence of the state's authority. The decision parts here from the legal norm, and (to formulate it paradoxically) authority proves that to produce law it need not be based on law."[74] Here, too, Schmitt suggests that, under extraordinary circumstances, law itself is produced *ex nihilo*, and, in its independence from legal norms governing law-making, law is not subject to legal limits. Extending the comparison to theology, Schmitt says that "the exception in jurisprudence is analogous to the miracle in theology."[75] The miracle breaks into the world, free from natural constraints, and thus is the truest demonstration of God's sovereignty. In an even stronger formulation, Schmitt states, "The decision frees itself from all normative ties and becomes in the true sense absolute."[76] This is a model of a sovereign in the mold of an omnipotent deity.

Along related lines, when Schmitt describes the emergency powers in a state of exception as "unlimited," he does not mean this merely as a technicality just because there is no practical, institutionalized way to limit the powers in that situation.[77] Rather, unlimited power is a feature of the nature of sovereignty in Schmitt's political theology, in which that power mirrors God's omnipotence. To be sure, none of this talk of unlimited power implies the absence of moral norms—we cannot say that the sovereign can never do anything wrong—only the absence of procedural constraints under the law. Just as an omnipotent God can still be subject to moral norms found in the natural law (as it exists in the divinely created world), a legally illimitable sovereign is still subject to moral norms. In fact, it is not only that the sovereign is subject to moral limits. In the bigger picture, it is also that authority is justified by virtue of the moral ends toward which it aims. Thus, we have a sovereign with the authority to issue binding directives, whose authority rests on that sovereign's alignment with the normative purposes of authority—a sovereign issuing commands that, on the whole, are oriented to the common good.

As Schmitt sets out in his thesis, politics and theology are not only related analogically but also genealogically. In the same vein, McCormick quotes Schmitt as saying that "the problem of legality and legitimacy must be interrogated both 'historically and conceptually.'"[78] To be sure, Schmitt is not focused on the question of whether God actually delegates authority to humans. Instead, Schmitt concentrates not on the pedigree of the actual authority but on the *concept* of authority, offering an intellectual history of sovereignty as an idea. For example, in keeping with his famous line from *Political Theology*, Schmitt states, "The juridic formulas of the omnipotence of the state are, in fact, only superficial secularizations of theological formulas of the omnipotence of God."[79] This sort of conceptual genealogy is very important for Schmitt because he argues that a proper understanding of the history of these ideas is necessary for diagnosing the problems of modern politics. More generally, for Schmitt, political concepts, which are derived from theological ones, can best be understood with reference to their theological antecedents.

Schmitt begins his account of that history of ideas (and institutions) with the transition from monarchy to constitutionalism (and, with that, to democratic forms of government), which corresponds to a theological shift from a more traditional theism to deism. "The idea of the modern constitutional state," argues Schmitt, "triumphed together with deism, a theology and metaphysics that banished the miracle from the world."[80] Just as the miracle is banished from theology in deism, so, too, the exception, which is the keystone of sovereignty, is banished from politics in constitutionalism: "The rationalism of the Enlightenment rejected the exception in every form."[81] This is why, for Schmitt, the modern concept of sovereignty is rootless. There is no longer the possibility of the decision that "frees itself from all normative ties and becomes in the true sense absolute," and, therefore, there is not real sovereignty as Schmitt recognizes it.[82] A different, modern approach is to locate all sovereignty within the boundaries of legal norms, which Schmitt clearly thinks fails. As McCormick writes, "Because there is no personal authority in this system, only norms, Schmitt claims that the legislative state assumes away the issue of 'obedience.'"[83] Of course, I, too, am taking aim at concepts of law and authority that do not entail an element of obedience. As I argue, obedience is definitional to the content independence of law because it is contained in the very idea of authority. Put another way, the absence of obedience is linked definitionally to the absence of genuine authority. If there is no obligation to obey, there is no authority. Law is not, as Hart has it, just what we happen to do around here, but the justified commands of an authority that confer obligation upon the subjects.[84] For Schmitt, assuming obedience away, as he sees the legislative state doing, is problematic. As McCormick explains, "In Schmitt's account of legitimacy, obedience is affiliated most closely with personal authority alone."[85] On this basis, "Schmitt avers that contemporary legality does not account for *why* authority is obeyed"—though, for McCormick, Schmitt can do this only by "ignoring all Kantian justifications of obedience to law as a form of self-rule."[86] While we do not need to go as far as Schmitt in linking obedience to *personal* authority, we can recognize the value in his point and maintain as he does that a proper concept of law must rest on commands and not merely impersonal norms: hence the impossibility of grounding authority in social practice.

To recast Schmitt's point in the context of Hart's concept of law, we can say that Schmitt's "decision" manifests in the form of social practice, which is the ultimate source of the authority of law behind the legal norms. Despite the importance of legal norms (including legal norms that explain legal norms, and so on) in Hart's theory, it is social practice, standing behind the legal norms, that finally accounts for why the first (or highest-order) legal norm is accepted and treated as authoritative. In Hart's case, social practice stands in place of Schmitt's decisionism as the explanation of final appeal— the answer to the final "why." Hart's "because that's the way we do things here" replaces Schmitt's "because I said so." Obviously, this does not mean that Schmitt and Hart endorse the exact same ideas using different terminology. Instead, I illustrate the parallel in order to draw lessons from where they diverge, namely a shift from authoritative decisions to authoritative (yet organic) social practices.

Schmitt attributes this sort of change in theories of law, from decision to social practice as the source of rules and ground of authority, in part to Rousseau's "politicization of theological concepts, especially with respect to the concept of sovereignty."[87] Schmitt explains, "The general will of Rousseau became identical with the will of the sovereign. . . . The people became the sovereign. The decisionistic and personalistic element in the concept of sovereignty was lost."[88] In the concept of command, I retain these elements just enough to make up for what Schmitt sees is missing in modern, liberal theory without requiring us to go all the way with him. In other words, the command model I employ captures just enough to address the problems Schmitt identifies, yet it does not necessitate a wholesale embrace of Schmitt's view.

In his critique of Rousseau, Schmitt calls into question whether the concept of sovereignty can be sustained without these elements. Schmitt, of course, thinks not. The problem is compounded by what Schmitt thinks is the inevitable result of a move to deism, politically and theologically, namely a further slide from deism to atheism, which finds its political analog in a shift from democracy to anarchy. In Schmitt's reading of history, "radicals who opposed all existing order directed . . . their ideological efforts against the belief in God altogether" while the people at large settled for "immanence pantheism or a positivist indifference toward any metaphysics."[89] For these radicals, "mankind had to be substituted for God," but this can only "end in anarchic freedom" with no real sovereignty.[90] These developments culminate in the fundamental challenge to the authority of law from the philosophical anarchists, who deny the justification of law's authority altogether. Their challenge is the touching-off point for Raz's theory of authority. As I demonstrate and as Schmitt effectively predicts, Raz's adoption of their premises makes it impossible to truly ground authority. In this way, Schmitt anticipates and diagnoses the problem ahead in jurisprudence and, in his evocation of divine authority as a model for human authority (and, consequently, religious obligation for legal obligation), points us toward the theoretical resources necessary for a successful concept of law.

AUTHORITY

The prima facie obligation to obey is conceptually essential for authority yet limited in force

The model of religious obligation I offer (commands without reasons) gives us a view of a content-independent obligation to obey that evades us when we have only moral obligation (reasons without commands) to consider. This is important in constructing a framework for legal obligation because it is the law's capacity to bind in a content-independent fashion that marks it as authoritative rather than merely advisory. There is no prima facie obligation if, so to speak, the burden of proof is on each law to show why one must obey rather than on the subject to show why not. In that case, the law is not truly authoritative because the reason for compliance in the face of disagreement—that is, when the subject does not agree with the law but complies—is the applicability to oneself of the reasons for the law and not the fact of being obligated by the law just because it is the law. There, it is the consequences of not adhering to the reasons that apply to oneself and not the violation of the law just as such that are the primary motivator of compliance and that make disobedience "wrong." And if it is mainly punishment that stands behind the authoritativeness of law, as in some earlier theories, then the concept of law reduces to coercion—the very thing that we must avoid in order to accept Hart's critical insight about obligation. In contrast, a better concept of law, by putting not coercion but obligation at the center, explains why people should take the law as a standard against which to measure their behavior. Even on the level of descriptive sociology (as opposed to moral philosophy), the turning point in analytic jurisprudence initiated by Hart depends on seeing the law as providing more-than-merely-instrumental reasons to obey and thereby serving as a reason in itself, creating an obligation apart from the reasons beneath it.

A prima facie obligation to obey the law means an obligation that comes with law just as such and stands independent of the content of the particular law. It is not, of course, an absolute obligation to obey, but it does mean that the law gets the benefit of the doubt, as it were, that there is an obligation to obey the law unless outweighed by a stronger obligation not to obey. In this respect, the claim that there is a prima facie obligation to obey is important and distinct. Simmons, Green, and others simply deny there is a prima facie obligation to obey the law.[91] Similarly, for theorists like Raz, the obligation to obey (which is not even really an obligation) always depends on an assessment of the reasons behind the law. For Raz, the justification of law's authority is always about the reasons behind the particular law, so the presence of an obligation is contingent upon the underlying reasons in each case. But the obligation to obey is never part of the law just because it is the law, whereas on my view there is an obligation to the law just as such. This is why Raz and others cannot meaningfully speak of the authority of law; law itself never carries obligation.

Although, as I show, Marmor's institutional conception of authority ultimately fails, Marmor does move past Raz in some important ways. One contribution is that Marmor's theory contains the implicit assumption that authority generates a prima facie obligation to obey the law. That is, once justified authority is identified, the normative power of the authority entails the ability to obligate those who are under it in a content-independent fashion. "Once these social practices are in place and conventionally practiced," Marmor explains, "voluntary participation is not a precondition of the reasons to participate in them."[92] This is an important counterclaim to normative theories in the Razian mode, which suggest that authoritativeness ultimately depends on the individual subject's assessment of justification in each case or at least that each directive is evaluated individually (rather than taken as obligatory in the context of a justified system). In contrast, Marmor understands that a proper theory of authority and obligation must entail some obligation to obey just as such, before any second-guessing takes place. As always, the obligation to obey can be overridden by stronger competing obligations. But a major motivation for resolving the dilemma of authority in the first place is to arrive at an explanation for social-institutional authority just as such. As Marmor says, he is aiming at "harmonizing a long standing divide in the literature about political obligation, that I think many have found unsatisfactory, between the question of the conditions for the legitimacy of practical authorities, and the question of the general obligation to obey the law."[93] And, indeed, he is right to want to harmonize them because they must go together if the justification of authority is to have any meaning.

At the same time, the obligation to obey the law that attends my theory is always conditional, or qualified, in some sense. The obligation to obey the law is a prima facie, or all-things-equal, obligation, not an absolute, or all-things-considered, obligation. That is, while there must be at least a prima facie obligation to obey the law in order to speak truly of authority, it is *only* a prima facie obligation. We only need the obligation to be prima facie in order to show that there is an obligation to obey the law just because it is the law and not (only) because of the overlap between the law and reasons that happen to apply to the subject already. There is never an absolute obligation because there can be competing moral obligations that trump the legal obligation, which is to say, that trump the moral obligation entailed in the legal obligation. In other words, like with any obligation, the obligation to obey the law is contingent upon the absence of a stronger moral obligation not to do what is required. One significant implication of understanding legal obligation this way is that a prima facie obligation to obey the law exists *even* when there is in fact a competing moral obligation not to do what the law says. In such a case, the prima facie obligation is overridden, but it is not absent. As long as the directive can be identified as part of a (justified) legal system, each particular law carries a prima facie (moral) obligation to obey, even if that obligation is ultimately defeated by a competing (moral) obligation.

Once again, the obligation to obey the law just because it is the law is only a prima facie obligation because there can be a stronger moral obligation to disobey the law. This view is supported by the ordinary usage of the phrase "lawful orders" in the sense of citizens being required to obey lawful orders of the police or soldiers of their commanders—but not unlawful orders. At first, the phrase seems redundant because validly issued orders are by definition "lawful" (and hence obligatory) in a system where there is a prima facie obligation to obey the law. But packed into the simple phrase "lawful (or unlawful) orders" is a sophisticated concept: that there is an obligation to do what the officer says unless there is a stronger obligation not to do so. In normal discourse, the term *lawful order* or *unlawful order* does not mean the kind of thing that fits with Hart's use of the term *law*. In Hart's world, *lawful* or *unlawful* means that the order is valid or invalid depending on whether it meets the criteria set by secondary rules. But in the ordinary and philosophically more correct sense, an order is an "unlawful order" because it is wrong to follow.

Any real conflict in determining whether to obey the law is always a case of competing moral obligations. In a case of conflict, the prima facie moral obligation to obey the law comes up against any separate moral obligation to refrain from what the law requires in that case. There is no need to discuss the supposed case of competing legal obligations because law itself resolves (or ought to resolve) the question of which requirement trumps the other. That is why it is legal to go through the intersection at a red light when directed to do so by a police officer. In those situations, the law is whatever the officer says it is, with those instructions trumping the usual requirement to stop at a red light. If the required action is already in the statute books, then the additional order by the officer is unnecessary. But, in this case, the law's reach is extended by the requirement to obey lawful orders that go beyond or supersede the statutes (a provision that can itself be found in a statute although it is understood implicitly even if not). Furthermore, the effective status as law of all "lawful orders" is why it is not necessary, for our purposes, to differentiate between statutes, decrees, measures, orders, and so forth, within the context of the law. In all these cases, the obligation to obey extends until it meets a moral obligation not to obey.

It is worth noting here that my concept of law has the advantage of helping us to make sense of civil disobedience. Borrowing Hart's core observation, we recognize that people do not relate to the law as a mugger—that is, out of fear of punishment—but instead see obedience to the law as a matter of obligation. Civil disobedience is not about shirking one's responsibility because one can get away with it, as in the case of an undetectable breach, but instead knowingly (and usually openly) breaking the law in acknowledgment of a contrary duty, namely the obligation to obey the law. This also explains, at least partly, why civil disobedience also includes accepting the punishment. It is precisely the thought that obeying the law carries a prima facie obligation to obey that makes civil disobedience so fraught. This is not unlike the key to understanding the trouble with the postwar German trials. There, people acted, if ultimately unjustifiably, in accordance with an obligation to obey the law (albeit one overridden by competing moral obligations). Here, people break the law justifiably because this obligation to obey, too, is overridden by competing moral obligations, yet the people do it openly, accepting the punishment for breaking the law. It is the prima facie obligation to obey the law that makes sense of this.

The question of undetectable breaches reveals key differences over the nature of authority

The debate between Raz and Finnis over the nature of law revolves, in a way, around the question of whether there is a prima facie obligation to obey the law, with Raz arguing in the negative and Finnis in the affirmative. Another manifestation of this division arises in the question of whether there is an obligation to obey the law even when there are no harmful consequences, which includes, by stipulation, that no one else will know (so that the lawbreaker is not caught; so that no one else's respect for the law is improperly diminished; and so on). Exploring this disagreement between Raz and Finnis both helps us understand why there must be an obligation to obey the law even in the case of so-called victimless crimes or undetectable breaches and helps us see how this relatively minor point maps onto the larger underlying debate about the nature of law.

For Finnis, the presence of a prima facie obligation entails that authority creates new reasons for action. Due to authority, there is a point in doing things that there is not otherwise a point in doing in the absence of the law—that is, the law creates new reasons that do not exist until the law exists. If there is no obligation to obey because the reasons behind the law do not apply, then the law cannot be said to have authority qua law. In the case of the mythical traffic light, with a red light and no other cars or pedestrians for miles, the case for compliance with the law depends entirely on the obligation to obey just as such. In other words, if there is a prima facie obligation to obey the law, then one must stop despite the absence of underlying reasons. On competing theories of law's authority, such as Raz's, a decision to stop at the red light depends upon having independent reasons for stopping (e.g., the presence of danger), so the decision whether to comply with the law has nothing to do with whether the law is authoritative. The assumption built into that way of thinking is that the law is not authoritative just as such.

To put it another way, individual decision-making about the law of the sort Raz has in mind largely defeats the purpose of authority, which serves to rule out private, individual decision-making. Presumably it does this because the introduction of individual decision-making ("Should I stop at the red light?") compromises the attainment of the goods that the law is seeking or protecting. If such decision-making does take place, there is nothing that we can meaningfully call a prima facie obligation to obey because Raz's position is that, in the absence of additional reasons beyond the command of the law, there is no obligation to obey. But the whole point of authority is to bind in the absence of a stronger, competing reason not to comply. Otherwise, there is nothing that we can meaningfully call authority because all decisions come down to private, individual assessments. To be sure, this does not preclude the possibility of individual judgments that result in civil disobedience and so forth in cases where there is a stronger moral obligation not to obey the law. The point is just that the absence of the underlying reasons for a particular law does not mean there is no reason to obey that law. There is a reason: the prima facie obligation to obey. Without that, there is *by definition* no authority of law.

Moreover, this correct understanding of the obligation to obey the law accounts for how the law can require people to put the public good before their own private good. This is important to add because the fact that the prima facie obligation to obey is a definitional requirement of genuine authority does not make any of that justified. On Raz's terms, the law is justified when it corresponds to the reasons one already has for action. If so, the case for sacrifice over self-interest is much harder to make and perhaps in many cases impossible. In theory, Raz can offer some attenuated explanation of how the public good is always implicated in the private good, but there are too many cases where the "math" does not work. This is because there are clearly many cases when the public and private good conflict. And even if the math does work (i.e., if the reasons that apply to a person always include reasons whereby the public good at which the law aims outweighs the private good), then, surprisingly, Raz's theory effectively yields all the same practical conclusions as the sort of theory he wishes to reject does. The force and novelty (and significance) of Raz's theory is greatly diminished if it effectively yields the same results as a theory in which the law is authoritative beyond the reasons in the particular case.

Finnis's argument is that one of the "features which are characteristic of 'the law'" is that "the law presents itself as a seamless web by forbidding its subjects to pick and choose."[94] There are instrumental reasons for this uniformity of obligation, such as a prudent distrust of individuals' ability to exercise sound judgment in determining when they ought to exempt themselves from the law and when not. It is a maxim as old as law itself that people are notoriously bad judges in their own cases. But there are deeper, intrinsic reasons why the law cannot be obeyed piecemeal, in principle. The very nature of law itself entails a systematic substitution of public judgment for private judgment and thereby excludes the possibility of individuals judging themselves to be outside the law's authority in particular circumstances. That is to say, the very meaning of being *law abiding* is following each applicable law, where each law is part of "a set coherently applicable to all situations and which exclude all unregulated or private picking and choosing amongst the members of the set."[95] Without this, it is hard to give meaning to the phrase "law abiding." One who determines on a case-by-case basis which laws are authoritative, meaning which are justified and generate a prima facie obligation to obey, cannot be said, in a true sense, to be law abiding. In Finnis's words, "Your allegiance to the whole set is put on the line: either you obey a *particular* law, or you reveal yourself (to yourself, if not to others) as lacking or defective in allegiance to the *whole*, as well as to the particular."[96] On this view, an individual who judges himself in some cases to be outside of the authority of the law, by definition, denies the authority of law just as such. Only with that sort of authority can the law do its coordinating work. If undetectable breaches are permitted, then the law cannot claim the authority necessary for securing coordination.

Raz, it is clear, has an entirely different conception of law. Because for Raz the authority of law depends entirely on reasons—that is, on the law's conformity with the reasons one already has independently for action—justification depends upon a case-by-case analysis. In his view, when the reasons for a particular law do not apply in a particular case, there is no obligation to obey.[97] The preemption of private judgment by public judgment depends entirely on one's assessment of the reasons that apply to oneself in that case (subject to limitations, but those only amount to rules of thumb, not obligations). In Raz's terminology, despite what he says, the law never really amounts to a second-order (exclusionary) reason to obey the law, or never offers a content-independent obligation to obey. Therefore, per his examples, if a pharmacist knows better than the drug regulators or if a potential polluter knows that everyone else is violating the environmental regulations, then there is no obligation to obey—the law has no authority in that case—because the reasons for the law do not apply to that individual in that situation.[98] Similarly, in any case where no one will know and there will be no harm done, such as our mythical traffic light, there is no obligation to obey. That is, when the reasons for the law do not apply, there is no obligation to obey.

Much of the disagreement between Raz and Finnis boils down to differing views of the purpose of law and particularly its role in coordination. Finnis sees a role for law in promoting the common good in "the need for individuals to be able to make reliable arrangements with each other for the determinate and lasting but flexible solution of coordination problems and, more generally, for the realizing of goods of individual self-constitution and of community."[99] Yet Raz wants to insist that those goods can be realized by obeying or by disobeying the law, depending on the circumstances. If the basis for disregarding the law is rooted not in a separate, countervailing reason (as with civil disobedience) but in the inapplicability of the law to that individual in that case, then it must mean that, for Raz, the law does not supply even a prima facie obligation to obey. So when Finnis writes that "the existence of the legal order creates a shared interest which gives everyone moral reason to collaborate with the law's coordination solutions, i.e., moral reason to regard the law as (morally) authoritative," Raz responds that that is true only *sometimes*.[100] Raz is prepared to view the law as authoritative only when the coordination solutions in fact advance the reasons that already apply to that person in that case, which is highly contingent. But, for Raz, the fact of a shared legal order itself does not have any purchase when the underlying reasons are not determinative. If Raz concedes that an overarching legal order necessarily entails a shared interest that gives everyone a moral reason to comply (that is, if law-abidingness is its own reason for action), then his position collapses into Finnis's position because all directives that are part of a broader scheme necessarily entail a prima facie obligation to obey.

Finnis maintains that there is reason to obey the law in general even when the reason for a particular law is absent, meaning that he sees a prima facie obligation to obey all particular laws as part of the institution of law. Finnis draws an analogy between obeying the law and keeping a promise, which he argues, contra Hume, there is an obligation to do even when no one else will know.[101] Promise-breaking is impermissible even in such situations because "the practice of promising gains much of its value, as a contribution to the common good, precisely from the fact that the obligations it involves hold good even when breach seems likely to be undetectable."[102] The implicit trust between the promisor and promisee is far weaker if the institution of promise-making does not entail an obligation to keep the promise even when failure to do so will go undetected. The mutual trust fostered by this practice is itself part of the common good rather than merely a means to other ends, so its absence damages the common good.[103] (Moreover, the good of the promisee is part of the common good itself because respect for that person, like respect for all persons, is "one of the conditions for the well-being of each and all in community."[104])

Raz, however, likely holds that there is no obligation to keep the promise if the promisee will never know because, in effect, the reasons for the promise no longer apply. If so, according to Raz, there is no obligation to keep promises just as such, only an obligation to act for the reasons that motivate the promise in the first place, where they still apply. It emerges, concomitantly, that Raz has a much narrower view of the common good. Presumably Raz does not deny that the common good figures into one's reasons for action in general. If he admits this, though, he has to deny that the common good includes these kinds of considerations, such as the importance of promise-keeping even when no one will know; otherwise, he has to accept the obligation to keep promises even in such circumstances and, *mutatis mutandis*, the obligation to obey the law even when there are no negative consequences. Instead, Raz must take a "what she doesn't know can't hurt her" approach, under which undetected breaches do not impair the common good.

To defend Raz, we can offer that the institution of promises can be damaged only if people know about the breaches and thereby learn that they cannot trust each other. By definition, the distrust can be established only by detectable breaches, so undetectable breaches are not a problem. At the same time, if the permissibility of undetectable breaches is normative, then it is probable that mere knowledge of the norm permitting undetectable breaches undermines the trust at the center of promise-making and therefore harms the common good. But this does not clinch the argument against Raz, who, with his more circumscribed view of the common good, can respond that people do not care about promises that are broken when no one will know because if the breach is undetectable, then they are presumably not affected by the breach. In that case, the permissibility of undetectable breaches need not necessarily undermine the institution of promise-making as a whole because there can still be a strong norm against breaking promises with detectable consequences for others. That is, if the obligation to keep promises rests solely on the reasons for the promise in the first place (and not also on the sheer fact that a person promises), then people can feel free to break promises undetectably, knowing that the undetectability effectively renders the promise void, but they also likewise know that people can generally be trusted in all cases where detection is possible, which are the only cases they care about. The upshot is that there is no faith in the institution of promise-making just as such, only in promises that people have other reasons to keep.

The understanding of promises that prohibits undetectable breaches applies to law as well. Like a promise, if the law binds on a case-by-case basis depending on the content of the law, then the law does not serve as a second-order reason, and the law's authority is not content independent. That is, there is no (authority and) obligation in the legal system per se, much as there is no obligation to obey promises just as such. On a better understanding of law and promises, the prima facie obligation attaches independent of the underlying reasons or content. Finnis explains why the alternative view must be flawed: "Part of the law's point is to maintain real (not merely apparent) fairness between the members of a community; and this aspect of law's point is unaffected by the detection or covertness of breaches of law. The institution of law gains much of its value, as a contribution to the common good, precisely from the fact that the obligations it imposes hold good even when breach seems likely to be undetectable."[105] Similarly, the "common good ... can be realized with reasonable impartiality *only* if the individual performs on his promise; and this necessity *is* the obligation of his promise."[106] Thus, with respect to both promises and the law, their very nature (as in, the point of their existence) must entail an obligation to fulfill their terms. The value that law or promising possesses as an institution, and especially its value to the common good, lies in the fact that it necessarily entails an obligation. Therefore, even though the obligation is not absolute, in cases of undetectable breaches, "Raz's claim that in those situations the law gives 'no reason' for doing what it commands, i.e., has *no* moral authority at all, seems extravagant."[107] Reprising the point but with further explanation, Finnis adds, "The reason (I suggested) for taking the law seriously to the full extent of its tenor and intended reach—*and never regarding it as giving* no *reason for doing what it commands*—is a reason connected with that irreducible multiformity of human goods (and that plurality of human persons) which imposes intrinsic limitation on human practical reasoning and makes nonsense (and injustice) of totalitarian projects."[108] As Finnis says, if there is an obligation to obey the law just because it is the law, then one can never see the law as providing *no* reason to obey, even when the underlying reasons do not apply; there is still the fact that it is the law. Once again, neither laws nor promises impose an absolute obligation; the obligations can always be outweighed by other factors. Finnis acknowledges that "in some circumstances an individual can serve fairness or other aspects of the common good better by breach than by conformity."[109] As an initial matter, though, keeping a promise or obeying the law is obligatory just as such.[110]

I focus on the disagreement between Finnis and Raz because it points us to something fundamental about the nature of law, namely how it is directed to the common good and not just the individual good. In order for Raz to reject Finnis's claims, Raz must deny that law has meaning beyond its role in advancing particular purposes in particular situations. As I demonstrate, for Raz, the law has no authority over an individual if it does not serve the reasons that person has for action (or better serve those reasons than he might on his own). In theory, promotion of the common good can be among those reasons for action. But, as before, reading that point into Raz means that there is always a reason (in the form of a prima facie obligation) to obey the law, which Raz denies. That sort of interpretation of the reasons that generally apply to a person brings Raz too close to Finnis's position and mostly vitiates the disagreement. This puts Raz in a very difficult position because surely Raz does not wish to deny that acting for the common good is ever a reason for action. Thus, instead, he must deny that acting for the common good entails an obligation to obey the law just because it is the law. In other words, he must claim that the law's value is relatively narrowly limited to advancing the more particular purposes of individuals (or groups), stemming from the law's potential to contribute expertise or efficiency to the furtherance of one's own purposes. In this light, we might interpret Raz to be saying that there is no such thing as "Law," just laws. That is, there is nothing about law that makes it special as a whole or even makes it a whole at all; instead, there are particular directives that are either rationally justifiable or not. In contrast, Finnis understands law itself to entail obligation because it is the obligation to obey that enables the law's contribution to the common good. In this respect, all directives bind precisely in respect of being "law," or being part of the whole known as "the law."[111]

The existence of prima facie obligation to obey matters more than its extent

If the prima facie obligation to obey the law depends upon the legal system's orientation to the common good, then one obvious question is how we know when a legal system is oriented to the common good. A challenge here is that the question of whether there is a prima facie obligation to obey the law is binary—either there is or is not. In contrast, it is easy to imagine that legal systems exist on a spectrum with respect to the degree to which they are oriented toward the common good. If so, perhaps the best approach here is to think in terms of focal and peripheral cases. The focal cases are the ones where a system is clearly sufficiently oriented to the common good or clearly not. In those cases there is little doubt as to whether the term "legal system" is appropriate. The peripheral cases constitute a gray area in which it can be difficult to tell, but this does not thereby detract from the main point. That is, the presence of some hard cases does not negate the existence of many easy ones. This allows us to classify candidates into the categories of "legal system" and "not a legal system" while acknowledging variation in justness on both sides of the (blurry) line.

Along these lines, it is possible to suggest that different degrees of orientation to the common good (among all legal systems that qualify as just) yield a prima facie obligation to obey of varying weights. But the precise details are tangential to my argument because the necessary claim is only that there is *some* prima facie obligation to obey, whether stronger or weaker. The nub of my argument is in rejecting the views, like Raz's, that suggest, in intent or in effect, that there is no prima facie obligation to obey the law. The fact that competing moral obligations can come up against prima facie obligations of varying weights is, for our purposes, beside the point.

Another reason we can leave this complication to the side is that the possibility of prima facie obligations of varying weights leaves my concept of law in no worse shape than any other theory does. A line-drawing (or other categorizing) problem exists whether we are looking at complete legal systems or individual laws. Deciding whether, on the balance of reasons, an individual law is to be obeyed is no less indeterminate than judging whether a system is sufficiently oriented to the common good to trigger an obligation to obey. So my theory does not introduce a further difficulty; it just moves the question of justification from the level of the individual law to the level of the legal system.[112] Plainly, my theory does add an additional layer of analysis because we must ask whether the legal system is oriented to the common good before we ask whether the balance of reasons (which includes the prima facie obligation to obey the law) speaks in favor of or against obeying. But this comes with the benefit of succeeding in the search for a coherent theory of law's authority. If a law has no force apart from an independent assessment of its merits irrespective of the source (meaning without treating the source as authoritative just as such), then there is no real authority of which to speak. This is exactly how Raz can arrive at the conclusion that individuals can disobey the law when they believe they know better than the officials or believe that their disobedience will have no effect.

Regardless of the exact extent of the prima facie obligation to obey, we can say that justified authority entails a prima facie obligation to obey in part because it provides reasons for action, specifically with respect to the advancement of the common good. In Finnis's words, law gives "all those citizens who are willing to advance the common good precise directions about what they *must* do *if* they are to follow the way authoritatively chosen as the common way to that good (it being taken for granted that having a defined and commonly adhered-to 'common way' is, presumptively, a peculiarly good way of advancing the common good)."[113] Clearly it is not authority that defines or creates the common good; the common good and some possibilities for its instantiation exist independent of authority. That is to say, the common good already gives reasons for action without authority because each individual has a reason to advance the common good whether or not there is a legal obligation involved. But authority creates unique possibilities for its advancement—unique because those possibilities are impossible, or absent, without authority. The existence of authority makes coordination possible, and, in cases where some forms of coordination were already possible, authority makes coordination much more likely and can very well open up new ways of coordination that are not otherwise available. Moreover, this opening up of new means can also result in the possibility of attaining ends that are not otherwise attainable. Therefore, authority creates reasons for action with respect to the common good, which are then reasons to obey authority. Critically, it is the obligation to obey that makes authority salient in this way. A nonauthoritative coordinating agent can offer various suggestions for advancing the common good, but authority, in virtue of the obligation to obey, opens up still new possibilities, and those are realizable only if the authority is authoritative. While more needs to be said about coordination, the key point here is that Finnis and Raz disagree about the existence of a prima facie obligation to obey because they disagree about the role of authority.

COMMON GOOD

The justified authority of the legal system stands or falls as a whole

How can we make the argument for a content-independent obligation to obey human authority? What is the justification for obeying the law just as such rather than taking individual laws on a case-by-case basis? Although religious obligation is instructive as a partial model, clearly the analogy between divine and human authority has its limits. Furthermore, there must be some value to law's authority that goes beyond the benefits of sound advice or rules of thumb that provide shortcuts in decision-making. Otherwise, as in my critique of Raz, obeying the law remains permissible or even prudent but not obligatory.[114] That is, we need a normative component in addition to the descriptive one (command) to provide justification and, as such, to generate the obligation to obey. This is why the concept of law must refer not simply to a set of commands but to a set of commands oriented to the common good.[115]

Here, our task is to explore that latter part, the orientation to the common good, and suggest how the law's unique relationship to the common good underwrites its authority. Specifically, to prove there is not merely good reason but actually an obligation to obey the law, we must show how authority is not just helpful for advancing the common good but necessary. This follows the argument of Elizabeth Anscombe that authority is necessary for the essential benefits it brings and that it is obligatory because it is necessary. Without the obedience that comes from obligation, authority is not able to achieve its necessary ends.[116]

The paradoxical challenge for a satisfactory concept of law is to explain how it is true *both* that the obligation to obey attaches to law just as such (content independence) *and* that the status of law as authoritative depends on meeting underlying normative criteria (content dependence). On one hand, rooting law's authority in normative criteria suggests that, when the normative criteria are not met, the law is not justified, in which case the obligation to obey is content dependent. This is how we can speak of law as either justified or unjustified—and, if unjustified, not really law. On the other hand, positing a content-independent obligation to obey the law, as in the prima facie obligation to obey, which by definition inheres in all law, suggests that the law is authoritative without reference to those normative criteria, or else it is a mistake to call it content independent. Critically, this content independence is necessary if we are to speak of real authority—that is, if the fact of something being commanded is to make a practical difference in one's reasons. At the same time, this seems to fly in the face of the normative requirement for justification. Moreover, although there must be content independence to have real authority, maybe we are chasing a phantom. That is, maybe real authority as I define it does not exist, just individual directives that must be weighed individually.

The solution for this conflict between normativity and content independence lies, for starters, in my claim that a legal system is justified (or not) as a whole. If the system as a whole is justified—and, therefore, rightly called a legal system—then there is a (prima facie) content-independent obligation to obey its individual directives. That is, the initial assessment of justification does not apply to individual laws but to "the law." The authority of the legal system as a whole is content dependent; its justification depends on its orientation to the common good. Accordingly, it can be true *both* that all the individual laws of a legal system carry a prima facie obligation to obey regardless of their content *and* that the legal system as a whole is justified—that is, counts as law with the accompanying moral force—only when it fulfills the normative criterion, namely an orientation to the common good. As Simon writes, "*The most essential function of authority is the issuance and carrying out of rules expressing the requirements of the common good considered materially.*"[117]

Obviously, the justification of the authority of the legal system as a whole cannot itself be content independent. Otherwise, we have authority without justification—in other words, raw power. Instead, the authority of the legal system is justified by its content and, specifically, its orientation to the common good. In turn, the goodness (or "justness") of the legal system as a whole entails a prima facie obligation to obey each of its particulars, as opposed to the obligation attaching to good laws individually. As I say, without the prima facie obligation to obey the law, there is no authority of law, meaning we do not really have law at all. But this only shows that, if there is to be law in this sense, then there must be the relevant obligation to obey. But perhaps there is no obligation and, therefore, no law with genuine authority. The fact that we must have a prima facie obligation in order to have authority does not logically require that we have either. Perhaps both are absent together. So, to defend the existence of law in the meaningful sense, we must show that there is a basis for this sort of system-wide justification and obligation. In other words, in addition to showing why the prima facie obligation to obey is definitional to the authority of law, I also need to show why there *is* a prima facie obligation to obey.

To do this, we need to explore the purpose of law and the good of authority. On one hand, if authority in the form of law is good, then we can understand why there is a prima facie obligation to obey, which is a requisite of such authority. Without the obligation to obey, we cannot reap the benefits of authority. On the other hand, perhaps true authority is unnecessary or even unjust in a world where people are to be guided by the light of their own reason. At least for Raz, this is a straightforward way out. To be sure, Raz is not making that point. The flaw in his work is not that he wishes to abandon authority and obligation altogether but that he undercuts them without realizing the extent of his argument. Even so, if authority is at times salutary but never necessary, then Raz's position has some merit. Raz does not deny that there are sometimes reasons to obey the law, only that there is no obligation to obey the law just as such. But if authority is necessary and good, then descriptive theories like Hart's and normative theories like Raz's fall short because, in their different ways, they deprive the law of true authority.

Despite John Rawls's view finally being different from my own, his prominent work on political legitimacy supports the key themes of justification being rooted in an orientation to the common good and of justification standing or falling for the system as a whole. In the *Law of Peoples*, Rawls tries to work out what it means for a regime to be morally good, or at least acceptably so, and this carries the implication that the authority of such a regime is justified. For our purposes, one important contribution of Rawls in this regard is that he recognizes that the assessment of justification of law, and therefore of law's (or laws') obligatoriness, takes place on the system-wide level. Rawls argues in *A Theory of Justice*, "The injustice of a law is not, in general, a sufficient reason for not adhering to it."[118] This is because Rawls recognizes that if the authority is justified, then its authoritativeness extends, prima facie, to all of its directives. As Rawls puts it, "When the basic structure of society is reasonably just, as estimated by what the current state of things allows, we are to recognize unjust laws as binding provided that they do not exceed certain limits of injustice."[119] To hold otherwise is to make it not a matter of the justification of the regime but, like for Raz, only a question of the coincidence of individual laws with other obligations that one has to do what the law also requires—that is, obligations rooted in reasons other than the say-so of the regime.

In criticizing Rawls, Simmons does not see that for authority to be justified it must be judged as a whole (say, the legal system as opposed to individual laws), which in turn enables us to explain the content-independent obligation to obey, a definitional feature of authority. Simmons asks, "Why does Rawls only disqualify *unjust* schemes, rather than all schemes which promote or aim at *immoral* ends?"[120] The reason is that the justification of the authority depends on an evaluation of the scheme as a whole. A legal system can promote some immoral ends yet, on balance, still be just. If, in contrast, the obligation to obey depends on a case-by-case analysis of the underlying reasons for acting in each case, then there is not any authority in the true sense because then everything depends on the balance of reasons that already apply to the subject.

Both Finnis and Simon show how authority and obedience can be reasonable and necessary. That is, both make a case for authority that is much stronger than Raz's and others'.[121] Simon notes that "some theorists would maintain that fear and self-interest account sufficiently for the fact of obedience in civil society," but, he adds, "any human experience, any knowledge of history, evidences the shallowness of this explanation."[122] Though Hart gets law wrong, he, too, grasps that there is much more to obedience than fear and self-interest: subjects are "obligated" and not merely "obliged" to obey the law. Of course, our task is not to show what accounts for people's actual obedience (a sense of obligation or a sense of fear) but to show that they have an obligation—regardless of whether and why they obey, if they do. Yet Hart puts us on the road to the conclusion that people do have an obligation when he insists that that is how people understand their relationship to the law, as one of being obligated.

The obligation to obey the law contributes to the upholding of just legal systems

The main normative claim embedded in the concept of law is that authority in the form of law is necessary in order to attain certain ends, or, put better, the very purpose of law is the attainment of those ends. Symmetrically, it is true both that authority is required if the law is to achieve its aims and that without adherence to those aims the law does not serve its purpose and is unjustified. That is, if the law is not, on the whole, oriented to those ends, then it is not authoritative because it is not justified, and so it is not law. Such an understanding of law makes possible a distinction between government and gangs that goes beyond questions of the scope of authority or the complexity of the rules and so forth and, instead, speaks directly to the question of justice.[123] Furthermore, this understanding shows how law's authority can be content independent in that justified authority attaches to the legal system as a whole despite problems within individual laws because of the way in which law as a whole aims at an overarching purpose that is not reducible to the ends of each individual law.

The law's architectonic purpose (its aim—though not in the sense of a goal that can be completed) is the promotion of the common good. Holding the correct conception of authority begins with seeing that the advancement of the common good provides a reason for action. This is because acting reasonably includes a requirement of (qualified) impartiality between one's own good and others, which means that each individual must care for the good of others and so the common good. As Finnis has it, "Every man has reason to value the common good—the well-being alike of himself and of his partners and potential partners in community, and the ensemble of conditions and ways of effecting that well-being—whether out of friendship as such, or out of an impartial recognition that human goods are as much realized by the participation in them of other persons as by his own."[124] Because authority plays an important role in advancing the good of its subjects, a demand for impartiality between one's own good and others' amounts to a claim that obedience to the law is reasonable because the law provides the framework for balancing among the competing goods of different people. But for obedience to be a definitional feature of law, we have to say that it is not just reasonable, which leaves room for it to be optional (in the form of voluntary compliance), but also necessary. With that in mind, we can join Finnis in arguing that law "represents to the subject an intelligible determinate pattern of action, which, having been chosen by the lawgiver to be obligatory, can actually *be* obligatory in the eyes of a reasonable subject because the ruler's *imperium* can (for the sake of the common good) be reasonably treated by the subject as if it were his own *imperium*."[125] This is true authority because the lawgiver's directives are treated as authoritative just as such, on the critical assumption that the directives are generally oriented to the common good. As I explain, the law cannot fulfill this function unless the directives are obligatory. It works only if it is obligatory, which is to say, the good can be instantiated only if the scheme is nonoptional.

In contrast, undermining the law evinces, generally, a lack of respect for the common good, which the law secures, and a deterioration or absence of law harms the common good because it harms the law's ability to secure it. Therefore, the goodness of the legal system as a whole, when it is good, gives us a (prima facie) reason to obey each law even when not each law is good. Upholding the system is part of enabling it to function. This is obvious in the plain sense that the more the system's directives are observed, the better it can function. Breaking the rules can cause the law's schemes to fail. Moreover, even when one believes there is good reason in a particular case to disobey, that can lead to the eroding of one's own or other's respect for the law, if such disrespect proves to be a consequence of one's disobedience. In this way, the law's relationship to the common good explains how the law can function as a second-order reason, excluding the consideration of other reasons for action, while also drawing its normativity from the first-order reason of promoting the common good. Although there is no specific directive that instructs people to contribute to the common good, the promotion of the common good serves to tie all the law together. The architectonic role of the common good in ordering the law turns the law's authority into a second-order reason, so the reasons to uphold the common good preempt the reasons against obeying individual laws, at least prima facie. Put simply, obeying the law upholds the system, which we have a prima facie obligation to do when the system is just. Once again, this depends on the law, as a whole, being oriented to the common good. If it is, the first reason for obedience does not depend on the reasons for particular laws but, instead, is rooted in something about law itself. If the system as a whole is just, then we can make sense of obedience to it because of the importance of upholding a just system, which manifestly cannot work if compliance is discretionary.

Importantly, while we can easily see the good in upholding a just system (contrasted with the deterioration or collapse of that system), we can also rule out that reason for obeying the law as a position that Raz can adopt to defend his own view. Raz is clear that there is no prima facie obligation to obey the law, so he cannot hold that the prima facie obligation to obey the law in order to uphold a just system is a reason that already applies to individuals, for, if he does, then there is an obligation to obey the law qua law. But that runs contrary to his conclusions. Because he does not hold the latter, he cannot hold the former. Moreover, if he does hold that, then he lacks any basis for his criticism of the prima facie obligation to obey the law because he effectively asserts it himself, and then, for all practical purposes, his position has the unenviable quality of completely overlapping with the view he is rejecting.

The necessity of law's authority is rooted in its ability to secure coordination

Of course, the role that a prima facie obligation plays in upholding the legal system already assumes a duty to uphold it. There must be some account of the legal system's initial justification—that is, an account of what law contributes to the common good that makes the system worth upholding in the first place. One main way law aids uniquely in advancing the common good is through coordination. For law to secure coordination (as part of promoting the common good), there must be a prima facie obligation to obey even when a person judges that the reasons behind the law do not apply. This is true in part because people are, as the dictum goes, poor judges in their own case. Even if Raz is right that authority is not justified when the directives do not coincide with the reasons that already apply to the subject, people can be expected to exercise bad judgment about when the appropriate conditions for disobedience obtain (i.e., when the reasons behind the law do not apply). One of the points of disagreement between Raz and Finnis that I explore is the case of undetectable breaches. One simple point about that example is that people cannot be trusted to discern well when no one will know about and no one will be harmed by disobedience to the law. Or, put more charitably, the possibility for honest mistakes (much less, consciously self-interested bias) is too high to adopt Raz's position—letting people judge for themselves as an initial matter—as a rule.

But, by extension, the bigger reason why Raz must be wrong in his main claim (of the lack of authority when the law's reasons do not apply) is that, without a prima facie obligation, the law cannot secure its aims owing to the ever-present possibility of reasonable disagreement about whether the reasons in fact apply. With unanimity usually impossible, authority is needed to secure coordination. Undoubtedly, reasonable people of good will can disagree in matters of judgment without anyone being guilty of bias. Finnis and Simon make the case for authority by framing the question in terms of whether authority is necessary in a society comprising entirely virtuous and intelligent members. They argue that authority is necessary even here, precisely because there is room for disagreement in matters of judgment. If a perfect society does not require authority, then law in practice—in our real world—comes down to enforcing what everyone already ought to be doing, in which case authority is necessary only insofar as people do not, for whatever reason, conform to obligations they already have. On that view, authority does not create new reasons; it just enforces the ones that already apply. But we must go further than this in recognition of the fact that authority can and does create new reasons for action, which are reasons that do not already apply to the subjects yet support good and necessary ends. The law *does* create reasons for action that do not exist before the law's say-so. For

Finnis and Simon, this is necessary in order to promote the common good regardless of the virtue or intelligence of the subjects.

Authority is necessary, at least in part, because it provides for coordinated action absent spontaneous unanimity. An obligation to obey is required for the success of authority because it ensures unity of action. Simon explains, "The unity of action which is supposed to be required by the pursuit of the common good will be ceaselessly jeopardized unless all members of the community agree to follow one prudential decision and only one—which is to submit themselves to some authority."[126] Unanimity can suffice in lieu of authority, but, plainly, unanimity does not arise in a community of any reasonable size. Any community with a "complex common good" and an "intelligent and interested membership" instead requires authority.[127] Indeed, "the greater the intelligence and skill of a group's members, and the greater their commitment and dedication to common purposes and common good, the *more* authority and regulation may be required, to enable that group to achieve its common purpose, common good."[128]

There are two basic reasons for this. First, people, in a manner neither vicious nor impious, pursue individual or local goods that are at odds with the common good. Second, because the good is so variegated, people, in good faith and without error, disagree about the best way to pursue the common good. With regard to the latter, the key point is that choosing among different paths requires a decision based in judgment. There is not a single correct solution in every case given the incommensurability of the tradeoffs. Therefore, in order for a decision to be made and action to be taken in the face of this multiplicity of choices (and, relatedly, to solve coordination problems), there must be authority.[129]

Accordingly, authority supports the common good in at least two ways, regulating the relationship between private goods and the common good and coordinating the disparate parts of the common good. In Simon's words, "The proposition that authority is necessary to the intention of the common good has a double meaning. It means, first, that authority is necessary in order for private persons to be directed toward the common good; it means, second, that authority is necessary in order for functional processes, each of which regards some aspect of the common good, to be directed toward the whole of the common good."[130] Thus, Simon, like Finnis, rejects what he calls the deficiency theory of government, that government is necessary only because people are selfish or stupid. On the contrary, "A society enjoying a supremely high degree of enlightenment would, all other things being equal, enjoy much more choice than ignorant societies and have to choose among many more possibilities," Simon writes, and, therefore, "it would need authority, *more than ever*, to procure united action, for, thanks to better lights, the plurality of genuine means would have increased considerably."[131] Simon is very clear that the need is fundamental, not incidental, because "authority has essential functions, i.e., functions determined not by any deficiency but by the nature of community."[132] Thus, authority is fundamental and does not arise from a negative feature of human nature: "Authority is neither a necessary evil nor the consequence of any evil, nor a lesser good, nor the consequence of some lesser good, but an *absolutely good* thing founded upon the metaphysical goodness of nature."[133] Because a "plurality of genuine means can be caused by excellence of knowledge and power," a "society made exclusively of clever and virtuous persons" needs authority, and, therefore, "authority is not devoid of essential function," especially "assur[ing] the unity of action of a united multitude."[134]

Simon firmly rejects the "rationalist" model that characterizes Raz's theory of authority. For Simon, authority is not ultimately "substitutional."[135] Skeptical of the "rationalistic enthusiasm for the possibilities of social science," Simon insists that the "indetermination of the means" is not merely "an appearance due to our inability to identify the appropriate means."[136] Simon thus rejects the idea that authority "substitutes for a determinate knowledge of a situation," as though, if we know more, then authority is not necessary.[137] It is, instead, "essential."[138] Here, Simon is arguing against those who believe that "thanks to social science, a rational society would be installed, in which the reign of reason would be the realization of anarchy" and, therefore, that "the progress of social sciences is, in fact, meant to enable us to do away, step by step, with authority."[139] In contrast, and in line with Finnis, Simon's own position is that "if the development of social sciences ever reaches a state of perfect achievement, authority will remain necessary then, just as it is now, as a social prudence, able to maintain the unity of society in its common action."[140]

We can further appreciate this aspect of the law's role in coordination (and the necessity of a better view of justification than Raz offers) through a likely dispute between Finnis and Raz. We can bring out their disagreement over law's role in coordination and the obligation to obey through my imagined case of the mythical traffic light — that is, the hypothetical example of the driver who arrives at a red light in the middle of the night in the middle of nowhere with a clear view in every direction and no one in sight for miles. This thought experiment is useful because it isolates the question of whether the driver must stop at the red light just because the law says so. Let us, for the moment, hold aside other considerations, such as whether running the light increases the driver's chances of running lights in less safe situations by accustoming her to exercising her own judgment rather than deferring to the traffic signal or whether the prioritizing of private judgment erodes her respect for the law in other areas altogether. Instead, we can focus on the main point of the example: the question of what is to be done when the normal reasons for stopping at the light do not apply and the only reason for stopping is that the law says so. We expect Finnis to say the driver must stop; we expect Raz to say she need not stop. Raz, though accepting some role for law in coordination, thinks that there is no reason to obey when the purposes of the coordination scheme do not obtain. Put simply, when there is no one around, none of the reasons for having the traffic light in the first place are present, and there is no obligation to stop. The law does not coincide with the reasons that apply to the subject, anyway. Finnis disagrees with Raz's conclusion, arguing that the very nature of law excludes such "private" or "individual" exceptions. Even so, Raz can argue right back that if law gains its authority from its coordinative function, then, in a case like this, where there is no coordinating to be done, there is no authority.[141]

Another hypothetical example, the case of a law passed against polluting a river, which Finnis and Raz debate in this context, addresses the issue of subjects deciding that the law's reasons do not apply. As Finnis acknowledges, "Raz accepts that a principal function of law is to secure morally desirable co-ordination" and that "law can be instrumental in securing desirable sorts of co-ordination."[142] Nevertheless, there remains a major divide between them. For Raz, a law against pollution creates an obligation to obey only when there is already a social practice of not polluting because the social practice (rather than the law) creates reasons not to pollute. (If everyone else is polluting, there is no reason apart from the law's say-so to comply whereas if the social practice to not pollute exists, then the choice to pollute or not can make a difference for the river.) But that is to say that the obligation to act a certain way arises not from the law but from other reasons that already apply to the person, which in the case of a coordination problem happen to obtain when others are participating in the same cooperative scheme. Finnis puts Raz's position this way: "But even when the law is thus instrumental in securing schemes of co-ordination with which everyone has moral reason to collaborate, it lacks moral authority. For the morally relevant reasons for complying with the scheme of co-ordination derive, he says, entirely from the practice of co-ordination, and not at all from the law; the moral situation is the same whether the practice exists by virtue of legal sanctions, government exhortations, pressure-group propaganda, or spontaneously emergent custom."[143] This is consistent, of course, with Raz's claim that there is no prima facie obligation to obey the law: the question of compliance depends entirely on reasons apart from the fact that the law says so. If that is the case, then it is inaccurate to speak of an obligation to obey the law (or obedience to it), which is why Raz has no conception of real authority in the law. The fact that it is the law makes no difference. It matters only, as Finnis says, whether the underlying reasons apply.

From this same scenario, a familiar problem for Raz emerges, providing us with yet more evidence that a better concept of law is required to justify its authority. Given what Finnis terms "the diversity of views about social 'problems,'" people can very reasonably disagree about whether the reasons behind any cooperative scheme do in fact apply.[144] With respect to the pollution example, "Some people think pollution no problem, some think it a lesser evil than the expense of avoiding it; some envisage one scheme for overcoming it, and others imagine different and incompatible schemes."[145] If the law itself is not a reason to obey, someone who doubts or denies the benefits of the chosen coordination scheme (or of any) has no obligation to obey on Raz's view. According to Raz, when the law requires what a person, on the balance of reasons, ought to do, anyway (i.e., what the person already has reasons to do without the law), then the authority is justified, and there is an obligation to obey. "But a *law* against pollution does, [Raz] contends, create a sufficient moral reason for even these dissenters to comply; that is to say, the law is (morally as well as legally) authoritative. But why?"[146] Despite Raz's modest concessions about the authority of law, by his logic, it is not only that one can pollute if everyone else does but also that one can pollute if one has a different view of pollution and its solutions (even if we allow only a limited range of reasonable views). Thus, because law's authority depends on the individual's judgment that the reasons in favor of complying outweigh the reasons against, Raz's model of law cannot necessarily even solve coordination problems. More precisely, it is the individual's compliance, not the law's authority, that depends on the individual's judgment because, for this very reason, there is no authority of which to speak. Another observer of the same situation can believe that the individual in question has the balance of reasons wrong due to the strong reasons for compliance created by the law's coordination of others' activity, but there still is no authority because it entirely depends on whether the individual happens to agree. To emphasize, this is not an accusation that Raz's theory underwrites willy-nilly disregard for coordination schemes. Rather, the problem exists in principle because it is possible for people acting entirely reasonably, even perfectly intelligent and virtuous people, to disagree in such matters of judgment.

Simon also recognizes the importance of law's coordinative function, relating it to law's function in promoting unity of purpose and of will. As Simon puts it, "Realizing that movement in any clear direction is better than unending idleness, we let authority decide which way we shall take, and we admire its ability to substitute definite action for endless deliberation."[147] Simon's observation echoes Schmitt's critique of deliberation in favor of "decisionism," but it is also aimed at Marx and others who believe that the perfection of the social sciences, when it arrives, obviates the need for authority.[148] For Simon, like for Finnis, authority is necessary in society, which is important for the argument that authority is truly good and not just a necessary evil and, accordingly, for the argument that authority can obligate.

This is true for coordination on very particular tasks as well as for more general, exalted ends: "The more effectively a society be united in its common action, the more perfect, happy, and free this society will be."[149] Authority, for Simon, necessarily plays a significant role in such unity. Moreover, authority is not just necessary in the bare sense of being essential for a common project to resolve a lack of unanimity. Even in the absence of an obligation to obey authority, one can at least imagine a cynical motive for securing coordination, where a dissenter complies "to spare himself and others the inconveniences following upon the breaking of the law."[150] But such an approach has its consequences. Although "outward anarchy and the violent disruption of society are avoided" and "external order is not delivered up to the fortuitousness of unanimity," "the inner dispositions of minds and hearts toward the law are subjected to such fortuitousness; this weakens dangerously the unity of society and corrupts the character of political life by substituting a law of utility and force for the law of voluntary co-operation whenever I happen not to be in the majority."[151] Simon is imagining two alternatives. In one alternative, authority is justified, and people obey the law because they recognize a moral obligation to do so. In this scenario, they see the law as justified, and they see their compliance as a necessary and warranted contribution to the functioning of a just regime. In the second alternative, people comply in the way Hart sees people complying with the demands of a mugger, just because they think it is better for them, as though to say: "I do nothing wrong if I do not comply, and if I can get away with not complying, all the better." Raz's approach is corrupting in a related way because it depends, at least in principle, on the judgment of the individual in each case. That individual can contemplate the common good, but, when she disagrees, her compliance is the fruit only of utility or force.[152] When cooperation comes just from utility, authority must rely on bare coercion when people disagree with the directives. Under the right understanding of law's authority, coercion is still a last resort in cases of disagreement. But the critical difference is that the coercion is justified because the coercion enforces a moral obligation whereas under other theories it merely imposes the will of those in charge. In other words, we have justice in one case and power in the other.

Only law can support the truly common nature of the common good

Understanding the nature of the common good as truly common helps illuminate the need for law, meaning for authority that is common. There is a tight relationship between the nature of law and the common good because law is the form that authority takes in the polity in the name of advancing the common good. Law is necessitated by the demands of the common good and serves it, and it is justified by filling that role. This raises the question of what constitutes the common good. On one hand, we can be agnostic as to the exact contours of the common good because my theory of law insists that a legal system be oriented to the common good, regardless of what, specifically, the common good is. On the other hand, we must have a general understanding of the term *common good* in order to appreciate its relationship to law. Finnis defines the common good in general as "the factor or set of factors (whether a value, a concrete operational objective, or the conditions for realizing a value or attaining an objective) which, as considerations in someone's practical reasoning, would make sense of or give reason for his collaboration with others and would likewise, from their point of view, give reason for their collaboration with each other and with him."[153] More specifically, as Finnis uses it throughout *Natural Law and Natural Rights*, the common good is "a set of conditions which enables the members of a community to attain for themselves reasonable objectives, or to realize reasonably for themselves the value(s), for the sake of which they have reason to collaborate with each other (positively and/or negatively) in a community."[154] Finnis differentiates this use of "common good" from the separate though related uses in which the good is common by virtue of the basic goods being good for all people and by virtue of "inexhaustible" possibilities for participation by one and all.[155] The different senses of "common good" closely entail one another because the shared goodness of the basic goods for all people means that it is possible to aim for a set of conditions that enables the flourishing of each person despite (and sometimes because of) their variegated participation in the basic goods.[156] In the case of a political community, "which (subject to the principle of subsidiarity) excludes no aspect of individual well-being and is potentially affected by every aspect of every life-plan," advancing the common good requires "securing of a whole ensemble of material and other conditions that tend to favour the realization, by each individual in the community, of his or her personal development."[157]

Finnis's theory can sound somewhat individualistic where the common good is understood as the aggregation of the good of individuals. In one sense, this is the case because basic human goods pertain to the good of persons as such. In another sense, though, it is reasonable to speak of the common good as the good of a community just as such. Finnis alludes to this when he notes the overlap between "common good" and "general welfare" or "public interest."[158]

While Finnis may intend this more collective meaning as well, it is Simon who really emphasizes the general, or public, character of the common good. He calls the "*pseudo-common good*" that which is the "sum of private goods which looks like a common good but is not" because "it lacks of the defining features of the common good, viz., the intelligible aspect by which the common good calls for communion in desire and common action."[159] Continuing, Simon explains, "In order that a good should be common, it does not suffice that it should concern, in some way or other, several persons; it is necessary that it be of such nature as to cause, among those who pursue it and in so far as they pursue it, a common life of desire and action."[160] This is critical to Simon's theory of authority because he argues that "whenever the good interesting several persons or groups causes (or, more precisely, is of such nature as to cause) such common life, it is a genuine common good and renders authority necessary."[161] As for Finnis, this commonness of the good is most vivid for Simon with respect to political life because "the state is the community which is so complete and self-sufficient that its good is not that of a particular subject—individual, family, township, etc.—but, unqualifiedly, the common good of men assembled for the sake of noble life."[162]

This, in turn, points to how authority plays a role in a common good that is truly common. First, there is the multiplicity of means for pursuing the common good, which creates the need for imposed unity of action, whether through unanimity or authority. With regard to the matter of disagreement even among virtuous, intelligent people, we can appreciate another role of authority in resolving conflicts between the good of individuals and the common good. Even if each individual wills and acts for the common good, "functional diversity causes a need for an agency relative to the common good as a whole."[163] But such an agency, namely authority, is necessary (and sensible) only if there is truly a common good that transcends the aggregate private good. This is because "the ground for the constitution of a society is either the attainment of a common good or that of interdependent private goods; in the first case there is need for authority; in the second, contract suffices."[164] In the case of a true common good, there is mere disagreement about how to arrive at it, which requires authority for its resolution.

Second, however, there is the possibility of genuine opposition between the common good and some private good, which, as Simon writes, "Aquinas considers altogether sound and honest."[165] This opposition is an important part of what renders authority necessary: "It is the proper concern of the public person to procure the common good materially understood, which the private person may virtuously oppose."[166] If such virtuous opposition is possible, then authority is further necessary even in a fully virtuous society—not only due to the aforementioned disagreements about the common good itself. Despite the possibility of virtuous opposition to the requirements of the common good, "the primacy of the common good demands that those in charge of particular goods should obey those in charge of the common good," with the result that "formal conformity may well be compatible with material disagreement."[167] For the primacy of the common good to be coherent, then, it must be that the requirement to submit to the common good does not depend on its overlap with any particular individual's good. Simon explains, "This rule of common action may coincide with my own preference, but this is of no significance, for the common rule might just as well be at variance with my liking, and I would be equally bound to follow it out of dedication to the common good, which cannot be attained except through united action."[168] This is why the law must be defined with reference to the common good and not as the expression of some set or combination of private goods that overpower other private goods.

The upshot of Simon's view is that the promotion of the common good requires sacrifice in that "excellent citizens, fully prepared to make all sacrifices required by the common good, should take one more step and, without assuming any new capacity, should will and intend the common good materially considered."[169] As Simon's view makes clear, this requires a view that sees the good located in something more than the individual, namely in communities: "The best way to perceive the ethical character of politics is to realize fully the political character of ethics. Indeed, whenever we achieve any understanding of man's social destiny, whenever we go beyond the cheap illusion that things social and political are merely means to the welfare of individuals, we virtually uphold the proposition that the ultimate accomplishments of prudence, of justice, of fortitude, and of temperance are not found in the individual man, but in the greater good of human communities."[170] Clearly, the law, as the authoritative coordinator, plays an indispensable role in determining the balance between individual and common good and in enforcing it. Accordingly, law is necessary for securing the common good, and its ability to do so clearly lies in its authoritativeness.

Authority and autonomy complement each other when the law is properly oriented

With an appreciation of the relationship between authority and the common good, we can now address how Finnis rebuffs Raz's underlying concern about the opposition between authority and autonomy. Raz's theory of authority is framed as a response to the worries of the philosophical anarchists about how authority can ever be legitimate because of the way it impinges on autonomy. Yet when authority is oriented toward the common good, authority and autonomy are not in opposition but rather serve the same end. Raz can perhaps lean toward agreement with Finnis when Finnis writes that a promise, "like the law, enables past, present, and predictable future to be related in a stable though developing order; enables this order to be effected in complex interpersonal patterns; and brings all this within reach of individual initiative and arrangement, thus enhancing individual autonomy in the very process of increasing individuals' obligations."[171] Raz is presumably enticed by the account of enhanced autonomy yet unable to admit increased obligation. Again, for Raz, the important thing is to show that authority is not in conflict with autonomy; he does not and cannot show that it is obligatory to obey. Finnis, in contrast, must insist that this obligation-increasing feature of the law is part of its very nature as being necessary for its operation and, therefore, that law is characterized by the imposition of obligation. If Finnis is right, then autonomy of this kind cannot be enhanced without real authority— that is, without its obligation-imposing aspect. Raz, at best, finds law to be obligatory only in certain circumstances and certainly not as a necessary element of law qua law.

Simon's theory, too, stands as a rebuttal to Raz and especially his concerns about autonomy. Simon takes a strong position on the relationship between authority and autonomy, arguing not for Raz's conditional compatibility—that is, that authority is justified only if it does not violate autonomy—but for necessary symbiosis. He writes, "Autonomy renders authority necessary and authority renders autonomy possible—this is what we find at the core of the most essential function of government."[172] This is true not least because, absent "an over-all direction toward the common good," "these autonomies would mean the disintegration of society."[173] Instead, for Simon, "The theory of authority as agency wholly concerned with the common good is connected with the excellence of particularity. Insofar as the particularity involved is that of the subject, not that of the function, the theory of authority comprises a vindication of autonomy on all levels."[174]

We can learn much about the benefits of authority not only to the community but to the individual by contrasting Simon's theory of authority with Raz's. Yet, because Simon himself emphasizes the intertwinement of authority and autonomy, it is important first to distinguish him clearly from Raz, lest we worry that Simon's theory is vulnerable to the same charges as Raz's. As we know, Raz tries to show how authority can be compatible with autonomy while Simon emphasizes how authority enables the freedom of the individual, notably in his line suggesting that authority vindicates autonomy. Consequently, we can easily but incorrectly take them to be more similar than they are. But, on closer inspection, it is apparent that Simon's defense of authority does not reduce to Raz's view.

The superficial similarities between them are easy to spot. Raz attempts to resolve the opposition between autonomy and authority by justifying authority when it requires one to do that which one's autonomy dictates, anyway. Autonomy is not violated when the authority's directives and one's separate reasons for acting coincide. Simon sounds similar when he speaks of the interiorization of the law. In a passage akin to what he says about freedom and obedience, Simon distinguishes between initial and terminal liberty. "Initial liberty," he writes, "is the sheer power of choosing, I mean the power of choosing the good and the evil as well."[175] As in the classic distinction between liberty and license, initial liberty, like license, "can be used rightly as well as wrongly" and "has the value of a means rather than that of an end."[176] In contrast, "Terminal liberty," which he calls "the glory of the rational nature," like liberty in the classical understanding, is "a power of choosing the good alone" acquired by "our endeavor to improve our nature by supplementing it with virtues."[177]

This state of using freedom to choose the good parallels the self-mastery that Simon says arises through obedience, so it is no coincidence that, in this context, Simon associates terminal liberty with obedience to the law. There is, presumably, a virtuous cycle whereby the acquisition of virtue and obedience to the law reinforce one another. In the mature stages of this process of personal development, according to Simon, "the virtuous man is no longer subjected to the law, since the law has become interior to him and rules him from within. The prescriptions of the law are truly identical with the dynamism of the virtuous nature. Terminal liberty does not mean only freedom of choice, but also autonomy."[178]

Does this edge too close to Raz's theory? Although authority ultimately produces autonomy through the interiorization of the law, this does not reduce Simon's concept of obligation to a Razian model in which the justification of authority depends on a convergence with the reasons one already has for action. One way to look at Simon's concept of the interiorization of the law is that obeying authority leads to autonomy because, once the law is interiorized, then the reasons *become* one's own. This is dissimilar from Raz because, for Simon, one adopts the law's reasons as one's own through interiorization. In contrast, for Raz, the law does not introduce new reasons; it is justified if it coincides with the reasons one *already* has. Clearly, they are not really considering autonomy in the same way.

To be sure, the view Simon is criticizing is not exactly the same as Raz's position. Simon's argument here is not a direct refutation of Raz because Raz's theory is an attempt to justify authority, not an attempt to do away with it. Nevertheless, Raz takes authority to be justified where it helps people act on their own reasons, so we can see his theory drawing on an ideal in which people successfully act on the reasons that apply to them without the assistance of authority. Raz's whole enterprise starts from the vantage point that authority must justify itself against the moral requirements of autonomy and that any justification granted to authority is a concession—one that is granted when authority does not violate autonomy. This does not mean that Raz envisions a utopian withering of the state, but it does suggest that authority is always second best, to put it lightly.

Another way to see this distinction between Simon and Raz is to recognize that their visions for society are, in a way, opposites. For Simon, the individual molds his will to the law whereas, for Raz, at least in broad terms, the law ought to be molded if not to the will then at least to the reasons or judgments of the individual to minimize its infringement on autonomy. This is not unfairly reductive of Raz's theory because the basic thrust of it is that authority is justified when it requires that which the subject already has reason to do. Hence, the subject's reasons become the reasons for following the law while, for Simon, the law's reasons become the subject's. Authority, in Simon's view, is not just substitutional, enabling one to achieve what one can in principle achieve independent of the authority (with more complete information).

Even so, considering Raz's emphasis on the need to reconcile authority with autonomy, we can find resonances of Raz in Simon when Simon says, "When a man is governed for his own good or for the common good of the society of which he is a member, this man is said to be free."[179] Simon's statement seems to overlap with Raz's solution to his concern, shared by the philosophical anarchists, over the threat that authority poses to autonomy. But we already know this cannot be the case because Simon thinks authority is essential and supplies something that is otherwise missing. He writes, "Two capacities are at work in the bringing about of the common good; individual good will procures the right form, authority determines the right matter. And thus *it is only by the operation of authority that the person enjoys the benefit of an orderly relation to the common good understood both with regard to form and with regard to matter.* No wonder that men of good will appreciate the privilege of working under a truly able leader. Thanks to his direction, the antimony is overcome; the man of good will who wants to do the thing that the common good demands, actually knows what that thing is and does it."[180] So Simon goes much further than Raz because he is not showing how authority can avoid violating autonomy where authority is essentially a necessary evil but, instead, how the individual good depends on authority for effecting "an orderly relation to the common good." Raz, in contrast, sees authority not as meeting a need but as jeopardizing autonomy unless it finds itself in line with the individual's preexisting reasons.

More generally, Raz sees the law remaining relatively agnostic with respect to questions of the good because the justification of authority depends on its correspondence to whatever reasons happen to be there already. Simon, however, sees the orientation to the common good as the essence of authority. For Simon, "The masterpiece of the natural world cannot be found in the transient individual. . . . Human communities are the highest attainments of nature, for they are virtually unlimited with regard to diversity of perfections and virtually immortal."[181] We do not need to go all the way with Simon on this point about individuals versus communities to share his view that attempting to account for law's authority while avoiding the deeper questions about the good leads to an impoverished notion of authority. This avoidance contributes to Raz framing authority effectively as a bad to be mitigated rather than a good to be valued. Instead, he espouses an understanding of obedience under which obedience is acceptable insofar as it can be effectively limited or eliminated by assimilating it to the reasons one already has for action. Put differently, Raz does not quite deny the need for authority, but what he contemplates is hardly authority at all.

Obedience can be good for its own sake in promoting self-mastery

Describing the ways in which law advances the common good is one way—indeed, the primary way—of justifying its authority. Another, related form of justification focuses on the good of obedience itself, namely the idea that obeying authority just as such can sometimes benefit the subject, supplying its own reason for action. This is as opposed to saying that obedience is good only when a directive's requirements coincide with what one ought to do, anyway, or when the *content* of the directives supplies new reasons for action. If there are distinct benefits that come from obedience, per se, then the availability of those benefits depends upon the existence of an obligation to obey because, without obligation, there is no true obedience. In the absence of an obligation to obey, compliance only appears to be obedience and is in fact more akin to volunteering or heeding advice. Without the obligation generated by authority, we have voluntary compliance, not obedience.

Simon offers a candidate for why obedience can be good in itself. As Vukan Kuic writes in his introduction to Simon's *A General Theory of Authority*, "To find ourselves, therefore, as well as to find our rightful place in the community, Simon suggests, we can hardly do better than make a practice, consciously and freely, of obedience."[182] Among other benefits, Simon puts the presence of authority and obedience at the heart of self-mastery. It is in this sense, at least, that Simon says "obedience may be chosen on account of some excellence of its own."[183] Importantly, the benefits in this regard are available only if there is truly authority and obligation, not autonomy masquerading as authority.[184] Simon gives the example of authority's "role in religious life," where "every religious ... is supposed to be lovingly concerned with the distinct merits of obedience, with the things it can do for him over and above the goods of spiritual training and those of community life."[185] Though religion seems unique because, there, obedience to God can be intrinsically valuable in a way that obedience to a human person might not be, religious life of that sort also includes obedience to human superiors, a religious order, and so forth. The value of obedience to those figures is not because they are stand-ins for God. The practice of obedience is itself valuable as a discipline. At the same time, it can seem like a stretch to suggest that everyone else, not living under vows of obedience, ought to turn to the law to provide content-independent discipline.

Simon's example sheds light more broadly on the relationship between obedience and true freedom. Simon's view on this part of the good of authority is perhaps best encapsulated in his statement that "obedience may well be the closest approximation to a general method for dealing with the weight of subjectivity in the uppermost part of our self."[186] For Simon, true freedom is "an uppermost kind of active indifference and mastery," which is to say, "a mastery over desire such that, for the sake of a law, for the sake of the good, for the sake of God, a man be free to choose, if he pleases, and without a struggle against overwhelming difficulties."[187] In that particular line, Simon is referring to choosing marriage over "free love," but we can assuredly take the point more generally.[188] In doing so, Simon unequivocally rejects "the philosophy which interprets freedom as spontaneity, and preferably as the spontaneity of animal desires," which he understands ultimately as enslavement to desire.[189]

This helps to explain why Simon speaks of the substitution of "a law of utility and force for the law of voluntary co-operation" (a substitution to which he objects, of course) rather than for a law of obedience.[190] Why do utility and force replace voluntary actions rather than obligatory ones in Simon's formulation? He writes of voluntary cooperation where we expect to see obligation because, in his understanding, voluntary cooperation and obedience to authority converge. Obedience, paradoxically (at least on the surface), makes freedom possible by displacing subjectivity, by nurturing a self-mastery that enables the subject to choose the good "freely." Such self-mastery is the fruit of conforming one's choices to the good via obedience to authority. On Simon's view, "Obedience is due to God alone in the domain of interior acts."[191] That is to say, only God can demand full assent of the will. Nevertheless, "There is one kind of judgment which is covered by a duty of obedience that man owes to man."[192] "True," Simon continues, "this judgment is not a purely interior act, since it is the form of an external action; yet its being covered by a duty of obedience implies a decisive surrender on the part of the self."[193] Thus, obedience leads to self-mastery because "whenever an act is done out of obedience, I will that any judgment and volition of mine should yield, if necessary, to the judgment and volition of those in charge of the common good. The decisive step has been taken."[194] Such yielding means putting the common good before one's individual desires, the ability to do so being necessary to be freed from enslavement to desires. Using Raz's terminology, it means taking the will of the other as an exclusionary reason, depriving base desires of the power to govern the decision. Simon concludes his point this way: "Inasmuch as the practical judgments, which are the forms of my exterior actions, also are acts of my mind and will, the rebellious moods of my subjectivity are curbed, and this happens voluntarily and freely. Whatever excellence is communicated in the exercise of authority uses ways of distinguished significance, for the ways of obedience are kept in order by a constant process of emancipation from the powers which threaten most profoundly my freedom to do what I please for the sake of the law, for the sake of the good, and for the sake of God."[195] Obedience, then, is good because it frees a person from "rebellious moods" to do what is right, and this need not apply only to obedience to God.[196] To be sure, this sort of benefit from authority need not come from the law specifically, yet the law is a good candidate not only because it is pervasive and has the power to "encourage" (enforce) but also because it is a sort of authority that balances content independence with normative limitations. On one hand, to yield blindly and totally to authority is problematic if the obedience is so complete that it turns people into unthinking automatons. On the other hand, authority's ability to confer the benefits of obedience is inefficacious if all decisions are personal and ultimately independent of authority. Under the authority of law, a prima facie obligation to obey yields the benefits of authority while the absence of an absolute obligation to obey leaves room for critical reflection. Once again, this is why it is suitable to speak of a disposition to obey. Obedience comes neither as an unthinking habit nor as unqualified submission.

If it is good to develop self-mastery, and if obedience to authority is essential for this development, then we have yet another way to see law's indispensable role in society. Yet, even without this, law's contributions in securing the common good account for why there must be genuine authority and obligation rather than the less compelling version of law's authority and legal obligation offered by Raz.

Klosko's and Estlund's theories of obligation fall short but point in the same correct direction

Although, in the contemporary literature, denial of a prima facie obligation to obey the law predominates, George Klosko argues that there is such an obligation. In his article "Multiple Principles of Political Obligation," Klosko addresses "the currently widespread view that there is no satisfactory theory of political obligation."[197] This part of Klosko's characterization of the current landscape is correct, as is his sense that it is worth seeking a satisfactory theory. Unfortunately, his own account of legal obligation comes up short. Yet it is also instructive because it reinforces the claim that the authority of law stems from law's relation to the common good.

Klosko attempts to construct a theory of obligation that rests on multiple moral principles. Green also takes into account multiple principles, writing, "Some of us have natural duties to obey, others duties of consent, still others may have only weak prudential ties, and some may have none at all."[198] But Green's theory, to the extent that he even accepts these principles as sources of obligation, is different because he sees different principles applying separately to different individuals. In contrast, for Klosko, multiple principles apply to the same individual at the same time, combining to generate an obligation where none of the principles alone suffices.[199]

Examining some of the standard accounts of obligation, Klosko determines, for example, that neither duties of fairness nor of mutual aid suffice to ground political obligation generally.[200] Instead, he proposes a "multiple principle theory," arguing that "a stronger theory can result from employing multiple principles of obligation, allowing them to work in combination, rather than attempting to develop a theory on the basis of a single principle."[201] Klosko recognizes that the authority of law necessarily entails a prima facie obligation to obey. "A successful theory," he explains, "establishes a strong presumption in favor of obedience."[202] Klosko is searching for the right object, but he does not quite get there. For one thing, his multiple-principles theory is not necessarily additive in the way he wishes. Klosko assumes that each of the principles, while insufficient on its own to establish political obligation, combines with the others in such a way as to make them sufficient as a whole. But it may very well be that principles that are insufficient on their own do not combine in this way. Instead of Klosko adding fractions to a sum of one, perhaps the more apt metaphor is that he keeps halving the distance to the goal without ever quite reaching it. Without more explanation, we simply do not have any reason to think the principles can add up to an obligation to obey the law because there is no true way to commensurate or quantify them.

This overarching problem notwithstanding, Klosko does point us in the right direction. Referring to the common good principle (CG), Klosko asserts, "CG does establish moral requirements to support the full range of governmental actions."[203] This is a curious concession because it seems to provide him with the single-principle solution he denies (or misses). Nevertheless, he insists on his multiple principles theory (MP) because "MP is a more convincing theory with the additional principles than without them."[204] This very strongly implies that, although MP is more convincing relatively speaking, CG can possibly be enough alone to explain political obligation. Yet, given that the main task is to discover what is minimally necessary to ground authority and obligation, Klosko undermines the search for a concept of law. In other words, while multiple principles can make for a more convincing theory, a more parsimonious theory, with fewer moving parts, is preferable (and perhaps less vulnerable) if it is available.

Either way, it is significant that Klosko lands upon the common good as the central driver of political obligation. He articulates the common good principle as follows: "The mechanism in place in society X to provide indispensable and other necessary public goods and to aid the unfortunate can also take reasonable measures to promote the common good in other ways."[205] In whatever formulation, this is the foundational principle because the authority of law is necessarily rooted in the common good because the common good is the end for which such authority exists. Without the law's orientation to the common good, the normativity of law is unintelligible.

The connection between authority and obligation on one hand and the common good on the other also supports my conclusion that the force of the common good principle depends upon the right overall orientation of the legal system and not the rightness of individual directives. In Klosko's words, "The appropriate standard is tolerable or reasonable justice. A government's actions must be on the whole defensible, though exceptions should be accepted."[206] Klosko is correct that there must be exceptions to the goodness of some laws. Otherwise, law can be authoritative only when it is perfect.

Like Klosko, David Estlund offers a theory of general (prima facie) obligation. Unlike Klosko, in *Democratic Authority*, Estlund focuses on a single principle to justify it. Although Estlund's account is ultimately incomplete, he, too, offers important contributions on the road to a better concept of law. Specifically, Estlund is right that authority can be justified without consent, and he is right that justification depends on features of the authority as a whole rather than on the content of individual laws.

Where Estlund gets authority right, he confirms several of our conclusions. Estlund clearly recognizes the importance of a content-independent theory of authority or, as he says, "the moral power to require action (to borrow a phrase from Raz) . . . just because you said so."[207] Without this moral power, there is no authority, per se, but only reasons for action one already has that overlap with the directives of the law. Estlund further recognizes one consequence of content independence, namely that "wrong" directives still obligate. In Estlund's words, "We should not assume that authority and legitimacy lapse just whenever the procedure gets a wrong answer."[208] With regard to democratic authority, he adds, "Owing partly to its epistemic value, its decisions are (within limits) morally binding even when they are incorrect."[209] Estlund is right that laws can be morally binding even when wrong though he is incorrect that this is limited to democracies. Indeed, notwithstanding his emphasis on the epistemic advantages of democracy, a close examination of Estlund's theory, which already admits that actual consent is not required, shows that democracy is not a necessary feature of justified authority. This accords with my own claims even though my concept of law remains fully compatible with democracy.

Estlund's theory contains essentially two parts: first, the claim that democratic decision-making yields epistemic advantages and, second, that those advantages matter normatively. This second part revolves around a concept he calls "normative consent." "Normative consent," he writes, "establishes the system's authority."[210] As Estlund describes it, normative consent means that "you are under my authority because you would be morally wrong to refuse to consent" and, because it is hypothetical, that "you would have consented if you acted morally correctly when offered the chance to consent."[211] The argument is best summed up by Estlund in this passage: "In light of all this, citizens would be morally required to consent to the new authority of such a democratic arrangement if they were offered the choice. Non-consent would be null, and so the fact that no such consent is normally asked or given makes no moral difference, and so any existing democratic arrangement that meets these conditions has authority over each citizen just as if they had established its authority by actual consent."[212]

The main problem with Estlund's theory is his framing of the justification of authority in terms of consent. Many theorists have demonstrated that consent cannot account for a general obligation to obey the law.[213] The presence of consent insuffices in both its breadth and depth. That is, we normally find that most of the people in question have not, in fact, consented. Or, when they have consented (or can be said to have consented), what they have (or would have) consented to is much less than what is necessary to justify the entire regime. Estlund is aware of this and, therefore, makes an adjustment with his introduction of normative consent. Normative consent is consent that is valid not because one has given it but because one is morally obligated to give it, whether or not one has given it and even whether or not it has been requested.

This addition of normative consent introduces an unnecessary wrinkle, however. Normative consent cannot be both the basis of justification and its result. On one hand, the "presence" of normative consent is the reason why the authority is justified. On the other hand, normative consent is owed because it is the type of authority to which one ought to consent. But it is circular to say that the authority is the type to which one ought to consent because normative consent is present. Instead of deriving political obligation from an obligation to consent (i.e., normative consent), we ought to ground justification in whatever it is that makes the authority the type to which one ought to consent.

If Estlund wants to say that we need normative consent *in order to* justify authority, then there must be something else about the authority that makes it the kind to which one ought to consent. For Estlund, that "something else" is the epistemic advantages of democratic decision-making. But if that is right, why not just say that democratic authority creates an obligation to obey instead of an obligation to consent? We must conclude that this is, in practice, what Estlund is saying. In other words, he is really arguing that the obligation to obey obtains whether or not people consent as long as the authority is otherwise justified. The consent part of the theory does no additional work unless normative consent is just his way of saying that one ought to consent to obligations one has, anyway. But that addition is an unnecessary complication. In describing his "hypothetical consent theory of authority," Estlund admits that "authority can simply befall us."[214] In that case, the focus ought to be more on the source (and entailments) of political obligation and not on shoehorning it into a model of consent. This attempt obscures more than it clarifies by suggesting that what matters most is translating obligation into a kind of consent, real or implied. And, in any case, Estlund's account of normative consent fails on its own terms.

Estlund's entire notion of normative consent is noticeably unstable. The idea of required consent is a curious one because it eliminates the very thing that consent normally accomplishes: self-binding. Consent is a meaningful or useful concept largely because it suggests that one takes an obligation upon oneself. If one is required to consent—and especially if one is obligated to obey regardless of whether one actually consents, as with Estlund's normative consent—then, once again, it is the source of the requirement to consent, not consent itself, that explains the obligation. If it makes sense at all to say that one is obligated to consent, then it is much more straightforward just to say one is obligated to act in accordance with the authority to which one is being asked to consent. In the case of law, this is simply an obligation to obey the law. For consent to serve any function conceptually, it seems there must be the possibility of valid nonconsent, even if such nonconsent is valid but illicit. If nonconsent is impossible in Estlund's theory—which it is because consent occurs automatically (and nonconsent is "null")—then his theory is really just positing the existence of an obligation, and the role of consent vanishes.

Presumably in view of these difficulties, Estlund tries to carve out a middle position, proposing symmetry between consent and nonconsent. According to this view, a person begins in a morally neutral position between consent and nonconsent such that normative consent can be binding even in the absence of consent because one is not in a state of nonconsent when consent is not given. But Estlund provides no good reason to reject the conventional, commonsense understanding of consent, namely that one begins in a state of nonconsent, normatively, and remains there until granting consent. One does not normally need to actively "nonconsent" (to coin a verb) in order to be violated by another person who acts upon oneself without consent.

In fact, Estlund makes this very point in offering his own counterexample from the case of sex. In a regular case of sexual activity, there is, of course, no obligation to consent, nor is there anything wrong with withholding consent. Estlund gives an example of sexual activity where nonconsent is wrongful yet still valid.[215] In that case, there is an obligation to consent to sex, yet nonconsent still works in prohibiting the other person from engaging in sexual contact. Under such circumstances, sexual engagement by the other person is wrong even though it is morally impermissible to refuse consent.[216] Here, normative consent does not work, and, contrary to the rest of Estlund's theory, one does not have an obligation to act as though one has consented when one has not. Estlund seems to prove more than he wishes here; his own example seems decisive against his theory.

One way out of this for Estlund is to show that legal obligation and sexual relations are not analogous. Perhaps wrongful nonconsent, while valid with respect to sex, is invalid with respect to the law. If so, the law is justified in coercing compliance in a way that the person who receives the valid but illicit nonconsent is not justified in coercing sexual congress. Alas, Estlund is not sure whether the disanalogy exists, conceding, "I do not know what the criterion is for when wrongful non-consent is, or is not, null."[217] Accordingly, Estlund accepts that the two may be the same, writing, "Maybe law is like sex in this way: even impermissible refusals are successful at forbidding the proposed action." Searching for a different way out, he continues, "In any case, normative consent is an account of authority, saying nothing about anyone's being permitted to do anything. Normative consent (without actual consent) can establish authority even if it cannot establish legitimacy."[218] But this amounts to Estlund saying that normative consent is not normative because it creates authority without creating legitimacy. This makes no sense. Fatally for this theory, he provides no solid account of what the authority of law is without legitimacy. And he skips over any explanation about how this distinction between authority and legitimacy applies to the case of normative consent in sexual relations, where its meaninglessness seems evident. In trying to square the circle, Estlund seems to land on authority merely in the sense of power, which does nothing with respect to sorting out justification. Once again, we see the specter of Hart's error arise in contemporary theories of authority. Estlund's failed attempt at explaining law's normativity ends in him dividing authority from legitimacy.

The unraveling of Estlund's theory is particularly jarring when we compare his premises and his conclusions. At the outset of his work, Estlund defines authority as "the moral power of one agent (emphasizing especially the state) to morally require or forbid actions by others through commands."[219] Yet he concludes that, thanks to normative consent, authority, or "the moral power to require action—can, in principle, be established even without a generally acceptable justification."[220] In other words, "There can be authority without legitimacy."[221] This is incoherent. If Estlund defines authority as the moral power to require action, which he does at the outset, then he cannot separate authority and justification, unless by "require" he means "require by force," which he clearly does not. People can be morally required to obey authority only if that authority is justified. Without justification, authority is power in the coercive, not moral, sense.

Despite the theory's heavy reliance on the epistemic advantages of democracy as the explanation for legitimate authority, there are intimations of a different path. Estlund argues, "Democracy is better than random and is epistemically the best among those that are generally acceptable in the way that political legitimacy requires."[222] Estlund's suggestion here is that democracy is better because of the superiority of the output (the results it produces), rather than because of the normativity of the input (i.e., the consent of the governed).

Clearly, there is some independent requirement of political legitimacy against which he is measuring democratic outcomes. Likewise, normative consent, the obligation to give one's consent, which binds whether or not one actually gives it, is premised on the idea that democracy has the epistemic advantages that Estlund attributes to it. The "duty to act as you would have been morally required to promise to act if you had been asked" is associated with the epistemic advantages of democracy insofar as democracy contingently advances the common good or other ends.[223] But if it is the output that is of concern, then any system that produces the appropriate results ought to possess justified authority. Other sources of obligation can potentially generate the same duty. To be sure, democracy can be an extremely useful proxy because its supposed epistemic advantages can mean that democratic decisions track the common good. Yet it is neither democracy nor consent that ultimately accounts for Estlund's conclusions. On the contrary, his insertion of consent is, at best, unsuited for the phenomenon he wishes to explain.

Estlund's claim is that democracy necessarily produces better results. But it is not necessarily the only system that produces results good enough to confer legitimacy. In principle, any arrangement ought to qualify if it advances the ends that Estlund thinks democracy advances best. Therefore, we can define justification by the ends the authority seeks or achieves and not by the means, even if we deem certain means more likely to succeed. One such possible end, and a very plausible candidate for the aim of law, which Estlund himself acknowledges as the benefit of democracy's epistemic advantages, is the advancement of the common good.

CHAPTER 5

We the Sovereign

DEMOCRACY

Law as a set of commands oriented to the common good remains compatible with democracy

Rawls's explanation for the obligation to obey a just regime is the subject of varied criticism. Smith, for example, is skeptical of some of Rawls's earlier formulations. Smith writes that, according to Rawls, "everyone who is treated by such a government with reasonable justice has a natural duty to obey all laws that are not grossly unjust, on the ground that everyone has a natural duty to uphold and to comply with just institutions."[1] Simmons has doubts about this, rejecting arguments both from the natural duty of justice and from the duty of fair play. Simmons opposes, for example, "his (unacceptable) claim that *all* obligations are accounted for by the principle of fair play."[2] On this point, I agree with Simmons. Fairness does not suffice, neither to explain why people have obligations based on benefits to which they do not consent nor to explain why one particular scheme that instantiates justice is authoritative over any other that also does so. Yet Rawls is off to a good start in recognizing that obligation comes fundamentally from the justice of the system.

Rawls refines his theory in the *Law of Peoples* when he describes the members of a minimally decent society who recognize "these duties and obligations as fitting with their common good idea of justice and do not see their duties and obligations as mere commands imposed by force."[3] Rawls hits upon an important point with his reference to the people's "common good idea of justice," to which he refers again when he sums up the characteristics of a decent society.[4] As a result, one unintended lesson we learn from Rawls, though, is that a decent regime probably does not need the political representation that Rawls suggests. If there is an obligation to obey the law and if it derives from obligations to a "common good idea of justice," then it does not necessarily matter whether the regime is representative or not. A regime that meets the requirements of justice is justified and, therefore, authoritative. Representation can aid the regime in meeting those requirements (in tracking the common good), but it is not a necessary condition of justification—unless Rawls's view is actually a theory of consent, in which case it is inadequate for other reasons.

In the same way, Simmons does not see that for authority to be justified it must be judged as a whole (say, the legal system as opposed to individual laws), and then it can have a place for imposing a content-independent obligation to obey. Without this content independence, we are not really speaking of authority. He asks, "Why does Rawls only disqualify *unjust* schemes, rather than all schemes which promote or aim at *immoral* ends?"[5] The reason is that the justification of the authority depends on an evaluation of the scheme as a whole. An authority can promote some immoral ends yet still be, on balance, just. If the obligation to obey depends on a case-by-case analysis of the underlying reasons for acting in each case, then there is not any authority in the true sense because then everything depends on the balance of reasons that already apply to the subject.

My concept of law defines law as a set of commands oriented to the common good. Given that I posit the command model as the best way to describe the form of law in its central case and given that the justification of authority depends on an orientation to the common good rather than on consent or something similar, we can anticipate a certain concern. Namely, we can wonder whether my concept of law comes at the expense of self-government and attendant desiderata such as liberty, autonomy, consent, and so on. In other words, in anticipation of such critiques, I wish to defend my concept of law against claims that, even if I have it right about law and authority, a justification of authority of this sort is a troubling invitation to authoritarianism. There are two closely related ways to formulate the anticipated critique. First, it can be erroneously thought that my theory explicitly prefers illiberal forms of authority because it centers on "command" and because it suggests that popular rule is not necessary for justification. Or, second, even if my concept of law does not explicitly endorse authoritarianism, my theory can erroneously be thought to have at least the tendency to undermine the importance of democracy merely by suggesting that the consent of the governed is not a strictly necessary component of justification.

Finnis and Simon address how authority contributes to the good and is not merely a necessary evil in conflict with the assumed good of autonomy. Nevertheless, is my concept of law weighted too heavily in favor of authority over self-rule? Technically, nothing in my formulation requires democracy given the theoretical, if uncommon, possibility of a nondemocratic system oriented to the common good. Therefore, to rebut these potential challenges, I wish to highlight the compatibility of my concept of law with self-government and limited government. Hart's argument notwithstanding, the command model is compatible with democratic governance. The normative aspect of an orientation to the common good at the very least serves as a limit on authority even if it does not strictly require the consent of the governed. Indeed, we can go further, with Simon, and see that the kind of authority entailed in my theory best supports and protects autonomy.

At a minimum, my view of law's authority is fully compatible with self-government, even if it does not require it. Going further, though, we can say that the requirement of the orientation to the common good protects liberty and autonomy because the requirement itself serves as a limit on authority. Going even further, we can consider how authority rightly understood actually supports autonomy and liberty. Drawing again on Simon, a strong proponent of authority, we can grasp "why authority and liberty are not irreconcilable and how they actually complement each other in all aspects of our lives."[6]

Authority's justification is rooted in the common good, not consent

The starting point for such worries begins with an acknowledgment that consent is not strictly necessary if law is defined as a set of commands oriented to the common good; non-elected officials can produce a legal system oriented to the common good. Consent can serve as a useful proxy for the common good; it may be a good indicator of laws or a legal system being oriented to the common good though it is not, in itself, a requirement. Finnis speaks of using consent as a rule of thumb.[7] While consent is not required for the justification of authority, consent is useful in deciding when to obey according to the following rule of thumb: "A man's stipulations have authority when a practically reasonable subject, with the common good in view, would think he *ought* to consent to them."[8] Finnis means that, when there is consent, it is likely, though not certain, that the law is oriented to the common good. This is because the common good, in part, comprises the good of all the individuals, and individuals can often recognize when the law coincides with their own good.

To be sure, individuals often cannot be counted on to offer or withhold their consent with an eye toward the common good. They can choose whether to consent based on the aspects of their own good that are in conflict with the common good. This is why consent can serve as an approximation but not as an assurance of authority's orientation to the common good. Even less does the justification of authority depend upon whether the subject in fact believes she ought to consent. Any actual individual can have bad information or bad motives, and so on. Finnis sensibly refers only to a practically reasonable person who is evaluating with an eye to the common good.

Justified authority is not coterminous with rule by consent because the determining factor is the orientation to the common good, which does not depend on consent. To the modern mind, it is appealing to suppose that justified authority traces back, at some level, to consent. Yet we know the familiar litany of reasons why consent cannot suffice. For example, most people do not actually consent to anything; their consent is at best tacit. Some who consent may do so under conditions that can be understood as duress, particularly in the sense of a lack of adequate exit options. Among those who consent freely, they can consent to different things, for instance, to different parts of the law or to different aspects of authority, and so on. Though consent can seem in principle like a good route for justification, it is very difficult to establish it in practice. And we know from a long history of critical literature that tacit consent hardly does better.[9] Instead, we need a normative explanation for authority other than consent.

Owing to the role that consent can play in tracking the common good, we can expect overlap between the will of the people, or the common will, and the common good. At the same time, such overlap is, of course, not assured. In that case, and if authority is justified by reference to the common good, then we must admit that justified authority does not require consent. Simon writes that "functional diversity causes a need relative to the common good as a whole," and that "decision pertains to a power which, inasmuch as it is responsible for order among the functions, necessarily controls all of them and commands all the functionaries."[10] If the ground of authority is this need, then authority cannot be justified because it conforms to the common will, which can stand against the common good. On the flipside, nothing about fulfilling that overarching function of authority requires consent.[11] Indeed, because the common good is more than the sum of individual goods and, more so, because the common good can conflict with particular goods, authority sometimes acts justly without consent. Another way to express this democratic-minded concern over consent is to ask what happens when the common will comes into conflict with the common good, and our answer is that the latter justifies authority while the former does not.

Sounding a rather sour note regarding the common will, Simon states, "An act of 'democratic faith' which would proclaim the wisdom of the many when the circumstances are such that the many cannot possibly know what it is all about would be obnoxious absurdity."[12] Here we might accuse Simon of offering an instrumental argument for authority based on epistemic elitism. But it serves to make the point nonetheless: Authority is not valuable simply because it reflects whatever a majority of people decide; it is valuable because it fulfills the function for which authority is necessary in the first place, namely the advancement of the common good. Apologists for autonomy can argue that a bad or even destructive course of action is still preferable over a good, productive one if that course of action is self-imposed rather than imposed from above. But, if that is correct, we must ask why any coordinated course of action is necessary at all. Surely we cannot say that a group is better off making a bad decision of its own accord, which is to say, acting in a coordinated though destructive fashion, than making no decision at all simply because the decision-making is in itself valuable. Sometimes a decision *can* be worse than no decision at all. Put another way, just as autonomy is not a basic good, not something good for its own sake but good only insofar as it is used to choose that which is good, so, too, for authority. Authority is not good just in virtue of some decision having been made but in virtue of a good decision having been made. This need not mean that the decision be the best possible one, but it at least needs to be better than no decision at all, for it cannot be good simply by virtue of being *a decision*.[13] So authority cannot be justified merely by reflecting the common will, for the common will might not be aligned with the common good. Hence, a thoroughly evil regime is not justified regardless of how large a majority supports it.

There is no denying that this relegation of consent is a difficult pill to swallow. But this is less idiosyncratic than it might seem at first: such a notion is built into most democratic theory, if quietly. As Finnis observes, all or most legal systems begin with an original unauthorized act.[14] Even the US Constitution, which was popularly ratified, depended upon an extralegal supplantation of the Articles of Confederation. At a minimum, we can say there was never a unanimous decision by the people approving any particular procedures for ratification of either system. Short of the extreme position that all polities are therefore illegitimate—not as the philosophical anarchists say because all authority is illegitimate but because unauthorized authority is illegitimate and, as it happens, all political authority is unauthorized for lack of unanimity—we can, instead, see if there is another route to justification. This, however, is not a concession to brute power but instead an observation that suggests that, unless we wish to deny the legitimacy of all political authority, the justification of authority cannot rest on consent.

The command aspect of law is compatible with democracy

Despite initial worries of the sort I describe, my concept of law is at least compatible with self-rule. As I argue in response to Hart's criticism of the idea of self-command, a concept of law that incorporates a command model remains compatible with popular sovereignty because of the possibility of people commanding themselves as they occupy different roles within the polity. For Hart, a concept of law rooted in command is incompatible with democracy. "Command" suggests a commander and a commandee, as it were, as opposed to self-government, in which people rule themselves and, therefore, for which the term *command* seems inapt in Hart's view. Yet, as I explain, this is a mistaken understanding of the notion of command. The persons of the commander and the commanded can reside in the same individual or group. The two can exist in the same body without contradiction or even strain. As Simon writes, even in the starkest case, one of a direct democracy, "The requirements of the concept of authority are entirely fulfilled in the case of a community governing itself directly, without any distinct governing personnel. Authority is not lacking; it resides in the community."[15] Simon is right that there is nothing odd or counterintuitive about the authoritativeness of the directives of a self-governing community. The people can be the authority, and therefore they can issue commands (directives).

To explain this duality, Simon suggests that, in assembly, "men undergo a qualitative change"; that is, "they are no longer a collection of private citizens minding their own affairs, they are the people minding common affairs."[16] More plainly, as I say in addressing Hart, this duality can be thought of quite ordinarily as people acting in different capacities. We can see this play out in real life, where a person serving as a legislator can vote against a piece of legislation, believing it to be bad policy, while that same person later serving as a judge can vote to uphold the same legislation, believing it to be constitutionally permissible. Similarly, a person might, as a legislator, act for the common good in a way she does not when contemplating only her private good. These intuitive examples illustrate that no deep metaphysics is necessary to conceive of people acting in different capacities, sometimes even opposed to one another, without contradiction or inconsistency.

Perhaps an even sharper example is that of the citizen who obeys a law despite opposing it or even having voted against it: "A citizen is considered law-abiding if, and only if, he considers his obligation independent from his personal opinion."[17] That is, a citizen serves in one capacity when rendering a judgment about the desirability (or other feature) of a law as a voter, or quasi-legislator, but serves in a different capacity when deciding as a subject of the law whether to obey. This is evident in the way that different factors weigh on those respective decisions. If the citizen simply consults her own opinion about the law in both instances (how to vote before it is a law and whether to comply once it is a law)—if the question of whether to follow the law is subject to no additional considerations beyond the merits of the directive in question—then there is no difference between the two perspectives.[18] But the fact that it is perfectly sensible for her to see it differently from the different perspectives shows that the salience of operating in different capacities is very real. The notion of capacities renders law as command compatible with self-rule, whether direct democracy or otherwise. The citizen serves in one capacity as commander and another as commanded.[19] And here is the connection back to one of our main points about authority: the fact that this measure becomes law must change the person's relationship to it, from one who considers (and casts a judgment about) the merits of the measure to one who accepts the judgment that has been rendered, with at least prima facie authority. If not—if the law is subject to the person's ongoing evaluation on the merits even as an initial matter—that is, with no credit given to the fact that it is the law—then the law cannot be said to be authoritative. On this flawed view, a subject is as free to disregard the law as she is to oppose it before it passes (whether as a voter or legislator or otherwise).

Even a robust transmission theory of authority remains compatible with democracy

The paradoxical seeming lesson from Simon is how there can be both genuine authority and a strengthening rather than a weakening of autonomy. Not to overstate things, but in some ways, the reconciliation of authority and autonomy is the challenge for modern political and legal theory. It is an animating concern both for Simon and for Raz (and for others) despite their strongly opposed perspectives. For Simon, as for Finnis, authority and autonomy (or liberty) work together to advance the common good. Simon writes, "As to their complementary character, it is quite clear that authority, when it is not fairly balanced by liberty, is but tyranny, and that liberty, when it is not fairly balanced by authority, is but abusive license. Each of these destroys itself at the very moment when it destroys the other term by its excess."[20] Both Simon and Finnis, in their own contexts, highlight the way in which regard for authority does not amount to a brief for authoritarianism. Instead, they paint a picture of limited government driven by the belief not that authority is bad but that the good can be best secured through a combination of public and private efforts.[21] Simon, who vigorously defends the benefits of authority, offers that the state "will discharge its duty best by concerning itself indirectly with such things as the maintenance and promotion of transcendent truth."[22] This is critical because it demonstrates that a defense of the need for authority is, by nature, balanced with a defense of individual initiative and prerogative. As Finnis explains, the "irreducible multiformity of human goods" mandates both authority and liberty or autonomy.[23] Simon outlines two principles that constitute this balance. There is the principle of authority: *"Wherever the welfare of a community requires a common action, the unity of that common action must be assured by the higher organs of that community."*[24] And there is the principle of autonomy: *"Wherever a task can be satisfactorily achieved by the initiative of the individual or that of small social units, the fulfillment of that task must be left to the initiative of the individual or to that of small social units.*"[25] Subsidiarity is often the name given to this idea that both private and public decision-making each have their places in advancing the aspects of the common good proper to them.

At the same time, in this light, these claims about authority and autonomy are especially surprising and their resolution especially illuminating when we appreciate just how robust Simon's view of authority is. Simon's characterization of authority, which rests with the people and devolves to officials in an act of transmission, also supports the notion of a qualified obligation to obey and thereby also helps to make sense of content independence with respect to obligation and obedience. On one hand, the authority possessed by the law imposes upon the subjects a prima facie obligation to obey irrespective of the content of particular directives. On the other hand, because authority ultimately rests with the people, there are circumstances in which the people can stand above, or outside of, the law. Simon favors an understanding of authority akin to transmission theory, whereby the people "have *designated* the ruling person, and they have *transmitted* to him the power given by God to the people."[26] Simon traces this understanding back at least as far as Aquinas, for whom "power belongs primarily to the people, who can use it to make laws for themselves."[27] Even without God in the picture, authority functions equivalently in a democracy. For Simon, the key element is a genuine transmission of authority from the people to officials, creating an obligation to obey. This obligation to obey in a democracy follows from an intuitive point about majority rule, namely that "everyone is bound to obey" and that "it is only by accident that one happens to be in the majority and to follow one's own judgment as one acts according to the decision of the majority."[28] If one obeys only when in the majority, then there is clearly no majority rule. This much is fairly uncontroversial. But, for Simon, it also follows that "transmission of sovereignty to a distinct governing personnel leaves to the people the character of a merely consultative assembly."[29] This is not a restatement of the view that citizens must obey authority; Simon goes further and critiques even expressions of opinion by the people that are, in intent or in effect, "calculated to deprive men in power of their right to command, of their duty to have a judgment of their own, of their responsibility, of their conscience."[30] This highlights the fullness of the transmission of authority from the people to the officials; the people's authority is restored only in extraordinary circumstances.

As Simon explains, transmission of authority not only disables the people's direct authority but even limits behavior that appears or aims to control the governing personnel: "Intense campaigns of opinion, which imply that the people has the power of decision, are lawful only when circumstances are so grave as to give the people a right to exercise, albeit in limited fashion, the power greater than that of the governing personnel which was suspended, but not nullified, by the act of transmission."[31] This is not, to be sure, an invitation to tyranny. Simon's view is fully consistent with his assertion that "every government has a duty to see the maximum of voluntary cooperation, to explain its purposes and methods," and so on.[32] This is important because authoritarianism is an obvious pitfall for a theory that seeks to justify content-independent authority.

At the same time, the government's responsibility to maximize voluntary cooperation and to explain itself is not to be mistaken for power held by the people, for "ungenuinely transmitted sovereignty implies constant rebellion."[33] Instead, Simon wants a version of authority, like the one embedded in my concept of law, that sees authority as both genuine (obligating) and limited. He contrasts his favored version of authority with the "coach-driver theory," reminiscent of Raz's theory, according to which the subject believes, "I really obey myself alone, and this is all that society needs and wants me to do."[34] On that view, even if there are elected officials, they entirely obey the people all of the time. The gap between transmission theory and the coach-driver theory is important for understanding just how robust Simon's idea of authority is—and, correspondingly, how revealing it is that he can reconcile his version of authority with autonomy. Under the coach-driver theory, "authority belongs not to the leaders but to the led," "not to the government but to the governed."[35] Simon recognizes the appeal of the coach-driver theory, as it "draws considerable power from its apparent ability to explain a number of phenomena pertaining to regular democratic practice."[36] Even so, despite its explanatory power, "The coach-driver theory is unlikely to be popular where there is a strong belief in a law of nature independent of the whims of man."[37] That is, authority's essential role in society recommends it against the simulacrum of authority presented by the coach-driver theory. Indeed, in holding forth authority in appearance only, the coach-driver theory can be downright dangerous, for it "flatters an instinct of disobedience from which no human heart is entirely free," an instinct that, when "uninhibited," "may lead to anarchism."[38] This is notable especially in light of Simmons's and Green's concerns about justifications of authority serving the ends of cynical officials rather than innocent subjects. Simon contends that the opposite problem, anarchism, is a real danger as well.

For Simon, the people transmit to officials the power to rule, but this is not unlimited power, for "the people, after having transmitted power and having placed itself in a position of mandatory obedience, retains a power greater than the power transmitted."[39] Still, this power retained by the people is a latent power because "in order for the transmission of power to be genuine, it suffices that the superior power of the people should be suspended by the act of transmission and should remain suspended until circumstances of extreme seriousness give back to the people the right to exercise it."[40] This is what makes the official(s) an actual authority rather than a "secretary or manager" as in the coach-driver theory.[41] The mechanics of this may be difficult to grasp at first because Simon's theory comprises the claims that the people possess superior power and that the transmission of power to the officials is "genuine."[42] This plays out through a very careful balance. On one hand, "the actual possession of a power does not necessarily entail the right to use it actually"; on the other hand, "the suspension of the right to use a certain power does not necessarily entail the loss of this power."[43]

How do the possession of a power and the suspension of the right to use it coexist? Simon elucidates this paradoxical notion by way of analogy to emergency powers, which "are given to the governor not by the emergency but by the constitution."[44] "What the emergency effects is the releasing of powers given by the constitution," he writes.[45] Therefore, the authority possesses the power to take extraordinary measures, but that power remains suspended until such time as its use is warranted by the circumstances. "Similarly," Simon continues, "the people who transmitted power to a king would be guilty of criminal disobedience if they decided to depose the king for no extraordinarily grave reasons. It would be like a constitutional ruler fancying to exercise emergency powers when there is no emergency."[46] So the people, too, retain "emergency" powers, the prerogative to defy the government when necessary—but only when necessary. Simon puts it this way: "Transmission is so genuine as to bind the superior power of the people, to tie it up in such a way that extraordinarily serious circumstances alone can untie it."[47] This ultimate power, which the people retain, is sometimes called revolution. In this sense, the officials' use of power is always tracked by the people, who sit aside silently most of the time but who have the authority to remove the officials from power should the threat become sufficiently grave. Moreover, because the possibility of revolution is not just a brute fact but also a right, this latent power exists not only de facto but also de jure, making it all the more conceptually relevant as a normative and not just practical constraint on authority. Revolution remains extralegal as it is not governed by anything found in the law, but it is still justified by virtue of the same principles that justify the authority of law. Thus far, we see that even Simon's robust understanding of authority coexists with the possibility of a self-governing (and therefore sovereign) people.

Revolution is justified when authority threatens the common good on the whole

That being said, the parameters of what justifies the invocation of the people's latent power (of revolution) are limited. In Simon's view, "The common right of deposition, which the transmission theory grants to every politically organized people, cannot be lawfully exercised without extraordinary circumstances, without dire and immediate threat to the common good."[48] Obviously, his rendering of the transmission view of authority supports the claim that an orientation to the common good is essential for justified authority, given that the purpose of authority is the promotion of the common good. Once authority no longer serves the common good, the transmitted power becomes unjustified and is replaced by the justly exercised power of the people to depose the officials. This formulation is significant because it clarifies that the right of revolution depends on more than widespread dissatisfaction with officials; it depends upon the authority failing to fulfill its justifying conditions. If authority depends on consent, then, all else being equal, consent can be withdrawn for lesser reasons and, therefore, revolution more easily justified. On Simon's view, though, the right of revolution, which is to say the ultimate authority of the people to govern themselves directly, is in fact suspended until such time as it is released, or reinstated, by the exigent circumstances. Specifically, such circumstances exist when the authority threatens, rather than promotes, the common good.

Under normal circumstances, however, there is an expectation that power will be transmitted to government officials rather than retained by the people. The need for genuine authority is a "demand of the common good."[49] When a community or society satisfies that demand by establishing a constitutional government "sanctioned by fundamental law, every attempt at corrupting transmission of power into an ungenuine process is sheer revolt against the fundamental law of the country."[50] For this reason, Simon emphatically rejects government by consent where it means that the people "are never obligated to obey."[51] In such cases, "The theory that government demands the consent of the governed expresses neither a political nor a democratic necessity but mere revolt against the laws of all community."[52] This theory of genuine authority presumably also denies a theory like Raz's, which sounds similar to the view Simon rejects here. In both cases, we can say that people are never *really* obligated to obey. Each person remains fully her own master, and compliance with the law can never be obedience, whatever else it is. While the insistence on real obligation can sound authoritarian, it is necessary if there is to be any real authority, which in turn is necessary for the common good.

Through its role in coordination and so forth, the government performs an essential function in helping to secure the conditions for human flourishing that uncoordinated individuals—that is, individuals without unanimity or authority—cannot secure for themselves. Thus, the advancement of the common good in a group of any reasonable size depends on authority. Put sharply, the common good both necessitates and justifies authority. Moreover, because authority exists for the sake of (is instrumental to) human flourishing, the justification of authority also serves as its limiting principle. Authority is justified only to the extent that it conduces to the common good.[53] As the needs of the common good both justify and limit authority, we can have genuine, robust authority without authoritarianism in either intent or effect.

The concept of law does not even undermine democracy in spirit, let alone in letter

If the law is not oriented to the common good, then its authority is unjustified. Even so, one can be forgiven for worrying about how this all sounds because authority, while limited by the common good, need not be understood in democratic terms. Thus, we want to address whether, even if my concept of law is fully compatible with democracy in letter, it is contrary to it in spirit. Even if the notion of command works in a democracy and even if the common good criterion fits easily with democracy, perhaps the concern is that my concept of law *tends* toward authoritarianism. If law fundamentally is command, does this imply that people are more "subject" than "citizen," the latter being the preferred democratic-republican nomenclature? Does this give encouragement to a (would-be) benevolent despot who cares for the common good? Does it plant a seed that over time tends to undermine self-government?[54]

The command aspect is not the problem, because it is married to the normative aspect, namely the one that requires the legal system to be oriented to the common good. Still, it is worth noting again that this orientation to the common good does not require democracy, strictly speaking. There are many prudential reasons that count in favor of a democratic regime, but if the justification of authority is rooted in the law's orientation to the common good, then democracy is not a necessary condition (nor a sufficient one, for that matter). This tracks the dispute between Finnis and Raz, where Finnis tries to buttress the concept of authority with moral obligation.[55] Some can misinterpret this type of thinking as tending toward authoritarianism. Finnis's aim is to render authority true by surpassing Raz's construction, in which authority is (only) an epiphenomenon of the subject's reason or will. Yet it is a misunderstanding of my view (or Finnis's) of authority to read in any authoritarianism—both a misunderstanding of what law *is* and what law is *for*.

Contrary to any concerns about an authoritarian-leaning theory, Finnis considers the obligation to obey the law to be of a piece with limited authority, writing, "The reason (I suggested) for taking the law seriously to the full extent of its tenor and intended reach—and never regarding it as giving *no* reason for doing what it commands— is a reason connected with that irreducible multiformity of human goods (and that plurality of human persons) which imposes intrinsic limitation on human practical reasoning and makes nonsense (and injustice) of totalitarian projects."[56] The limitations of practical reasoning account both for the need for authority and for authority's limits. With respect to their responsibility for the common good, officials "do well to regard it as quite other than a goal which could be defined and attained by skillful disposition of efficient means, like a bridge or an omelet."[57] Thus, the common good is not an objective to be accomplished, a state of affairs to reach if only the government wields enough power with enough wisdom. This means that the normative component of my theory, which requires an orientation to the common good, invites authoritarianism neither by commission nor omission. It does not do so by omission because the absence of a democratic criterion does not leave authority without normative limits. And it does not do so by commission because the requirement to uphold the common good is precisely the thing that necessitates limitations on authority because of any authority's (or anyone's) inability to realize the complete common good of a community by fiat. On the contrary, "Attempts to absorb the individual or particular groups into a vast overall co-ordination 'solution,' so as to eliminate all *private* purposes and all enterprises launched for reasons other than the advancement of the public co-ordinative scheme, confuse the idea of a national common good with the idea of a national common enterprise or scheme of co-ordination. Such attempts, indeed, thereby do grave damage to the common good. Their injustice *is* a reason for regarding laws made pursuant to them as morally *ultra vires* and devoid of law's generic moral authority."[58] Given that he is making a different point, Finnis does not frame it the following way, but his comment suggests the question of when such schemes lack justification altogether. In such cases, absent an orientation to the common good, a system lacks the quality of law altogether. In Finnis's example here, it is not a case of finding countervailing moral obligations that outweigh the obligation to obey the law but a case where there is no obligation to obey in the first place because we are not truly dealing with law. Thus, as above, the limits on law's authority are built into the normative aspect of the concept of law.

Properly construed, authority provides a way to avoid both anarchism embraced in the name of self-interest and totalitarianism perpetrated falsely in the name of the common good. On one hand, authority is limited in what it can do. On the other hand, authority remains necessary as a balance against the individual will. In the (appropriate) absence of an all-encompassing scheme of coordination, people best advance the common good by pursuing their own good and fulfilling their responsibilities to others, not because "otherwise everyone suffers" but because, in part, "the common good *is* the good of individuals, living together and depending upon one another in ways that favour the well-being of each."[59] Favoring the well-being of each does not guarantee unanimity of opinion or action. Even taking into account the demands of impartiality between persons, individuals or groups reasonably put their own good first in keeping with the principle of subsidiarity. They are best equipped to know and instantiate this individual (or local) good. Yet precisely because individuals are inclined and empowered to pursue this individual good, which can yield disagreement despite universal good faith, there is also the need for coordination at higher levels in authority that sees to the broader common good.[60]

Again, this authority is inherently limited by what it can in fact accomplish for the sake of the common good, which is far less than what it attempts in the name of a misplaced national enterprise, where all common activity is, as Finnis says, like building a bridge or making an omelet.[61] In other words, the higher authority does not attempt to direct all activity, much less direct all activity toward a certain goal or function. Under a proper arrangement, not only does authority not attempt to supplant all private purposes (instead seeking an appropriate balance between individual and common good), but it also frees individuals and groups to pursue the good in the best way they can: "Generally speaking, an individual acts most appropriately for the common good not by trying to estimate the needs of the community 'at large,' nor by second-guessing the judgments of those who *are* directly responsible for the common good, but by performing his particular undertakings and fulfilling his other responsibilities to the ascertained individuals who have contractual or other rights correlative to his duties."[62] In this way, there is a complementarity that manifests as specialization between individuals or local groups and an overarching authority. Individuals attend to aspects of the good that they know best, and higher authorities attend to aspects of the good that come into view only from their vantage point.

Simon and Raz's disagreement about Rousseau parallels their disagreement over authority

We see, then, that authority is limited by the demands of the common good, which includes the prerogatives of individuals and groups, but this does not resolve the concern about authority's limits entirely. For one thing, the contours of the common good remain to be specified, and, in practice, that specification falls to the authority responsible for the common good, so we can see an obvious danger wherein the authority is limited by the demands of the common good while also, in practice, identifying those demands. In that case, remaining within proper limits likely depends upon the good sense of the authority. In a community, Simon writes, "Happiness depends on the ability of its head to determine exactly the right limits of his authority, together with the ability of those who must obey to recognize that their claim for freedom cannot reasonably exceed certain limits."[63] This is tantamount to saying that institutional constraints alone never suffice. Indeed, striking the right balance between authority and autonomy requires a full complement of virtues that culminate in or at least support prudence: "Inquiring into the nature of this ability to delineate the boundaries of one's field of action, let us say that it consists in a particular form of the virtue of prudence, in a wisdom which is practical in the full sense of the term, and proceeds from the virtuous dispositions of the will, justice, moderation, and charity."[64]

Both Finnis and Simon recognize the limits of authority all the while defending authority against critics, like Raz, who question it. Simon closes an essay on authority by citing Jefferson's political thought in contrast to the "abomination" of the totalitarian state, which, "materializing a dream of Rousseau, indefatigably pursues the destruction of every social group within the state, so as to establish an absolute domination over a crowd of individuals that no autonomic organization is able to protect."[65] In an arresting parallel, Raz closes his introduction to his edited volume *Authority* with a reference to Rousseau as well — yet a favorable one. Raz claims that "the aim of political philosophy since Rousseau" is "a theory of participatory government in a society in which conditions exist that enable each to see his own well-being as tied up with the prosperity of others."[66] Rendering his judgment on this program, Raz adds, "Its achievement is eagerly awaited."[67] In one respect, this is an interpretive argument over Rousseau whether, as in Raz's view, Rousseau inspires personal investment in the common good or whether, as in Simon's, he underwrites the totalizing state. But, looking deeper, we can offer that it is no coincidence that what Raz sees as shared prosperity Simon reads as the totalizing state. On one hand, Raz surely does not disagree with Simon's condemnation of the totalizing state. On the other hand, Simon, like Finnis, is concerned with the multiformity of the human good and therefore resists the idea of a state that sees the common good like an omelet or a bridge. And perhaps Simon sees Rousseau's vision as one in which the state ensures (or attempts to ensure) that everyone wants or gets the same bridge or omelet.

Put another way, Simon's account of authority is not about what kind of authority it takes to keep people from tearing each other apart, as it is for the social contract theorists (like Rousseau). It is about what kind of authority makes human flourishing possible, as it is for the natural lawyers. This, in turn, is an argument not only about why authority is necessary and good but also about why authority is necessarily limited by the requirements of human flourishing. There cannot be a complete melding of autonomy and authority, which Rousseau sees in the emergence of the general will, and which is echoed as well in Raz's convergence between autonomy and authority. Ironically, it is not Raz but Simon, the stout defender of authority, who protects individual prerogative because his understanding of authority is coupled with his recognition of the variegated nature of the good.

DECISIONISM

Schmitt's argument against neutrality points to a normative basis for law

Although my concept of law recognizes command as the paradigmatic form of law and locates its normativity in an orientation to the common good rather than in some form of democratic legitimacy, it remains fully compatible with democracy and is ultimately symbiotic with the ends expressed in concerns for democratic legitimacy. To reinforce both law's inescapable normativity (its rootedness in substantive ends) and my theory's compatibility with popular sovereignty, I return to the once-again unlikely source of Schmitt. First, as I explain, despite his "decisionism," Schmitt is not a positivist. Second, not only is Schmitt not a positivist, but he is also a strident critic of neutrality, ruling it out as a possibility in politics and law. On the contrary, he insists on law's normativity (its directness toward substantive ends) and frames it in a way that resonates with our idea of law's necessary relationship with the common good.

Moreover, Schmitt's opposition to neutrality notwithstanding, his theory is compatible with democracy (and, like my theory, more than just compatible). Although Schmitt attacks liberalism, this is not because he opposes democracy, per se. Indeed, for our purposes, his critique is quite important because it targets majoritarianism unmoored from substantive aims. The point here is only to show that we cannot see the law in nonnormative terms as Hart and other positivists wish to do. To avoid the incoherence of functionalism, a democracy must be oriented toward, and constrained by, certain values that lie behind the procedural aspects. Although Schmitt certainly formulates it differently, he helps to make the case for a concept of law that depends upon the legal system being oriented to the common good.

Embracing the command model in my concept of law is not an adoption of positivism because it is only one part of the bipartite definition of law as a set of commands oriented to the common good. Austin's version of the command model is thoroughly (and intentionally) positivist because he defines the law as a form of command largely independent of the content (or any normative judgment of the content) of the command. To the extent that Carl Schmitt's political-theological model of sovereignty supports the command model of law and suggests the need for a commander, there is danger of mistaking Schmitt for a positivist. His emphasis on the need for "decision" and on decisiveness can seem to imply a nonnormative basis for legality, as though what matters is that a decision be made rather than the content of any decision. More broadly, seeing law as command does fit a positivist model of the law, if the command model means that we look only at the form of the law and ignore the content. But Schmitt is not a positivist, and he actually stands against positivism. Despite his "decisionism," Schmitt does not take the route that identifies law by its form without respect to content. On the contrary, for our purposes, Schmitt's work is instructive for his attack on positivism.

Schmitt does advocate for decisiveness in sovereignty. He favors the idea of a leader acting decisively over ongoing, seemingly interminable discussion in a legislative body, and his emphasis on decision over deliberation sometimes sounds as if the fact of making a decision—any decision—is more important than the content of what is decided. Nevertheless, the more assuredly we grasp his opposition to positivism, the more we can see how Schmitt's work supports the notion of law as a set of commands oriented to the common good.

In my definition of law, the notion of law as command is married to justification through an assessment of the legal system's orientation toward the common good. And, to repeat, the latter is not primarily a criterion to distinguish between individual just and unjust laws but, rather, is an inextricable part of legality itself.[68] Even though Schmitt does not write of the common good in our terms, he also does not think that the authority of the sovereign is without (normative) substance. He leaves the power of the sovereign unlimited, but this is not because law has no normative aspect. On the contrary, Schmitt is emphatic about the impossibility of true neutrality in the law and in politics precisely because he believes that politics is defined by normative judgments.[69] In practice, the sovereign is legally illimitable, but this must be true by definition because the sovereign makes the rules. The key normative point for Schmitt is that there are no legal limits on the sovereign because the sovereign may (and ought to) do whatever is necessary to preserve the existing order.[70] Put another way, the sovereign's legitimacy comes from the defense of certain goods (the common good, we might say), and it is the sovereign's responsibility to defend those goods.[71] Because it cannot be known what measure will be necessary to defend the very things whose defense legitimates the sovereign, there are no legal limits on what the sovereign can do. But, in this way, the legitimacy of the sovereign is indeed constrained not in the means it can use but in the ends it can pursue.

Schmitt argues most forcefully against positivism in *Legality and Legitimacy*. In essence, his charge against positivism, understood here as a claim of neutrality in the law between competing values, is twofold. First, positivism is incoherent for its inability to hold to the neutrality it espouses. Second, even if positivism is coherent and therefore actually neutral, without any substantive commitments, it is self-defeating because it lacks the resources to maintain itself. Schmitt demonstrates that there is no such thing as true value neutrality in politics. Every choice in politics and law is a choice for some value. Even a liberal democratic society run by majoritarian rule, ostensibly neutral between outcomes of any given vote, does not come without some underlying principle(s). For example, for those who favor parliamentarism, the underlying normative judgment can be in favor of equality, or what Schmitt calls "equal chances." For those with more Schmittian sensibilities (for whom parliamentarism has, at best, instrumental value), it can be for the sake of stability. Schmitt distinguishes liberalism from pure functionalism, but we can apply Schmitt's logic even to functionalism. For starters, there must be some reason why functionalism is the right choice in the first place. One way or another, functionalism must have some answer to the question of why functionalism is preferable, so even a choice for functionalism is not neutral.

First, for Schmitt, neutrality is impossible, and, therefore, any system that purports to maintain it is incoherent. His concept of the political necessarily rules out the possibility of neutrality because "any decision about whether something is *unpolitical* is always a *political* decision."[72] Indeed, Schmitt locates sovereignty first and foremost in the power to determine both when an emergency exists and what to do about it: "Sovereignty (and thus the state itself) resides in deciding this controversy, that is, in determining definitively what constitutes public order and security."[73] This ever-present ability to declare and respond to an emergency leaves no room for neutrality. It means there is always a standing judgment on whether it is a time of normal operations or a "state of exception" (what we can call in ordinary terms a state of emergency but which has more severe connotations in Schmitt's usage).[74] On the contrary, the exercise of sovereignty depends on a commitment to particular substantive values, in defense of which the sovereign is prepared to declare a state of exception and utilize emergency powers outside of the law. That is, the state of exception exists when there is a threat to the fundamental values to which the state is committed. This point is at the heart of Schmitt's critique of the functionalist-legislative state, which purports to uphold no more than value-neutral procedures. As he adds in the afterword to *Legality and Legitimacy*, "Value neutralization belonged to the general functionalization at work and made democracy into a worldview of fundamental relativism."[75] A strictly procedural system embraces relativism, lacking any mechanism to distinguish among, and defend, values.

Furthermore, while such a system proclaims neutrality, it remains nonneutral all the same. The farce of neutrality is revealed, for example, in some legislative states' adherence to substantive values that promote or ensure their self-preservation. Though not known for fondness toward the liberalism of his day, Schmitt accepts that, for liberals, "the bourgeois-legal system itself, with its concepts of law and freedom, is at least still sacred, and liberal value neutrality is viewed as a value, while fascism and bolshevism are openly termed the political enemy."[76] He contrasts this with pure functionalism, where "the value neutrality of a still only functional system of legality is taken to the extreme of absolute neutrality toward itself and offers the legal means for the elimination of illegality per se."[77] Under such circumstances, there are "no unconstitutional goals," and "value neutrality is pushed to the point of system suicide."[78] This is a functionalism that cannot even defend and sustain itself. For this reason, McCormick understands Schmitt as advocating for the government's authority to preserve itself—for example, in moving to exclude antidemocratic parties, in which case "an unconstitutional act in fact proves to be constitutionally faithful" whereas "open legality invites the triumph of absolutely illegality."[79]

Another example of the nonneutrality of the legislative state is the appeal to equal political participation as a value or even justification for authority. This is not what Schmitt recommends as the basis for legitimacy, but it does show that even purported functionalism likely depends on some nonprocedural value. And here, too, a Schmittian friend-enemy distinction applies: "One can hold open an equal chance only for those whom one is certain would do the same"; otherwise it is "suicide in practical terms but also an offense against the principle itself."[80] That is, even the allegedly neutral principle of equal participation must make substantive judgments about who can participate. If it attempts to refuse even this, then it is in high danger of not even being able to sustain itself. Declining to exclude those who aim to destroy the system sacrifices long-term political equality in the name of giving would-be tyrants, anarchists, and so on an equal chance. Thus, Schmitt's unheeded position in 1932 Germany "aimed at banishing extreme political movements from the political arena."[81]

Schmitt's claim that politics cannot be neutral rests first and foremost on his friend-enemy distinction.[82] He proclaims the need for recognizing the value judgments inherent in all political choices and, as he says, the impossibility of making only nonpolitical choices. As a result, Schmitt concludes, "State and politics cannot be exterminated," adding further that "this allegedly non-political and apparently even antipolitical system serves existing or newly emerging friend-and-enemy groupings and cannot escape the logic of the political."[83] In a related essay, "The Age of Neutralizations and Depoliticizations," Schmitt expands on this theme, using the example of technology as the tool of modernity's futile attempt to suppress, avoid, or deny the political. Technology is not the only vehicle for ill-fated attempts to escape the political, but Schmitt believes that the pursuit of this avenue prominently characterizes the modern age.[84] "The evidence of widespread contemporary belief in technology," Schmitt claims in his essay, "is based on the proposition that the absolute and ultimate neutral ground has been found in technology, since apparently there is nothing more neutral."[85] Relying on technology to advance neutrality is doomed to fail, however, because "the neutrality of technology is something other than the neutrality of all former domains."[86] Modern democracies can place all of the emphasis on technological progress in the hope of eschewing central moral questions, but Schmitt insists that those questions must be asked and that judgments must be made—especially those pertaining to the friend-enemy distinction. A society that fails to ask and answer such questions is poorer for it, and this eventually spells its demise. A society that pretends it need not ask such questions is only deluding itself.

Schmitt's rejection of neutrality in politics extends similarly to his discussion of law, so we can see his clear antipositivism there as well. Schmitt opposes what he refers to as the functionalist approach to law, which attempts to achieve neutrality by valuing procedure but not substance: "Comprehending law and statute without relation to any content as the present conclusion of the transitory parliamentary majority corresponds to a purely functional manner of thinking. In this way, law, statute, and legality become 'neutral' procedural mechanisms and voting procedures that are indifferent toward content of any sort and accessible to any substantive claim."[87] In this functionalist state, "The written constitution of the parliamentary legislative state must ultimately limit itself to organizational and procedural rules" in the name of "neutrality."[88] This position is untenable, though. McCormick reads Schmitt to mean that "law placed in the service of democratically responsive policies of regulation and redistribution necessarily descends into arbitrariness and incoherence."[89] McCormick writes that, for Schmitt, merely following "the new legal policies of the latest party or interest-group coalition that formulated them constitute[s] a kind of revolution approximating an illegitimate assault on the very structure of state and society."[90] So even if the functionalist state is not neutral between functionalism and any alternatives, functionalism's commitment to majoritarianism is still a problem. Schmitt acknowledges that the legislative state "may not be 'neutral' toward itself and its own presuppositions."[91]

Yet where the state's values extend only to majority rule, "all guarantees of justice and reasonableness, along with the concept of law and legality itself, end in an internally consistent functionalist view without substance and content that is rooted in arithmetic understandings of the majority."[92] In that case, there is no reason to assume that the majority will be sensitive to the common good. For Schmitt, the legitimacy of such a system depends on homogeneity in society. This "method of will formation," he says, "is sensible and acceptable when an essential similarity among the entire people can be assumed."[93] Under conditions of homogeneity, "There is no voting down of the minority."[94] Rather, "The vote should only permit a latent and presupposed agreement and consensus to become evident" because "all those similarly situated would in essence will the same thing."[95] But, in the absence of homogeneity, an arithmetic approach to law is "the opposite of neutrality and objectivity"; it is, instead, "forced subordination of the defeated and, therefore, suppressed minority."[96]

While Schmitt's critique begins (conceptually) with the claim that neutrality is mistaken because of functionalism's incoherence, it points to a deeper problem, namely that even allegedly neutral systems are not truly so. In his paradoxical-sounding formulation, Schmitt asserts, "Should only neutrality prevail in the world, then not only war but also neutrality would come to an end."[97] Schmitt explicates further, "But in the dialectic of such a development one creates a new domain of struggle precisely through the shifting of the central domain. In the new domain, at first considered neutral, the antithesis of men and interests unfold with a new intensity and become increasingly sharper. Europeans always have wandered from a conflictual to a neutral domain, and always the newly won domain has become immediately another arena of struggle, once again necessitating the search for a new neutral domain."[98] In the arena of the political, neutrality always gives way to nonneutrality, or struggle, and, in Schmitt's analysis, the new conflict is normally worse than the old one. At the most basic level, even a choice for neutrality is a substantive choice, much as, to quote again, "any decision about whether something is *unpolitical* is always a *political* decision."[99] Schmitt writes, "In regard to the question of neutrality and non-neutrality, whoever intends to remain neutral has already decided in favor of neutrality. Value assertion and value neutrality are mutually exclusive. Compared to a seriously intended value assertion and affirmation, conscientious value neutrality means a denial of values."[100]

And even if one does not take this route in the interpretation of functionalism as nonneutral, there is still the question of *why neutrality*: What substantive principle motivates *it*? Why choose neutrality? According to McCormick, Schmitt maintains that the legislative state, if not purely functionalist, can be saved by acknowledging "preconstitutional and prelegal substantive values or concrete decisions" that undergird the system and by recognizing that "these, and not the law itself, as liberals hope, are the source of the regime's legitimacy."[101] McCormick explains that, at the barest minimum, Schmitt believes that "even the most formally neutral constitution cannot espouse neutrality toward its own existence."[102]

Furthermore, a constitution that espouses neutrality toward its own existence is a recipe for disaster. This returns us to Schmitt's second lesson about attempted neutrality: it is self-defeating. Schmitt argues that a concept of legality that can be used against itself to destroy the law (the constitution) is not only incoherent in principle but also unstable in practice. For Schmitt, neutrality in politics and the law is unsustainable and prone to ending in oppression.[103] In his view, failure to suppress extreme political movements allows for their triumph. A political and legal order that claims to ensure procedural fairness while remaining substantively neutral cannot endure or at least cannot justify itself because it has no value to which to appeal for justification.

A regime that cannot survive or cannot give a reasonable account of its own authority is undesirable, to say the least. Still, there is a more profound claim embedded in Schmitt's argument: that preservation of the regime is built into the logic of the law. Implicit in any particular political and legal system is the idea that the current arrangement is preferable to other arrangements and perhaps preferable to all other feasible arrangements (which otherwise would be adopted). Even if it is not the best of all possible arrangements, it is at least part of a set of possibilities that are better than all of the possibilities not in the set. In this way, we can see again that, strictly speaking, claims of substantive neutrality are not correct. It can technically be possible to argue that a given arrangement is not taken to be superior to any other choice and that the only thing keeping it in place is that it is *some* choice. This is a weak rejoinder, though, because that is such a poor reason for keeping a system in place because it is to defend the system on no other grounds than that it is better than nothing. Few have the incentive to uphold such a system, meaning that few have a reason to support it other than the fact of it being the one they have. This sort of self-understanding in a political system portends serious instability or worse. There can be no neutrality because all politics and law entail some judgment about the good. The fact that there can be differing views about the good does not negate the fact that judgments about the good are at the heart of politics and law.

Schmitt's theory is compatible with democracy despite his objections to functionalism

Schmitt contends that the disappearance of true authority accompanies the rise of modern parliamentarism. Furthermore, he is highly critical of Rousseau's equation of the will of the sovereign with the will of the people. Adding those points to Schmitt's commitment to the decisionistic and personalistic elements of sovereignty, we can wonder whether Schmitt is compatible with democracy. I investigate Schmitt's compatibility with these because I want to draw on Schmitt to support my concept of law and also insist that my concept of law is compatible (and more than just compatible) with liberalism and democracy. We can maintain that Schmitt is important for his critique of positivism even if we have to accept that he is not fully compatible with some common versions of democratic norms. The sovereign, according to McCormick's interpretation of Schmitt, "possesses a world-making, God-like fiat of exceptional legislative authority."[104] But the question is whether this can include the people as the sovereign or whether the sovereign must be like a deity that sits above and apart from the people. In the end, while Schmitt rejects parliamentarism, his objection is limited to certain forms of popular rule; he does not oppose democracy in general.

Another concern to address if I wish to rely on Schmitt for support is whether my concept of law risks self-contradiction of the very kind Schmitt rejects in *Legality and Legitimacy*.[105] Clearly, it does not do to rely on Schmitt in explaining law if it turns out that Schmitt's understanding of law is sufficiently different altogether as to be inapplicable here and especially if my theory is ultimately incompatible with his political-theological model. Yet we can draw on one part of Schmitt's work and not another if those parts are severable. So, in addition to showing how Schmitt supports my view, I must also show that there is enough overlap to deploy him fairly to my ends despite some important differences.

Schmitt's rejection of positivism is distinct, if not unique, because it is intertwined with a rejection of what he calls functionalism or parliamentarism. For this reason, Schmitt's idea of authority is less easily reconciled with democratic norms than is, for example, a natural law understanding of authority. To be sure, attempting to reconcile Schmitt's decisionism with democracy can seem misguided altogether, given that his account of sovereignty locates authority in a single, decisive powerholder. But, in fact, his view is only a dismissal of a particular kind of participatory politics: he favors a plebiscitarian democracy that avoids the problems of parliamentarism.[106] For Schmitt, a deliberative body characteristic of the latter sort cannot offer the kind of decisiveness necessary to defend the polity in times of trouble. But that rules out only one form of participatory government; it does not rule out political participation entirely.

Schmitt's opposition to the legislative state is really twofold. First, its functionalism attempts to vest authority in rules rather than in people.[107] For Schmitt, the legislative state is characterized chiefly by the "separation of law and legal application, the legislative and the executive," which is the product of the "directly necessary, constructive, fundamental principle of the legislative state, in which not men and persons rule, but rather where norms are valid."[108] This is unacceptable to Schmitt because "laws do not rule; they are valid only as norms."[109] "There is no ruling and mere power at all anymore," insists Schmitt. He condemns the legislative state as one in which there is "no longer any government or obedience in general because only impersonal, valid norms are being applied."[110] One can clearly see here a prospective criticism of Hart, who dramatically reorients the understanding of law away from the personalistic element and "mere power" to the validity of rules and norms. Law, for Hart, is grounded in norms that emerge from social practice. In making law, officials conform to rules that already exist and come from "nowhere."

Schmitt's point about rules versus people is a significant one because, in his view, a rule-based state is what makes deep value-pluralism possible for liberals because the system is founded on procedures rather than substantive commitments. That is, each alternative form of government entails foundational claims about the nature of the state. As Strong puts it in his commentary on Schmitt's *Political Theology*:

> This claim is at the basis of Schmitt's rejection of what he calls "liberal normativism" — that is, of the assumption that a state can ultimately rest on a set of mutually agreed-to procedures and rules that trump particular claims and necessities. Pluralism is thus not a condition on which politics, and therefore eventually the state, can be founded. Politics rests rather on the equality of its citizens (in this sense Schmitt is a "democrat") and thus their collective differentiation from other such groups: this is the "friend/enemy" distinction, or more accurately the distinction that makes politics possible. It is, one might say, its transcendental presupposition.[111]

Pluralism of the sort Schmitt decries no more serves as an adequate foundation for a state than neutrality (and, indeed, they are essentially the same). Schmitt argues throughout that the formalist, or proceduralist, neutrality to which the legislative state aspires is impossible. It is both inadequate and self-defeating. It cannot serve as a proper conceptual basis for a political community, which must distinguish between members and nonmembers, and, in any case, it must end in some form of substantive distinction-making.

In addition, the legislative state is flawed because its parliamentarism places special interests ahead of the will of the people. Under the legislative state's "absolute, 'value-neutral,' functionalist and formal concept of law," the law "is only the present decision of the momentary parliamentary majority."[112] As a result, Schmitt favors a plebiscitary form of democracy, instead. It is here that Schmitt is at his most paradoxical, favoring popular voting and a decisive sovereign but ultimately revealing himself to be a democrat, in the sense that Strong suggests, if not a liberal.

On one hand, Schmitt maintains a certain opposition to popular rule. As he writes, "In the struggle of opposing interests and coalitions, absolute monarchy made the decision and thereby created the unity of the state. The unity that a people represents does not possess this decisionistic character; it is an organic unity, and with the national consciousness the ideas of the state originated as an organic whole."[113] For this reason, according to George Schwab, Schmitt "determined to reinstate the personal element in sovereignty and make it indivisible once more."[114] In this, Schmitt sounds undemocratic. Moreover, it is not only in response to liberalism's or parliamentarism's failure that Schmitt advocates decisionism. The main point for Schmitt is that the decision is the true mark of sovereignty, prior to and independent of the flaws of any system in which authority is institutionalized.

On the other hand, Schmitt reserves his ire not for popular rule, per se, but specifically for nonpersonalistic, parliamentary forms of democracy that he believes follow from liberalism, for, with Donoso Cortés, he sees in "continuous discussion a method of circumventing responsibility."[115] In contrast to decisionism, which takes "the immediately executable directive as a legal value in itself," the "parliamentary legislative state's tendency toward endless discussion" is the true danger.[116] Under such circumstances, Schmitt writes, "It still holds true: 'The best thing in the world is a command.'"[117] Proponents of parliamentarism suffer under the same illusion of nonjudgment, as it were, as those who hold out hope for true neutrality and the elimination of making divisive, substantive decisions: "The essence of liberalism is negotiation, a cautious half measure, in the hope that the definitive dispute, the decisive bloody battle, can be transformed into a parliamentary debate and permit the decision to be suspended forever in an everlasting discussion."[118] Schmitt knows, however, that conflict cannot be avoided indefinitely, that a "decision" always has to be made eventually. And he recognizes that the outcome of indefinite, indeterminate deliberation may be dictatorship (in response to the desperation that arises from prolonged indecision), which is "the opposite of discussion."[119] When real authority is no longer possible, the "logical conclusion" is "political dictatorship."[120] For Schmitt, liberalism of a certain sort paves the way for dictatorship due to the absence of the kind of decisionism possible under proper monarchies. Ironically, in Schmitt's view, those who cherish liberal values ought not to scoff at his preferred form of authority, which he proposes to be less of a threat than certain forms of liberalism.

Again, Schmitt is not against the rule of the people; he endorses self-rule in a plebiscitary form of democracy. This is critical because it further enables us to reconcile Schmitt's work with popular government.[121] Plebiscitary democracy is superior to parliamentary democracy, according to Schmitt, because "the logical consistency of a system built on the idea of a representation is different than that of the plebiscitary-democratic sovereign people, which is directly present and thus not represented."[122] McCormick explains Schmitt's position as follows: "According to Schmitt's logic, if the people attempt to actually *participate* politically, they will be merely represented by parties that supposedly threaten popular unity. If they simply *acclaim* the President and his policies, however, they can be represented, embodied, as a whole, because *he* is a whole."[123] Thus, while Schmitt apparently holds to a minimalist view of popular rule through representation, he still grounds authority in the will of the people as a whole. For Schmitt, McCormick claims, the key is not the depth of the people's participation but its directness: "The people are more directly and thereby more faithfully represented by the President than the parliament."[124] Rule by a parliament, says McCormick, is "a subjection to a particularistic, legalistically empowered party" whereas rule by a president is "a subjection to the general, democratically legitimate will."[125] For the functionalist-pluralist, government is naturally composed of special interests. But Schmitt argues that plebiscites offer a different, and more robust, kind of legitimacy. For him, "the referendum is always a higher form of decision."[126] He elaborates on this idea to the effect that "the meaning of the plebiscitary expression of will is, however, not norm establishment, but decision through one will, as the word 'referendum,' or popular decision, aptly expresses."[127] The expression of a singular will is channeled through a president, in whom the people are united, or "present." For this reason, "plebiscitary legitimacy is the single type of state justification that may be generally acknowledged as valid today."[128]

McCormick sums up Schmitt's point, writing, "The people are more directly and thereby more faithfully represented by the President than [by the] the parliament."[129] And he adds an important point on Schmitt's behalf, that the "will of the people as a whole more closely approximates justice than that of some party in parliament."[130] This dovetails well with our idea that the justification of authority must come back to justice and the common good, even if there is room for disagreement with Schmitt about how we can advance them. Ironically, then, in Schmitt's counterintuitive way, he prefers the presidential system, like referenda, because he sees it as more democratic, not less, and more in keeping with the requirement to pursue justice.

The difference between voting for a parliament and voting for a president is a key distinction, not merely a difference of institutional design, in Schmitt's theory. The concept of a referendum helps us see this because of the way it, too, is a reflection of decisionism: "The people can only respond yes or no. They cannot advise, deliberate, or discuss. They cannot govern or administer. They also cannot set norms, but can only sanction norms by consenting to a draft set of norms laid before them. Above all, they cannot pose a question, but can only answer with yes or no to a question placed before them."[131] McCormick adds, though, "Plebiscites are self-limiting and actually demonstrate a leader's dependence on the people."[132] Plebiscites show the direct dependence of authority on the people. Even so, this does not jeopardize the sovereign's illimitability because "Schmitt proposes as the only limit on the authority of plebiscites the faith in its administrators to ask the appropriate question."[133] These two competing themes, the dependence on the people and the seemingly meager limitation on authority, point to an apparent tension in Schmitt's theory between democracy and sovereignty, which can be reconciled only through the plebiscite. McCormick concludes, "If government is going to be legitimate in contemporary circumstances—circumstances of mass democracy, pluralist interests, and complex bureaucratic governance—authority must be justified plebiscitarily."[134]

Yet we can still doubt whether we have fully accommodated Schmitt to democracy if sovereignty lies truly with the person in charge and not with the people in general. This doubt arises not only because, according to Schmitt, the people, until they are unified in the sovereign, lack the decisiveness of a ruler but also because, in principle, the sovereign is legally illimitable, which seems to put her beyond the control of the people. At the same time, in my own theory, justification does not ultimately trace back to the consent of the people but to the common good. So it is only fitting that we can find support in Simon's explication of designation theory for seeing how Schmitt's plebiscitarianism links to the common good. It seems that, according to Simon, sovereignty can rest only with God or the people, and God gives people authority to rule over people, not unlike people giving other people authority to rule over them. Simon writes that "designation theory is a more moderate, less paradoxical form of the divine-right theory; it holds that in temporal power the only thing traceable, *in any sense*, to human power is the designation of the ruling person."[135] The distinction between the justification of authority and the designation of authority is helpful because it shows how, in designation theory, it is not justification of authority, per se, that comes from the people. Rather, what comes from the people is the designation of the particular person who justifiably exercises authority. The justification itself, though, derives from a separate source, namely the advancement of the common good.

The election or selection of a sovereign in a Schmittian plebiscite is not exactly what most theorists have in mind for a robust democracy. Similarly, what Simon describes as designation theory is democratic mainly insofar as power traces back to the people etiologically, and democratic power is exercised by them only in this constrained sense. Simon confirms this in writing that the obligation to obey, having "its roots in the nature of things, in the very nature of man and of human society," is "completely independent of my casual belonging to the majority or the minority. This is why the coach-driver theory is unlikely to be very popular where there is a strong belief in a law of nature independent of the whims of man."[136] Majorities can have an important role to play in government, but they are neither the source of authority nor the arbiters of justice just as such.

Despite popular approval not being necessary for authority, the fact that (in the case of human authority) there needs to be a designation of some individual or group as the authority means that there may be many contingent reasons why the best body to do this designating is the people. Although Schmitt seems to resist this, in the ordinary case, the people can be both the authority and the subjects, acting in different capacities as commander and commanded. Anscombe notes that Hart "attacks the notions of 'sovereign' and 'subject' where we have a democracy."[137] Hart rejects the idea that there can be sovereign and subject where the people rule themselves because he denies the possibility of sovereign and subject existing within the same entity. Perhaps Hart overly associates those terms with habits of obedience (and coercion) and therefore thinks it does not make sense for a self-governing people to be considered subjects. But the utility of conceptualizing authority in terms of sovereign and subject does not come from any relation to notions of habits or coercion but, rather, to obligation. It is neither habits of obedience nor coercive power that makes the sovereign the sovereign or the subject the subject. Therefore, we are able to retain the terms *sovereign* and *subject* in a meaningful way, thus drawing upon theorists with robust conceptions of sovereignty, such as Schmitt and, separately, Simon, yet still insist that my concept of law remains compatible with democracy.

Admittedly, Schmitt's view of presidents and plebiscites, including his distaste for parliamentary deliberation, makes him at least an unconventional democrat. But perhaps we can narrow the gap between parliamentary and plebiscitary government.[138] Schwab speculates that, for Schmitt, "the condition of his acceptance of political parties and parliament would be that they be united with the sovereign—the popularly elected president—in seeking solutions necessary for the welfare of the entire civil society."[139] This means that the parliament has to be realigned away from special interests—a core concern for Schmitt—such that it, too, seeks the common good. Schmitt's point is that, when the law embodies nothing more than majority will, it is the fruit of functionalism and lacks legitimacy. Schmitt thus argues, contra the positivists, that legality and legitimacy are conceptually and institutionally inseparable. Legality without legitimacy is effectively meaningless because law exists for certain ends.[140] The common good, or, for Schmitt, the will of the people, is an integral part of sovereignty; without it, there is no real sovereignty, which is to say, no justified authority. In other words, even if we concede on the question of Schmitt's compatibility with liberal democracy, there is a critical point in Schmitt's emphasis on the common good's centrality to legitimacy.

Schmitt has a less capacious view of law but agrees on the fundamental point of law's normativity

In addition to ensuring that Schmitt is not a positivist and that his view is reconcilable with democracy, we have to start all the way at the beginning, as it were, and ask whether his concepts of politics and law are sufficiently compatible with my theory. If we cannot make that work, then all the more specific, subsidiary issues do not even come into play. For our purposes, there is no meaningful difference between political and legal obligation, and a satisfactory theory of legal obligation can be rather capacious in its understanding of law. As long as we are referring to requirements imposed by the system, there is no meaningful difference between different types of legal obligations: all commands under justified authority are, for all intents and purposes, law. Any obligation that exists due to the binding directives of a commander is the functional equivalent of a law. It may not take the form of a statute, but it is law just the same. A coherent concept of law does not need the common distinction between, say, constitutional provisions and the instructions of a policeman at an intersection. An order from a police officer is not a statute, but the obligation to obey her is a legal obligation, implicitly or explicitly. A concept of law that makes sense of authority's normativity encompasses all directives generating legal obligations. While some wish to distinguish between political obligations and legal obligations, the former usually refers to moral obligations of the political sort, such as the moral obligation to vote (if there is one). But everything the political system requires of subjects can reasonably be construed as a legal obligation, whether or not it comes in the form of a statute and the like.

We must not take this loose definition of law for granted, however. Austin, for one, argues that certain measures, depending on certain descriptive features, are not properly called law. In his view, an order can be too particular to be a law. If, for example, the legislature prohibits the exportation of a particular shipment of corn, that "would not be a law or rule, though issued by the sovereign legislature."[141] It makes sense that an order that is insufficiently general does not qualify as a rule because the idea of a rule and especially of law is that it creates standards that can be applied to similar circumstances across different instances. In the corn example, the order applies only to the particular case. Nevertheless, in the sense that there is an obligation to obey (if there is) and that the authorities are justified in enforcing it (if they are)—and that anyone subject to the law ought to take it as a standard or measure of behavior, as Hart puts it—the order is very much a law, and violations can be properly called "illegal." The application of the concept of law does not depend on the scope of directives as long as they are of the authoritative type. This allows us to capture everything that rightly falls under the title of law.

Like Austin, Schmitt addresses the need for the legislative state to distinguish between statutes and measures if it is to maintain its coherence:

> In terms of constitutional theory, the actual basis of confusion in both public and constitutional law lies in the degeneration of the concept of law. There can be no legislative state without an accepted, distinct concept of law. Most importantly, such a state must insist that law and statute, statute and justice, stand in a meaningful relation to one another, and, consequently, that the legislature's norm creation, undertaken on the basis of its legislative powers, is something other and higher than a mere measure. In a legislative state, whose entire system of legality rests in the priority of such statutory sets of norms, it is not possible to issue a measure as a statute and a statute as a measure.[142]

In contrast to a statute, a measure is the "consideration of just the singular circumstances of a case."[143] Schmitt laments that "the legislature itself has long abandoned the inner distinction between statute and measure," having failed to see that this narrower scope is part of the "essence of the measure" and not just determined by varying statutory language.[144]

Schmitt's insistence on the distinction between statutes and measures is an important challenge if we wish to draw on his theory of law to support our own; we need to be sure we are speaking of compatible concepts of law. The scope of the directive does not matter in the context of our analysis. This element of Schmitt's thinking, distinguishing between different types of directives, makes it more difficult to draw Schmitt into my modified version of the command model because I want to claim that all are commands (and law) in the relevant sense. However, Schmitt's notion of decrees leaves room for a broader concept of law that works for here as well. Schmitt doubts the coherence of the legislative state, for which, in a "state of exception," "the 'measures' of the office empowered for extraordinary action are not contrary to law, but they also do not have the force of law."[145] In a presidential system, which escapes this incoherence, there is a third category beyond statutes and measures: decrees. In essence, the decree is to the president what the emergency measure is to the legislature. But just as the president has far greater legitimacy for Schmitt than the parliament, so, too, decrees have higher standing than these measures.

In fact, because decrees, insofar as they are emergency actions, emerge from the paradigmatic expression of sovereignty, they can even surpass statutes in their legitimacy (or "lawness"—i.e., the extent to which they embody law in its central, or essential, form) for Schmitt. McCormick explains, "In terms that recall 'the exception' from his *Political Theology* written a decade before, Schmitt declares that the extraordinary circumstances lend decrees more than normative equality with statutes; decrees have acquired a normative superiority such that 'law' now means a measure and not a statute."[146] This is, as McCormick points out, an inversion of the ordinary liberal understanding, whereby the considered judgments of a representative legislature in the form of statutes command the most legitimacy (relative to emergency actions).[147] In part, the primacy of decrees is because, in McCormick's words, "the increasing bureaucratization of society gives presidential decrees a more stable and enduring quality than parliamentary statutes that merely reflect transitory legislative majorities."[148] Going further, Schmitt "justifies presidential decrees that would have a permanent and not just temporary force of law," which demonstrates his willingness to see decrees as law.[149] In turn, this means that, for Schmitt, the scope of a decree, whether in duration or breadth, is not determinative of whether it is "law." This is important because, in principle, there is no reason under the command model why decrees or emergency measures issued by the sovereign are not "law" (again in the relevant sense) and no reason why they are any less so than statutes ratified by a legislature. Accordingly, Schmitt's willingness to see decrees as law means that Schmitt's concept of law is capacious enough to be compatible with and, therefore, useful for, my own.

Beyond the difficulty of appropriating Schmitt given his distinction between decrees and statutes is a deeper, related difficulty: whether we can appropriate Schmitt given his distinction between the concept of law and the concept of the political. On one hand, Strong argues that, to understand Schmitt's view of sovereignty, one must see that "politics (or here, 'the political') is not the same for Schmitt as 'the state.'"[150] Rather, the state is just the most common modern "concretization" of the political.[151] On the other hand, politics and the state are intertwined: Schmitt, in his book on the concept of the political, claims, "The concept of the state presupposes the concept of the political."[152] Where the state is the "concretization" of the political, there is, for Schmitt, an important distinction between the state and the law. Drawing out this distinction, Schmitt writes, "What characterizes an exception is principally unlimited authority, which means the suspension of the entire existing order. In such a situation, it is clear that the state remains, whereas law recedes."[153] Schmitt is quick to add that the recession of the law does not mean "anarchy and chaos"; on the contrary, "order in the juristic sense still prevails."[154] But if decrees can be law just like statutes, then all authority exercised in an exception can be seen as a form of law. Therefore, Schmitt is likely using the term *law* in this context to refer to the set of rules that govern under ordinary circumstances—that is, statutes. As he says in *Legality and Legitimacy*, extraordinary measures are every bit as authoritative as, if not more than, statutes. They are law, then, in the sense of being authoritative directives (commands that obligate), assuming they emanate from justified authority. That these directives are not law in the sense that characterizes the directives of the state in ordinary times is not a problem for our purposes. As long as the directive is authoritative, then it shares the relevant features of law. The absence of legal constraints on the sovereign does not mean the absence of law in this broader sense. Indeed, Schmitt's idea of the exception actually helps to make the general point about law and authority. The "principally unlimited authority" of which he speaks is authority without legal constraints—that is, not subject to the normal procedures of the state. But there are still moral constraints, to which the sovereign (or the state) is always subject. Those constraints reflect the moral purposes that motivate the declaration of the state of exception. As seen in Schmitt's attack on neutrality, there must be some moral substance at stake that justifies the use of emergency powers (which is to say, extraordinary measures for the preservation of the state) in the first place. Therefore, once again, we see Schmitt making the critical point that we cannot understand authority (and law) apart from the substantive ends for which it exists.

Conclusion

STUDYING THE CONCEPT OF LAW OPENS DEEPER QUESTIONS ABOUT POLITICS AND CIVILIZATION

As I tell my students, one of the central questions in political philosophy is whether politics is ultimately about justice or power. This debate is one way to describe the arc of the field from its earliest core texts to some of its most prominent postmodern figures. "What is justice?" is the animating question for Socrates's discussions in Plato's *Republic*, and the quest to define justice is at the heart of understanding politics. About two and a half millennia later, riffing on Carl von Clausewitz, Michel Foucault observed that, while "it may be that war as strategy is a continuation of politics," "it must not be forgotten that 'politics' has been conceived as a continuation, if not exactly and directly of war, at least of the military model as a fundamental means of preventing civil disorder."[1] Foucault's position is that all laws (and not just laws) are a form of subjugation of one group by another.

But we do not need to reach across the ages to find this dichotomy. On the contrary, Socrates's most adamant foil in the *Republic* is Thrasymachus, who contends that justice "is nothing other than the advantage of the stronger."[2] Thrasymachus serves as Socrates's most significant opponent precisely because he represents a polar-opposite approach to justice, essentially reducing "justice" to power, much like Thucydides has the Athenians do in the Melian Dialogue with their "might makes right" stance.

This division between competing interpretations of politics is absolutely critical because it determines whether political competition is about advancing different visions of the common good or merely about seeking to dominate the rest, whether through strength of numbers in a democracy or otherwise. If politics is about justice, then even when we disagree—even when we disagree passionately and even when we disagree all the way down—we believe we are working for the good of all, however imperfectly. Ideally, this also tames politics if all sides are and see each other as enacting some vision of the common good. Moreover, law's connection to the common good serves as a check on those advancing an agenda in good faith because it demands an account of how that agenda contemplates the good of all. For this reason, grasping the connection to the common good teaches us that we owe each other reasons—reasons rooted in a final appeal to justice—for the restrictions we impose upon each other through the law. If politics is about power, then it just comes down to defeating or being defeated. Reasons are nice, but they are not an essential ingredient in deciding who rules or what the rules are.

A parallel problem is inherent in positivism. To take one version of sovereignty, if authority resides with the one who is regularly obeyed and who regularly obeys no one, then authority is fundamentally about power. Positivism functions precisely by identifying authority apart from consideration of why the individual (or group) is habitually obeyed and habitually obeys no one. While this does not necessarily mean there is no normative for the authority in this case, positivism does not and cannot require that there be such. Maybe the authority just has all the guns. Indeed, this sort of positivism is not too far off from Max Weber's famous formulation of the state as the entity that claims "the monopoly of legitimate force for itself."[3] To be sure, the word "legitimate" is doing a lot of work in that phrase, but it is telling that one of the most influential modern definitions of the state relies on a primary association between the state and violence. This does not have to mean that the state is unnecessarily violent, but it does mean that the state is characterized first and foremost by its capacity for violence—that is, its power.

This defect of positivism persists even with the redefinition of law (and, by extension, sovereignty) by Hart. For Hart, law rests on social rules, or rules based on social practice. This means, recast less elegantly, that law is just what we do around here; or at least the rules that underlie the law, allowing us to recognize what is a law, are just what we do around here. In other words, even for contemporary positivists, we can identify law without respect to any requirements of justice. As long as a law conforms to a given society's rules for recognizing law, namely the rule(s) of recognition, then it is in fact a law, regardless of what that society's rules for such happen to be. This is still a power-based argument, the main difference being that power lies with social rules rather than a commanding body.

In our current time, we can sense in certain quarters a waning commitment to the obligation to obey the law. We can be forgiven for wondering whether this is connected to the polarization that feeds this very idea of politics as a contest for power rather than a quest for justice. After all, the more one sees one's political opposites as enemies, the harder it is to see the other side as purveyors of a competing vision of the common good rather than opponents in zero-sum struggle for control. As the latter perspective crowds out the former, it is sometimes expressed nowadays in a "not my president" attitude or calls to defy court decisions, among other dangers. Simmons's worries notwithstanding, the health of our society is not improved by a declining appreciation for our obligation to obey the law. This means that a renewed understanding of the authority of law and the corresponding obligation to obey can serve not only our pursuit of the truth for its own sake but also a much-needed revival in civic mindedness, public spiritedness, and the elements of human flourishing supported by the political common good.

Hannah Arendt, in her essay "What Is Authority?," sees clearly the need to find some basis for law's authority outside of the fact of where power resides. Arguing for some normative criterion that stands outside of political power, Arendt writes:

Behind the liberal identification of totalitarianism with authoritarianism, and the concomitant inclination to see "totalitarian" trends in every authoritarian limitation of freedom, lies an older confusion of authority with tyranny, and of legitimate power with violence. The difference between tyranny and authoritarian government has always been that the tyrant rules in accordance with his own will and interest, whereas even the most draconian authoritarian government is bound by laws. Its acts are tested by a code which was made either not by man at all, as in the case of the law of nature or God's Commandments or the Platonic ideas, or at least not by those actually in power. The source of authority in authoritarian government is always a force external and superior to its own power; it is always this source, this external force which transcends the political realm, from which authorities derive their "authority," that is, their legitimacy, and against which their power can be checked.[4]

Although not sitting with the tradition of analytic jurisprudence or in the natural law schools of Simon and Finnis, Arendt grasps, in her own language, the key distinction between power and the potential for legitimacy from an external referent. This is markedly different from Hart's concept of law, which is, in this respect, self-referential. Law is identified by rules that identify law. Those rules have no necessary relationship to justice. "What we happen to do around here" has a certain status because it is accepted. This makes sense if positivism aims to identify law without reference to normative criteria. But there is nothing about positivism that offers Arendt any critique of totalitarianism.

One of the key points in Arendt's essay is the importance of religion, authority, and tradition. Arendt states:

Thanks to the fact that the foundation of the city of Rome was repeated in the foundation of the Catholic Church, though, of course, with a radically different content, the Roman trinity of religion, authority, and tradition could be taken over by the Christian era. The most conspicuous sign of this continuity is perhaps that the Church, when she embarked upon her great political career in the fifth century, at once adopted the Roman distinction between authority and power, claiming for herself the old authority of the Senate and leaving the power—which in the Roman Empire was no longer in the hands of the people but had been monopolized by the imperial household—to the princes of the world. Thus, at the close of the fifth century, Pope Gelasius I could write to Emperor Anastasius I: "Two are the things by which this world is chiefly ruled: the sacred authority and the royal power."[5]

What is so striking about this passage is Arendt's usage of the quote from Gelasius. Ordinarily, Gelasius's invocation of the two swords is taken to indicate a protoseparation of church and state. The pope has his sword, and the king has his. Yet Arendt reads the papal line not for this distinction but instead as a distinction between authority and power. The king surely has power, and that power emanates from the sword (at the time, quite literally the swords of the king's armies). But, unlike the monarchy, the church has authority, which is quite different from, though not exclusive of, power.

What, then, is authority? Arendt opens by declaring a crisis of authority in her day: "Little about its nature appears self-evident or even comprehensible to everybody, except that the political scientist may still remember that this concept was once fundamental to political theory, or that most will agree that a constant, ever-widening and -deepening crisis of authority has accompanied the development of the modern world in our century."[6] One wonders what Arendt would say today. Do we have too much authority? Not enough? Is desire for more authority now a cause of the political left or right? Arendt thinks we have lost the concept of authority, adding, "In order to avoid misunderstanding, it might have been wiser to ask in the title: What was—and not what is—authority? For it is my contention that we are tempted and entitled to raise this question because authority has vanished from the modern world."[7] Further: "Practically as well as theoretically, we are no longer in a position to know what authority really *is*."[8]

Although Arendt was writing in a separate context, her concerns about the loss of authority and of knowledge of it as a concept dovetail with positivists' identification of law independent of justification. For positivists, we can identify law as law without respect to whether the law is justified and, therefore, whether there is a moral obligation to obey it. This means law can have authority in that other sense—power—without having legitimacy. But what, really, is the point of that? As Finnis shows in "Law and What I Truly Should Decide," the very purpose of law as an enterprise must have something to do with justice.[9] A concept of law does not get us very far without the component of *justified* authority and the concomitant moral obligation to obey. Whatever added value positivists see in a "scientific" (nonnormative) concept of law seems minimal compared to the problems introduced by it. Leo Strauss covers this well in his rejection of the distinction between political philosophy and political science, where he details the distorting effects of the artificial division.[10]

Alternatively, the positivists' view can take us in the opposite direction to the conclusion that all law is authoritative and obligatory just because it is the law. That is, on one hand, if the existence of de facto authority (power) says nothing about the existence of de jure authority (justification), then the ability to identify de facto authority provides little analytic benefit. On the other hand, if the existence of de facto authority implies, indicates, or proves the existence of de jure authority, then we find ourselves back at might makes right and Thrasymachus's collapsed distinction between power and justice. In that case, it is not only that an unjust law is a law, but also that all unjust law is law. Plainly, such an approach leaves us unable to distinguish between the authority of the most benevolent and most malevolent rulers.

This rather extreme view is, understandably, not embraced in the literature. Instead, analytic jurisprudence tends to favor a position that is, in a different way, also opposite to the idea that law is authoritative just because it is law. This is Raz's view that the authority of law depends on the reasons behind the law already applying to the subject. It is opposite in the sense that, instead of potentially positing that all law is authoritative just because it is law, this theory suggests that no law is authoritative just because it is law. It always depends upon the reasons applying. So this leaves us with the question of whether there is something in between, something that validates the authority of law as law yet without underwriting a totalitarian form of law.

Here, again, Arendt is instructive. Speaking in her own idiom, she writes that authority cannot be reduced to "coercion" or "persuasion": "Since authority always demands obedience, it is commonly mistaken for some form of power or violence. Yet authority precludes the use of external means of coercion; where force is used, authority itself has failed. Authority, on the other hand, is incompatible with persuasion, which presupposes equality and works through a process of argumentation. Where arguments are used, authority is left in abeyance. Against the egalitarian order of persuasion stands the authoritarian order, which is always hierarchical. If authority is to be defined at all, then, it must be in contradistinction to both coercion by force and persuasion through arguments."[11] The stakes are high in the search for authority and a coherent, compelling concept of law. As I also tell my students, "You may not care about politics, but politics cares about you." Arendt links the loss of authority to the brokenness of politics in her age, a brokenness that I dare say has hardly abated: "With the loss of authority, however, the general doubt of the modern age also invaded the political realm, where things not only assume a more radical expression but become endowed with a reality peculiar to the political realm alone. What perhaps hitherto had been of spiritual significance only for the few now has become a concern of one and all. Only now, as it were after the fact, the loss of tradition and of religion have become political events of the first order."[12] Arendt sees "the elements of the Roman trinity" as intrinsically linked, such that, "whenever . . . religion or authority or tradition . . . was doubted or eliminated, the remaining two were no longer secure."[13] She goes on to explain the crushing consequences of the decline in various elements: "Thus, it was Luther's error to think that this challenge of the temporal authority of the Church and his appeal to unguided individual judgment would leave tradition and religion intact. So it was the error of Hobbes and the political theorists of the seventeenth century to hope that authority and religion could be saved without tradition. So, too, it was finally the error of the humanists to think it would be possible to remain within an unbroken tradition of Western civilization without religion and without authority."[14] According to Arendt, both tradition and religion are compromised in the absence of authority.

Though the loss of tradition and religion does not sound like bad news to everyone, such a dismissal fails to appreciate the broad way in which Arendt invokes these notions and the ways in which, in the broader sense, they are fundamental to human life. Arendt unsparingly equates the loss of authority to "the loss of the groundwork of the world":

> Some similar qualifications seem to me to be necessary regarding the modern loss of authority. Authority, resting on a foundation in the past as its unshakeable cornerstone, gave the world the permanence and durability which human beings need precisely because they are mortals—the most unstable and futile beings we know of. Its loss is tantamount to the loss of the groundwork of the world, which indeed since then has begun to shift, to change and transform itself with ever-increasing rapidity from one shape into another, as though we were living and struggling with a Protean universe where everything at any moment can become almost anything else.[15]

Despite the despairing words, Arendt concludes that passage with a glimmer of hope: "But the loss of worldly permanence and reliability—which politically is identical with the loss of authority—does not entail, at least not necessarily, the loss of the human capacity for building, preserving, and caring for a world that can survive us and remain a place fit to live in for those who come after us."[16] Somehow, despite the brokenness of the world, there remains the possibility of renewal. We take one step toward that renewal with a renewed understanding of the concept of law and the authority and obligation entailed therein.

NOTES

INTRODUCTION

1. This maxim is famously cited by Augustine and Aquinas, among others. Augustine writes, "Surely we will not dream of calling these laws unjust—or rather, not to call them 'laws' at all, for a law that is not just does not seem to me to be a law" (Augustine, *On the Free Choice of the Will*, 10). Aquinas, following Augustine, states, "The like are acts of violence rather than laws; because, as Augustine says, *a law that is not just, seems to be no law at all*" (Aquinas, *Summa Theologica*, 1020 [*ST* I-II, q. 96, a. 4]).

2. It is impossible to mention this topic without referring to Plato's *Crito*, a classic text on the question of whether there is an obligation to obey the law. The profound importance of the *Crito* even in our time shows that this enduring human question is relevant in all ages.

3. Hart, *Concept of Law*, 7.

4. Following the convention in jurisprudence, I normally employ the term *justification* when discussing whether law is authoritative in the relevant sense, namely from a normative perspective. As far as I am concerned, though, the language of *legitimacy* serves equally well, so I occasionally alternate between the terms for the sake of clarity, such as to conform to the vocabulary of a particular author under discussion. For our purposes, both *justification* and *legitimacy* carry the same meaning of creating an obligation to obey. Furthermore, because I understand justification as a necessary part of law properly so called, it is redundant to call a legal system just or justified—though, of course, I do so when it adds clarity.

5. This is similar to the language Marmor uses in laying out the dilemma of authority. See Marmor, "Dilemma of Authority."

6. This is extremely consequential in real life because the difference between having justified authority and not having justified authority is the difference between justice and raw coercive power.

7. Marmor, "Dilemma of Authority," 25.

8. Marmor, "Dilemma of Authority," 2.

9. I refer to this as the focal (or central) case of obedience because I am trying to get at cases in which the reason for acting is the directive itself. In any real-life scenario, one can have additional reasons for acting besides the command (i.e., content-dependent reasons), but to act for those reasons is not to obey precisely because it is to act for those other reasons. (It is also not to disobey, to be sure.)

10. This is exactly the title of Smith's article ("Is There a Prima Facie Obligation to Obey the Law?"). See Smith, "Is There a Prima Facie Obligation."

11. As famously defined by Raz, an exclusionary reason is a specific kind of second-order reason that is a reason for not acting (i.e., a reason for refraining from acting) for a reason. See, for example, Raz, *Practical Reason and Norms*.

12. Going forward, for simplicity, I generally prefer to collapse "to act or to not act" and especially "to act or to refrain from acting" into "to act," justifying this stylistic improvement with the plain premise that "to act" refers to whatever one chooses to do whether one chooses to do the thing or not to do the thing.

13. Here, of course, I am invoking the well-known phrase of Richard Weaver. See Weaver, *Ideas Have Consequences*.

14. Although the word *positivism* has varied uses, I intend here only the sense that law can be defined without respect to normative criteria.

15. See Raz, *Practical Reason and Norms*, 35–48.

16. Finnis, *Natural Law and Natural Rights*, 318.

17. Finnis, "Law and What I Truly Should Decide," 114.

18. To be clear, I am not arguing, finally, that every instance of law is best understood as a command, but I am arguing that the notion of command best captures the *central case* of law and that the command aspect can be seen in much more of law (more kinds of law) than is generally accepted in contemporary legal theory.

19. Wright, *Vindication of Politics*, 8.

20. Wright, *Vindication of Politics*, 16.

21. I have a bit to say about this elsewhere. See Mark, "New Natural Law Theory."

22. Wright, *Vindication of Politics*, 78.

23. Wright, *Vindication of Politics*, 13.

24. Wright, *Vindication of Politics*, 72.
25. Bertea, "Contemporary Theories of Legal Obligation," 13.
26. Bertea, "Contemporary Theories of Legal Obligation," 13. Bertea's theory of legal obligation rests on intersubjective reasons, under which "the necessities of everyone concerned count equally." In his words, "One uses intersubjective reasons to take into account the needs of each subject impartially, give full weight to each need, and make each need matter in practical deliberation" (Bertea, *Theory of Legal Obligation*, 220). It is surely no accident that this follows the natural law position developed by Finnis and others on the requirements of practical reasonableness. See Finnis, *Natural Law and Natural Rights*, 100–127.
27. Bertea, *Theory of Legal Obligation*, 58.
28. Bertea, *Theory of Legal Obligation*, 60.
29. Bertea, *Theory of Legal Obligation*, 13–42.
30. Wright, *Vindication of Politics*, 9, quoting Aquinas, *ST* I-II, q. 94, a. 4.
31. Bertea, *Theory of Legal Obligation*, 352.
32. Bertea, *Theory of Legal Obligation*, 225.
33. Bertea, *Theory of Legal Obligation*, 57.
34. Bertea, *Theory of Legal Obligation*, 58.
35. To be fair, we must note that what is at issue here with respect to commands is the matter of sanctions, which I also reject, but the correspondence remains striking.
36. Bertea, *Theory of Legal Obligation*, 222.
37. I will refer mainly to his original work, *A Theory of Legal Obligation*, but a similar taxonomy appears in his introductory essay to his edited volume, *Contemporary Perspectives on Legal Obligation*. See Bertea, *Theory of Legal Obligation*, 43–73; Bertea, "Contemporary Theories of Legal Obligation," 1–16.
38. Simmons and Wellman, *Is There a Duty*, 95.
39. Simmons and Wellman, *Is There a Duty*, 94.
40. Bertea, "Contemporary Theories of Legal Obligation," 14.
41. Pennock, introduction, xv.
42. Bertea, *Theory of Legal Obligation*, 3.
43. Bertea, *Theory of Legal Obligation*, 3.
44. Pennock proposes there are "at least two respects in which obligations to the state are unique" (Pennock, introduction, xvii). For one thing, "the obligation to obey the law ... derives much of its force from the fact that it supports other obligations" (xvii). I am happy to stipulate that that is true, but I am not persuaded that it is unique to legal obligation. For another thing, "law achieves its 'legitimacy,' its claim to our obedience, and at least part of

its morally obligatory force from a peculiar recognition that it receives from those, or the bulk of those, to whom it is supposed to apply" (xvii). Here, I am more inclined to differ. Law functions in part because people recognize it, but I do not agree that law's obligatoriness stems from that recognition.

45. Bertea, *Theory of Legal Obligation*, 4.
46. Bertea, *Theory of Legal Obligation*, 5.
47. Bertea, *Theory of Legal Obligation*, 1.
48. Bertea, *Theory of Legal Obligation*, 1.
49. Bertea, *Theory of Legal Obligation*, 217. Bertea develops this point extensively. Some examples: "Obligation is best conceived as a practically normative requirement that makes a noticeable and yet resistible claim on us, who in turn are bound to, and accountable for, conforming to it, since acting otherwise would be prima facie wrong" (6). "The main hypothesis underpinning my treatment of legal obligation is the proposition that in order for a conception of legal obligation to be theoretically tenable, it must show that, as a bare minimum, legal obligation (a) is *normative* in a *practical way* ... ; (b) *requires* us to do (or not do) something in this or that circumstance by making a claim on us ... ; (c) entails that any disregard of, or noncompliance with, such claim would amount to a wrong on our part such we [*sic*] can be held accountable if we do fail to comply with that ... ; and (d) has its source in law" (44). "Legal obligation should be understood as inextricably bound up with justification" (216). "Legal obligation is essentially defined by justificatory reasons" (216). "Intersubjective reasons, by contrast, play their justificatory role largely (though not exclusively) by establishing that certain undertakings can be demanded to, or required from, an acting subject, since those undertakings are singled out as the right thing for someone to do" (217). "Something is legally obligatory only if the sanction that accompanies, or is likely to accompany, the non-compliant behavior can be argued to be justifiable, or legitimate" (228). This comports entirely with the sense I develop of law as inescapably normative.

50. Bertea, *Theory of Legal Obligation*, 72.
51. Bertea, *Theory of Legal Obligation*, 46.
52. Bertea, *Theory of Legal Obligation*, 48, 50, 47.
53. Bertea, *Theory of Legal Obligation*, 48.
54. Bertea, *Theory of Legal Obligation*, 55.
55. Bertea, *Theory of Legal Obligation*, 54.
56. Bertea, *Theory of Legal Obligation*, 56.
57. Bertea, *Theory of Legal Obligation*, 57.
58. Bertea, *Theory of Legal Obligation*, 58.
59. Bertea, *Theory of Legal Obligation*, 58.
60. Bertea, *Theory of Legal Obligation*, 58.

61. Bertea, *Theory of Legal Obligation*, 59.
62. Bertea, *Theory of Legal Obligation*, 59.
63. Bertea, *Theory of Legal Obligation*, 350.
64. Bertea, *Theory of Legal Obligation*, 350.
65. Bertea, *Theory of Legal Obligation*, 349.
66. As I show, Marmor adopts the same confused stance.
67. Bertea, *Theory of Legal Obligation*, 165.
68. Bertea, *Theory of Legal Obligation*, 21.
69. Bertea, *Theory of Legal Obligation*, 199.
70. Bertea, *Theory of Legal Obligation*, 199.
71. Bertea, "Contemporary Theories of Legal Obligation," 2.
72. See Bertea, *Theory of Legal Obligation*, 225.
73. Bertea, "Contemporary Theories of Legal Obligation," 2.
74. Bertea, *Theory of Legal Obligation*, 66.
75. Bertea, *Theory of Legal Obligation*, 66.
76. Despite notable exceptions for self-harm and self-incrimination, Hobbes nearly takes this view. But if Hobbes generally takes legal obligation to be absolute, then we can fairly say that no one credible follows him today. A demand to follow the law *no matter what* is tyrannical and, frankly, implausible.
77. Bertea, *Theory of Legal Obligation*, 199–200.
78. Simmons and Wellman, *Is There a Duty*, 101.
79. Bertea, *Theory of Legal Obligation*, 12.
80. Bertea, *Theory of Legal Obligation*, 41.
81. Bertea, *Theory of Legal Obligation*, 41–42.
82. Bertea, *Theory of Legal Obligation*, 201.

CHAPTER 1 Obligation

1. Hart, *Concept of Law*, 82.
2. Hart, *Concept of Law*, 90.
3. Hart, *Concept of Law*, 19–20.
4. Austin, *Province of Jurisprudence Determined*, 1.
5. Hart, *Concept of Law*, 20.
6. Hart, *Concept of Law*, 20.
7. Hart, *Concept of Law*, 7. On the imperative model, see, for example, Bentham, *Of Laws in General*; and Austin, *Province of Jurisprudence Determined*. Gerald Postema raises an important question about differences between figures such as Bentham and Austin, but those are not germane here. See Postema, "Law as Command."

8. Austin, *Province of Jurisprudence Determined*, 9, 14.
9. Austin, *Province of Jurisprudence Determined*, 17.
10. Hart, *Concept of Law*, 6.
11. Bertea makes a similar point, noting that "a distinction remains between the psychological states of 'believing to have a legal obligation' and 'feeling to have a legal obligation,' on the one hand, and the condition of 'having legal obligation,' on the other" (Bertea, *Theory of Legal Obligation*, 230).
12. For this reason, I am not arguing simply for a return to thinking about law as commands rather than as rules based in social practice. The normative component is necessary as well.
13. As I explain, although it is possible for Hart to allow for law's authoritativeness without explaining it, because Hart defines law as rules based in social practice, he must recognize as law directives (and systems) that plainly lack justification on any plausible normative account. This means that, by definition, Hart's concept of law swings free of justified authority.
14. Hart, *Concept of Law*, 100.
15. Hart, *Concept of Law*, vi.
16. Hart, *Concept of Law*, 83.
17. Hart, *Concept of Law*, 12.
18. So, too, if officials carry out their duties not with a sense that they *ought* to follow the rules but, instead, simply with an awareness of doing so, then the theory is nearly back to prediction. If the theory cannot provide a reason why officials ought to take the law as a reason for action—that is, if officials do not believe they are doing the "right thing"—then the best the theory can do is give a description of what they are likely to do under any given circumstances. On this reading, the officials do not take the law as an authoritative reason for action, or, if they do, Hart cannot say why they do because they are just going along with the way things are done.
19. Hart, *Concept of Law*, 59.
20. Hart, *Concept of Law*, 60.
21. Hart, *Concept of Law*, 56.
22. Hart, *Concept of Law*, 57.
23. Hart, *Concept of Law*, 180.
24. Hart, *Concept of Law*, 179.
25. Hart, *Concept of Law*, 67.
26. Hart, *Concept of Law*, 61.
27. Hart, *Concept of Law*, 193.
28. Hart, *Concept of Law*, 117.
29. Hart, *Concept of Law*, 192.
30. Hart, *Concept of Law*, 193.

31. Hart, *Concept of Law*, 98.
32. Hart, *Concept of Law*, 90.
33. Shapiro, "What Is the Internal Point of View?," 1157.
34. Hart, *Concept of Law*, 92.
35. Hart, *Concept of Law*, 98.
36. Hart, *Concept of Law*, 40.
37. Hart, *Concept of Law*, 8.
38. Hart, *Concept of Law*, 8.
39. Hart, *Concept of Law*, 8.
40. Hart, *Concept of Law*, 11.
41. Hart, *Concept of Law*, 145.
42. Hart, *Concept of Law*, 145.
43. The same problem applies both to the accounts of sovereignty that rely on habits of obedience, which Hart criticizes, and to Hart's own replacement for this idea.
44. Hart, *Concept of Law*, 147.
45. Hart, *Concept of Law*, 94.
46. Hart, *Concept of Law*, 92–93.
47. Hart, *Concept of Law*, 94.
48. Hart, *Concept of Law*, 92.
49. Hart, *Concept of Law*, 94.
50. Hart, *Concept of Law*, 92.
51. Hart, *Concept of Law*, 95.
52. Hart, *Concept of Law*, 93.
53. Hart, *Concept of Law*, 97.
54. See, for example, Hart, *Concept of Law*, 100–117.
55. Hart, *Concept of Law*, 100–117.
56. Hart, *Concept of Law*, 95.
57. There can be multiple rules of recognition.
58. Hart, *Concept of Law*, 103.
59. This means that some of the same problems that Hart attributes to the use of habits in defining law also plague his view. Moreover, Hart writes: "There are therefore two minimum conditions necessary and sufficient for the existence of a legal system. On the one hand, those rules of behaviour which are valid according to the system's ultimate criteria of validity must be generally obeyed, and, on the other hand, its rules of recognition specifying the criteria of legal validity and its rules of change and adjudication must be effectively accepted as common public standards of official behaviour by its officials" (116).

The fact that a legal system requires obedience to the law and acceptance of the rules of change and adjudication does not address why anyone ought to obey the law. If Hart's answer is that no one has to obey the law, then it seems he is collapsing the distinction between law and custom, given that both can constitute widespread, socially accepted practices. While Hart can still claim important differences between law and custom, the fact of law but not custom being obligatory cannot be one of them, and this partly defeats the purpose of his theory.

60. There also must be rules of change and rules of adjudication that apply at least to the lowest-order rule of recognition as well as a rule of recognition that applies to those.

61. Or, in other words, it's turtles all the way down.

62. Hart, *Concept of Law*, 114.

63. Hart, *Concept of Law*, 211.

64. Hart, *Concept of Law*, 198.

65. From this, it is also clear that Hart does not think that the justification of authority rests on consent.

66. Hart, *Concept of Law*, 201.

67. Hart, *Concept of Law*, 203.

68. Hart, *Concept of Law*, 203.

69. If they do not believe that they are under any obligation, then, surely, they do not believe the objects of their coercion are, either.

70. Hart, *Concept of Law*, 117.

71. Hart, *Concept of Law*, 117.

72. Hart, *Concept of Law*, 117.

73. See Simmons, *Moral Principles and Political Obligations*.

74. Simmons, *Moral Principles and Political Obligations*, 195.

75. Simmons, *Moral Principles and Political Obligations*, 196.

76. Simmons, *Moral Principles and Political Obligations*, 201.

77. Hart cannot have it both ways. Once we admit that the internal point of view reveals something true and important, Hart cannot privilege the fact that people take the law as a standard or guide while ignoring the question of moral obligation to obey the law, or *why* the standard or guide ought to count in people's deliberations.

78. Finnis argues that law, in its nature, is necessarily normative. See Finnis, "Law and What I Truly Should Decide." Leo Strauss makes a parallel point in his criticism of "social science positivism" and its aspiration to "ethical neutrality," pointing to "the impossibility of a 'value-free' political science" (Strauss, "What Is Political Philosophy?," 16, 18). For Strauss, politics is intrinsically normative, so political science must be normative as well. Similarly, he writes, "The objects of the social sciences are constituted by reference to values. Reference to values presupposes appreciation of values" (Strauss, *Natural Right and History*, 63).

79. It is too weak to say that every decision that is accepted counts as social practice because then Hart is not saying anything interesting, just that what is accepted is accepted. For example, if a democratic society holds a popular referendum outside of the normal political and legal processes—i.e., against the rule of recognition—then the majority's decision does not count as law.
80. See Marmor, "Dilemma of Authority."
81. Marmor, "Institutional Conception of Authority," 238.
82. Marmor, "Institutional Conception of Authority," 241.
83. Marmor, "Institutional Conception of Authority," 254.
84. Marmor, "Institutional Conception of Authority," 254.
85. Marmor, "Institutional Conception of Authority," 260.
86. Marmor, "Institutional Conception of Authority," 240.
87. Marmor, "Institutional Conception of Authority," 246, 247.
88. Estlund, *Democratic Authority*, 134; Marmor, "Institutional Conception of Authority," 241.
89. Marmor, "Institutional Conception of Authority," 240.
90. Marmor, "Institutional Conception of Authority," 248.
91. Marmor, "Institutional Conception of Authority," 247.
92. Marmor, "Institutional Conception of Authority," 247.
93. Marmor, "Institutional Conception of Authority," 260.
94. Shapiro, *Legality*, 48.
95. Shapiro, *Legality*, 48.
96. Shapiro, *Legality*, 116.
97. Shapiro, *Legality*, 116.
98. Shapiro, *Legality*, 49.
99. Shapiro, *Legality*, 17.
100. Shapiro, *Legality*, 50.
101. Shapiro, *Legality*, 7.
102. Shapiro, *Legality*, 171.
103. Shapiro, *Legality*, 171.
104. Shapiro, *Legality*, 171.
105. Shapiro, *Legality*, 119.
106. Shapiro, *Legality*, 119.
107. Shapiro, *Legality*, 156.
108. Shapiro, *Legality*, 3.
109. We can say that, at a minimum, Shapiro must think that planning is better than not planning, but even this is incorrect if the plans are evil.
110. Hart, *Concept of Law*, 193–99.
111. Shapiro, *Legality*, 214.
112. Shapiro, *Legality*, 215.

113. Shapiro, *Legality*, 215.
114. To be sure, we can also understand crime syndicates to have a moral mission (or at least to believe that they have one), whether it be protection of the "family" or of some ethnic subgroup, but here I give Shapiro the benefit of the doubt for the sake of argument.
115. Shapiro, *Legality*, 101.
116. Shapiro, *Legality*, 100–101.
117. Shapiro, "What Is the Internal Point of View?," 1157.
118. Shapiro, "What Is the Internal Point of View?," 1157.
119. Shapiro, *Legality*, 96.
120. Shapiro, *Legality*, 96.
121. Shapiro, *Legality*, 96.
122. Shapiro, *Legality*, 124.
123. Shapiro, *Legality*, 231.
124. Shapiro, *Legality*, 392.
125. Shapiro, *Legality*, 217.
126. Finnis, "Law and What I Truly Should Decide," 114.

CHAPTER 2 Commands versus Rules—and Nazis

1. Hart, *Concept of Law*, 77.
2. Hart, *Concept of Law*, 20.
3. Hart, *Concept of Law*, 20.
4. Separately, we can point out that Hart is misguided in his positivistic search for a purely descriptive concept of law.
5. Hart, *Concept of Law*, 20.
6. I agree with Hart that obligation is central to law (though I criticize his theory for undermining his own claim). Without the obligation to obey, the authority of law is not authority in the relevant sense, and obedience to the law is not compliance with authority *as authority*. Rather, it is closer to Raz's version of authority, in which, as I show, directives serve more as suggestions or expert advice.
7. Austin, *Province of Jurisprudence Determined*, 24.
8. Austin, *Province of Jurisprudence Determined*, 13.
9. Austin, *Province of Jurisprudence Determined*, 25; see also 24–25.
10. Hart, *Concept of Law*, 91–99.
11. Austin, *Province of Jurisprudence Determined*, 133.
12. Hart, *Concept of Law*, 155.
13. Hart, *Concept of Law*, 84.
14. Hart, *Concept of Law*, 115.

15. Hart, *Concept of Law*, 80.
16. Hart, *Concept of Law*, 53.
17. And this is just the beginning of the questions—which we need not discuss here to deliver the key points—raised by reliance on the idea of habits of obedience. Even if habits are not so complicated to observe and assess, there can be doubt about sovereignty if many commands are obeyed habitually but some or even one is disobeyed habitually.
18. Hart, *Concept of Law*, 59.
19. Hart, *Concept of Law*, 63.
20. Hart, "Commands and Authoritative Legal Reasons," 100.
21. Hart, *Concept of Law*, 57.
22. Hart, *Concept of Law*, 56.
23. Hart, *Concept of Law*, 56.
24. Neither consent nor utility gives the rules normative force.
25. Hart, *Concept of Law*, 60.
26. Hart, *Concept of Law*, 54.
27. Hart, *Concept of Law*, 59.
28. Widespread adherence to a particular practice must not be confused with consent, though that is not to say, either, that consent necessarily equals justified authority. The fact that everyone knows who the officials are in North Korea and behaves accordingly does not mean that those officials govern with consent (in the normatively salient sense).
29. Hart, *Concept of Law*, 23.
30. Hart, *Concept of Law*, 51, 54.
31. "Charismatic authority" is Weber's term. See, for example, his following statement: "In principle, the inward justifications, i.e., the grounds of *legitimacy* of rule, to start with them, are three in number. . . . Then there is the authority of the special personal *gift of grace* (charisma), absolutely personal devotion, and personal trust in revelation, in heroism or in other leadership qualities of an individual. This is 'charismatic' authority, such as that exercised by the prophet or—in the political sphere—by the elected warlord or the plebiscitary ruler, the great demagogue and the party leader." Weber, "Politics as a Vocation," 157.
32. Hart, *Concept of Law*, 59.
33. Hart, *Concept of Law*, 63.
34. Hart, *Concept of Law*, 26.
35. Hart, *Concept of Law*, 75.
36. Hart, *Concept of Law*, 113.
37. Hart, *Concept of Law*, 113.
38. Hart, *Concept of Law*, 43.
39. Hart, *Concept of Law*, 43.

40. Alternatively, we can say that Hart is wrong about the unsuitability of command because legislating differs from promising. If the law is sufficiently similar to a promise, then Hart has a hard time accounting for the variety within the law that is critical to his theory. A practice of self-binding (of which promising is a key form) does not capture well the nature of power-conferring rules as Hart wishes to understand them. (I address separately Hart's idea of power-conferring and duty-imposing rules.) Self-binding appears to entail an element of imposing duties on oneself that Hart does not want to build into the definition of law because he does not believe that power-conferring rules, one of the two main types of rules in the law (for him), fit that description. If, contra Hart, power-conferring rules do entail an element of obligation, they can be more easily construed as a form of promise or command. But this is just the sort of understanding Hart is at pains to reject because he wants to distinguish strongly between duty-imposing and power-conferring rules. Furthermore, while it is intuitive to see how one can impose duties on oneself in an act of self-binding, it is less clear how one can confer powers on oneself in an act of self-binding (or why it makes sense to do so).

41. Hart, *Concept of Law*, 58.

42. It is also worth noting that promises are different from laws because promises generally have a promisee (one who is owed the duty of the promise) whereas the natural form of legislation is for the subjects of the law to be bound to the law but not in a way that creates a duty to a specific party distinct, in principle, from those who are bound.

43. Hart, *Concept of Law*, 42.

44. Ladenson, "In Defense of a Hobbesian Conception," 45.

45. In rejecting this possibility, Hart contends that combining the command model and popular sovereignty makes "the distinction between revolution and legislation untenable" (Hart, *Concept of Law*, 78). What Hart seems to mean is that if there are no legal limits on what the people can do, then the term *revolution* does not carry the extralegal status that otherwise seems to define it. But a revolution entails going outside the rules the people have set for themselves. While it is true that the people can, through legislation, effectively achieve the same results as a revolution by changing the rules as they please and even by changing the rules about how to change the rules (that is, by changing secondary rules), as with a constitutional amendment, such action does not constitute a revolution. Even then, the people still must follow the rules about how such changes are made. At most, the term *revolution* can be used figuratively to describe such events in the sense that the changes are momentous, but they are not extralegal.

46. Hart, *Concept of Law*, 67.

47. Hart, *Concept of Law*, 61.
48. Hart, *Concept of Law*, 61.
49. Hart, *Concept of Law*, 60.
50. Hart, *Concept of Law*, 61.
51. Hart, *Concept of Law*, 209.
52. Hart, *Concept of Law*, 209.
53. Hart, *Concept of Law*, 32.
54. Hart, *Concept of Law*, 209.
55. Hart, *Concept of Law*, 32.
56. Hart, *Concept of Law*, 32.
57. Hart, *Concept of Law*, 27.
58. Hart, *Concept of Law*, 80.
59. Hart, *Concept of Law*, 28.
60. Hart, *Concept of Law*, 27.
61. Hart, *Concept of Law*, 80.
62. In fairness to Hart, the errors of older versions of the command model possibly obscure how an improved model can accommodate duty-imposing and power-conferring rules, but we can assume for the sake of argument that Hart wants to resist this, too.
63. Hart, *Concept of Law*, 41.
64. Hart, *Concept of Law*, 38.
65. This claim about the binding nature of agreements, including contracts, calls to mind the position of Chief Justice John Marshall that "contracts derive their obligation from the act of the parties, not from the grant of government" (*Ogden*, 354). In his separate opinion (assenting to the judgment yet dissenting in part), Marshall explains, "If the answer to these questions must affirm the duty of keeping faith between these parties, and the right to enforce it if violated, the answer admits the obligation of contracts, because, upon that obligation depends the right to enforce them. Superior strength may give the power, but cannot give the right. The rightfulness of coercion must depend on the pre-existing obligation to do that for which compulsion is used" (*Ogden*, 345).
66. Hart, *Concept of Law*, 96.
67. Hart, *Concept of Law*, 96.
68. To be sure, in Hart's taxonomy, rules about how to create contracts are in the same category as rules about how to create legislation, but the two examples serve differently to better illustrate the two points about how power-conferring rules track duties.
69. In claiming there are certain moral features of law, per se, this argument is akin to Lon Fuller's logic regarding the moral requirements of legal validity in *The Morality of Law*.

70. There is already a duty to refrain from acting unjustly. The power-conferring rule about how to legislate specifies one way of not violating that duty in the exercise of power. Different societies can have different standards that all meet the abstract requirements of justice. But this is not because power-conferring rules are different from duty-imposing rules. Duty-imposing rules against assault can also vary according to cultural norms, which can all be consistent with a duty to refrain from assaulting. For example, societies might differ about whether spitting on another person constitutes physical assault. Or societies might differ on whether, despite the general duty to refrain from assaulting another, "assaults" in the form of self-defense are justified in response to physical attacks only or also to certain verbal insults. Furthermore, the specific mechanism required for law-making can be intrinsically just, or justice can simply require adherence to whatever mechanism is decided. A rule that allows decisions to be made by 40 percent of the legislature still has to uphold that threshold because it is unjust to deviate from whatever is decided.

71. Hart, *Concept of Law*, 69.
72. Hart, *Concept of Law*, 69.
73. Hart, *Concept of Law*, 68.
74. See, for example, Fuller, *Morality of Law*.
75. Hart, *Concept of Law*, 33–35.
76. See, for example, Austin, *Province of Jurisprudence Determined*, 9, 14.
77. Hart, *Concept of Law*, 35.
78. Hart, *Concept of Law*, 35.
79. Hart, *Concept of Law*, 35.
80. So, for example, the law can say that agreements are binding unless one of the parties has her fingers crossed on her left hand while the two parties shake hands with their right hands. Ordinarily, one party can insist that a shook-upon agreement is binding regardless of any silly gestures the other party makes with her left hand. But, under this power-conferring rule, it is understood that this handshake is not binding.
81. Hart, *Concept of Law*, 35–36.
82. Hart, *Concept of Law*, 35n1, quoting Kelsen, *General Theory of Law and State*.
83. Hart, *Concept of Law*, 35–36.
84. Hart, *Concept of Law*, 37.
85. Hart, *Concept of Law*, 39.
86. See, for example, Genesis 24:2, 9.
87. Hart, *Concept of Law*, 12.

88. It cannot be the presence of secondary rules that makes the difference because other forms of social rules besides law generally lack something like secondary rules. So, too, it cannot be that the rules' internal aspect (or their reflective nature) is what distinguishes power-conferring rules from habits because other social practices, such as customs, can possess an internal aspect without being law.
89. Hart, *Concept of Law*, 32.
90. Hart, *Concept of Law*, 38.
91. Hart, *Concept of Law*, 32.
92. Hart, *Concept of Law*, 32.
93. Hart, *Concept of Law*, 8.
94. Shapiro, *Legality*, 15–16.
95. Hart, *Concept of Law*, 209. At the same time that his theory ensures that nothing that belongs is left out of the category of law, Hart also thinks it enables us to properly exclude much that can improperly qualify as law, such as the orders of a mugger and various nonlegal practices, such as customs.
96. "Valid law" is somewhat redundant in this context because, according to Hart's view, the guiding maxim is "an invalid law is no law." Validity is the marker of whether it is a law at all, so the term *law* implies the term *valid*.
97. Hart, *Concept of Law*, 157.
98. Hart, *Concept of Law*, 211.
99. This is not to say that unlawful behavior must always be a necessary and/or sufficient condition for justifiable punishment, but it is to say that Hart sets it up as a relevant factor because he insists that the key question is whether it is just to punish people for acts that are lawful at the time they commit them.
100. Hart, *Concept of Law*, 211.
101. Hart, *Concept of Law*, 211.
102. Hart, *Concept of Law*, 211.
103. Hart, *Concept of Law*, 209.
104. Hart, *Concept of Law*, 116.
105. Hart, *Concept of Law*, 211.
106. I address separately the matter of what constitutes a legal system and why a legal system has force in the way I describe here.
107. Hart, *Concept of Law*, 19.
108. Hart, *Concept of Law*, 19.
109. Simmons, *Moral Principles and Political Obligations*, 158, quoting Murphy, "In Defense of Obligation," 42–43.
110. See Marmor, "Institutional Conception of Authority."

111. Marmor, "Institutional Conception of Authority," 254.
112. Marmor, "Dilemma of Authority," 15.
113. Marmor, "Dilemma of Authority," 15.
114. See Finnis, "Law and What I Truly Should Decide," 114.
115. As Augustine writes, "Remove justice, and what are kingdoms but gangs of criminals on a large scale?" (Augustine, *Concerning the City of God*, 139 [4.4]).

CHAPTER 3   Justification

1. We can play out a similar argument with respect to theories that define the commander's authority by the subjects' habitual obedience.
2. As I show, nothing about the overlap between one's independent reasons for acting and the law's requirements produces an obligation to obey the law just because it is the law. The truth of this is manifest when one considers whether there is an obligation under such theories to obey the law when it does not overlap with the independent reasons: there is not. In these theories, it is not law's authority but other reasons that underwrite the "obligation to obey" (which is, in the end, not an obligation to obey).
3. Other normative factors, such as democratic legitimacy, cannot account for authority in Hart's theory. If they can, then Hart's theory cannot explain the authoritativeness of social practices that are not democratically legitimate nor the legality of democratically legitimate rules that are not adhered to widely in society.
4. In the command model, there is effectively a substitution of the commander's will for the subject's because the fact of the command being the commander's will alone suffices to justify it. In Raz's model, the fact of the law being anyone's will in particular is effectively irrelevant to its authoritativeness.
5. Austin, *Province of Jurisprudence Determined*, 24–25.
6. Hart, *Concept of Law*, vi.
7. Raz, *Authority of Law*, 9.
8. To be sure, law can have legal effect without moral authority insofar as officials or others treat the law as obligatory even when it is not.
9. Raz, *Authority of Law*, 3.
10. Wolff, "Conflict between Authority and Autonomy," 27. See also Wolff, *In Defense of Anarchism*; Wolff, "Conflict between Authority and Autonomy," 28.
11. Wolff, "Conflict between Authority and Autonomy," 29.

12. Wolff, "Conflict between Authority and Autonomy," 29.
13. Raz, introduction to *Authority*, 4.
14. Raz, introduction to *Authority*, 4. Raz often frames the issue of law's authority in terms of the challenge of the philosophical anarchists. See, for example, Raz, "Authority and Consent," 105; Raz, "Obligation to Obey," 139; Raz, "About Morality," 1.
15. Raz, *Morality of Freedom*, 46.
16. Raz, *Practical Reason and Norms*, 39–45.
17. Raz, *Morality of Freedom*, 47. Raz is quick to point out that the dependence thesis does not entail the no difference thesis, which he rejects. The no difference thesis states that "the exercise of authority should make no difference to what its subjects ought to do" (*Morality of Freedom*, 48).
18. Raz, *Morality of Freedom*, 41. The term *dependent reasons* can be counterintuitive and therefore misleading. To be clear, dependent reasons, despite their name, apply to the subject *independent* of the exercise of authority. For its justification, authority is dependent upon tracking the independently applicable reasons (reasons that apply to the subject already apart from the directives in question).
19. Raz, *Morality of Freedom*, 53, 47.
20. Raz, *Morality of Freedom*, 53.
21. Raz, *Morality of Freedom*, 53.
22. Raz, *Authority of Law*, 233. For further examples, see also the following: "My starting point is the assumption that there is no general obligation to obey the law, not even a prima facie obligation and not even in a just society" (Raz, "Authority and Consent," 103); "A good deal of common ground seemed to have been established among many of the political and moral theorists who did and still do attend to the issue. It is summed up by the view that every citizen has a prima facie moral obligation to obey the law of a reasonably just state. . . . I have joined several theorists who challenge this consensus" (Raz, "Obligation to Obey," 139); "The final section of the chapter . . . denies the existence of a general obligation to obey the law even in a reasonably just society, though it is argued that just governments may exist, and that in certain circumstances their existence is preferable to any alternative method of social organization" (Raz, *Morality of Freedom*, 70); "The fact that normative language is used to describe the law helped to perpetuate two of the great fallacies of the philosophy of law. One is the fallacious belief that laws are of necessity moral reasons (or that they are morally justified or that there are always moral reasons to obey each one of them)" (Raz, *Practical Reason and Norms*, 154–55).
23. Raz, *Morality of Freedom*, 69.

24. I use "better outcomes" as shorthand for what Raz means when he says "more likely to act successfully for the reasons which apply to him" (*Morality of Freedom*, 71) and "better to conform with reason" (73).

25. Raz, *Morality of Freedom*, 64–65, 67–68.

26. Of course, my use of the analogy is not meant to suggest that laws, properly understood, carry no more authoritativeness than advice.

27. That is true unless Raz believes there is a moral obligation to choose better outcomes over autonomous decision-making (and that making a decision autonomously cannot itself be constitutive of a "better" outcome). But it can be rational to decline expert advice, and it can be morally permissible even if it is not the most "rational" course of action under a certain constrained definition of *rational*.

28. Raz, *Morality of Freedom*, 100. We can see here reference to the same idea underlying the normal justification thesis.

29. Raz, *Morality of Freedom*, 78.

30. Raz, *Morality of Freedom*, 100.

31. Raz, *Morality of Freedom*, 71.

32. Raz, *Morality of Freedom*, 73.

33. Raz, *Morality of Freedom*, 56.

34. Raz, *Morality of Freedom*, 67.

35. The phrase "the reasons that apply to them" signifies the reasons that apply to the subjects before they receive (apart from their receiving) instructions from the authority. For clarity, we can also render it as "the reasons that already apply to them" or "the reasons that apply to them, anyway."

36. Raz, *Morality of Freedom*, 74.

37. Raz, *Morality of Freedom*, 75.

38. Raz, *Morality of Freedom*, 75.

39. Raz, *Morality of Freedom*, 75.

40. Raz, *Morality of Freedom*, 75.

41. Raz, *Morality of Freedom*, 75.

42. Raz, *Morality of Freedom*, 75.

43. Another inevitable conclusion is that the government "may have more authority over one person than over another" (Raz, *Morality of Freedom*, 74).

44. Raz, *Morality of Freedom*, 73.

45. Raz, *Morality of Freedom*, 74.

46. Raz, *Morality of Freedom*, 78. Raz is quick to point out that the laws in these situations are in no way unjust. The lack of justified authority here over those subjects does not speak to the topic of unjust laws and civil disobedience.

47. Raz, *Morality of Freedom*, 78.

48. Raz, *Authority of Law*, 248.
49. Raz, *Authority of Law*, 249.
50. There are possible exceptions, which is why Raz, too, uses the word "normally." For example, if the government is off to a successful start in a pollution-awareness campaign to change the current practice of polluting the river, there can be a moral obligation to refrain from polluting because the subject's actions can make a difference for others' actions (Raz, *Authority of Law*, 248n13).
51. Raz, *Morality of Freedom*, 52.
52. Raz, *Morality of Freedom*, 56.
53. Raz, "Obligation to Obey," 141.
54. Raz, "Obligation to Obey," 141–42. To be sure, Raz believes the paradox is "overstated" because "sometimes the law makes a moral difference." There are some cases where "it is morally obligatory to act as the law requires because it so requires," but "in some fairly central cases there is no such obligation" (142).
55. Raz, *Authority of Law*, 249 (emphasis added).
56. Raz, *Morality of Freedom*, 103–4. In the case of the river pollution, this assumes that the social practice of not polluting the river creates an independent moral obligation where none exists before (when everyone does pollute the river), but that assumption is not at issue here.
57. Raz, "Obligation to Obey," 143.
58. Raz, "Obligation to Obey," 143.
59. Raz, "Obligation to Obey," 143 (emphasis added).
60. As a reminder, the moral obligation is "independent" in that it does not exist because the law requires it, even if the law *also* requires it. It exists apart from and prior to the law's requirements.
61. Raz makes the same point elsewhere using the example of legal enforcement of antidefamation laws. His formulation, denying the need for authority, is unambiguous: "It is worth pausing here momentarily to observe that such legally provided remedies can be morally justified even when applied to people who are not subject to the authority of the government and its laws.... One need not invoke the authority of the law over the defamer to justify such action. The law may not have authority over him. It makes no difference. The importance of the law in such matters is in creating a centre of power which makes it possible to *enforce moral duties*. It does so through the authority it exercises over government officials, and because the population at large is willing to see morality enforced, even in matters in which they are not subject to the authority of the government" (Raz, *Morality of Freedom*, 103 [emphasis added]). Even more straightforwardly, Raz writes, "It is important to remember that a government's power can and

normally does quite properly extend to people who do not accept its authority. They are subject to its power partly because those who accept its authority are willing to obey its instructions, even when they affect people who do not accept its authority" (102). The idea of people being subject to the power of the law partly because others are willing to enforce it against them comes very close to the "de facto" side of the distinction between de facto and de jure authority. Or, more sharply, it seems very close to unjustified authority.

62. In a striking line, Raz explains, "They are subject to its power partly because those who accept its authority are willing to obey its instructions, even when they affect people who do not accept its authority" (Raz, *Morality of Freedom*, 102). This is different from Locke's discussion of foreigners, who "by living all their lives under another government, and enjoying the privileges and protection of it, though they are bound, even in conscience, to submit to its administration, as far forth as any denizen; yet do not thereby come to be subjects or members of that common-wealth" (Locke, *Two Treatises of Government*, 177). In Locke's case, tacit consent justifies the authority, and the foreigner presumably acknowledges the justified authority of the host government. In Raz's case, there is no requirement of tacit or explicit acceptance of authority or its benefits (and, actually, quite the contrary).

63. This is probably not Raz's argument even if it is true that anyone can enforce moral obligations against anyone else, which, too, is unlikely.

64. Raz, *Authority of Law*, 249.

65. Raz, *Authority of Law*, 248.

66. Of course, a belief in the obligation to obey the law need not entail an actual obligation to obey the law. Still, there is no indication that Raz favors widespread deception about the obligation to obey the law in order to get a social practice off the ground.

67. If there actually is such a moral obligation (and not just a belief in one—though, for these purposes, the two coincide), then the law can justifiably enforce it, too.

68. Raz, *Authority of Law*, 253–58.

69. Raz, *Authority of Law*, 255.

70. Raz, *Morality of Freedom*, 91.

71. Raz, *Authority of Law*, 259.

72. Raz, *Authority of Law*, 260.

73. Raz, *Morality of Freedom*, 55.

74. Raz, *Authority of Law*, 253.

75. Raz, *Morality of Freedom*, 98.

76. Raz, *Morality of Freedom*, 98.

77. Raz, *Morality of Freedom*, 89. Presumably, the recognition and the obligation are qualified because one's respect can be qualified and because the law itself can be respectable only in certain aspects.
78. Raz, *Morality of Freedom*, 98.
79. Raz, *Morality of Freedom*, 93.
80. See, for example, Raz, *Morality of Freedom*, 98.
81. Raz, *Morality of Freedom*, 92.
82. Raz, *Morality of Freedom*, 89.
83. Raz, *Morality of Freedom*, 98.
84. Raz, *Authority of Law*, 260.
85. Raz, *Authority of Law*, 250.
86. Raz, *Authority of Law*, 259.
87. Raz, *Authority of Law*, 260.
88. Raz, *Authority of Law*, 260.
89. Raz, *Authority of Law*, 261.
90. Raz, *Authority of Law*, 261.
91. Again, the point of calling it a prima facie obligation or some similar term is to make clear that it is not an absolute obligation but rather one that obtains only until it is defeated by a stronger contrary obligation.
92. Smith, "Is There a Prima Facie Obligation," 976.
93. Smith, "Is There a Prima Facie Obligation," 976.
94. Smith, "Is There a Prima Facie Obligation," 958. If Smith thinks that, despite his conclusion that there is no obligation when no one benefits, such conditions never arise (because of the law's relation to the common good), then his position collapses into one in which there *is* a prima facie obligation to obey the law. We know he does not hold that, so we can rule out that interpretation of Smith.
95. Smith, "Is There a Prima Facie Obligation," 958.
96. Smith, "Is There a Prima Facie Obligation," 971.
97. Smith, "Is There a Prima Facie Obligation," 971.
98. Smith, "Is There a Prima Facie Obligation," 971.
99. Smith, "Is There a Prima Facie Obligation," 972.
100. Smith, "Is There a Prima Facie Obligation," 972.
101. Smith, "Is There a Prima Facie Obligation," 976.
102. Elsewhere, in direct contrast to my view, Simmons writes, "The mere fact that an action is legally required or that a stable government holds power within a reasonably just state is insufficient to establish a moral presumption in favor of legal compliance" (Simmons and Wellman, *Is There a Duty*, 101).
103. Simmons, *Moral Principles and Political Obligations*, 193.
104. Simmons, *Moral Principles and Political Obligations*, 23.

350 Notes to Pages 180–193

105. Simmons, *Moral Principles and Political Obligations*, 39, quoting Pitkin, "Obligation and Consent II," 49.
106. Simmons, *Moral Principles and Political Obligations*, 39.
107. Simmons, *Moral Principles and Political Obligations*, 198, 200.
108. Green, *Authority of the State*, 262.
109. Green, *Authority of the State*, 263.
110. In cases of severe injustice, which rightly worry Green, the obligation not to commit the injustice outweighs the obligation to obey the law, for it is only prima facie, but content independence is preserved because the obligation to obey the law does not vanish. The fact that the subject has to make a content-dependent decision about whether to obey the law does not eliminate the content-independent obligation to obey; it merely overcomes it.
111. Green, *Authority of the State*, 263.
112. Green, *Authority of the State*, 265.
113. Green, *Authority of the State*, 266.
114. Green, *Authority of the State*, 266.
115. In addition, Green appreciates insufficiently the need for and good of authority, even in a virtuous society, in which case a full answer to him explains not just how authority can be rationalized but also why it is affirmatively good.

CHAPTER 4   Authority and the Good

1. Marmor, "Institutional Conception of Authority," 245.
2. This is why Marmor believes there needs to be an institutional relationship. He is correct to argue that authority must entail this conventional component, but, because he stops there, he, too, cannot explain why this authority-by-convention can obligate.
3. This does not justify any sort of consequentialism, to be sure. It just means that a government renders such decisions with justified authority that a spontaneous leader does not possess.
4. Marmor, "Dilemma of Authority," 23.
5. Marmor, "Dilemma of Authority," 12.
6. Marmor, "Dilemma of Authority," 12.
7. Marmor, "Dilemma of Authority," 25.
8. See, for example, Finnis, "Law as Co-ordination," 102.
9. This is especially vivid from a law-and-economics standpoint but not exclusive to it.
10. The view that sees the law in this way justifies what we ordinarily call punishment as a restoration of the balance of benefits and burdens, but

we need more to say why, from the perspective of the law, one cannot blamelessly opt for the "punishment" in lieu of compliance with the law, meaning why the law is not simply offering a choice. If the law is doing that (offering a choice), then, to take an everyday example, we ought not to call it a parking fine but a parking fee. Similarly, there ought to be no such thing as a "moving violation" but rather a "moving option." Indeed, the law can put a price (monetary or otherwise) on everything and make all directives optional, but that makes law a very different creature.

11. See, for example, Friedman, "On the Concept of Authority," 57.

12. I emphasize "loosely" because the term *an authority* can refer solely to expertise, and it is wrong, as I say extensively in my critique of Raz, to think of expertise as the justification of authority (except, perhaps, in the sense that statesmanship can be a form of expertise in advancing the common good).

13. Finnis, *Natural Law and Natural Rights*, 249.

14. Finnis, *Natural Law and Natural Rights*, 249.

15. Finnis, *Natural Law and Natural Rights*, 249.

16. To be clear, this does not overlook the difference between "being oriented to the common good," which is part of the definition of law, and "being able to advance the common good," which is important but not definitional. If the purpose of authority is to promote the common good, then a government in exile or a government with weak enforcement powers is seriously handicapped. But subjects recognizing the obligation to obey can in fact obey, thereby demonstrating the government's ability to promote the common good even without enforcement power.

17. Finnis, *Natural Law and Natural Rights*, 246.

18. Finnis, *Natural Law and Natural Rights*, 247.

19. Finnis, *Natural Law and Natural Rights*, 246.

20. Simon, *General Theory of Authority*, 144.

21. Simon, *General Theory of Authority*, 145, 146.

22. Simon, *General Theory of Authority*, 143, 145.

23. As I show, this is also necessary for properly understanding civil disobedience. See chapter 3, under "Smith's theory of law's authority exemplifies Raz's errors."

24. To be sure, the proposed harm to the intended victim also threatens the common good, but, even if—counterfactually—the death of the victim serves the common good, the injustice involved in the killing negates the obligation to obey the law.

25. Aquinas teaches that there can be prudential reasons to obey even an unjust law, but this is, possibly, not identical to saying that there is a prima facie obligation to obey an unjust law within a just legal system. Although the

two produce similar results, Aquinas's version—again, possibly—supposes that the prudential reasons to obey exist apart from the authority of law, per se. Still, insofar as those prudential reasons involve obligations to the common good, the positions become vanishingly close. See Aquinas, *Summa Theologica*, 1020 [*ST* I-II, q. 96, a. 4].

26. Finnis, *Natural Law and Natural Rights*, 318.
27. Finnis, *Natural Law and Natural Rights*, 318.
28. In this sense, the phrase "just legal system" is redundant, and it is more precise to speak simply of legal systems and systems of rules that are not legal systems.
29. This, for instance, allows us to see correctly what was at stake in the postwar trials of German perpetrators. See chapter 2, under "Hart's errors about law undermine his analysis of postwar German war-crime trials."
30. A major challenge to this is the presumably commonsensical observation, which serves in a way as a starting point for Hart (and others), that the Nazis obviously have a legal system. An observer can wonder, if the legal system in Nazi Germany is sufficiently oriented to the common good to meet the standard for my concept of law, then what does not meet that standard? A correct understanding of the concept of law affects our classification of candidates for the title of "legal system" by ruling out a truly arbitrary or brutal tyranny, a government that exists for the benefit of the few and oppresses most of the people rather than just some. Of a legal system in such a regime we can say either that it cannot (because of its caprice) or does not (because of its cruelty) serve the common good. This extends to, but is not limited to, the kind of system that Lon Fuller depicts in *The Morality of Law*, where retroactive laws and the like make it impossible for the system to serve its functions (38).
31. Just as the authority of law and legal obligation are two sides of the same coin, divine authority and religious obligation are similarly linked, so I often use the two terms in tandem.
32. Even some new natural law scholars argue that God can command people to commit acts that are otherwise intrinsically evil. See, for example, Brugger, "Capital Punishment Is Intrinsically Wrong."
33. The better the advice (assuming one can know it is better), the better the reason one needs to justify choosing another course, but as long as that other course can be justified, the person who demurs from taking the advice avoids even the accusation of acting irrationally here.
34. Austin, *Province of Jurisprudence Determined*, 10.
35. In this way, Austin provides a strong counterpoint to Hart and is, unsurprisingly, a primary target of Hart.

36. This is, for example, the understanding of Islam that the Byzantine emperor holds in Pope Benedict XVI's famous Regensburg address: "But for Muslim teaching, God is absolutely transcendent. His will is not bound up with any of our categories, even that of rationality. Here Khoury quotes a work of the noted French Islamist R. Arnaldez, who points out that Ibn Hazm went so far as to state that God is not bound even by his own word, and that nothing would oblige him to reveal the truth to us. Were it God's will, we would even have to practise idolatry" (Benedict XVI, "Faith, Reason, and the University").

37. Here, it is easier to speak of religious obligation, rather than divine authority, in parallel to moral obligation because moral obligations do not stem from any authority, properly speaking, in the way that religious or legal obligations do.

38. In other words, I am not using these terms in any unusual or idiosyncratic way but, rather, in an ordinary way with the meaning we normally give to them.

39. This is especially relevant for our examination of Carl Schmitt, who claims that political concepts derive from theological ones. See Schmitt, *Political Theology*, 36.

40. Of course, in addition, there still needs to be the normative aspect that enables us to distinguish between justified and unjustified authority.

41. Finnis describes the good of religion as "the establishment and maintenance of proper relationships between oneself . . . and the divine" or the bringing of "one's life and actions . . . into some sort of harmony with whatever can be known or surmised about" the "transcendent origin of the universal order-of-things and of human freedom and reason" (Finnis, *Natural Law and Natural Rights*, 89–90).

42. It does no harm to the argument here, however, if Finnis's take is not compatible with the voluntarist view of divine authority.

43. Finnis, *Natural Law and Natural Rights*, 90, 89–90.

44. *Natural Law and Natural Rights*, 90.

45. Given the transcendent nature of such a God, divine commands are instructions of how to properly engage in that relationship.

46. Of course, they can also serve the person performing the actions in various ways.

47. *Natural Law and Natural Rights*, 405.

48. *Natural Law and Natural Rights*, 404.

49. *Natural Law and Natural Rights*, 404.

50. *Natural Law and Natural Rights*, 404.

51. *Natural Law and Natural Rights*, 405.

52. The model loses nothing to claims that such a being does not in fact exist; the only relevant challenge is that such a being cannot exist, but such a claim seems to entail premises no less problematic (and likely more problematic) than the ones it wishes to repudiate.

53. In a related vein, though not speaking of God, Arendt writes, "The authoritarian relation between the one who commands and the one who obeys rests neither on common reason nor on the power of one who commands; what they have in common is the hierarchy itself, whose rightness and legitimacy both recognize and where both have their predetermined stable place" (Arendt, *Between Past and Future*, 93).

54. Simon, *Philosophy of Democratic Government*, 154.

55. Simon, *Philosophy of Democratic Government*, 154.

56. Simon, *Philosophy of Democratic Government*, 154.

57. Simon, *Philosophy of Democratic Government*, 154. I address Simon's transmission theory separately. See Simon, *Philosophy of Democratic Government*, 158.

58. Simon, *Philosophy of Democratic Government*, 145.

59. Unlike with government, obedience to God can be good for its own sake just because of the kind of being God is. Obedience, in that case, is the mode most appropriate to the kind of relationship that the God-person relationship is.

60. Finnis used this language of "public judgment" and "private judgment" in a conversation with me at Princeton University on 14 October 2010.

61. Finnis, *Natural Law and Natural Rights*, 406.

62. Finnis, *Natural Law and Natural Rights*, 406–7.

63. Finnis, *Natural Law and Natural Rights*, 407.

64. Finnis, *Natural Law and Natural Rights*, 409.

65. Even in a case of coordination, where law creates additional reasons for action that do not exist before the law proposes a coordinating solution, the reasons that the law provides are not necessarily to be privileged over the reasons provided by anyone else who offers a solution.

66. From another angle, the insertion of substantive considerations (here, about the common good) actually strengthens the point that there is real authority in this model. The requirement in the definition of authority that subjects treat directives as authoritative is relevant precisely where there is the possibility for disagreement. If there is no room for disagreement, then decision-making is not so much a matter of authority as of reasonableness. One major purpose of authority is to give direction where there is not otherwise unanimity, which includes cases where unanimity remains elusive even with perfect information. This is often the case because many decisions are

not a matter of appealing to irrefutable facts but of judgment in situations where reasonable people of good will can disagree. This is another way of getting at my main charge against Raz: Any time compliance with authority is primarily about acting for the reasons that are independent of the authority's directive, it is not really a matter of authority. There is authority and obedience only when there is some content-independent obligation to obey. In this way, it is the possibility of obedience in spite of disagreement that makes authority possible.

67. Schmitt, *Political Theology*, 36.
68. Schmitt, *Political Theology*, 36.
69. Schmitt, *Political Theology*, 5.
70. Schmitt, *Political Theology*, 31–32.
71. In a perhaps unintended way, this parallels Finnis's reference to an original, unauthorized authority. Finnis does not mean it as a reference to God's primordial authority, but the resonance is notable.
72. Strong, foreword to Schmitt, *Political Theology*, xxvii.
73. McCormick, introduction to Schmitt, *Legality and Legitimacy*, xxxv.
74. Schmitt, *Political Theology*, 13.
75. Schmitt, *Political Theology*, 36.
76. Schmitt, *Political Theology*, 12.
77. Schmitt, *Political Theology*, 7.
78. McCormick, introduction to Schmitt, *Legality and Legitimacy*, xvi. Schmitt's own sentence reads, "With regard to the concept of legality, one must keep in mind, both historically and conceptually, that it is a product and a problem of the parliamentary legislative state and its specific type of normativism" (10).
79. Schmitt, *Concept of the Political*, 42. Schmitt writes famously, "All significant concepts of the modern theory of the state are secularized theological concepts" (Schmitt, *Political Theology*, 36).
80. Schmitt, *Political Theology*, 36.
81. Schmitt, *Political Theology*, 37.
82. Schmitt, *Political Theology*, 12.
83. McCormick, introduction to Schmitt, *Legality and Legitimacy*, xxiv.
84. This works even if the sovereign and the subjects are the same people operating in different capacities.
85. McCormick, introduction to Schmitt, *Legality and Legitimacy*, xxiv.
86. McCormick, introduction to Schmitt, *Legality and Legitimacy*, xxiv.
87. Schmitt, *Political Theology*, 46.
88. Schmitt, *Political Theology*, 48.
89. Schmitt, *Political Theology*, 50.

90. Schmitt, *Political Theology*, 51.
91. See Simmons, *Moral Principles and Political Obligations*; Green, *Authority of the State*.
92. Marmor, "Dilemma of Authority," 22.
93. Marmor, "Dilemma of Authority," 25.
94. Finnis, "Law as Co-ordination," 101.
95. Finnis, *Natural Law and Natural Rights*, 317.
96. Finnis, *Natural Law and Natural Rights*, 317.
97. As I have been saying, Raz can posit that all persons at all times have other reasons that support a prima facie obligation to obey the law, but that makes nonsense of what he is trying to do in his account of the authority of law precisely because he denies the existence of a prima facie obligation to obey in that way. If there is always a general reason to obey the law just because it is the law, then none of the rest of his theory about law's authority applies.
98. Raz, *Morality of Freedom*, 74.
99. Finnis, *Natural Law and Natural Rights*, 306.
100. Finnis, "Law as Co-ordination," 102.
101. Finnis, *Natural Law and Natural Rights*, 302.
102. Finnis, *Natural Law and Natural Rights*, 304.
103. Finnis, *Natural Law and Natural Rights*, 306.
104. Finnis, *Natural Law and Natural Rights*, 305.
105. Finnis, "Law as Co-ordination," 102.
106. Finnis, *Natural Law and Natural Rights*, 307.
107. Finnis, "Law as Co-ordination," 103. See Raz, "Obligation to Obey," 149.
108. Finnis, "Law as Co-ordination," 103 (emphasis added).
109. Finnis, "Law as Co-ordination," 102–3.
110. At the same time, the limits of practical reasoning mean that both private and public judgment (authority) must be constrained. The limits of practical reasoning guarantee that individuals will err, and, particularly in light of the multiformity of good, the state (or anyone else) can never succeed in truly comprehensive planning and control. Furthermore, even in the completely hypothetical case of a society of perfectly intellectual and virtuous people, prediction remains impossible and so, too, perfect planning.
111. If Raz holds, however, that an individual always has reasons to comply with the law for the sake of the common good regardless of the particular circumstances, then his position collapses into Finnis's and offers no practical difference.
112. Obviously, this does not create an absolute obligation to obey every individual law in a justified legal system.

113. Finnis, *Natural Law and Natural Rights*, 325.

114. Directives or rules can often be useful as such shortcuts because they guide subjects' actions in cases where the time or opportunity to consider from scratch all the relevant factors is lacking. But, without something more, the fact that this can be very useful does not necessarily mean that compliance is obligatory.

115. To be sure, the orientation to the common good alone does not characterize law. Authority not only must have justificatory reasons but also be specified in commands. Otherwise, there is no way to distinguish between different proposals for advancing the common good.

116. Anscombe, "On the Source of the Authority of the State."

117. Simon, *General Theory of Authority*, 57.

118. Rawls, *Theory of Justice*, 308.

119. Rawls, *Theory of Justice*, 308.

120. Simmons, *Moral Principles and Political Obligations*, 110.

121. This is what we expect because Raz is mainly concerned with the challenge from the philosophical anarchists who champion autonomy, which Raz answers by showing how obeying authority can be permissible. But, as I argue, he falls short of showing it can be obligatory.

122. Simon, *Philosophy of Democratic Government*, 145.

123. See, for example, chapter 1, under "Marmor's and Shapiro's attempts to improve upon Hart end up replicating the same critical error."

124. Finnis, *Natural Law and Natural Rights*, 303.

125. Finnis, *Natural Law and Natural Rights*, 341.

126. Simon, *Nature and Functions of Authority*, 27–28.

127. Finnis, *Natural Law and Natural Rights*, 233.

128. Finnis, *Natural Law and Natural Rights*, 231.

129. Finnis, *Natural Law and Natural Rights*, 231–32. To be sure, none of this is to suggest that Finnis and Simon are of exactly one mind on this subject. My emphasis here is on the synthesis of the two.

130. Simon, *Philosophy of Democratic Government*, 59. This latter point is not the exact same point that Finnis is making, but the gist is the same, and the two points complement one another.

131. Simon, *Philosophy of Democratic Government*, 33.

132. Simon, *Philosophy of Democratic Government*, 10.

133. Simon, *Nature and Functions of Authority*, 28 (emphasis added).

134. Simon, *Philosophy of Democratic Government*, 35, 19; Simon, *Nature and Functions of Authority*, 17.

135. Simon, *Philosophy of Democratic Government*, 30.

136. Simon, *Philosophy of Democratic Government*, 31.

137. Simon, *Philosophy of Democratic Government*, 31.

138. Simon, *Philosophy of Democratic Government*, 30.
139. Simon, *Nature and Functions of Authority*, 30.
140. Simon, *Nature and Functions of Authority*, 31.
141. See Finnis, "Law as Co-ordination," 102; Raz, "Obligation to Obey," 149.
142. Finnis, "Law as Co-ordination," 100.
143. Finnis, "Law as Co-ordination," 101.
144. Finnis, "Law as Co-ordination," 101.
145. Finnis, "Law as Co-ordination," 101.
146. Finnis, "Law as Co-ordination," 101 (note omitted).
147. Simon, *General Theory of Authority*, 18.
148. Simon, *General Theory of Authority*, 18.
149. Simon, *General Theory of Authority*, 44.
150. Simon, *Philosophy of Democratic Government*, 153.
151. Simon, *Philosophy of Democratic Government*, 153, 153–54, 154.
152. This does not entirely negate the role of individual judgment in the final decision whether to obey the law or engage in civil disobedience, as there is no absolute obligation to obey the law. But, with a proper concept of law, the starting point for determining what to do is the prima facie obligation to obey. In that case, law's authority is outweighed only by a stronger moral obligation not to comply, not by contrary preferences or alternative proposals.
153. Finnis, *Natural Law and Natural Rights*, 154.
154. Finnis, *Natural Law and Natural Rights*, 155. See also 154–56.
155. Finnis, *Natural Law and Natural Rights*, 155.
156. Finnis, *Natural Law and Natural Rights*, 156.
157. Finnis, *Natural Law and Natural Rights*, 233, 154.
158. Finnis, *Natural Law and Natural Rights*, 156.
159. Simon, *Philosophy of Democratic Government*, 49.
160. Simon, *Philosophy of Democratic Government*, 49.
161. Simon, *Philosophy of Democratic Government*, 49.
162. Simon, *General Theory of Authority*, 61. As I write elsewhere, Finnis rejects some other natural lawyers' views of the "completeness" of the political community, but that does not affect our point here. See Mark, "New Natural Law Theory."
163. Simon, *General Theory of Authority*, 62.
164. Simon, *Philosophy of Democratic Government*, 50.
165. Simon, *Philosophy of Democratic Government*, 41.
166. Simon, *Philosophy of Democratic Government*, 42.
167. Simon, *Philosophy of Democratic Government*, 57, 42. Clearly, Raz cannot account for such a situation. Insofar as he can accept that a case exists where an individual's good genuinely conflicts with the common good, there

is no accounting for the primacy of the common good. Perhaps Raz denies it can ever occur, but more likely he just thinks that individuals need not submit to the common good. This conclusion is, perhaps, another undesirable feature of Raz's theory. Alternatively, if promoting the common good counts within the reasons that already apply to a person, then the distinction between the individual and common good collapses for Raz, and he also must accept a prima facie obligation to obey the law.

168. Simon, *General Theory of Authority*, 47–48.
169. Simon, *General Theory of Authority*, 60.
170. Simon, *General Theory of Authority*, 141–42.
171. Finnis, *Natural Law and Natural Rights*, 303.
172. Simon, *Philosophy of Democratic Government*, 71.
173. Simon, *Philosophy of Democratic Government*, 71.
174. Simon, *General Theory of Authority*, 158.
175. Simon, *Nature and Functions of Authority*, 40.
176. Simon, *Nature and Functions of Authority*, 40.
177. Simon, *Nature and Functions of Authority*, 42, 41, 40.
178. Simon, *Nature and Functions of Authority*, 41.
179. Simon, *Nature and Functions of Authority*, 32.
180. Simon, *General Theory of Authority*, 144.
181. Simon, *General Theory of Authority*, 29.
182. Simon, *General Theory of Authority*, 11.
183. Simon, *General Theory of Authority*, 154.
184. Simon makes a related point when he differentiates between the Razian version of law's authority, in which the law takes the subject's reasons as its own, and his own version, in which the subject takes the law's reasons as her own.
185. Simon, *General Theory of Authority*, 154n19.
186. Simon, *General Theory of Authority*, 153.
187. Simon, *General Theory of Authority*, 150, 149–50.
188. Simon, *General Theory of Authority*, 149.
189. Simon, *General Theory of Authority*, 150, 148–49.
190. Simon, *Philosophy of Democratic Government*, 154.
191. Simon, *General Theory of Authority*, 156.
192. Simon, *General Theory of Authority*, 156.
193. Simon, *General Theory of Authority*, 156.
194. Simon, *General Theory of Authority*, 156.
195. Simon, *General Theory of Authority*, 156.
196. It is in a similar sense of "free" that Simon writes that a society more united in common action is also freer. The structure that facilitates good choices is liberating, not restricting. Surely Simon does not envision the sort

of totalizing state for which he criticizes Rousseau, but neither does his idea of unity reduce to straightforward tasks of coordination such as bridge building. On the contrary, there is a transcendent(al) purpose here, but an all-encompassing state is neither the means nor the end.

197. Klosko, "Multiple Principles of Political Obligation," 802.

198. Green, *Authority of the State*, 246–47.

199. While Green does not explicitly deny that multiple principles can apply to the same person, he does not take it up.

200. Klosko, "Multiple Principles of Political Obligation," 807, 809.

201. Klosko, "Multiple Principles of Political Obligation," 801.

202. Klosko, "Multiple Principles of Political Obligation," 802. I leave aside the question of what Klosko means by "strong" and whether that is necessary.

203. Klosko, "Multiple Principles of Political Obligation," 818.

204. Klosko, "Multiple Principles of Political Obligation," 818.

205. Klosko, "Multiple Principles of Political Obligation," 812–13.

206. Klosko, "Multiple Principles of Political Obligation," 816.

207. Estlund, *Democratic Authority*, 118.

208. Estlund, *Democratic Authority*, 7.

209. Estlund, *Democratic Authority*, 8.

210. Estlund, *Democratic Authority*, 11.

211. Estlund, *Democratic Authority*, 10.

212. Estlund, *Democratic Authority*, 157.

213. See, for example, Simmons, *Moral Principles and Political Obligations*, 57–100; Green, *Authority of the State*, 158–87.

214. Estlund, *Democratic Authority*, 117.

215. Estlund outlines such a case as follows: "Consider a committed sexual relationship. Normally, each partner will have a moral duty to be sexually available to the other to some degree. . . . When sex is proposed, the partner can still prevent it from being permitted by refusing to consent" (*Democratic Authority*, 126). My purpose in raising this is not to defend the conclusions he draws here. Rather, as I say, I believe Estlund's own example highlights what is wrong with his notion of normative consent.

216. Estlund, *Democratic Authority*, 126.

217. Estlund, *Democratic Authority*, 127.

218. Estlund, *Democratic Authority*, 127.

219. Estlund, *Democratic Authority*, 2. Notwithstanding the rest of my critique of Estlund, I am happy to accept his use of the term *commands* to describe how authority obligates.

220. Estlund, *Democratic Authority*, 134.

221. Estlund, *Democratic Authority*, 134.

222. Estlund, *Democratic Authority*, 8.
223. Estlund, *Democratic Authority*, 155.

CHAPTER 5   We the Sovereign

1. Smith, "Is There a Prima Facie Obligation," 959.
2. Simmons, *Moral Principles and Political Obligations*, 109.
3. Rawls, *Law of Peoples*, 66.
4. Rawls writes: "The meaning of decency is given in the same way. As I have already said, a decent society is not aggressive and engages in war only in self-defense. It has a common good idea of justice that assigns human rights to all its members; its basic structure includes a decent consultation hierarchy that protects these and other rights and ensures that all groups in society are decently represented by elected bodies in the system of consultation. Finally, there must be a sincere and not unreasonable belief on the part of judges and officials who administer the legal system that the law is indeed guided by a common good idea of justice. Laws supported merely by force are grounds for rebellion and resistance. They are routine in a slave society, but cannot belong to a decent one" (*Law of Peoples*, 88).
5. Simmons, *Moral Principles and Political Obligations*, 110.
6. Simon, *General Theory of Authority*, 12.
7. Finnis, *Natural Law and Natural Rights*, 251.
8. Finnis, *Natural Law and Natural Rights*, 251.
9. See, for example, Simmons, *Moral Principles and Political Obligations*, 79–100.
10. Simon, *General Theory of Authority*, 62, 63.
11. Consent can play a role in determining who is in authority (who the commander is), but that does not mean that the authority lacks justification when it is identified in a different manner.
12. Simon, *Philosophy of Democratic Government*, 16.
13. There can be cases in which any decision is better than no decision, but when we say that, we really mean "any decision" among a set of choices from which many bad options are already ruled out. In other words, we really mean any decision among the options that remain on the table. This is important for understanding Schmitt's preference for decision over deliberation.
14. Finnis, *Natural Law and Natural Rights*, 249.
15. Simon, *Philosophy of Democratic Government*, 152–53.
16. Simon, *Philosophy of Democratic Government*, 151.
17. Simon, *Philosophy of Democratic Government*, 153.

18. As I say, in that case, there is no true authority of law because she does not obey laws with which she disagrees. More to the point, she cannot be said to be *obeying* the law in any meaningful sense.

19. Self-rule through command also mitigates concern over the rejection of consent as a necessary criterion for justified authority. If the commander and commanded are the same person or people, then presumably there is consent.

20. Simon, *Nature and Functions of Authority*, 2.
21. Simon, *Philosophy of Democratic Government*, 5.
22. Simon, *General Theory of Authority*, 130.
23. Finnis, "Law as Co-ordination," 103.
24. Simon, *Nature and Functions of Authority*, 45.
25. Simon, *Nature and Functions of Authority*, 45.
26. Simon, *Philosophy of Democratic Government*, 158.
27. Simon, *Philosophy of Democratic Government*, 159.
28. Simon, *Philosophy of Democratic Government*, 186.
29. Simon, *Philosophy of Democratic Government*, 189.
30. Simon, *Philosophy of Democratic Government*, 187.
31. Simon, *Philosophy of Democratic Government*, 190.
32. Simon, *Philosophy of Democratic Government*, 194.
33. Simon, *Philosophy of Democratic Government*, 187.
34. Simon, *Philosophy of Democratic Government*, 146.
35. Simon, *Philosophy of Democratic Government*, 146.
36. Simon, *Philosophy of Democratic Government*, 149.
37. Simon, *Philosophy of Democratic Government*, 154.
38. Simon, *Philosophy of Democratic Government*, 149. For Simon, such a position is flawed down to its core, for "the obligation to obey has its roots in the nature of things" (154). Moreover, this is true for any political arrangement: "In a direct democracy as well as in any other organization the nature of society demands that man should obey man" (154).
39. Simon, *Philosophy of Democratic Government*, 179.
40. Simon, *Philosophy of Democratic Government*, 182.
41. Simon, *Philosophy of Democratic Government*, 182.
42. Simon, *Philosophy of Democratic Government*, 182.
43. Simon, *Philosophy of Democratic Government*, 183.
44. Simon, *Philosophy of Democratic Government*, 183.
45. Simon, *Philosophy of Democratic Government*, 183.
46. Simon, *Philosophy of Democratic Government*, 183.
47. Simon, *Philosophy of Democratic Government*, 183.
48. Simon, *Philosophy of Democratic Government*, 180.

49. Simon, *Philosophy of Democratic Government*, 186.
50. Simon, *Philosophy of Democratic Government*, 186.
51. Simon, *Philosophy of Democratic Government*, 194.
52. Simon, *Philosophy of Democratic Government*, 194.
53. In the same way, autonomy (or liberty) is instrumental to human flourishing—in both senses of "instrumental." Some measure of autonomy is necessary for human flourishing, but it is valuable only to the extent that it conduces to human flourishing. Therefore, once again, the common good both necessitates and justifies autonomy, and, under good government, we find both authority and autonomy in proper measure.
54. This can seem like a tenuous objection because such a possibility depends on how much this legal-philosophical concept affects the political and legal culture (and it is unwise to overestimate such effects), but it is not an unreasonable concern for that reason.
55. See, for example, Finnis, "Law as Co-ordination."
56. Finnis, "Law as Co-ordination, 103.
57. Finnis, "Law as Co-ordination, 103.
58. Finnis, "Law as Co-ordination, 103.
59. Finnis, *Natural Law*, 305.
60. Finnis, *Natural Law*, 233.
61. Finnis, "Law as Co-ordination," 103.
62. Finnis, "Law as Co-ordination," 103.
63. Simon, *Nature and Functions of Authority*, 2–3.
64. Simon, *Nature and Functions of Authority*, 3.
65. Simon, *Nature and Functions of Authority*, 45–46.
66. Raz, introduction, 17.
67. Raz, introduction, 17.
68. See, for example, Finnis, "Law and What I Truly Should Decide," 111.
69. Although Schmitt insists that politics is normative, he also regards ethics as a different domain from politics. Schmitt writes, "The political enemy need not be morally evil or aesthetically ugly.... But he is, nevertheless, the other, the stranger; and it is sufficient for his nature that he is, in a specially intense way, existentially something different and alien" (Schmitt, *Concept of the Political*, 27). Relatedly, Schmitt adds, "Thereby the inherently objective nature and autonomy of the political becomes evident by virtue of its being able to treat, distinguish, and comprehend the friend-enemy antithesis independently of other antitheses" (27). For our purposes, I leave aside whether Schmitt's distinction between politics and ethics holds up. The key here is that Schmitt sees politics as a realm in which neutrality is necessarily impossible.

70. See Schmitt, *Political Theology*, 5–15.
71. We can take it as an assumption here that the existing order is worth preserving because it serves the common good.
72. Schmitt, *Political Theology*, 2.
73. Schmitt, *Political Theology*, 9.
74. See Schmitt, *Political Theology*, 5–15.
75. Schmitt, *Legality and Legitimacy*, 96.
76. Schmitt, *Legality and Legitimacy*, 48.
77. Schmitt, *Legality and Legitimacy*, 48.
78. Schmitt, *Legality and Legitimacy*, 48.
79. Schmitt, *Legality and Legitimacy*, xxvii.
80. Schmitt, *Legality and Legitimacy*, 33.
81. Schmitt, *Political Theology*, xlviii.
82. Schmitt, *Concept of the Political*, 26.
83. Schmitt, *Concept of the Political*, 78, 79.
84. Schmitt, "Age of Neutralizations and Depoliticizations," 80–96.
85. Schmitt, "Age of Neutralizations and Depoliticizations," 90.
86. Schmitt, "Age of Neutralizations and Depoliticizations," 90.
87. Schmitt, *Legality and Legitimacy*, 27.
88. Schmitt, *Legality and Legitimacy*, 25.
89. McCormick, introduction to Schmitt, *Legality and Legitimacy*, xvi.
90. McCormick, introduction to Schmitt, *Legality and Legitimacy*, xvi.
91. Schmitt, *Legality and Legitimacy*, 27.
92. Schmitt, *Legality and Legitimacy*, 27.
93. Schmitt, *Legality and Legitimacy*, 27.
94. Schmitt, *Legality and Legitimacy*, 28.
95. Schmitt, *Legality and Legitimacy*, 28.
96. Schmitt, *Legality and Legitimacy*, 28.
97. Schmitt, *Concept of the Political*, 35.
98. Schmitt, "Age of Neutralizations and Depoliticizations," 90.
99. Schmitt, *Political Theology*, 2.
100. Schmitt, *Legality and Legitimacy*, 47.
101. Schmitt, *Legality and Legitimacy*, xvi.
102. Schmitt, *Legality and Legitimacy*, xix. Even the great positivist Hart has a similar line in discussing the so-called minimum content of law: the law must at least ensure its own survival (Hart, *Concept of Law*, 193).
103. See, for example, Schmitt, "Age of Neutralizations and Depoliticizations," 95.
104. Schmitt, *Legality and Legitimacy*, xxxv.
105. See, for example, Schmitt, *Legality and Legitimacy*, 9–10, 47.
106. Schmitt, *Legality and Legitimacy*, 59–66.

107. This echoes my critique of Hart and the difference between rules and commands.
108. Schmitt, *Legality and Legitimacy*, 4.
109. Schmitt, *Legality and Legitimacy*, 4.
110. Schmitt, *Legality and Legitimacy*, 4.
111. Strong, foreword to Schmitt, *Political Theology*, xvi.
112. Schmitt, *Legality and Legitimacy*, 25.
113. Schmitt, *Political Theology*, 48–49.
114. Schwab, introduction to Schmitt, *Political Theology*, xlii.
115. Schmitt, *Political Theology*, 63.
116. Schmitt, *Legality and Legitimacy*, 9.
117. Schmitt, *Legality and Legitimacy*, 9.
118. Schmitt, *Political Theology*, 63.
119. Schmitt, *Political Theology*, 63.
120. Schmitt, *Political Theology*, 66.
121. Some theories of justification depend on this. Where justification depends on an orientation to the common good, compatibility with popular sovereignty is not strictly necessary but is helpful, not least in making it attractive for contemporary politics.
122. Schmitt, *Political Theology*, 62.
123. McCormick, introduction to Schmitt, *Legality and Legitimacy*, xxxvi.
124. McCormick, introduction to Schmitt, *Legality and Legitimacy*, xxxv.
125. McCormick, introduction to Schmitt, *Legality and Legitimacy*, xxx.
126. Schmitt, *Legality and Legitimacy*, 63.
127. Schmitt, *Legality and Legitimacy*, 89.
128. Schmitt, *Legality and Legitimacy*, 90.
129. McCormick, introduction to Schmitt, *Legality and Legitimacy*, xxxv.
130. McCormick, introduction to Schmitt, *Legality and Legitimacy*, xxxii.
131. Schmitt, *Legality and Legitimacy*, 89.
132. McCormick, introduction to Schmitt, *Legality and Legitimacy*, xli.
133. McCormick, introduction to Schmitt, *Legality and Legitimacy*, xli.
134. McCormick, introduction to Schmitt, *Legality and Legitimacy*, xli.
135. Simon, *Philosophy of Democratic Government*, 157.
136. Simon, *Philosophy of Democratic Government*, 154.
137. Anscombe, "On the Source of the Authority of the State," 169.
138. Schmitt, *Legality and Legitimacy*, 63.
139. Schwab, introduction to Schmitt, *Political Theology*, l.
140. See, for example, Finnis, "Law and What I Truly Should Decide," 111.

141. Austin, *Province of Jurisprudence Determined*, 20.
142. Schmitt, *Legality and Legitimacy*, 79–80.
143. Schmitt, *Legality and Legitimacy*, 81.
144. Schmitt, *Legality and Legitimacy*, 82.
145. Schmitt, *Legality and Legitimacy*, 73.
146. McCormick, introduction to Schmitt, *Legality and Legitimacy*, xxxv.
147. McCormick, introduction to Schmitt, *Legality and Legitimacy*, xxvi.
148. McCormick, introduction to Schmitt, *Legality and Legitimacy*, xxiii.
149. McCormick, introduction to Schmitt, *Legality and Legitimacy*, xxiii.
150. Strong, foreword to Schmitt, *Political Theology*, xv.
151. Strong, foreword to Schmitt, *Political Theology*, xv.
152. Schmitt, *Concept of the Political*, 3.
153. Schmitt, *Political Theology*, 12.
154. Schmitt, *Political Theology*, 12.

CONCLUSION

1. Foucault, *Discipline and Punish*, 168.
2. Plato, *Republic*, 15 (1.338c).
3. Weber, "Politics as a Vocation," 156.
4. Arendt, *Between Past and Future*, 97.
5. Arendt, *Between Past and Future*, 126.
6. Arendt, *Between Past and Future*, 91.
7. Arendt, *Between Past and Future*, 91.
8. Arendt, *Between Past and Future*, 92.
9. Finnis, "Law and What I Truly Should Decide," 111.
10. Strauss, "What Is Political Philosophy?"
11. Arendt, *Between Past and Future*, 92–93.
12. Arendt, *Between Past and Future*, 93.
13. Arendt, *Between Past and Future*, 128.
14. Arendt, *Between Past and Future*, 128.
15. Arendt, *Between Past and Future*, 94–95.
16. Arendt, *Between Past and Future*, 95.

BIBLIOGRAPHY

Aiyar, S. "The Problem of Law's Authority: John Finnis and Joseph Raz on Legal Obligation." *Law and Philosophy* 19, no. 4 (July 2000): 465–89.
Anonymous. "H. L. A. Hart on Legal and Moral Obligation." *Michigan Law Review* 73, no. 2 (December 1974): 443–58.
Anscombe, Elizabeth. "Authority in Morals." In *Ethics, Religion and Politics: Collected Philosophical Papers*, 3:43–50. Oxford: Blackwell, 1981.
———. "On Frustration of the Majority by the Fulfillment of the Majority's Will." *Analysis* 36, no. 4 (June 1976): 161–68.
———. "On the Source of the Authority of the State." In Raz, *Authority*, 142–73.
Aquinas, Thomas. *Summa Theologica*. Translated by Fathers of the English Dominican Province. Westminster, MD: Christian Classics, 1981.
Arendt, Hannah. *Between Past and Future*. New York: Penguin Books, 2006.
Augustine. *Concerning the City of God against the Pagans*. Translated by Henry Bettenson. New York: Penguin Books, 2003.
———. *On the Free Choice of the Will, On Grace and Free Choice, and Other Writings*. Edited by Peter King. Cambridge: Cambridge University Press, 2010.
Austin, John. *The Province of Jurisprudence Determined*. Amherst, NY: Prometheus Books, 2000.
Bayles, Michael. *Principles of Legislation: The Uses of Political Authority*. Detroit: Wayne State University Press, 1978.
Benedict XVI. "Faith, Reason, and the University: Memories and Reflections." 12 September 2006. Available via the Vatican website. https://w2.vatican.va/content/benedict-xvi/en/speeches/2006/september/documents/hf_ben-xvi_spe_20060912_university-regensburg.html.

Bentham, Jeremy. *Bentham's Political Thought.* Edited by Bhikhu Parekh. New York: Harper & Row, 1973.
———. *Of Laws in General.* Oxford: Oxford University Press, 1970.
———. *The Principles of Morals and Legislation.* Amherst, NY: Prometheus Books, 1988.
Bertea, Stefano. "Contemporary Theories of Legal Obligation: A Tentative Critical Map." In *Contemporary Perspectives on Legal Obligation*, edited by Stefano Bertea. Abingdon, Oxfordshire: Routledge, 2022.
———. *A Theory of Legal Obligation.* New York: Cambridge University Press, 2019.
Brugger, E. Christian. "Capital Punishment Is Intrinsically Wrong: A Reply to Feser and Bessette." *Public Discourse*, 22 October 2017. https://www.thepublicdiscourse.com/2017/10/20341/.
Cover, Robert. *Justice Accused: Antislavery and the Judicial Process.* New Haven: Yale University Press, 1975.
Coyle, Sean. "Hart, Raz, and the Concept of a Legal System." *Law and Philosophy* 21, no. 3 (May 2022): 275–304.
Darwall, Stephen. "Authority and Reasons: Exclusionary and Second-Personal." *Ethics* 120, no. 2 (January 2010): 257–78.
Dworkin, Ronald. *Law's Empire.* Cambridge, MA: Belknap Press, 1986.
Edmundson, William. "State of the Art: The Duty to Obey the Law." *Legal Theory* 10, no. 4 (December 2004): 215–59.
Estlund, David. *Democratic Authority: A Philosophical Framework.* Princeton: Princeton University Press, 2008.
Finnis, John. "The Authority of Law in the Predicament of Contemporary Social Theory." *Notre Dame Journal of Law, Ethics, and Public Policy* 1, no. 1 (1984): 115–38.
———. "Law and What I Truly Should Decide." *American Journal of Jurisprudence* 48, no. 1 (2003): 107–29.
———. "Law as Co-ordination." *Ratio Juris* 2, no. 1 (March 1989): 97–104.
———. *Natural Law and Natural Rights.* Oxford: Oxford University Press, 2011.
———. "On the Incoherence of Legal Positivism." *Notre Dame Law Review* 75, no. 5 (1999–2000): 1597–1611.
———. "Religion and State." Notre Dame Legal Studies Paper No. 06-34, Notre Dame Law School, Notre Dame, IN, 9 November 2006. http://ssrn.com/abstract=943420.
Foucault, Michel. *Discipline and Punish: The Birth of the Prison.* Translated by Alan Sheridan. New York: Vintage Books, 1995.
Friedman, R. B. "On the Concept of Authority in Political Philosophy." In Raz, *Authority*, 56–91.

Fuller, Lon. *The Morality of Law*. New Haven: Yale University Press, 1969.
George, Robert, ed. *The Autonomy of Law: Essays on Legal Positivism*. Oxford: Oxford University Press, 1999.
——. "Kelsen and Aquinas on 'The Natural-Law Doctrine.'" *Notre Dame Law Review* 75, no. 5 (1999–2000): 1625–46.
Gilbert, Margaret. "Social Rules: Some Problems for Hart's Account, and an Alternative Proposal." *Law and Philosophy* 18, no. 2 (March 1999): 141–71.
Green, Leslie. *The Authority of the State*. Oxford: Oxford University Press, 1988.
——. "The Concept of Law Revisited." *Michigan Law Review* 94, no. 6 (May 1996): 1687–1717.
Greenawalt, Kent. "The Rule of Recognition and the Constitution." *Michigan Law Review* 85, no. 4 (February 1987): 621–71.
Hart, H. L. A. [Herbert Hart]. "Commands and Authoritative Legal Reasons." In Raz, *Authority*, 92–114.
——. *The Concept of Law*. Oxford: Oxford University Press, 1994.
——. *Essays in Jurisprudence and Philosophy*. Oxford: Oxford University Press, 2001.
——. *Essays on Bentham: Studies in Jurisprudence and Political Theory*. Oxford: Oxford University Press, 2011.
——. "Positivism and the Separation of Law and Morals." *Harvard Law Review* 71, no. 4 (February 1958): 593–629.
Himma, Kenneth. "Bringing Hart and Raz to the Table: Coleman's Compatiblity Thesis." *Oxford Journal of Legal Studies* 21, no. 4 (2001): 609–27.
——. "Law's Claim of Legitimate Authority." In *The Postscript: Essays on the Postscript to "The Concept of Law,"* edited by Jules Coleman, 271–309. Oxford: Oxford University Press, 2001.
——. "Positivism, Naturalism and the Obligation to Obey Law." *Southern Journal of Philosophy* 36, no. 2 (Summer 1998): 145–62.
——. "Revisiting Raz: Inclusive Positivism and the Concept of Authority." *APA Newsletters* 6, no. 2 (Spring 2007): 20–27.
Hook, Sidney, ed. *Law and Philosophy: A Symposium*. New York: New York University Press, 1964.
Jouvenel, Bertrand de. *Sovereignty: An Enquiry into the Political Good*. Translated by J. F. Huntington. Cambridge: Cambridge University Press, 2012.
Kelsen, Hans. *General Theory of Law and State*. Translated by Anders Wedberg. Clark, NJ: Lawbook Exchange, 2009.
——. *Pure Theory of Law*. Translated by Max Knight. Clark, NJ: Lawbook Exchange, 2009.

Klosko, George. "Multiple Principles of Political Obligation." *Political Theory* 32, no. 6 (December 2004): 801–24.
Kramer, Matthew. "Of Final Things: Morality as One of the Ultimate Determinants of Legal Validity." *Law and Philosophy* 24, no. 1 (January 2005): 47–97.
Ladenson, Robert. "In Defense of a Hobbesian Conception of Law." In Raz, *Authority*, 32–55.
Locke, John. *Two Treatises of Government*. North Clarendon, VT: Tuttle Publishing, 2000.
MacCormick, Neil. *H. L. A. Hart*. Stanford, CA: Stanford University Press, 2008.
———. *Legal Reasoning and Legal Theory*. Oxford: Oxford University Press, 2003.
MacIntyre, Alasdair. *Secularization and Moral Change*. Oxford: Oxford University Press, 1967.
Mark, Daniel. "The Failure of Joseph Raz's Account of Legal Obligation." *American Journal of Jurisprudence* 61, no. 2 (December 2016): 217–36.
———. "New Natural Law Theory and the Common Good of the Political Community." *National Catholic Bioethics Quarterly* 19, no. 2 (2019): 293–303.
Marmor, Andrei. "An Institutional Conception of Authority." *Philosophy and Public Affairs* 39, no. 3 (2011): 238–61.
———. "The Dilemma of Authority." USC Legal Studies Research Paper No. 10-6, University of Southern California, Los Angeles, CA, 20 April 2010. http://ssrn.com/abstract=1593191.
McCormick, John. Introduction to Schmitt, *Legality and Legitimacy*, xiii–xliii.
Murphy, Jeffrie. "In Defense of Obligation." In *Political and Legal Obligation*, edited by John W. Chapman and Roland Pennock, 36–45. New York: Atherton Press, 1970.
Murphy, Mark. *An Essay on Divine Authority*. Ithaca, NY: Cornell University Press, 2002.
———. "Natural Law Jurisprudence." *Legal Theory* 9, no. 4 (2003): 241–67.
———. "Surrender of Judgment and the Consent Theory of Political Authority." *Law and Philosophy* 16, no. 2 (1997): 115–43.
Oberdiek, Hans. "The Role of Sanctions and Coercion in Understanding Law and Legal Systems." *American Journal of Jurisprudence* 21, no. 1 (1976): 71–94.
Ogden v. Saunders. 25 US 213 (1827).

Pennock, Roland. Introduction to *Political and Legal Obligation*, edited by John W. Chapman and Roland Pennock, xiii–xxiii. New York: Atherton Press, 1970.
Perry, Stephen. "Hart on Social Rules and the Foundations of Law: Liberating the Internal Point of View." *Fordham Law Review* 75, no. 3 (2006): 1171–1209.
———. "Law and Obligation." *American Journal of Jurisprudence* 50, no. 1 (2005): 263–95.
Peters, Richard. "Authority." In *Political Philosophy*, edited by Anthony Quinton, 83–96. Oxford: Oxford University Press, 1967.
Pitkin, Hanna. "Obligation and Consent II." *American Political Science Review* 60, no. 1 (March 1966): 39–52.
Plato. *Five Dialogues: Euthyphro, Apology, Crito, Meno, Phaedo.* Translated by George Grube. Indianapolis: Hackett, 2002.
———. *The Republic of Plato.* Translated by Allan Bloom. New York: Basic Books, 2016.
Postema, Gerald. "Law as Command: The Model of Command in Modern Jurisprudence." *Philosophical Issues* 11 (2001): 470–501.
Rawls, John. *The Law of Peoples.* Cambridge, MA: Harvard University Press, 2002.
———. *A Theory of Justice.* Cambridge, MA: Belknap Press, 1999.
Raz, Joseph. "About Morality and the Nature of Law." *American Journal of Jurisprudence* 48, no. 1 (2003): 1–15.
———, ed. *Authority.* New York: New York University Press, 1990.
———. "Authority and Consent." *Virginia Law Review* 67, no. 1 (1981): 103–31.
———. "Authority and Justification." In *Authority*, 115–41.
———. *The Authority of Law: Essays on Law and Morality.* Oxford: Oxford University Press, 2009.
———. *The Concept of a Legal System: An Introduction to the Theory of a Legal System.* Oxford: Oxford University Press, 2003.
———. *Ethics in the Public Domain: Essays in the Morality of Law and Politics.* Oxford: Oxford University Press, 2001.
———. Introduction to *Authority*, 1–19.
———. *The Morality of Freedom.* Oxford: Oxford University Press, 1986.
———. "The Obligation to Obey: Revision and Tradition." *Notre Dame Journal of Ethics and Public Policy* 1, no. 1 (1984–85): 139–55.
———. "On Respect, Authority, and Neutrality: A Response." *Ethics* 120, no. 2 (January 2010): 279–301.
———. *Practical Reason and Norms.* Oxford: Oxford University Press, 1999.

———. "The Problem of Authority: Revisiting the Service Conception." *Minnesota Law Review* 90 (2006): 1003–44.

Sartorius, Rolf. "Political Authority and Political Obligation." *Virginia Law Review* 67, no. 1 (February 1981): 3–17.

Schmitt, Carl. "The Age of Neutralizations and Depoliticizations." In *Concept of the Political*, 80–96.

———. *The Concept of the Political*. Translated by George Schwab. Chicago: University of Chicago, 2007.

———. *Legality and Legitimacy*. Translated by Jeffrey Seitzer. Durham, NC: Duke University Press, 2004.

———. *Political Theology: Four Chapters on the Concept of Sovereignty*. Translated by George Schwab. Chicago: University of Chicago Press, 2005.

Schwab, George. Introduction to Schmitt, *Political Theology*, xxxvii–lii.

Shapiro, Scott. *Legality*. Cambridge, MA: Belknap Press, 2011.

———. "What Is the Internal Point of View?" *Fordham Law Review* 75, no. 3 (2006–7): 1157–70.

Simmons, John. "The Anarchist Position: A Reply to Klosko and Senor." *Philosophy and Public Affairs* 16, no. 3 (Summer 1987): 269–79.

———. "Associative Political Obligations." *Ethics* 106, no. 2 (January 1996): 247–73.

———. "Consent, Free Choice, and Democratic Government." *Georgia Law Review* 18 (1983–84): 791–819.

———. *Moral Principles and Political Obligations*. Princeton: Princeton University Press, 1979.

———. "Tacit Consent and Political Obligation." *Philosophy and Public Affairs* 5, no. 3 (Spring 1976): 274–91.

———. "Voluntarism and Political Associations." *Virginia Law Review* 67, no. 1 (February 1981): 19–37.

Simmons, John, and Christopher Wellman. *Is There a Duty to Obey the Law?* Cambridge: Cambridge University Press, 2005.

Simon, Yves. *A General Theory of Authority*. Notre Dame, IN: University of Notre Dame Press, 1980.

———. *Nature and Functions of Authority*. Milwaukee: Marquette University Press, 1948.

———. *Philosophy of Democratic Government*. Notre Dame, IN: University of Notre Dame Press, 1993.

Singer, Marcus. "Hart's Concept of Law." *Journal of Philosophy* 60, no. 8 (April 1963): 197–220.

Smith, Malcolm. "Is There a Prima Facie Obligation to Obey the Law?" *Yale Law Journal* 82, no. 5 (April 1973): 950–76.

Strauss, Leo. *Natural Right and History*. Chicago: University of Chicago Press, 2000.

———. "What Is Political Philosophy?" In *An Introduction to Political Philosophy: Ten Essays by Leo Strauss*, edited by Hilail Gildin, 3-57. Detroit: Wayne State University Press, 1989.

Strong, Tracy. Foreword to Schmitt, *Political Theology*, vii–xxxv.

Waldron, Jeremy. "Authority for Officials." In *Rights, Culture, and the Law: Themes from the Legal and Political Philosophy of Joseph Raz*, edited by Lukas Meyer, Stanley Paulson, and Thomas Pogge, 45–69. Oxford: Oxford University Press, 2003.

———. "*Lex Satis Iusta.*" *Notre Dame Law Review* 75, no. 5 (1999–2000): 1829–58.

———. "One Law for All." *Washington and Lee Law Review* 59 (2002): 3–34.

Weaver, Richard. *Ideas Have Consequences*. Chicago: University of Chicago Press, 2013.

Weber, Max. "Politics as a Vocation." In *Max Weber's Complete Writings on Academic and Political Vocations*, translated by Gordon Wells, edited by John Dreijmanis, 155–207. New York: Algora Publishing, 2008.

Wolff, Robert. "The Conflict between Authority and Autonomy." In Raz, *Authority*, 20–31.

———. *In Defense of Anarchism*. Los Angeles: University of California Press, 1998.

Wright, Matthew. *A Vindication of Politics: On the Common Good and Human Flourishing*. Lawrence: University Press of Kansas, 2019.

INDEX

A
absolute obligation to obey, 9, 224, 231, 232, 241, 270, 349n91, 356n112, 358n152
adjudication, rules of. *See* rules of adjudication
"Age of Neutralizations and Depoliticizations, The" (Schmitt), 303
agreement
    binding, 126–27, 341n65, 342n80
    coercion emerging from, 69
    governance, 119
    handshake as, 129
    imposing legal duty, 118
    legal enforcement, 118–19
    morally obligatory nature, 118
    prelegal, 118
    private, 126, 128
    promise as, 118
    self-government, 119
    See also contracts; power-conferring rules
all-things-considered authoritativeness, 138
all-things-considered decision to obey, 18

all-things-considered obligation, 9, 30, 132, 137, 138, 181, 232
all-things-considered reason to obey, 173–74
all-things-equal authoritativeness, 138
all-things-equal obligation, 9, 30, 132, 135, 137, 147, 199, 232. *See also* prima facie obligation to obey
anarchism, 290
    philosophical, 149–50, 185–86
    Wolff on autonomy and, 149–50
Anscombe, Elizabeth, 245, 314
Aquinas, Thomas, 4, 22–23, 33, 261, 288, 329n1, 351n25
Arendt, Hannah, 354n53
    loss of authority, 326, 327–28
    "What Is Authority?," 40, 323–28
Aristotelian-Thomistic ethical tradition, 19
Arnaldez, R., 353n36
Articles of Confederation, 284
atheism, 214, 229
Augustine, 91, 140, 329n1
Austin, John, 189, 201, 315–16
    on authority, 143, 146

Austin, John (*continued*)
   command model, 43, 45, 47–48, 52, 94, 97, 99, 143, 186, 188, 299
   divine vs. human command, 207
   on sanctions, 99
authoritarianism, 281, 287, 289, 293, 294, 324
authoritative directives, 6, 18, 47–48, 150–51, 153, 190, 222, 285, 316, 319, 354n66
authority, 4, 230–44
   Arendt's theory of, 323–28
   autonomy and (*see* autonomy)
   being in vs. being an, 193–94
   charismatic, 106, 339n31
   content independence (*see* content independence)
   de facto and de jure, 103, 162, 194–97, 291, 326
   dilemma of, 6–8, 10, 13, 35, 37, 77, 82, 231–32
   expertise, 9, 32, 37, 155, 157–60, 191, 194, 351n12
   justification (*see* justification)
   legitimacy (*see* legitimacy)
   limits, 296–97
   normative power, 78–83, 180, 191, 231
   normative valence, 18
   political, 144, 145, 159
   practical, 6, 78, 79–81, 139, 232, 285
   Raz's theory of (*see* Raz, Joseph)
   role in religious life, 268
   Simon's theory (*see* Simon, Yves)
   terminological usage, 8–9
   undetectable breaches, 234–42
   unlimited in principle, 318, 319
   See also common good
Authority (Raz), 297
autonomy, 263–67
   common good and, 263–67, 281–82, 363n53
   deferring to authority, 152–53
   human flourishing and, 363n53
   outcomes, 153–55
   preserving, 152
   Raz's theory of authority and, 149–55, 263–67
   Simon's theory of authority and, 263–67, 287–88

B
Benedict XVI, Regensburg address of, 353n36
Bentham, Jeremy, 47, 59, 94, 143, 186, 189
Bertea, Stefano, 20
   on Hart's theory, 21
   theory of legal obligation, 21–30, 40–41, 332n49
Bible, 209
binding agreement, 126–27, 341n65, 342n80. *See also* agreement

C
capacities, 36, 109–12, 266, 286, 314
   rational cultivation, 19
   rules of adjudication, 64
change, rules of. *See* rules of change
charismatic authority, 106, 339n31
civil disobedience, 15, 177–78, 233–34, 235
civility, 182–83
Clausewitz, Carl von, 321
coach-driver theory, 289–90, 313
coercion/coercive power, 4, 50, 90, 191, 230, 314
   Arendt on authority and, 327

Hart's critique of, 5, 16, 43, 45, 46, 47, 48, 50, 55–56, 59, 60, 67, 68–72
legal obligations and, 80
legal power vs., 80, 90
moral obligation and, 259
rightfulness of, 341n65
voluntary co-operation and, 69
command, 14, 32, 38, 93–113
attendant theory, 38
Austin's model/theory, 43, 45, 47–48, 52, 94, 97, 99, 143, 186, 188, 299
common good and (*see* common good)
depsychologized, 104, 109
as descriptive theory, 98
diversity within law and, 113–17
habits of obedience and, 101–3 (*see also* habits of obedience)
Hart's critique or rejection of, 14, 36, 44, 45, 47, 48, 50, 93–113, 187–88
identifying legally valid rules, 94
as instructive framework, 94
internal point of view and, 51
justified, 51, 194–95, 228
notion, 94
obligation and, 94, 95–96, 98–99, 109
as orders backed by threats, 47–48
reasons without, 33–34, 186–87, 188, 203–6, 212 (*see also* moral obligation)
without reasons, 33, 186–87, 188, 202, 203, 206–12, 217, 230 (*see also* religious obligation)
rules based in social practice vs. (*see* rules)
sanctions and, 36, 47–48, 97, 98–101, 112, 124, 144, 331n35

self-government and, 108–12
self-rule, 285–86, 362n19
succession and persistence, 104–8
as useful component of law, 93
as a whole to common good, 14–15
common good, 14–15, 32–33, 38, 39, 79, 187–201, 244–78, 298, 323, 351n16, 357n115
agency relative to, 261
architectonic role, 249, 250–51
autonomy and, 263–67, 281–82, 363n53
common will vs., 283–84
consent and, 282–85
coordination and, 251–59, 293, 295–96
democracy and, 279–98
Estlund's general obligation theory and, 273–78
Finnis on, 19, 195, 196, 237–39, 241, 242, 249–50, 259–60, 261
human flourishing and, 19–20
Klosko on, 272
legal system, 198–201
nature of, 259–62
Nazi law and, 138, 140
nondemocratic system and, 281
political, 20
Raz's theory and, 239–42, 263, 266–67, 356n111, 358n167
Schmitt and, 299–300, 304, 312, 313, 314–15
second-order reason, 250–51
Simon on, 139, 246, 253–54, 260–62, 264, 266, 297–98
threat to, 291–93
transmission theory, 291–92
truly common nature of, 259–62
virtuous opposition to, 261–62

common good (*continued*)
　Wright on, 19–20
　See also justification; prima facie obligation
common good idea of justice, 280, 361n4
common will, 283–84
Concept of Law, The (Hart), 48, 52, 69
consent, 273
　common good, 282–85
　common will, 283–84
　Finnis on, 282
　justification of authority and, 282–85
　as meaningful/useful concept, 275
　nonconsent and, 275–76
　normative, 273–78
　respect and, 169–71
　sexual activity and, 276
　tacit, 283
　theory of, 280
content-dependent decision, 350n110
content-dependent theory of authority, 186
content independence, 38–39, 186–87, 270
　authoritarianism and, 289
　concept/notion, 9–10
　Estlund's theory, 273
　Green's theory of authority, 181–83, 350n110
　justified authority, 6–13, 231, 244–48, 249
　obedience, 220, 228, 268
　reasons for action (*see* reasons)
　religious obligation (*see* religious obligation)
　Shapiro's recognition of, 89
　Simmons on, 280

theory of justification, 77
transmission of authority, 288
unlimited authority, 39
See also prima facie obligation to obey
contracts, 178
　Marshall on, 341n65
　obligation of, 341n65
　power-conferring and duty-imposing rules, 117–20, 125–27, 128–29
　private agreement vs., 128, 129
　rules about, 341n68
coordination, 157, 295
　common good and, 251–59, 293, 295–96
　Finnis's theory, 238, 252, 253, 254, 255–57, 258
　Raz's theory, 252, 254, 255–59
　Simon's theory, 252, 253–55, 257–58
Cortés, Donoso, 319
Crito (Plato), 329n2
customs, 5, 129, 205, 206
　Hart's critique of, 5, 47, 54, 57, 58, 61, 75, 95, 335n59
　See also habits of obedience

D

decent society, 280, 361n4
decision and decisionism, 284
　deliberation vs., 300
　nonnormative basis for legality, 299
　plebiscites, 308, 309, 311–14
　referendum, 311, 312, 337n79
　sovereignty, 225–26, 298–319
decrees, 317–19
deficiency theory of government, 254
deism, 227, 229

democracy, 279–319
　command aspect of law being compatible with, 285–87
　common good, 279–98
　consent, 282–85
　decision and decisionism (*see* decision and decisionism)
　direct, 285, 286
　epistemic advantages, 273, 274, 277–78
　plebiscitary, 308, 309, 311–14
　Rawls's theory, 279, 280
　Simon's theory (*see* Simon, Yves)
　transmission theory, 288–92
　See also sovereignty
dependence thesis, 151
descriptive sociology, Hart's theory as, 5, 49, 52, 59–60, 67–68, 69, 74, 77, 134, 146, 230
designation theory, 313
dilemma of authority, 6–8, 10, 13, 35, 37, 77, 82, 231–32
directives, 14, 18
　authoritative, 6, 18, 47–48, 150–51, 153, 190, 222, 316, 319, 354n66
　content of, 6, 7, 9, 10, 17–18, 181, 267, 288
　decrees, 317–19
　useful as such shortcuts, 357n114
　wrong, 273
divine authority, 188, 202, 203, 206, 216–19, 223–25, 229–30, 352n31, 353n37
　content-independent obligation, 207–13
　rationalist understanding, 210
　Raz's theory of authority and, 210–12
　See also religious obligation
divine law, 4, 33, 203, 207, 209, 211, 218, 223. *See also* religious obligation
due process, 123
duty-imposing rules, 14, 31, 36, 117–30
　as commands, 114–15
　concept, 115
　contracts and, 117–20, 125–27, 128–29
　Hart's concept of law, 36, 114–15, 117–30
　legal obligation, 120
　nullity and, 122–27
　self-binding and, 340n40
　See also power-conferring rules

E

emergency powers, 291–92
　state of exception and, 226, 301
empowerment, 27, 295–96, 311, 317
equal chances, 301
Estlund, David, 16, 21
　authority, 273, 277
　content independence, 273
　democracy's epistemic advantages, 273, 274, 277–78
　Democratic Authority, 272–73
　moral power, 273, 277
　normative consent, 273–78
　theory of general (prima facie) obligation, 272–78
evil legal systems, 83–84, 91–92, 132
expertise, 220, 242
　authority, 9, 32, 37, 155, 157–60, 191, 194, 197, 351n12
　law, 146, 171, 173

F

Finnis, John, 21, 29, 34, 39, 91, 177
　common good for, 19, 195, 196,

Finnis, John (*continued*)
  237–39, 241, 242, 249–50, 259–60, 261
  coordination, 238, 252, 253, 254, 255–57, 258
  equal obligation of each law, 18, 199
  locating authority, 195, 196
  moral obligation, 18, 199, 294, 295
  Natural Law and Natural Rights, 213, 259
  prima facie obligation to obey, 234–35, 238, 243–44
  religious obligation, 213–15, 220–23
first-order reason, 10–13, 17, 18, 150, 151, 211, 250
  concept, 10–13
Foucault, Michel, 321
Fuller, Lon, 341n69, 352n30
functionalism, 299, 301–5
  liberalism vs., 301
  as right choice, reason for, 301–2
  value neutralization, 302

G
gangs, 87
  vs. government, 82, 90, 91, 140, 203, 249
Gelasius, Pope, 325
General Theory of Authority, A (Simon), 268
German postwar trials of Nazis. *See* Nazis, postwar German court trials of
God, 352n32, 353n36
  authoritative superiority, 215
  commands, 207–13
  Finnis's notion of religion, 213–15, 220–23
  goodness, 207, 209–10, 218–19, 221
  harmonizing or cooperating with, 214, 222–23
  human law and, 207, 223–24
  intrinsic authority, 209
  laws set by (*see* divine law)
  obedience to, 208–24, 268–70, 354n59 (*see also* religious obligation)
  omnibenevolence, 210
  as omnipotent lawgiver, 225
  Schmitt's political theology, 225–30
  Simon's theory, 215–16, 268–70, 288
  sovereignty and, 225–27, 313
  as subject to moral norms, 226–27
  transcendence, 214
  will of, 208, 214
government, 293
  autonomy, 263–64
  binding agreements and, 126
  common good principle (CG), 272
  crime boss's henchmen vs. officials of, 136
  de facto authority in, 91
  deficiency theory of, 254
  deserving support, 179, 180
  due process of law and, 123
  in exile, 194–96, 198
  vs. gangs, 82, 90, 91, 140, 203, 249
  justified authority, 164, 166, 175
  legitimacy, 4, 175, 178
  moral obligation, 123
  nullity, 123
  obedience to, 216–18
  obligation to obey the law as propaganda of, 72
  participatory, 297
  philosophical anarchists, 153
  Raz's theory of authority, 157, 159–60, 164–66, 169–71

Schmitt's political theology, 225, 227
self, 36, 108–12, 119, 281, 285
Simmons on, 179, 180, 216
Simon on, 289–92
voluntary cooperation, 289
See also democracy; sovereignty
Green, Leslie, 16, 21
The Authority of the State, 181
civility, 182–83

H
habits of obedience, 144, 217, 218, 314, 339n17
Hart's critique of, 5, 36, 43, 47, 53–58, 61, 75, 98, 99, 101–8, 112–13, 116, 314
law-as-command approach and, 36
social rules and, 53–58, 103–8
sovereignty and (*see* sovereignty)
Hart, H. L. A., 4, 30–31, 35–37
command model/theory and, 14, 44, 45, 47–48, 50, 93–113
The Concept of Law, 48, 52, 69
dangers, 68–73
descriptive sociology, 5, 49, 52, 59–60, 67–68, 69, 74, 77, 134, 146, 230
habits and (*see* habits of obedience)
illegal for, 316
injustice, 83–84, 134–35, 137–38
internal point of view (*See* internal point of view)
judges, 61–63
justification and, 16, 17, 46, 48–52, 56, 62, 63–76, 131, 132–42
obligation to obey the law and, 5
obliged-obligated distinction, 31, 44–45, 46, 48–50, 51, 67, 70, 80, 82, 88, 100, 136–37, 138, 144, 147, 190, 212, 248
power-conferring rules, 31, 36, 48, 114–16, 118, 128
questions surrounding law's authority and, 48–50
reducing law to coercion, 69–72
rules based in social practice (*see* rules)
sanctions and, 36, 43, 45, 56, 60, 69, 71, 93, 100–101, 112, 113, 124, 127, 130
on sovereignty, 43, 97
homogeneity, 304–5

I
initial liberty, 264
injustice, 295
Green on, 181–83, 350n110
Hart's theory and, 83–84, 134–35, 137–38
objection to legal enforcement of, 177–78
Rawls on, 247–48
instructions to officials, 127–30
internal point of view (Hart's concept of law), 31, 114
defined, 43, 57
external point of view vs., 58
failure to account for obligation, 47, 57–61
mass delusion, 73, 75
obliged-obligated distinction, 31, 44–45, 46, 48–50, 51, 67, 70, 80, 82, 88, 100, 136–37, 138, 144, 147, 190, 212, 248
sense of obligation, 46, 50, 52–53, 56, 58, 60–61, 74, 95, 114, 119, 248
Shapiro on, 88

J

judges, Hart's treatment of, 61–63
  command model and, 62
  decision making, 62–63
  rule as a guide, 62
judgment, normative, 83, 87–88, 89, 140, 299–301
justice, 3, 48, 67, 91, 162, 249, 304, 342n70
  coercive power vs., 4, 330n6
  common good idea of, 280, 361n4
  fairness and, 279–80
  justification and, 312
  law and, 132, 323, 324, 326
  majorities and, 313
  politics and, 321–22, 323
  power-conferring and duty-imposing rules, 121–24
  Rawls's theory, 247–48, 279, 280
  Schmitt's theory, 312
  Simmons's theory, 279
  Thrasymachus on, 321–22, 326
justification, 6, 103, 106, 365n121
  command model and, 143–45
  common good and (*see* common good)
  content independence and (*see* content independence)
  good of obedience, 267–70
  Green's theory of authority, 181–83
  Hart's theory and, 16, 17, 46, 48–52, 56, 62, 63–76, 131, 132–42
  independent, 32
  legal obligation (*see* legal obligations)
  Marmor's theory and, 77–83
  moral obligation (*see* moral obligation)
  as necessary condition for law, 51
  nondemocratic, 39
  normative, 32–33
  rational, 22–23
  Raz's theory of authority, 8, 17, 37, 145–74
  Shapiro's theory and, 86, 90–91
  Simmons's theory of authority, 178–80
  Smith's theory of authority, 174–78
  Wright on, 20
  See also legitimacy
justified authority, 4, 5
  absence of, 91, 180
  authoritative directives (*see* authoritative directives)
  consent and, 273–78, 282–85
  content independent, 8–13
  divine authority (*see* divine authority)
  Estlund's theory, 273–78
  expertise, 197
  generating obligation to obey (*see* obligation)
  government in exile, 194–96, 198
  government with, 164, 166
  Green on, 181, 182
  legal system, 244–48
  Marmor on, 8, 77–83, 231
  moral obligations and, 86, 164–65
  normative, 17
  philosophical anarchists on, 180
  power and, 194–97
  Rawls on, 247–48
  Raz's theory (*see* Raz, Joseph)
  reasons and, 6, 8–13 (*see also* reasons)
  Simmons on, 180, 248, 258, 280
  Smith on, 175

K

Kelsen, Hans, 27
  Hart's criticism of, 127–28

legal obligation for, 23
nomological conception of normativity, 23, 27
Klosko, George, 16, 21
  common good principle (CG), 272
  "Multiple Principles of Political Obligation," 270
  multiple principles theory, 271, 272
  on political obligation, 270–72
Kuic, Vukan, 268

L
law
  architectonic purpose, 249
  authority (*see* authority)
  as coercion/coercive force (*see* coercion/coercive power)
  as command (*see* command)
  common good and (*See* common good)
  evolving organically, 205
  form and content, 14
  Hart's concept (*see* Hart, H. L. A.)
  justice and, 132, 323, 324, 326
  Nazi (*see* Nazi law)
  normative valence, 14
  obligation-imposing aspect, 205, 249
  obligation to obey (*see* obligation)
  as orders backed by threats, 4, 44, 45, 47, 99, 108, 113, 180, 189
  planning theory, 16, 84–92
  as prediction, 99–100
  as rules (*see* rules)
  traffic (*see* traffic laws)
  unjust (*see* unjust law)
lawful orders, 232–33
Law of Peoples (Rawls), 247, 280
legal disabilities and limitations, 122–23

Legality (Shapiro), 83
Legality and Legitimacy (Schmitt), 225, 300, 302, 307, 318–19
legal norms, 226, 228
legal obligations, 4–5, 33, 201–30
  Bertea's theory of, 21–30, 40–41
  commands and reasons for, 203
  concept, 203–4
  dilemma of authority (*see* dilemma of authority)
  moral obligation and (*see* moral obligation)
  nature of, 4, 13, 35, 39
  Pennock on, 25
  political vs., 315
  Raz's failure to account for, 204
  as religious and moral obligations combined, 203
  religious obligation and (*see* religious obligation)
  Simmons's denial of, 178–80
  Weinrib on, 40
legal power, 85, 122
  coercive power vs., 80
legal realism, 62, 100
legal system
  authority of, 246
  evil, 83–84, 91–92, 132
  goal/purpose, 84, 200
  justified authority, 244–48
  moral mission, 86–87, 90–91
  Nazi Germany, 140
  orientation to common good, 198–201
  Shapiro on, 83–92
  See also common good
legal validity, 63–68, 71, 112, 133–35, 138, 335n59
  descriptive features, 64
  establishing, 65
  obligation and, 68

legal validity (*continued*)
  popular acceptance, 112
  See also rules of recognition
legislating, 110, 111
legislative state
  decrees vs. statutes, 317–19
  nonneutrality, 302–3
  Schmitt's critique of, 228, 301–5, 308–9, 316–19
  self-preservation, 302
  statutes vs. measures, 316–17
  See also sovereignty
legitimacy, 324, 339n31
  authority and, 80–82, 156, 157–58, 175, 178, 263, 273, 276–77, 285
  belief in, 90–91
  claiming vs. having, 148
  de facto authority, 148, 196
  democratic, 34, 74, 277–78, 298, 344n3
  emergency actions and, 317
  government, 4, 175, 178
  Hart's theory of legal validity vs., 134–35
  legality without, 314
  legal system, 18, 90–91
  moral, 85–86, 88, 134–35
  normative theory, 82
  plans without reference, 85–86
  plebiscites, 311
  political, 247, 277–78
  practical authorities, 6, 232
  presidential system, 317
  Schmitt's theory, 227, 228, 300–319
  sovereign, 300
  See also justification
liberalism, 307
  Schmitt on, 299, 301, 302, 310

M
majoritarianism, 299, 304
Marmor, Andrei, 5–6, 8, 16, 21
  dilemma of authority, 6–8, 10, 13, 35, 37, 77, 82, 231–32
  institutional conception, 78–83, 139–40
  justification, 78, 80, 82–83
  moral right to rule (S-power), 79, 81–82
  normative power, 78–83
  obligation, 78, 79, 80
  power-conferring norms, 78
  practical authorities, 6, 78, 79–81, 139, 232
McCormick, John, 225, 227, 228, 302, 304, 305–6, 307, 311–12
  on decrees, 317–18
  on plebiscites, 312
  on rule by a parliament, 311
measures
  emergency, 317–19
  statutes vs., 316–17
morality and moral mission, 85–87, 90–91. *See also* planning theory of law
Morality of Law, The (Fuller), 341n69, 352n30
moral mission, 86–87, 90–91
moral obligation, 4–5, 18, 22, 25, 26, 37, 38, 77, 100, 129, 201, 326, 348n67
  absence of, 74–75
  concept, 33–34, 202
  Finnis and, 18, 199, 294, 295
  government, 123
  Hart's concept of law and, 55, 65, 68, 70, 74–75, 132–33, 135–38, 140–41, 147
  independent, 167, 179, 347n56, 347n60

justified authority, 86
Marmor and, 78, 79, 80
nonlegal, 116, 205
Pitkin's right to command, 180
political obligations as, 315
power-conferring and duty-imposing rules, 118–22
prima facie obligation to obey and, 132, 230, 232–34, 243
Raz's theory of authority, 147, 148, 160–67, 171
reasons without commands, 33–34, 188, 203–6, 212
religious vs., 202–3, 206, 212 (*see also* religious obligation)
as self-specifying, 205
Simmons's perspective, 139, 179
traffic light regulations, 1–2
moral power, 273, 277
Moral Principles and Political Obligations (Simmons), 178
moral right to rule (S-power), 79, 81–82
"Multiple Principles of Political Obligation" (Klosko), 270
multiple principles theory, 271, 272
Murphy, Jeffrie, 139
mythical traffic light, 1–2

N
Nazi law, 1, 2–3
all-things-equal obligation, 137
as coercive orders, 137
common good and, 140
as a legal system, 138
philosophical study of, 3
unjust, 3
See also unjust law
Nazis, postwar German court trials of, 36–37, 133–42
lawfulness of acts committed, 133
legal validity, 133–34
obligation to obey unjust laws, 135–41
neutrality
absolute, 302
constitution espousing, 306
functionalism and, 304, 305
liberal value, 301, 302
McCormick on, 305–6
political domain, 305
positivism and, 300–301
Schmitt's opposition to, 298–307
as substantive choice, 305
technology, 303
true value, 301
normal justification thesis, 151
normative consent, 273–78
normative judgment, 83, 87–88, 89, 140, 299–301
normative power, 78–83, 180, 191, 231
nullity, 122–27
concept, 122
contracts, 125–27
role of duty, 123–24
as sanctions, 124
See also power-conferring rules

O
obedience, 4, 5, 7–8
being good, 268–70
to God, 208–24, 268–70, 354n59
to government, 216–18
habits of (*see* habits of obedience)
self-mastery and, 265, 268, 269–70
obligation, 1–8, 43–92
authority and (*see* authority)
content independence (*see* content independence)
dilemma of authority, 6–8, 10, 13, 35, 37, 77, 82, 231–32

obligation (*continued*)
   Estlund's theory, 273–78
   as government propaganda, 72
   Hart's concept of law (*see* Hart, H. L. A.)
   Klosko's theory, 270–72
   legal (*see* legal obligations)
   moral (*see* moral obligation)
   obedience and, 4, 5, 7–8 (*see also* obedience)
   prima facie (*see* prima facie obligation to obey)
   as a psychological phenomenon, 52–53
   religious (*see* religious obligation)
   sense of, 46, 50, 52–53, 56, 58, 60–61, 74, 95, 114, 119, 248
   threat of force and, 44
   traffic laws (*see* traffic laws)
obliged-obligated distinction, 31, 44–45, 46, 48–50, 51, 67, 70, 80, 82, 88, 100, 136–37, 138, 144, 147, 190, 212, 248
order, 45, 315–16
   Austin on, 315–16
   Hart on, 316
   lawful, 232–33
orders backed by threats, 4, 44, 45, 47–48, 99, 108, 113, 180, 189

P
pantheism, 229
parental authority, 209
parliamentary legislative state. *See* legislative state
Pennock, Roland, 25, 26, 331n44
persistence, 104, 105–8. *See also* succession
Pitkin, Hanna, 180
planning theory of law, 16, 84–92
   authoritativeness, 86, 89
   defined, 84–85
   morality and moral mission, 85–87, 90–91
   nonlegal forms, 85
plebiscites/plebiscitary democracy, 308, 309, 311–14
political authority, 144, 145, 159
political community, 260, 309
political dictatorship, 310
political institutions, 182, 183
political legitimacy, 247, 277–78
political movements, 303, 306
political obligations, 6, 80, 265, 274
   Klosko on, 270–72
   legal vs., 315
   Marmor on, 232
   as moral obligation, 315
   Pennock on, 25
   Simmons on, 72, 139
political theology, 38, 224–30, 299, 309
Political Theology (Schmitt), 225, 227, 309, 317
politics
   competing interpretations, 322
   justice and, 321–22
   neutrality, 298–307 (*see also* neutrality)
   power and, 321–27
   religion and, 224–30
   See also democracy; Schmitt, Carl; sovereignty
positivism, 322–23
   Schmitt's attack on, 299, 300–301
Postema, Gerald, 333n7
power
   coercive (*see* coercion/coercive power)
   emergency, 226, 291–92, 301
   justified authority and, 194–97
   normative, 78–83, 180, 191, 231

suspension of the right, 290
transmission, 290–91, 292
power-conferring rules, 127–30, 131, 341n62, 341n68, 342n70, 342n80
concept, 115
contracts/agreement, 117–20, 125–27, 128–29
duty to act justly, 119–22
Hart on, 31, 36, 48, 114–30
imposing duties, 14, 36, 115, 116, 117–22
as instructions to officials, 128
Marmor on, 78
nullity, 122–27
obligations, 115, 116–19
private law, 119
public law and, 119–20
self-binding and, 340n40
See also duty-imposing rules
practical authorities, 6, 78, 79–81, 139, 232
practical reasoning, 149, 161, 162, 223, 259
legal validity and, 138
limits/limitations, 241, 294, 356n110
preemption thesis, 150–51
presidential decrees. *See* decrees
prima facie obligation to obey, 14–15, 209, 220
as all-things-equal obligation, 9
being important and distinct, 231
benefits of authority, 247, 270
civil disobedience and, 15, 177–78, 233–34, 235
concept, 9, 14, 231
content independence, 9–10, 38–39, 231, 240, 245–46
Estlund's theory of, 272–78
existence of, 232, 242–44
Finnis on, 234–35, 238, 243–44

German postwar trials, 132, 135, 136–41
Green's denial of, 181–83
justified authority, 236, 237, 243
Klosko's theory of, 270–72
lawful orders, 232–33
legal system, 242, 243, 246, 250, 251–52
moral obligation and, 132, 230, 232–34, 243
overridden/overriding, 18, 232
Raz's denial of, 32, 37, 148, 152, 156, 159, 166–67, 169, 174, 234, 235, 236, 238, 251, 252, 256
Simmons's denial of, 180
Smith's theory, 174–78
unjust law, 15, 72, 135, 198–99, 351n25
varying weights, 242–43
promising, 110–11, 118, 119, 238–41, 263. *See also* self-government
pseudo-common good, 260. *See also* common good
punishment, 3, 31, 44, 52, 59, 62, 64, 87–88, 98, 99–100, 123, 125, 133–35, 141, 144, 147, 179, 193, 194, 206, 214, 233–34, 343n99, 350n10

Q
Queen-in-Parliament, 87

R
Rawls, John, 279
common good idea of justice, 280, 361n4
decent society, 280, 361n4
Law of Peoples, 247, 280
on political legitimacy, 247
theory of consent, 280
A Theory of Justice, 247

Raz, Joseph, 8, 12, 15, 16, 17–18, 21, 31–32, 37, 77, 90
  autonomy and authority, 148, 149–55, 263–67
  coordination for, 252, 254, 255–59
  denying prima facie obligation, 32, 37, 148, 152, 156, 159, 166–67, 169, 174, 234, 235, 236, 238, 251, 252, 256
  dependence thesis, 151
  divine authority and, 210–12
  moral obligation and, 147, 148, 160–67, 171
  normal justification thesis, 151
  obligation to obey the law, 145–74
  preemption thesis, 150–51
  respect, 146, 168–73
  river pollution, hypothetical case of, 160–67, 255–57, 347n50, 347n56
reasoning, moral, 160. *See also* practical reasoning
reasons (for action), 8–13, 17–18, 204
  commands without, 33, 202, 203, 206–12, 217, 230 (*see also* religious obligation)
  without commands, 33–34, 186–87, 188, 203–6, 212 (*see also* moral obligation)
  first-order, 10–13, 17, 18, 150, 151, 211, 250
  second-order (*see* second-order reason)
  See also authority
recognition, rules of. *See* rules of recognition
referendum, 311, 312, 337n79
religion, 201–30
  Arendt on, 324–25, 327–28
  biblical, 209

Finnis on good of, 213–15, 220–23, 353n41
  obedience to God, 268
  politics and, 224–30
religious obligation, 22, 33, 34, 38, 353n37
  as commands without reasons, 33, 188, 202, 203, 206–12, 217, 230
  divine authority and, 188, 202, 203, 206–13, 216–19, 223–25, 229–30, 352n31, 353n37
  Finnis's account of, 213–15, 220–23
  moral obligation vs., 202–3, 206, 212 (*see also* moral obligation)
  as partial model for legal obligation, 33, 38, 188, 202, 209, 216, 218–20, 223–25, 244
  Schmitt's work and, 224–30
  Simon's theory, 215–16
Republic (Plato), 321–22
respect
  acceptance of authority, 168–69
  analogy to friendship, 168
  as an attitude to law, 172–73
  as belief in an obligation to obey, 171–72
  consent and, 169–71
  as loyalty to society, 172, 173
  Raz's theory of authority, 146, 168–73
  as reason to obey, 169, 172
revolution, right of, 292
river pollution, hypothetical case of, 160–67, 255–57, 347n50, 347n56. *See also* moral obligation
Rousseau, Jean-Jacques, 297–98
  general will, 229, 298
  Schmitt being critical of, 229, 307
rules, 113–31
  commands vs., 46, 48, 50, 94, 96, 98

duty-imposing (*see* duty-imposing rules)
habits vs., 53–58, 129–30
Hart's concept of law and, 19, 28, 31, 32, 36, 43, 44, 45–89
justification of obligation and, 46–47
obligation and, 46–47, 50–57
power-conferring (*see* power-conferring rules)
succession and persistence, 104–8
as a valid law, 46
rules of adjudication, 64, 134, 335n59, 336n60
rules of change, 64, 66, 134, 335n59, 336n60
rules of recognition, 52, 63, 74, 76, 87, 97, 133, 336n60, 337n79
as authoritative, 66
defined, 64
determining, 66–67
identifying rules as valid, 65–66
jurisprudential analysis and, 65
legal validity (*see* legal validity)
rules of change and, 66
as secondary rules, 64
social acceptance and, 66
rules of the game, 100–101

S
sanctions, 146
Austin's theory, 99
commands and, 36, 47–48, 97, 98–101, 112, 124, 144, 331n35
Hart on, 36, 43, 45, 56, 60, 69, 71, 93, 100–101, 112, 113, 124, 127, 130
Kelsen on, 127
nullity as, 124, 125
power-conferring rules as, 124, 125, 128

referendum and, 312
Schmitt, Carl, 39, 298–319
authority unlimited in principle, 318, 319
concept of law, 34–35, 224
decisionism, 35, 225–26, 298–319
decrees, and statutes vs. decrees, 317–19
divine authority, 224, 225, 229–30
Legality and Legitimacy, 225, 300, 302, 307, 318–19
legal norms, 226, 228
liberalism for, 299, 310
plebiscites/plebiscitary democracy, 308, 309, 311–14
political theology, 38, 224–30
Political Theology, 225, 227, 309, 317
religious obligation (*see* religious obligation)
Simon's transmission theory, 288–89
sovereignty, 224–29, 298–319
statutes vs. measures, 316–17
technology for, 303
Schwab, George, 310, 314
secondary rules
absence of, 64
legal system and, 64
second-order reason, 14–15, 35, 150–51, 240, 250–51
authoritative directive, 18
concept, 10–13
exclusionary reason as, 17
See also first-order reason
self-command, 36, 111, 285
legal obligation and, 111
self-government, 36, 108–12, 119, 281, 285
commitment, 111–12

self-government (*continued*)
  legislating, 110, 111
  promising, 110–11
self-mastery, 268, 269–70. *See also* obedience
self-rule
  command, 285–86, 362n19
  Schmitt and, 311
Shapiro, Scott, 21
  evil legal systems, 83–84, 91–92
  Legality, 83
  natural law theory, 83–84
  planning theory of law, 16, 84–92
Simmons, John, 16, 21, 40
  absence of an obligation to obey, 72
  denying legal obligation, 178–80
  designation theory, 313
  Moral Principles and Political Obligations, 178
  obligation as government propaganda, 72
Simon, Yves, 21, 34, 281–82
  autonomy and authority, 263–67, 287–88
  coach-driver theory, 289–90, 313
  common good for, 139, 246, 253–54, 260–62, 264, 266, 297–98
  common will for, 283–84
  direct democracy for, 285, 286
  A General Theory of Authority, 268
  obedience for, 268–70
  totalitarian/totalizing state, 297
  transmission theory, 288–92
  true freedom for, 268–69
  voluntary cooperation, 269
Smith, M. B. E., 16
  civil disobedience, 177–78
  "Is There a Prima Facie Obligation to Obey the Law?," 174–75, 349n94

legitimacy of government, 175, 178
  theory of authority, 174–78
social rules, 28, 53, 55, 71, 96, 104, 129–31, 145, 323, 343n88
Socrates, 321–22
sovereignty, 34
  command model and, 101–3
  commitment to particular substantive values, 301
  decisionism, 225–26, 298–319
  emergency and, 301
  habits of obedience, 101–8, 112–13, 143–44
  Hart on, 43, 97
  Hobbesian view of, 112
  illimitability, 300, 312–13
  legal limits, 300
  legitimacy, 300
  plebiscites, 308, 309, 311–14
  referendum, 311, 312, 337n79
  Schmitt's theory, 224–29, 298–319
  Simon's transmission theory, 288–89
S-power (systemic power), 79, 81–82
state of exception, 317, 319
  emergency powers in, 226, 301
  See also sovereignty
statutes, 205
  decrees vs., 317–19
  measures vs., 316–17
Strauss, Leo, 326, 336n78
Strong, Tracy, 225
subsidiarity, 260, 288, 295
succession, 104–5, 106. *See also* command; persistence

T
technology, 303
terminal liberty, 264–65

theology. *See* political theology
Theory of Justice, A (Rawls), 247
Thrasymachus, 321–22
totalitarian/totalizing state, 297
tradition, 75, 76
   ancient, 226
   Arendt on, 324–25, 327–28
traffic laws, 1–2, 4, 35, 121
   being conventional, 2
   being instructive, 3
   Hart's view, 45, 58
   moral obligation, 2
   mythical traffic light, 1–2, 12–13, 235, 237, 255
   Nazi, 138–39
   reasons for, 1
transmission theory of authority, 288–92
   coach-driver theory vs., 289–90
   common good, 291–92
   common right of deposition, 291

U
unjust law, 200, 248, 326
   being obligatory, 3, 198
   civil disobedience and, 15, 177–78, 233–34, 235
   moral obligation to disobey, 137–38
   Nazi law (*see* Nazi law)
   prima facie obligation to obey, 15, 72, 135, 198–99, 351n25
   understanding of, 199
"unjust law is no law" maxim, 3, 132, 134, 187, 188
unlimited authority
   content independence and, 38–39
   See also authority: unlimited in principle
US Constitution, 284

V
voluntary co-operation, 69, 258, 269

W
Weber, Max, 322, 339n31
"What Is Authority?" (Arendt), 40, 323–28
Wolff, Robert, 149–50
Wright, Matthew, 19–20, 22

Daniel Mark is associate professor of political science at Villanova University.

This book was selected as the recipient of the
2024 FIRST-TIME AUTHOR AWARD.

The First-Time Author Fund underwrites the promotion and production costs of one book per year and provides a grant directly to the author to aid their scholarship, professional development, or promotion of the book.

The University of Notre Dame Press and the author thank the following donors for their generous support.

Anonymous
Paul and Allegrita Ashenfelter
Dr. Matthew and Amy Dowd
Fritz Heinzen
James Kee
Steffi and Reed Marchman
Wendy and Joseph McMillen
Oluwatomisin Oredein
Grant Osborn
Jayne B. Riley
Mark Roche
Michelle Sybert and Jordan Allen
Stephen Wrinn